DO-IT-YOURSELF ADVERTISING AND PROMOTION

DO-IT-YOURSELF ADVERTISING AND PROMOTION

How to Produce Great Ads, Brochures, Catalogs, Direct Mail, Web Sites, and More!

Third Edition

Fred E. Hahn

With Tom Davis, Bob Killian, and Ken Magill

WILEY

JOHN WILEY & SONS, INC.

Copyright © 2003 by Fred E. Hahn. All rights reserved.

Published by John Wiley & Sons, Inc., Hoboken, New Jersey.
Published simultaneously in Canada.

For general information on our other products and services please contact our Customer Care Department within the United States at (800) 762-2974, outside the United States at (317) 572-3993 or fax (317) 572-4002.

Wiley also publishes its books in a variety of electronic formats. Some content that appears in print may not be available in electronic books. For more information about Wiley products, visit our web site at www.wiley.com.

Library of Congress Cataloging-in-Publication Data:

Hahn, Fred E., 1925–
  Do-it-yourself advertising and promotion : how to produce great ads, brochures, catalogs, direct mail, web sites, and more! / Fred E. Hahn; with Tom Davis, Bob Killian, and Ken Magill.—3rd edition.
      p. cm.
  Includes bibliographical references and index.
  ISBN 0-471-27350-3 (pbk. : alk. paper)
    1. Advertising—Handbooks, manual, etc. I. Davis, Tom II. Title.

HF5823.H187 2003
659.1—dc21   2002192267

Printed in the United States of America.

10 9 8 7 6 5 4 3 2 1

Dedicated with love,
to my wife, Alice J.,
without whom there could not have
been the athletically gifted brilliant*
Frederick M., Ph.D., and Lisa C., MS, LLD.

---

*Despite what A.J. says, half their astonishing good looks do too come from me!

If it's a bright idea, that's good.
If it's well executed, that's good too.
But if it's a persuasive execution of
a terrific idea . . . that's advertising
                                    —BOB KILLIAN

Preface

THREE NEW CHAPTERS: THREE NEW AUTHORS!

So much has changed in advertising in the past five years since the second edition of this book, that almost every chapter needed—and received—major revisions and updating. Not only have advertisers changed what they do, but even when they do the same thing, often it's called something else. Even more important there are now new chapters on subjects not covered before: branding and Yellow Pages advertising plus a totally new approach to basic Internet advertising. Here's a quick overview of these new additions:

Branding, by Bob Killian

Branding tells the world who you are, but before you can launch an effective branding campaign, you have to know how the world actually sees you. That's why we begin this new edition with Bob's do-it-yourself, self-grading Branding Report Card.

Bob Killian, CEO of the Chicago integrated marketing agency that bears his name, is an author, lecturer, creative director, graphic designer, and marketing and branding consultant. His white papers on branding, which explore this methodology in detail, have become popular course material in a number of graduate schools of business. Over his career, Bob has provided branding, company and product naming, advertising, and marketing counsel to companies in almost every category, from startups to AT&T and McDonald's, from barbecue grills to bourbon, financial services to frozen foods, software to bulldozers. In addition to our new Chapter 1, you'll find him online at www.killianadvertising.com.

Successful Yellow Pages Advertising, by Tom Davis

Tom's contribution is our new Chapter 8. Yellow Pages advertising is the most overlooked and frequently most cost-effective way for the smaller business to make themselves known. As Tom shows, businesses of all sizes can use Yellow Pages and advertising to boost their visibility.

Nationally recognized as "Mr. Yellow Pages," Tom has over 30 years' experience in the Yellow Pages industry. As president of Better Business Builders of Maitland, Florida, he brings the former Yellow Pages seller's expertise to buyers through consultant services and workshops for buyers of Yellow Pages advertising.

Since retiring from the Reuben H. Donnelley, his consulting clients have included the Disney Corporation, franchises such as Purofirst International, and Truly Nolan Pest Control, and major names in the telecommunication industry, such as BellSouth. You can reach Tom at (407) 647-3990 or e-mail truthp@aol.com.

Basic Internet Advertising:
It Doesn't Have to Start on the Internet, by Ken Magill

Ken is founding editor since March 1999 of *IMarketing News*, and Internet marketing editor of *DM News*, the direct marketing industry's No. 1 newspaper for 20 years. A frequent business group speaker, he is broadly experienced in direct marketing and its Internet applications. Magill began writing full-time about Internet marketing in January, 1997. In addition to our new chapter 11, you can read his articles in the magazine and online at www.dmnews.com.

MAJOR REVISIONS AND ADDITIONS

Every chapter or subject section that contains major revision or review for up-to-date accuracy begins with a boxed heading like this. It names the reviewer, his or her company, and a bit about their expertise. Chapters without such a headline are the full responsibility of the author, **Fred Hahn**. E-mail him at adwizfred@aol.com.

Some Major Revisions

Major revisions include:

- The transformation from telemarketing to teleservicing for even greater profits.
- How audiovisuals from commercials to films have been transformed by "media" revolution in technology and techniques. What you can do now and what you shouldn't even try.
- How to take advantage of new computerized creative and production for preprint and the latest in printing technology and what's coming tomorrow . . . maybe later today.
- The ever-more confusing problems, and solutions, of mass mail with lots of ways to make it still affordable.
- *Every* chapter has been updated and revised as needed.
- Lots more web site, e-mail, and telephone numbers are given throughout. I've checked each before going to press, but of course these are subject to change.
- New—and even better—Insights, Applications, Case Histories, Charts and illustrations.

Lots more

Every aspect of this new edition is better, stronger, and more valuable to your advertising and promotional needs. That's why I want to use this preface and the acknowledgments that follow to give everyone the credit and thanks their contributions deserve. If anyone has been left out, *please* forgive.

Fred E. Hahn
February 2003

Acknowledgments

I COULDN'T HAVE DONE IT WITHOUT . . .

This book would not be nearly as valuable to the reader if individual chapters had not been read, critiqued, and updated by the experts and their organizaitons cited throughout. It also would not be as valuable without the help of the following who deserve my acknowledgment and the readers' thanks.

Here and There

Mindy Weissler, Advertising Checking Bureau. **Maury Kauffman,** Fax technology and services consultant. **Lindsay Morrison / Christine Pokomy** SRDS,. **Bob B. Swick,** Anchor Computer, Inc., rbsemperfi@aol.com. **Andrew Arthur,** Mediamark Research, Inc. **Henry Hoke III,** *Direct Marketing* Magazine. **Anna Chernis,** Publication Research Coordinator, Direct Marketing Associaton, NYC. **Shelli Sommariva,** Bacon's Information Inc.

The Whole Book

Michael Snell, literary agent, without whom there would not have been a first edition,[1] much less this third. Maureen Drexel, Wiley Managing editor; Linda Indig, Senior Associate Managing Editor; Susan Alfieri, Creative Services Project Supervisor; Reeves Hamilton, copywriter; Airie Stuart, Editor; and Jessica Noyes, Editoral Program Coordinator: hand-holders beyond the calls of duty. Claire Huismann, Senior Project Coordinator; Laura Poole, copyeditor; plus all the others at Impressions Book and Journal Services, Inc., in Madison, Wisconsin. Shellie Rounds, Ladd, IL, creator of all the checklists and other wonderful charts (815-894-3207, dsrounds2@insightbb.com). Nancy Willson, Winnetka, IL, authors' creative director, production artist, miracle worker (847-446-5003). Evanston, IL public library research staff who always knew where to find the answer. Morton L. Levin, who once upon a time asked me: "Have you ever thought of working in advertising?" He has a *lot* to answer for!

---

[1]Before I began writing that book, I sent a two-page preliminary outline to 15 literary agents who specialized in business subjects. "Would they be interested in representing me?" I asked. All 15 replied! Seven wrote to say they saw no market for the book. Seven wrote to say they liked the concept, but it was not for them. Michael Snell wrote a brief, positive note enclosing directions on how to prepare a book proposal for a publisher's consideration. Six months and six copies of the 137-page proposal later, Snell called to tell me "Four publishers want to do the book. Keep writing!" He's also called several times since.

Introduction

This book is a step-by-step guide to the creation or supervision of the most widely used advertising and promotional activities. Four kinds of audiences will find it particularly helpful:

1. The business, corporation, or organization that must do its own advertising and promotion.
2. Persons newly appointed or promoted to positions in advertising, promotion, marketing, or marketing services with little or no experience in those fields.
3. Managers with supervisory responsibility for advertising and promotion.
4. Adult education and in-house training directors who find traditional textbooks unsatisfactory for their needs.

The book works equally well as a blueprint for the do-it-yourselfer, amateur or professional, or as a checklist for managers and supervisors. It is not a complete course in advertising. Each chapter covers a specific type of activity or project and is complete in itself. It focuses on just those things you must know and do to accomplish that specific objective—produce an ad, prepare a catalog, supervise a television commercial, and so on. Ordinary English is used as much as possible. When technical terms are introduced, they are defined immediately, in context. Like every other profession, advertising has its own language, and certain "ordinary" words can prove confusing to the uninitiated. ("Light" for "short" in advertising copy was my first such experience.)

ADVERTISING AND PROMOTION

Because "advertising" and "promotion" are often used interchangeably, even by professionals, some definitions may be helpful.

In ordinary use, "promotion" is everything that is done to help sell a product or service in every step of the sales chain, from the presentation materials a salesperson uses during a sales call to the television commercial or newspaper advertisement that tries to get the customer to think favorably about what is being advertised. Technically speaking, however, "advertising" is responsible for "space" or "print"—that is, newspaper and magazine ads, Internet advertising, radio and television commercials, and direct mail and other "direct response" activities, plus catalogs and billboards. "Promotion" is responsible for everything else in this area except public relations and publicity. These last two may be assigned to an independent department or to either advertising or promotion, depending on the make-up of the company or organization. Because job titles and department designations are quite arbitrary, a detailed job description is highly desirable to avoid turf battles when more than one person or department does any of the above.

Throughout this book, you will find "insights" that are meant to be both aids to memory and actual guidelines to action. Since many of them are applicable to more than one type of project, browse through these pages and read them all, even if the help and information you need are contained in a single chapter. For example, here are the "Three S's"—the insight that is basic to all of the how-to knowledge you will find in these pages:

INSIGHT 1

Keep it Simple . . . keep it Specific . . . and you're likely to keep Solvent. You won't go far wrong by sticking to these three!

HOW TO USE THE CHECKLISTS

The checklists are practical on-the-job help developed for use by my clients as well as by my agency. They can be applied by you for in-house advertising, for working with multiperson staffs, for working with advertising agencies and other outside sources, or any combination of all three. Please note that the checklists are suggested models only. Modify them to fit your own work needs.

A Systems Approach

APPLICATION

Every ad or other promotion must have its own checklist to guarantee control and to ensure a final checkoff on each individual project.

Items on each checklist are numbered for ease of multiperson use. ("Let's look at point 8" rather than "Let's find the line about the offer.") Following each checklist, the numbered items are annotated, with the exception of six that would repeat the same annotation throughout (see Figure I.1). To save space and repetition, those annotations are given here.

Six Uniform Annotations

All annotations are written for multiperson use with you as the project administrator. For one-person, do-it-all-yourself items, or total projects, just translate every "we" into a "me" and work accordingly.

NEWSPAPER/MAGAZINE ADVERTISING CHECKLIST

Project title/description _____   Date _____
_____   Project # _____
_____   Checklist # _____
Overall Supervision by _____   Deadline _____
Budget _____   Start-up Date _____   Completion Date _____

MANAGEMENT DECISIONS	ASSIGNED TO	DUE	IN	MUST APPROVE	BY DATE	IN	INFO COPY ONLY	SEE ATTACHED
1. Quotations	_____	___	☐	_____	___	☐	_____	☐
2. Budget approval	_____	___	☐	_____	___	☐	_____	☐
3. Project approval	_____	___	☐	_____	___	☐	_____	☐

Figure I.1   The basic format used with minor variations on all checklists.

- **Project title.** The *title* is the project's headline or name.
- **Project description.** The *description* is a brief explanation of the project. For instance, "32-item, 2-color Thanksgiving 4-page insert" or "1/2-page Shopping News ad."
- **Project supervisor.** Some *one* person has to be in charge. This is the person who assigns to individuals responsibility for each of the numbered items and, when absolutely required, resolves conflicts.
- **Budget.** The *allocated* cost of the project. *How* budgets are set and approved can have a major impact on the time needed for a project. Allow for this in determining the next two items.
- **Completion date.** Since start-up is controlled by when the project must be done, completion dates are set first; then, working backward through the "time lines" (the time required for each step), a start-up can be set. The start-up to completion dates is called the "time frame." What happens within that frame is spelled out in detailed time lines.
- **Start-up date.** When work *must* begin on the project. In many organizations, multiple projects are assigned at the same time. Depending on the time needed for each, the number of simultaneous start-ups often determines how many outside resources must be used *and paid for.*

APPLICATION

Make all due dates at least three hours before the end of that work day, not—as is normal—one minute before closing. Have the work delivered by the person who did it. This allows time for immediate inspection to check for obvious omissions and errors, and, if necessary, to return it *on the same day it was received* for modification or correction. Since practically no one else works on anything the day they get it, this saves *two* days—the one it would otherwise take to return the material and the day more it would take to get it restarted.

Assigning Responsibilities

In any organization where the assignment of working or supervisory responsibility is not routine, such assignment for a group of projects is best done at a single meeting. The advertising director precedes the meeting by preparing and distributing a checklist with all known information and *likely* due dates for each project. At the meeting, objections to scheduling can be raised and resolved. Should one or more persons be unable to attend, the advertising director fills in the missing due dates and circulates to those absent a clearly marked *Preliminary Working Copy* of the checklist, highlighting due dates assigned to that particular person or department.

If any of those assigned dates present a problem, *that person must contact the project supervisor* and negotiate a workable schedule. The project supervisor sets an absolute deadline for when the schedule should be approved or renegotiated by everyone involved. Based on those negotiations and agreements, the advertising director issues a *Final Checklist.*

Five Vertical Checklist Columns

The checklists, as seen in Figure I.1, are divided into five vertical columns:

1. **Decisions.** The first column is the numbered list of individual project subdivisions. The subheads within that column, such as "Management Decisions" and "Creative Decisions," are used to divide the checklists into easy-to-work-with sections. If this causes a political problem, take them out!

2. **Assignment.** The "Assigned to" column tells who is *responsible* for getting that item done, not who actually does it (unless they are the same). "Due" shows the due date. The "In" box can be checked when work is delivered. In one company's system it is checked only when material is completed or delivered on the actual due date. A "minus" or "plus" number shows that it was completed early or late. Thus, "+3" means three days early; "−2" shows two days late.

3. **Approvals.** In many organizations, different persons and departments must approve part or all of a project. The more such approvals are involved, the more time must be allowed *for that step.* The "By date" is the due date for these approvals.

4. **Information only.** Certain persons and departments get copies of parts of the project as they are completed. The "Info copy only" column shows who they are and what they get. Such copies are clearly marked as *Information Only.* (A self-inking stamp works wonders here.)

5. **See attached.** *Everything* that bears on a project must be *in writing* and kept in a central physical or computer file. If there must be telephone or E-mail information or instruction, the person receiving it puts it in writing ("Phone from JK 3–7. Price changed to $47.55.") and files that, too, sending a copy to the person from whom it originated. A list of all changes is attached to the checklist, with the "See attached" box checked for each change.

> ## INSIGHT 2
>
> In assigning due dates, always assign a specific calendar date. Do not permit completion "ASAP" (as soon as possible). ASAP most often means *never*.

Make "Final" FINAL!

If at all possible, avoid issuing *revised* "final" checklists; they are an invitation to make all future finals translate to "preliminary." But if you absolutely must do so, be sure that the new checklist is dated and clearly marked as "Revised" and that the original "finals" are equally clearly marked as "See Revised Copy Dated __."

Remind everyone that getting something perfect is no substitute for getting it done!

Note: The checklists in this book are copyrighted. They may, however, be reproduced for personal use. For ease of use on standard $8^{1}/_{2}'' \times 11''$ paper, copy them at 135 percent of their printed size.

Contents

Checklists and Key Charts

1 | Branding and Your Brand Asset Assessment

This chapter by **Bob Killian** has been modified, with his approval, to fit the format of our book. For more information about branding and the Brand Asset Scorecard developed by Killian, see his Web site at www.KillianAdvertising.com.

INSIGHT 3

No business is too small—local retail store, shoe shiner—or too large—General Mills, General Motors—to focus on the importance of branding. Every one must create expectations that promise value: What do customers think when they think of you? What do noncustomers expect? In other words, what is *your* brand?

Undoubtedly you have heard the legend of the seven blind MBAs vacationing in India. Their path blocked by an elephant, they feel different parts of the animal . . .

The one feeling the elephant's side declared that an elephant was "very like a wall." Another felt a leg, and concluded that an elephant was "very like a tree." A third grasped the elephant's tail and decided that it was "very like a rope." And so on.

This task force failed to achieve consensus because they got hung up on seven different Situation Analyses.

Like the study of this legendary beast, a brand performing below expectations often is approached from multiple directions, with marketing experts tugging and probing and prescribing, based on whatever portion of elephant anatomy is at hand.

The ad agency offers an advertising solution; the brand manager's spreadsheet proves that retailers are at fault; the sales promotion agency knows a sweepstakes contest will jump-start sales; the packaging experts say a redesign will save the brand; the regional sales managers want an extra 5 percent for a new trade deal, and the CFO says it's a brand in decline, so quit spending on it.

This is not a case of literal blindness; instead, you should recognize the limitations of strategies based on narrow perspectives.

This chapter offers a brief overview, with reader participation, of a way to see the bigger picture of brand asset management. So make a copy of the Brand Asset Scorecard on page 3, sharpen your pencil, and keep score.

Brand Asset Management is a new discipline for most brand holders. It's a perspective that differs sharply from the viewpoint that values brick-and-mortar more highly than, say, the knowledge and skill of a sales force. It's that bias that confidently accounts for a paper clip, but suspiciously discounts a company's reputation.

TRADITIONAL BRAND ANALYSIS

Most brand managers focus on tangible, easily quantified assets. When you combine that with "next-quarter-itis," the national penchant for focusing on short-term numerical goals, regardless of the impact on brand equity, you get systemic long-term problems. In this mind-set, for example, volume will always seem more important than market share, and easy-to-measure quarterly results will matter more than hard-to-measure customer satisfaction.

Add to those institutional biases the short-term perspective of brand managers at General _____ (fill in the blank) who know they'll be on X Brand for 18 months, tops, before moving on to Y Brand (or field sales, or something). They know their career path is paved with short-term fixes. Is it any wonder that budgets for indiscriminate high-value couponing (and other brand de-motions) are growing far faster than budgets for brand-building?

Come, Let Us Assess Together

Focus on your brand. (Sometimes, in a small business, it's the business as a whole.) If you have more than one brand from which to choose, pick the one that makes you lose sleep at night. Grab a pencil and keep score as we review 16 of your brand's vital assets. Use additional copies of the Scorecard (Figure 1.1), if you want someone else to go through this for the sake of comparison. (And you do.)

YOUR BRAND'S VITAL ASSETS

1. Brand Name

A brand's most valuable asset can be the name itself. For one thing, a name can have inherent selling power when the word(s) stand for something that showcases and explains the uniqueness of the product or service. By this measure, for example, Vapo-Rub is more valuable, more descriptive, than Formula 44, and Mercury Cougar promises much more than Hyundai Elantra.

Long-Term Power
But that value of "name" pales in comparison to the enormous power of those brands that have built equity after decades of consistent brand-building activities. "Diet Rite," for example, no matter how descriptive and colorful, can't approach the equity in "Diet Coke," a heritage built on a gazillion dollars of investment ad spending.

Brand Asset Assessment Scorecard		
Vital Asset	**Range**	**Points**
1. Brand Name		
A. Inherent value	0 to 5	_____
B. Consumer awareness	0 to 10	_____
2. Packaging and Point of Purchase	0 to 10	_____
3. Reach and Frequency		
A. Smart segmentation	0 to 10	_____
B. Share-of-Voice	1, 2, or 3	_____
4. Ad Content		
A. What you say	0 to 10	_____
B. How you say it	0 to 10	_____
C. 4A + 4B × 3B	0 to 60	_____
5. Promotion		
A. Strategically-sound policy	0 to 5	_____
B. (*Deduct* coupon promotions)	0 to –12	_____
6. Consistency	0 to 5	_____
7. Distribution		
A. Geographic breadth	0 to 6	_____
B. Depth and cost	0 to 6	_____
8. Newsworthiness / Public relations	0 to 5	_____
9. Likeability	0 to 5	_____
10. Trade Support	0 to 5	_____
11. Sales Force	0 to 10	_____
12. User Profile	0 to 5	_____
13. Product Performance	0 to 5	_____
Customer perception of	0 to 5	_____
14. Repurchasing	0 to 5	_____
15. Actionable Research	0 to 5	_____
(*Deduct* for useless research)	0 to –5	_____
16. Value / Pricing	0 to 10	_____
	Total	_____

Figure 1.1 The Brand Asset Assessment Scorecard. Copy this and use it as you read this chapter.

INSIGHT 4

The function of branding is to make it difficult and expensive for competitors to try to enter or compete in your market. Successful branding makes that practically impossible. Think of Bayer™ aspirin, Rand McNally's road atlases, Adobe Photo-Shop. Others may sell in their markets, but only as fringe products.

———

"Branding" defined by Dr. Rolf Weil, president emeritus and emeritus professor of finance, Roosevelt University, Chicago.

In any brand asset audit, we give a lot of weight to the use (and occasional misuse) of a name. Investigating the practical limits of line extensions, for example, forces you to distinguish between those new product efforts that reinvest brand equity, versus those that dilute it.

In #1 on your Scorecard, give your brand anywhere from 0 to 5 points for the salesmanship built into the meaning of the name. Add from 0 to 10 points for its top-of-mind consumer awareness, a fair measure of the value of your prior investment in the brand's reputation.

2. Packaging

Packaging is the ultimate final dialog with the consumer. It must call attention to itself, set the product apart from the category and other products in its own line. We don't know why packaging is so often regarded as separate from the selling process, a stepchild in the marketing family. Think of packaging and POP (Point of Purchase) as brand assets to be invested in and deployed like other managed assets. That will help focus on how important they are to the final sale. A family of packages can reassure consumers by projecting a persuasive brand personality and value-added consistency. At their most effective, packages can jump off the shelf and close the sale.

(Note: Be creatively flexible here. If you're a service business, your "packaging" might be your selling tools, brochures, truck signs, whatever you use to speak to your customers. If you're a retailer, it's you store front and store atmosphere.)

On your Scorecard, give your brand from 0 to 10 points for packaging and POP strengths. If you have a strong retail presence compared to your competitors, but not one that can be compared to the best of the best, don't give yourself more than 5.

3. Reach and Frequency

When most people think of advertising effectiveness, they tend to think in terms of an ad budget. So some are deluded into believing that if we spend twice as much on our advertising, we will get twice the results. This was never true, and it is getting even less true every year. In an age where niche markets are proliferating and mass markets are mostly myth, it is very helpful to think of reach, frequency, and ad content as *related but separate* assets in your advertising portfolio.

The New Importance of Reach
With so many new marketing tools available to target specific audience segments, reach has become relatively more important than frequency. Niche marketing has created efficient new ways to get to specific consumer affinity groups and increasingly accurate psychographic slices of the almost-extinct mass audience. (Remember when there were general-interest magazines?)

Frequency still is basically deploying money against markets, boxcar numbers flexing budgetary muscle. Market segmentation strategies can, however, deliver more leveraged results with equal frequency but (relatively) smaller budgets.

Give yourself 0 to 10 points for smart segmenting. Then record 1, 2, or 3 for Share-of-Voice media spending: (1) below, (2) the same, or (3) above the spending level of competitors.

4. Ad Content

The greatest leverage of advertising is in its creativity. A great ad can be, and often is, 10 times more effective than a mediocre one.

It's possible, for example, to cut a media budget by 25 percent and know that you will lose roughly 25 percent of your effectiveness. But if you cut advertising production costs by 25 percent, you can't possibly know the impact. You might lose up to 90 percent of your effectiveness.

Invest in Production Values
We are not talking about throwing money around. It's true that dazzling production values can't rescue a nonidea. But it's also true that if, say, a TV spot has poor camera work, cheesy lighting, and an awkward, overly loud spokesman who would never be hired as a spokesperson for anybody else (you know, that local used car dealer in your market,) it can turn off an audience's receptors to even the strongest ideas. Even on radio, you can tell the difference between a national spot and a homemade local spot in the first few seconds—the false bargain of amateurish production values strikes again.

Think of media spending as an unleveraged investment and ad content as highly leveraged. You will be less tempted to steal budget from the creative process to buy a few more spots in Lubbock.

Candidly, score 0 to 10 points for what your ads say, plus 0 to 10 for how memorably and unexpectedly they say it. Then multiply that total by the Share-of-Voice score you gave yourself above. This is the single biggest score you'll get, because these assets are the biggest equity builders. It stands to reason: more leverage = more importance = more points.

5. Promotion

Can promotion kill brand equity? Yes!

Can promotions build brand equity? Yes, if one sees to it that the promotional activities enhance and reinforce the basic brand image. In other words, don't needlessly, blindly switch on a marketing autopilot, drop millions of high-value coupons, and call it a plan. To put it bluntly, sometimes FSI (Free-Standing Insert) stands for Failed to Search for Ideas

Score 0 to 5 for a strategically sound promotion policy. Then subtract one point for every coupon promotion in the last 12 months. Range = −12 to +5.

6. Consistency

There are two kinds of consistency, and both are important for brands: consistency from year to year and consistency across all communications vehicles.

Long-Term Consistency

If your brand changes its personality every few years, it runs the risk of having no image at all. (What does Canada Dry stand for, anyway? How is a Plymouth different from a Dodge?) The Marlboro Man, on the other (tattooed) hand, suffers from no such confusion after five decades of consistent messaging, building to market dominance.

Usually, two or three years into any brand-building campaign, a firm grip is needed to keep the agents of change-for-the-sake-of-change on a short leash. Just because *they* are tired of doing "the same old thing," doesn't mean it's penetrated into the heads and hearts of your target audience.

Integrated Consistency

The second kind of inconsistency that erodes brand equity is advertising, promotion, packaging, and public relations people who aren't reading from the same sheet of music. They each pursue their own vision, losing the single focus that successful branding demands and rewards.

Score 0 to 10 for across-the-disciplines consistency, and 0 to 5 for across-the-years consistency.

7. Distribution

The Consumer Products Problem

In the conventional view, the single greatest problem for most consumer products brand holders is to get, hold, or expand retail shelf/floor space. So the conventional (that is, easiest) solution is to "buy" the distribution.

Buying Distribution

Pay the slotting fees, display allowances, baksheesh, and listing fees to get the shelf space, then discount like crazy to keep your facings. Run an avalanche of coupons and rebates and similar margin-reducing activities to keep the inventory turning. That makes the retailer (not to mention the coupon delivery system) happy and prosperous.

For many smart marketers, however, establishing a retail presence by *pushing* with big trade deals and *pulling* with big coupons can be prohibitively unprofitable (and not altogether consistent with developing a brand). There are alternatives, such as smarter advertising, publicity, word of mouth, and the many aspects of promotion detailed throughout this how-to-book.

Score 0 to 6 for breadth of distribution (are you in all the geography you want?), plus 0 to 6 for the depth and cost of that distribution. (Are you overspending to maintain marginal regions? Channels? Markets? Customers?)

8. Newsworthiness

Being in tune with the times offers lots of opportunities for "unpaid advertising."[1] Clearly defined, strategically oriented public relations can be a powerful tool. They are assets that can induce trial, enhance brand image, and build brand equity, if it is consistent with your other messages. Do remember, however, that such unpaid advertising takes just as much skill to produce and place as the paid version! As in item no. 4, "Ad Content," it's the production that's critical, so budget your PR accordingly.

Give yourself 0 to 5 points for how well you've exploited this brand asset.

9. Likeability

Yes, likeability matters! And yes, it's measurable. If your communications (and therefore your brand) are likeable, then people will welcome your message. It's a fundamental truth: People buy from people (read: brands) they like. In consumer buying, there are no rational purchases. None.

Give yourself up to 5 points for a refreshing brand "attitude."

10. Trade Support

Leverage over competitors is the best result of enthusiastic trade support. For many brand holders, of course, that leverage can be enormous: In some industries, trade support can be life or death. Remember, in today's environment, you can achieve your goals only by making your trade network believe that you are helping them achieve theirs. Every sales force worth its salt cultivates relationship sales.

Score 0 to 5 points for how your brand is supported (versus competitors) by the trade.

11. Sales Force

You'd think that the scores you recorded for distribution would tell you all you need to know about your sales force. That is usually true, but any major change in a selling organization brings a dynamic to established distribution. Adding reps, changing sales management, or altering compensation programs—really, any substantial change—can weaken the strongest distribution or (conversely) pay big dividends. Should you plan such a change, test its outcome—on a regional basis, if possible. Testing permits you to reverse course before an impending disaster.

---

[1]See Chapter 12, "Publicity and Public Relations."

A CASE HISTORY

Britannica Films hoped to sell a fire prevention film, produced for elementary schools, to municipal fire departments for their community outreach programs. To sweeten the offer, they tested the choice of a *free* popcorn popper or a set of top-quality steak knives with each film. The result was immediate outrage! How dare Britannica assume a fire department would purchase a public safety film just to get something else for free! The subsequent nonpremium mailing was a huge success.[2]

Give yourself up to 10 points for the strength and discipline of your front-line troops.

12. User Profile

Certain user groups and market segments carry more significance and impact than others. Distinguish between high-index users (that's research-speak for the delightful 10 percent of your customers who buy 60 percent of your product) and merely high-potential users. For example, people with developing or changeable brand images are highly important.

This translates in many cases into pursuit of the young, in hopes of securing a long-term predisposition toward a brand. If it works, when it works, the benefits can roll on for decades. Consider Honda. They pursued and nurtured a relationship with a whole generation of consumers and continued to fine-tune the product line to meet their changing needs.

Beer marketers, too, know the value of a lifetime customer. Of 100 people loyal to a beer brand at age 21, 50 will still be loyal to that brand at age 30.

On the other hand, narrow appeals mean narrowing markets. People who buy fur coats, Cadillacs, and shelf liner paper are dropping out faster than they're being replaced. This is not, however, irreversible. Whole categories (like gourmet coffee) have been rejuvenated by young trendsetters.

Add 0 to 5 points to your score for having enough good research to know your user intimately.

13. Product Performance

What You Get Is What You See
It almost goes without saying that product performance is a key factor in a buyer's decision to repurchase. If the world were rational, the objective realities of product performance would generate trial, too. The key factor in a consumer's decision to try a product in the first place, however, is its *perceived* product performance.

---

[2]The testing of nonschool sales, the testing of the premiums, and the immediate recognition of the no premium results were all "outside *its* box" practices, introduced to Britannica Films by Hahn's advertising agency.

Although it's up to you to maximize actual product performance, many different components of brand image influence consumers' perceptions of anticipated performance. That's a shared responsibility of advertising, promotions, packaging, POP—everything that "talks" to consumers.

Score 0 to 5 for actual performance; add 0 to 5 for consumer perceptions of performance.

14. Repurchasing

Frequency of use equals frequency of brand-affirming (or brand-switching) decisions. That's a key equation, because it helps explain why loyalties grow stronger to Snickers candy bars (bought three days a week) than to oatmeal (bought once every first snowfall.) It also helps you know how many trials you have to induce to conquer competitive users.

You can never know too much about purchaser behavior. Do repurchase patterns change by time of day, time of year, retail environment, competitive pressure, or promotional activity? Can these behaviors be altered? What are your use-up rates? Do users take themselves out of the market for a considerable time with each purchase?

Who Deserves Loyalty from Whom

Too many marketers bask in the glow of so-called brand loyalty, which has the unintended consequence of taking good customers for granted. Nobody should count on the continued (blind) loyalty of people who have chosen a brand in the past. Brand owners should be loyal to their customers, not the other way around. Consumers will buy and rebuy only those brands that continue to live up to their perceptions of added value

How well have you planned and exploited ways to promote additional uses/occasions, which tend to increase the velocity of repurchase? Score 0 to 5.

15. Actionable Research

In an age of computerized databases, and number-crunching machines of awesome speed, there is little or no problem with the quantity of information available to us. Indeed, the problem is the opposite. It's analysis paralysis.

INSIGHT 5

Decide on the action(s) to be taken, based on possible results, before authorizing the research. If it's "None; I just want to know," why not use the money to throw a party *everyone* can enjoy?

From Data to Decisions

The key is how to turn data into decisions. The key to the key (to murder our metaphor) is to recognize and use *actionable* research. Do your findings lead to action or just to filling PowerPoint slides? Can you make the leap from raw tabs to real insight? Can you learn how to use your brand assets more creatively, more unexpectedly? If not, save the research money.

The ongoing fascination with focus groups (and concurrent neglect of quantitative studies) has had unfortunate side effects. Some marketers suffer because they broke rule one: They tried to project quantitative results from qualitative research. We call it the "But-that's-what-the-woman-in-Walla-Walla-said" syndrome. The absurd number of new product offerings is a monument to this kind of wishful thinking.

INSIGHT 6

If your focus group moderator ever asks for a "show of hands," find another moderator.

One of your most valuable functions is to act as if an alien visitor arrived from another marketing planet. Question every old assumption, all research, any comfortable ritual. If your research is aging (or missing), or it's been a while since your corporate assumptions have been challenged, it's time to restate all your questions and question all your answers.

Subtract 5 points for wasting money on useless research, score 0 points for no research, and give yourself up to 5 for actionable results that make you say "Aha!"

16. Value

In a rational world, price would equal value. (Of course, in a rational world, there'd be no civil wars or salad shooters. But we digress.)

Price is just one element in the complex, nonrational perception tug-of-war within consumer buying decisions. Value equals perceived quality, divided by actual price.

Perceived quality, of course, is what you hope to establish with your other assets.

Pricing decisions, insofar as a brand holder can actually control (or even influence) them, have to be handled with much more skill and attention then simply throwing coupons or rebates at potential buyers. They require continuing attention to each and every one of the first 15 points in your Brand Asset Assessment. That's how you get to no. 16: Value!

Score 0 to 10 based on your pricing. If you can establish and maintain a value-added premium price versus competition, give yourself credit for being perceived as a value-added brand. It's a judgment call, of course. Sometimes it takes heroic measures just to maintain price parity.

WHAT'S YOUR TOTAL SCORE?

Have you projected wishful thinking (or natural optimism) onto the numbers? Most people tend to be a bit on the overly optimistic side. Not that the objective total matters. *But now put someone else through this same exercise.* Would your staff come up with the same numbers? Your distributors? Salespeople? Consumers? Competitors? Where are the most obvious disagreements? Where can you find consensus? Which assets are clearly performing beyond their potential? Which need a little hand holding, or a bandage, or major surgery? Which are a drag on your brand equity?

The fact is, every brand asset has to contribute to a value-added brand image to make the machinery work at peak efficiency. But prudent asset deployment calls for putting money, people, time, and energy against the assets with the most leverage. Don't polish the one bright spot if a crucial asset needs repair.

Although analysis based on the 16 points is a critical beginning, correction may require help. To get that, it's often an outside professional who can convince management and employees that not only brand assessment but brand *action* is necessary.[3] So check with your current advertising or marketing agency about their experience in brand asset assessment. Don't ask *if* they have the expertise—nobody ever says, "No, we don't."

INSIGHT 7

You know your company is a brand. *But so are you.* When you meet with prospects or customers or enter a meeting, what do people expect? Are you sure you know? Can you improve it? At some point, reread this chapter with that point in mind.

EXTRA CREDIT

Most companies and nonprofit organizations have a Mission Statement. Translate that into a Branding Statement—a Branding Commandment—by which every one of the 16 Brand Assets can be judged, then make sure that every brand-related action conforms to that law.

---

[3]Should you decide you need outside objectivity, Killian & Company Advertising provides a unique convergence of disciplines and capabilities, built around a new perspective: the Brand Equity Agency. (And, as we emphasize throughout our book, never leave without asking for the order!)

2 | Newspaper and Magazine Advertising

The process of preparing newspaper and magazine advertising described in this chapter serves the same function as a blueprint or detailed drawing in the construction of a garden shed. Using identical plans, the professional builder should construct a somewhat sounder and better looking structure than you—but the shed you produce on your own will be immeasurably improved by following the drawing rather than trying to make things up as you go along.

WHY YOU ADVERTISE

Preparation and Inspiration

When Thomas Edison was asked the secret of his success, he replied, "Two percent inspiration, 98 percent perspiration." You won't have to work nearly that hard. Think of your task as "90 percent preparation, 10 percent inspiration." That preparation starts with a systematic look at why you advertise and what you expect to get out of advertising.

Put It in Writing

Put into writing your reasons for advertising—*all* the reasons—and the results you expect the advertising to bring. You need this list to give a sharper focus to the ads you are going to create and, probably even more important, to have a method of evaluating results. Don't expect any one ad to do ten different things or you'll get one-tenth the results . . . or none at all! Set priorities, then focus on the most important.

How to Set Goals for Your Advertising

In setting goals for your advertising, remember at all times that your *results must be quantifiable.* Depending on your competitive situation and specific business goals, list the expected results as a definite number or percentage—not "more sales," but, for instance, "5 percent more sales during the week following the ad." If you, like many newcomers to a certain kind of business, have no idea what to expect, put down the number that will justify the cost of the ad *if it meets your list of objectives.* Regardless of the actual results, *whether you like them or not,* keep a record *in writing.*

It is your benchmark for future planning and programs. How to use such a record will be discussed shortly.

Typical Advertising Goals

Following are some goals a retailer might set. Analogous goals would be set for a manufacturer or a service organization. The sample percentages are arbitrary and are not based on actual case histories.

Short-Term Goals

- **Increase total store traffic** by 5 percent during the week following advertising.
- **Increase the sale of advertised items** by 15 percent over the previous week. If you are advertising more than one item, you will want to know how each individual item sold, as well as how all the advertised items sold as a whole. This knowledge gives you information for future promotions, even when sales as a whole do not live up to expectations. Be sure to make a special note of purely seasonal successes, such as pumpkins sold just before Halloween. Make a note of the weather—from great to terrible—plus special occasion successes . . . or failures. A traffic-stopping fire two blocks away can affect business just as much as a hailstorm can.
- **Increase the sale of nonadvertised merchandise** by 5 percent over the previous week. Advertising is usually meant to increase traffic, and that should be reflected in increased sales throughout your establishment.

Long-Term Goals

- **Maintain an increase in store traffic** of 2 percent in the month following the advertising, as against the previous year.
- **Increase customers' satisfaction** with products and services. Often it is impractical for a smaller firm to afford professional research on customer or client satisfaction. But informal research is always possible. When customers phone, ask about their satisfaction with your products and service, and whether they are getting the information they want from your advertising and promotions. Make certain *you* get and *read* any letters of complaint as well as those of praise. Make sure everyone associated with you knows you are serious about customer satisfaction. Make it your personal priority, and you'll be astonished at the positive results.

Where to Get Help in Setting Goals

If you are a novice in setting advertising goals, here are some sources of help:

1. **Media.** The publications in which you advertise, the media, have expert representatives who often have information about advertising campaigns such as yours. Whether you plan a single ad or a yearlong series, speak with these reps about what you might expect from your ads. But remember that their jobs depend on their convincing you of the effectiveness of their publications, so check their suc-

cess stories with the people who did the actual advertising—even if they are now your competitors!

2. **Your competitors.** Take your competitors to lunch—one at a time—and ask them what kind of results they get from their advertising. Chances are, they'll tell you. Almost everyone shows off by talking too much. Analyze your competitors' promotions. Even if they tell you everything you want to know, check.

3. **Trade associations.** Your trade association probably has an entire library of advertising case histories. Call and ask for this and any other help the association might give.

4. **Colleges and universities.** Contact the head of the advertising or marketing department (advertising is usually taught as part of marketing and is also located in journalism and communications schools). Explain what you are trying to learn, and ask whether that information is available from either staff or research materials. Expect to pay a consultant fee. (You don't work for free, do you?) The faculty will help if it can.

5. **Libraries.** Explain your need to the research librarian at your public or professional library. These are extraordinarily knowledgeable professionals with access to networks of information through computer linkups.

6. **Build your own research base.** If no other information is available, run your ads, set "best guess" goals, and begin to build your own records. You'll quickly have the best database in town and might even be invited to lecture to those whom you previously asked for information. But don't disclose too much. Remember what we said about your competitors. You be the one who does know how to keep your mouth shut, even when you'd much rather show off. Brag about your bank statement, not your ad results.

SUMMARY

- Know why you advertise.
- Put the reasons in writing.
- Analyze your competitors' budgets, promotions, and appeal.
- Set goals that can be quantified.
- There's lots of help available. Use it.

HOW MUCH TO PAY FOR ADVERTISING

How to Budget for Advertising

How much you can, will, or must spend on advertising should be decided as objectively as possible; that is, base your decision on reasoning rather than luck or "hoped for" results. To do this, take your advertising goals and calculate, as well as you can, both the "static" percentage-of-sales and the "dynamic" objective way of establishing your overall advertising budget. Both methods are explained below and have devoted followers. After you've become familiar with them, begin by using the one with which you feel most comfortable—*but stay with it only as long as it gives you the expected results!*

A case history. Gaining additional profit by *not* advertising has been attempted by a number of companies and brands, usually with disastrous results. The nonchocolate milk flavoring, Ovaltine, my childhood favorite, never recovered from such a decision. Not advertising to gain dollars to fight, or profit from a corporate takeover is not an advertising consideration.

1. **"Static" percentage-of-sales method.** Historically, "percentage of sales" was the way to establish advertising—and most other—budgets. In many businesses it still is. A specific percentage of *last* year's gross sales, often suggested by industry standards, is allocated for promotional activities. Objectives are proposed but must be modified by the reality of such budgets.

Despite the static aspect of percentage-of-sales budgeting, many managers welcome its protection from unrealistic sales projections. Most of them recognize that it "protects" them from realistic projections as well. They simply prefer the relative safety of the known to the projected.

2. **"Dynamic" objective method.** The objective method is more dynamic and requires a certain daring by management—especially if it's spending its own money. Unlike percentage of sales, which locks in budgets regardless of the current year's goals, the objective method expands promotional budgets to meet what management believes are realizable objectives, regardless of previous years' sales.

APPLICATION

Budgeting based on objectives rather than previous sales is especially important in promoting for new business—what direct marketing calls "the cost of buying a new customer." In many businesses, such a first sale will cost 100 percent of the merchandise sold or, in higher-priced items, 100 percent of the regular profit. An objective promotional budget permits even a major effort in this direction without "eating up" the total percentage-of-sales advertising dollars, thereby eliminating a regular advertising budget.

Budgeting for Individual Ads

Using some of the advertising goals suggested earlier, an individual ad plan might look like Figure 2.1. It charts four points to consider in planning:

1. Advertisement goal.
2. Percentage of total ad dollars allocated to your goal.
3. The dollar value for achieving the goal.
4. The time allowed for achieving the goal.

Advertising Planning & Record of Results (To be kept with copy of ad)

Subject or Headline: July 4 Picnic Special. 14 "Sale" items; 21 regular   Ad # 51-629/72–03

Media	Size	Date	/	Day	Cost	Coop $	Our $	Coop With
Daily Mail	Tab page	6-29		Thu	$ 600	$300	$300	Frank's Franks
Sunday Mail	Tab page	7-02		Sun	800	400	400	Frank's Franks
Sunday Herald	Tab island	7-02		Sun	1200	600	600	Sandy's Soaps

Production
Art & Design   400
Type   300
                                                      $2600 $1300 $2000

Ad Goal: 6-29/7-5	Last Week	Projected $	& %	Actual $	Actual %	% of Goal
Sale Items 50% over last week	$ 35,000	$ 52,000	+50%	$ 53,622	51%+	+1%
Nonsale Items 10% over last week	165,000	181,500	+10%	177,662	7.6%+	−2.4%
Traffic for Week 5% over last week	11,859	12,451	+ 5%	12,706	7.2%	+2.2%

WEATHER: Perfect for picnicking. About 85°

SPECIAL NOTE: Lots of positive customer comments! "Best sale of year," etc.

Figure 2.1 *Spending on advertising.* A typical record combines the advertising goals, the media used, the various costs (including co-op contributions explained on pages 38–40), and the results. In our example, dollar goals are compared to a single time period that makes sense for that particular business. A more complete comparison by week, month, quarter, and year(s) is easy and practical with computerized spreadsheet records. The "Ad #" at the top right shows that the 51st ad of the year (51) ran on June 29 (629) and July 2 (72), 2003 (03). For record purposes, this number must appear in the ad. Try to put it the same place each time.

Evaluating Advertising Results

In evaluating the success of your ad, as charted in Figure 2.1, the calculation might seem quite simple; however, what if your overall goal is reached but your individual subgoals are not? Does it really make any difference?

The answer depends both on the type of establishment you have and the reasons you set your goals. If you are advertising loss leaders to bring new customers to your store, and only regulars show up, you're in a different position from having a sale where your inventory costs have been reduced by a manufacturer, leaving profits the same as at the regular price. These and similar considerations should enter into developing your advertising goals. You want sales, of course, but it requires a different perspective to plan advertising for a funeral home or accounting service than for a hardware store or a farm equipment dealership. In fact, without prohibitively expensive research, how *can* you get a short-term fix on advertising that aims at long-term results? Fortunately, there is a fairly easy, practical, and inexpensive way to do just that.

Getting a Preview of Short-Term Results

Where there is high customer traffic, such as shopping malls, individual stores, banks, and so on, display *large-enough-to-read* copies of possible future promotions and track the results. These can be fairly simple "nonadvertised specials" or copies of complete possible ads. The preview secret is to give your prospects a benefit for acting *now!* Your reward is immediate positive, negative, or neutral test results. Two examples show how this works.

1. *Ad previewing in a bank.* Three possible ads, offering what the bank believes are benefits wanted by its customers, are mounted and placed in the bank's windows and high-traffic lobby. Each ad offers in-person or written information. Each test produces a clear winner, which then becomes part of the bank's advertising campaign.
2. *Offer preview.* A talk with the sales representative brings a free coffee cup personalized with the prospect's name as Executive of the Year. Hundreds of office managers listen to the sales pitch. Far too few buy for the time spent by the sales force. A different offer is previewed and proves a winning success—both in producing sales and in earning a major advertising award.

Getting a Preview of Long-Term Results

Although the need you fill may lie months or years in the future, try for *some* immediate response to your advertising *now.* If you establish a good relationship before the need arises, you're much more likely to get the call when it does. So do what the movie moguls do before they spend millions on promoting a film: Check it out with a sneak preview.

How to Sneak a Preview

Purchase or produce a helpful hints flyer along the lines of "10 reasons why you should meet your banker *before* you need a loan" or "10 things to look for when you're ready to buy a house." The help should be specific rather than general and be directly related to what you do (where to look for dry rot and how to tell it's there rather than "check for dry rot"). The more valuable the advice, the more likely that it will be kept and consulted when a service such as yours is needed.

Informational flyers may be available from your trade or professional organization and often are advertised in trade journals. They tend to be inexpensive and may be customized with your name, address, and telephone number at a small additional cost. You can, of course, also produce your own.

If several suitable flyers are available, offer a different one free each time you advertise, to see which one gets the best response. Then use that flyer as long as the level of response continues. If your budget is limited to fewer ads than the number of different kinds of flyers available, ask the supplier which one has gotten the most repeat orders. Then use that, providing that it meets your other criteria.

The least expensive and often the best research is to learn from the experience of others.

SUMMARY

- Allocate specific dollar amounts to each advertising goal.
- Don't just wait for long-term results to happen. Offer information or use a premium to jump-start results.

No matter how successful your response, vary the offer occasionally to attract a different audience and to check whether what has been your best draw continues its appeal. Take *nothing* for granted if you can test to make sure.

BUT MICE DON'T BUY MOUSETRAPS: HOW TO FIND THE AUDIENCE YOU NEED

Targeting by Building Profiles

Profile building can be critically important for many different kinds of business and the success of their advertising and promotions. If you are a retailer, your customer profile may seem obvious, but there is a simple and inexpensive way to make sure: *Ask your customers why they bought what they did at your shop.* Since they may not want to tell *you,* use the same approach suggested for getting help in defining advertising objectives. Ask the marketing department of a nearby college or community college for help in wording the questions and doing the actual interviews. For instance:

- Did your customers check advertising before purchasing a product or service and if so, in which medium?
- Which publications do they buy and/or get delivered, actually check the ads, read, or just skim?
- Which publications do they like best? (This is a check against the "which they read" answers.)
- Demographic information, where appropriate, such as age, education, and income, given in approximate ranges. As stressed in the chapter on telemarketing, it is astonishing what people will tell you, when they are asked politely.

Often the answers are not at all what you expected and lead to changes in advertising plans. Perhaps equally important, it never hurts to show professional concern for your customers' wants and needs!

Manufacturing may require more sophisticated research—and often gives equally surprising results. For example, when a film company produced a series that would explain upcoming surgery to patients, the company "knew" its customer profile. It consisted of family doctors who make the initial diagnoses and surgeons specializing in those fields. But before the filmmaker's advertising agency did anything about creating ads, it did a routine check to corroborate the customer profiles. It took only a very brief telemarketing survey to learn that the true customer—ready and eager to order, immediately, over the phone—was *not* the doctor. It was the hospitals' senior floor nurses, who were responsible for putting the patients at ease before surgery.

The client saved tens of thousands of dollars in two ways: by not advertising to the wrong audience and through earning profits by advertising to the right target audience. Even more important, the company gained insight into the importance of verifying a customer profile—even when you "know" that you know the result before you begin.

There's much more about profile building and its use in the chapter on direct mail.

So decide to whom you will be advertising before you write a single word. Often, it's not as obvious as it seems. Suppose you have a baby product. Will you advertise to parents, grandparents, pediatricians, toy store owners, supermarket buyers, and so on? Don't work on what to say until you're absolutely clear about two things:

1. **The audience you're trying to reach.** This may, in fact, be a variety of audiences. The question then becomes one of how many different messages you can get into one ad. Generally, you are better off to concentrate your advertising on one specific target—the "rifle" rather than the "shotgun" approach. To repeat: Don't expect any one ad—or any one medium—to do 10 different things or you'll get one-tenth the results . . . or none at all.

2. **What you want your audience to do.** Rush to your shop . . . call for an appointment . . . invite you to their office or home . . . send money . . . send for information . . . authorize a trial subscription . . . Vote! Buy! Try! Call! Write! Drive! Fly! Run! Walk! Taste! Imagine! Sleep! And that's just a sampler to get you started.

DESIGNING THE AD

This chapter will guide you in writing a competent advertisement; however, only God can gift you with the talent to be a designer. Therefore, in the hope that we will be forgiven, we do what real designers do. We borrow. Or as a number of great designers are credited with saying: "The art of creativity is not to reveal one's sources."

How to Design Your Ad without Being a "Designer"

Look through the publications in which you expect to advertise, and pick out those ads which you feel are well designed and are aimed at your audience. Equally important, they must be the same size as the ad you wish to produce. Try to find several examples, especially those with different amounts of manuscript—what copywriters call "light," "medium," or "heavy."

Now pick two or three you like best. These will be your models. Everything you do to create your ad will be based on one of them. The reason for choosing several originals is to give you flexibility in how much you say. But whatever the original has—light copy or heavy, large type or small, with a picture or without—plan to do the same. Avoid the temptation to mix and match—to take design elements from several ads and combine them into a new whole. That is what professional designers often do, but those of us who aren't pros usually botch it up.

Eventually, you'll give your manuscript, along with your design model, to a typesetting service and ask them to *approximate* the original. (You want to avoid lawsuits whenever possible.) Do not do this on your own computer, unless it has a true typesetting program. It won't work! This aspect of advertising is called *production* and needs a manuscript as well as a design. That's why writing the ad is next. Production, including the wisdom of setting your own ads, follows right after.

SUMMARY

- When it comes to design, don't. Find a true designer . . . or follow a real designer's lead.

WRITING THE AD: THE IMPORTANCE OF BENEFITS

The key to writing successful ads lies in training yourself to turn features into benefits—and then to use benefits to sell the product or service.

A **feature** is anything inherent in your product or service, for instance, punctureproof tires on a bicycle, large type in an insurance policy, nonpolluting soap in a laundry. In essence, a feature is what *you* have put into your product or service.

A **benefit** tells the potential buyers what's in it for them if they use your product or service. For example:

- Are your bicycle tires punctureproof because they're made from uncomfortable solid rubber, or is the benefit that these state-of-the-art tires are so safe that riders won't need to carry patching kits and pumps?
- Large type in an insurance policy seems an obvious benefit for the elderly, but is it necessary if you're trying to sell to newlyweds? How about "No eye-straining tiny type, but a policy designed to be read and understood!"
- Surely you can develop six additional benefits of even greater value to the person you are trying to persuade, no matter what you wish to sell.

How to Develop Benefits

Even though you want to end up with benefits, begin with features, because they are what you are likely to know best. List each individual feature at the top of a 5″ × 8″ index card. Start with what *you* know, then enlist the help of anyone who has knowledge you may lack or who might catch an item you've overlooked. Once you're satisfied that you've captured all the features, call an old-fashioned brainstorming session and explain your problem. You have all these great features, but the people you're trying to sell keep saying, "So what? What's in it for *me?*" It's the answer to these two questions that are your *benefits.*

THINGS TO REMEMBER IN BRAINSTORMING, WHETHER YOU DO IT BY YOURSELF OR IN A GROUP

1. Use a tape recorder so that you can keep note taking to a minimum.
2. There are no dumb suggestions.
3. Do not discuss individual answers now; that will inhibit the free flow of thought and force participants to defend something they may not quite understand themselves.
4. Bring in a new feature the moment the benefit stream dries up. Keep the action lively.
5. If someone suddenly suggests a benefit for a feature that's already been covered . . . great!
6. Don't let *anything* negative get in the way of the process.

Once you and your features are exhausted, type each one, along with its suggested benefits, into your computer, print them on individual sheets of paper, and distribute copies to the brainstorming participants. Now is the time for critical scrutiny—and for the addition of those benefits that brought you awake in the middle of the night two days after the original session. Ask everyone to criticize, add to, change, edit, or otherwise modify anyone's suggestions and return the lists to you for a final compilation. Whether you'll have another meeting to discuss this final list will be determined by your working situation, but the end result should be a series of features and their benefits, in order of importance *for specific audiences.* Thus, the same benefit may appear more than once but be given different emphasis, as in details of nutritional value in selling puppy food to veterinarians and careful feeding instructions in selling it to the general public.

SUMMARY

- Features instruct. Benefits sell!

Features Instruct, Benefits Sell!

Practically no one buys anything solely because of its features—it's the benefits that sell. Thus, you do *not* say, "the world's best seeds," but "the world's best lawn!" *Not* "777-horsepower engine," but "from 0 to 135 mph in 3 seconds!" And ask yourself where and how anyone is actually going to want to speed up like that and what other uses there can be for a machine with that much power. You'll continue to discover benefits that will surprise even you—and delight you with their pulling and selling power.

Beware of Overkill

Make sure that the benefits you claim are actually those *the buyer* gets. You are legally responsible for any claim made in your promotional materials—for *anything* that appears in print or on electronic media and for which you may be assumed to have given approval. There are some exceptions, such as an innocent mistake in a price that is corrected immediately at the place of purchase—although not a price designed to mislead! In case of doubt, consult your attorney, or better yet, change the benefit to something else. Advertising is not a game to see what you can get away with; it's one of the few ways of communicating what you hope to sell to potential buyers. The end goal is *not* to avoid going to jail. It's to make an honest sale from which the buyer will receive genuine benefits and the seller will earn a profit.

Developing Your Offer

Suppose you've listed every *feature* you can possibly discover in your product or service and overwhelmed the skeptic's "so what" question about each with a flood of irresistible *benefits*. Now it's time to consider the *offer*—the agreement between you and your customers, the promise you make when they buy your product or service.

Planning the Offer

In planning your offer, three different factors need to be considered:

1. **What do you want the reader of the ad to do?** For example, go to your store or shop? Telephone for information? Invite you to make an estimate? Send money?

2. **What will the customers get if they accept your offer?** Offers range from discounts (10 percent off) to service (oil changed while you wait) to promises (service with a smile) to guarantees (unbreakable or your money back). Offers can be implied (Swiss quality) or trumpeted (world's best roofing shingles). They can be limited (offer ends Wednesday) or universal (lifetime guarantee). Whatever the offer, try to match it to the needs and interests of your particular audience. If you're not sure and have no other good way to find out, run two or more versions of the same ad at the same time, changing only the offer, and see what happens. How to do this is covered under advertising production's "A/B Split" a bit later in the chapter.

3. **Can you afford it? Can you afford to offer less?** Obviously, you will make your offer as inexpensive to you as possible. However, the key is not cost as such, but cost effectiveness or cost per sale. So before deciding on what you can afford, get the best answers possible to four more questions:

   A. Is this a one-time sale, or are you trying to establish an ongoing customer relationship, and how much is each of these worth?

   B. How fast must you get your return on the dollars spent for promotion, and will that return come faster if you make the offer more attractive?

    C. What do your competitors offer, and should you match that or make your offer even more attractive? What are the likely consequences to them—and you—of an "offer war"?

    D. What are the immediate costs of these options, what are their break-even points, and what are their payoffs if they succeed?

The chances are that you'll have to make an educated guess at some of the answers to these questions. Do it, but keep your guesses on the conservative side. If there are to be surprises, let them be happy ones.

SUMMARY

- Load up with benefits to hit your target.
- Plan your offer for your customers' wants, not yours.
- When you can't afford the offer, can you afford to offer less?

WRITING THE AD: WHERE TO START

Every ad is made up of four elements:

1. The *headline,* commonly called "the head."
2. *Body copy,* which is everything except the headline and the identifying signature, or "logo."
3. The *offer,* which is part of the body copy but has to be thought out separately.
4. The *logo,* or signature, which identifies you and is generally the same as or very similar to your letterhead.

My personal way of working is to begin with the offer, go to the body copy, and do the headline last. The offer forces me to understand *exactly* what I am trying to sell and what the buyer gets in return. Chicken at 49¢ a pound, when the competitors are charging 55¢, requires no explanation; but an HMO or the 27th new restaurant to open this month needs a different kind of enticement.

After a rough (preliminary) draft of the offer, I do the body copy. My best headlines have generally grown out of a seed planted in the body, which I suddenly realize would make the perfect head. Of course, once the headline is in place, the entire ad may have to be fine-tuned to fit it, but that won't matter, as long as you work within the ARM framework, which I will tell you about next.

Where *You* Should Start

Where *you* start really makes no difference. Many writers begin with the headline or body copy instead of the offer and work from there. But no matter where you *start,* the headline is of such crucial importance that we'll treat it in detail first.

The Headline (and Illustrations)

The headline (and illustrations, if any) are your grabbers. They are the way to catch readers' fleeting attention and get them actually to read what you have to say. To do this, your advertisement, as every other marketing communication, must achieve the three ARM factors.

INSIGHT 8

The Three ARM Factors Every Ad Must Have
A Attract attention.
R Retain interest, so that the reader will become aware of your overall message.
M Motivate the reader to take the action your ad is designed to produce.

Think of these as the ARM portion of "I'd give my arm if only they'd buy." So arm yourself with the best headline you can develop to attract attention.

Two things your headline must do:
1. Attract the audience that will actually buy the product or at least influence its purchase. Buyers and influencers are not necessarily the end users. Young children neither buy nor influence their parent's purchase of cough syrup, but they are a major factor in deciding on purchases of toys, games, and cereals. Know for whom you write . . . and why!
2. Have carry-over power that will get readers from the headline into the ad itself.

Let's assume that you are writing an ad for a bicycle shop that has added a line for senior citizens. In writing your headline, don't try to be clever or funny. That usually fails, even when attempted by professionals. Rather, begin by stating the most obvious fact and let your ad develop from there. For instance, you might try

BIKES FOR SENIOR CITIZENS

This approach will keep you out of trouble, but is unlikely to attract very many from the audience you want, unless you spice it up with some *benefits.* Two of the all-time best benefits are "new" and "free," so let's try to get at least one of those into the ad, perhaps as easily as this:

NEW! BIKES FOR SENIOR CITIZENS

Notice the difference between "NEW BIKES and "NEW! BIKES." In this instance, the second version is probably preferable. With a different product—insurance, for instance—"NEW BENEFITS" might well do better than "NEW! BENEFITS." Always think of what will appeal to your specific audience and write accordingly.

But there is still nothing in the headline to get very many readers from "A" to "R"—to motivate Attention into Readership. So let's strengthen the headline with stronger benefits and, if room permits, more of them, like this:

NEW! SPECIAL OFFER
FOR 50-PLUS BIKERS

or

FREE TEST DRIVE OF SENIORS'
NEW RECREATIONAL BIKES
Free Lessons For Nonbikers Who Purchase

Note the change from "SENIOR" to "50-PLUS" in the first headline, and think about how you might make a similar change in the second. In writing headlines, keep refining, with three goals in mind:

1. **Broaden the appeal where possible, but take care not to lose your targeted audience.** "50-PLUS" may well capture the attention of seniors, plus attract a bonus group in the close-to-senior years. But broaden one step further to "ADULT," and not only have you lost the focus on your real audience, but you've picked up a number of possible meanings of "adult" that will simply confuse your message. In writing your ad, every single word must be considered for the effect it has on the total message, and nowhere is this more true than in the headline.

2. **Get at least one major benefit into your headline.** "NEW" and "SPECIAL OFFER" show benefits in the first example. The offer might well be the test drive and free lessons spelled out in the second sample, or it might be something entirely different.

3. **Fit the headline into the basic design you've elected as your model.** Count the number of letters and spaces in the headline rather than its words, and work within that limitation. Don't cheat.

A Note on Guarantees, Promises, and Offers

If there is to be *any* limitation or qualification on an offer—such as free lessons only to those who make a purchase—state this immediately in conjunction with the offer. Unless qualified, a "free" offer is legally free to *anyone* who requests it.

SUMMARY

- Start writing your ad wherever in the copy you feel most comfortable; you'll get to the headline soon enough.
- Follow the ARM (Attention/Retention/Motivation) rule for successful copy.
- Stick to the basic design of your models in writing—especially in your headline.

WRITING THE BODY OF THE AD

All your hard work in developing benefits will now pay you back, because this part of the ad should just about write itself.

1. Take the benefits you've put on individual cards or sheets of paper, and arrange them *in order of importance to the person you are trying to sell.*
2. Check your design model, and see how much room you have for copy.
3. Within your space limitation, put as many benefits as will fit, using a ☐ small box, • bullet, or √ check for each. This is the "telegraphic" style and gives a feeling of importance and urgency to your ad:

   - Lets you write incomplete sentences.

   - Gets the most benefits in the fewest words.

IF YOUR ORIGINAL USES
A STANDARD PARAGRAPH FORMAT

If your models use a paragraph format, count the letters in each line, and then use the same space for the telegraphic style. Copy in paragraph format takes a "writer," just as original design takes a "designer." And in most instances, the telegraphic style will be more effective, regardless of writing skill. So stick to what you can do.

---

4. Highlight each benefit with its own bullet, box, or check. You want your readers to know how much they will get. Don't be afraid to pile it on!
5. Separate the benefits from the offer by the use of a "subhead," a smaller headline within the body of the ad. (See Figure 2.2).
6. Your offer can be a continuation of the bullet/box/check format, or it can go to a normal paragraph format. Which it does will depend on the room available and the details of the offer. The goal is to make the offer easy to understand and impossible to resist. Always edit yourself with that in mind.

Features, Too!

What does your audience *have* to know about technical specifications, size, weight, colors, materials, packaging, and so on, to anchor the benefits to reality? Consider "Available in blue only" versus "A rainbow of 14 color selections." Or "1/4-hp motor" versus "3/8-horsepower, three-speed motor with reverse option." Or "All standard sizes" versus "20-gallon drums only." Recall how irritated you get when you respond to an advertisement, only to learn that it left out the one key factor that would have told you it wasn't for you (or when you didn't respond and found out too late that it was for you). Benefits, yes! Pile them on. But don't forget the features. They'll help draw the right customers in and, equally important, keep the wrong audience out.

NEW! Ad Pros' secrets for successful copy
Find out the way to write selling ad copy
the way professionals do in the newly revised 3rd Edition of
Do-It-Yourself Advertising and Promotion.
■ How to know exactly what to say
■ How to get the most sell into least space
■ How to work with layouts
■ How to get started . . . and keep going!
■ How to get results like a creative
genius without being one!
TRY IT FOR 30 DAYS. IT'S *GUARANTEED!*
Get your copy of **Do-It-Yourself**
Advertising and Promotion directly from the publisher.
Follow the step-by-step directions for 30 days to create your
own ads. If you're not satisfied for any reason,
return the book for full credit or refund. This handbook
works for you or we take it back and refund your money.
000 pages. 21 Checklists.
Illustrations. Index.
only $00.00
Available wherever books are sold
JOHN WILEY & SONS
111 River St., Hoboken, NJ 07030

Figure 2.2 Manuscript copy for advertisement for *Do-It-Yourself Advertising and Promotion* before final price and number of pages is known.

A Sample

Figure 2.2 shows how the manuscript might look for a small ad for this part of *Do-It-Yourself Advertising and Promotion.* Instructions for type sizes would be given in the margin.

Check out how this sample is loaded with benefits. The headline contains three (new, secrets, success). Every point begins with the benefit of "how to" and then adds one or two more. Even the subhead offers the clear benefits of a 30-day trial and a guarantee; what could be a clearer benefit than a no-nonsense, no-quibble guarantee? Aim for that if your product or service permits; if not, come as close as you can. The features are there, too, with the number and size of pages, checklists, illustrations, and an index.

INSIGHT 9

Keep a single, clearly marked master copy of any manuscript. Use it to show all changes and corrections, and hold it along with all supporting documents that show when and where the changes originated. On computerized systems, use a printed (hard copy) manuscript for this purpose. Neatly redone versions will, of course, exist, but the final check is always against the master.

Identifying Yourself: Your Advertising Signature or Logo

Somewhere in every advertisement, the advertiser's logo—the particular way you show your name, address, and telephone number—has to appear. No matter how fancy or plain, be sure that your logo does include your address, phone number, fax, e-mail, and web site, if applicable. Don't assume that the ad is so appealing that your readers will look them up. They won't. Rather, they'll go to your competitors—the ones who make it easy to do business with them. Always remember that no one *has* to buy from you, so . . .

- Make it simple.
- Make it easy.
- Make it a benefit for the buyer.
- Prepare to laugh all the way to the bank.

SUMMARY

- Use a telegraphic style for the body of the ad.
- Concentrate on benefits, but don't forget the features.
- Let the offer itself determine its writing style.
- Complete you logo with all the ways someone can contact you: address, phone, fax, e-mail, and website, if applicable. Your readers won't do it for you.

ONE FINAL CHECK BEFORE TYPESETTING

You know the audience you need to reach, and you have developed a cornucopia of benefits and offers that should make them buy. Now is the time to analyze your finished copy and layout for its appeal to that particular audience. Answer the following ARM questions:

- Does your headline shout for *Attention* from your specific audience?
- Do your benefits *Retain* and heighten the interest of that same audience?
- Does your offer *Motivate* the audience to the action you want it to take?

If the answers are all "yes," and if the amount of copy matches the model ad you've chosen, you're ready to go to production.

PRODUCTION: FROM MANUSCRIPT AND LAYOUT TO FINISHED AD

You've picked a design and written the copy. Now all you have to do is set the type and get it to the media in a form acceptable to them. Fortunately, that's the easiest part, and the next few pages will tell you how.

Typesetting Options

1. **Outside production service.** Turn over the ad to an outside service and let them do everything else. This is the easiest way to go, and not too expensive.

2. **Desktop publishing.** If you are very skillful at using your computer to set type, try to typeset the ad yourself. But unless the end result looks as good as professional typesetting, turn it over to the pros.

3. **Typesetting by your medium.** If your advertisement will run in a single magazine or newspaper, find out if the publication offers a typesetting service and at what cost. Often, this is free or low-cost, and many publications take pride in doing a fine job as part of their overall service. Some of these publications will even permit you to run ads they set in other media, so check on that, too.

4. **Professional typesetting.** Professional typesetting, which was a thriving industry when our book was first published, has largely disappeared as a stand-alone enterprise. Designers and design studios have taken this business in-house and the remaining "typesetters" now tend to offer design services also. Typesetting does exist at many quick printing and copy locations, but the majority lack the knowledge of typography that made old-fashioned typesetters such a valuable helper to the do-it-yourselfer.

Whether your type is set in-house or outside, here are a few things you should do and know in dealing with typesetters:

Things You Should Do
- Explain that you are using your sample ad as a model only; it must not be copied so exactly that you might get sued.
- Get a cost quotation. Find out if the cost includes any changes and, if not, how changes are charged.

Things You Should Know
- **Typos.** Mistakes by the typesetter, called typos, are corrected without any charge to you.
- **Alterations.** Alterations are the changes you make after the manuscript and layout are delivered and the type is set. They are at your expense. There will be a minimum charge for any alteration—even a single comma.
- **Manuscript.** The best way to avoid charges for alterations is to make sure that your manuscript is clean, that is, exactly as you want it. But be prepared to make a few changes even so. Typesetting seldom comes out exactly as we'd like. So make whatever changes you must, but try very hard to make them all at once. That minimum charge comes back each time you request another set of alterations!

Before deciding which typesetting option to choose, you may wish to know more about type itself. What's involved in deciding on a particular typeface and why you might pick one over another are covered in the next section.

SUMMARY

- Use a professional-quality typesetting source. It's the cheapest way to get a professional look.
- Give your typesetter a letter-perfect manuscript. It's the best way to keep your typesetting inexpensive.

Type: Faces, Weight, and Sizes

There are thousands of different styles (faces) of type from which to choose, but there is no need to work with more than a very few. To see some obvious differences among them, see Figure 2.3. You may not find the exact same faces on your computer, but they will be close.

Major Type Families

Every typeface belongs to one of three families:

- **Cursive** type imitates script or handwriting. It has little use in the body of an ad but is sometimes used for headline or logo.
- **Serifs** are the small curlicues or fine lines at the tops and bottoms of letters. This book is set in a serif face.
- **Sans serif** means "without serif" and is any type in that family. The "Major type Families" above is a sans serif face.

The Serif Advantage.   Most adults find serif type easier to read than sans serif, with a group of serif designs known as "reader faces" easiest of all. Of the tens of thousands of books, magazines, and newspapers published in the United States, practically every one uses such a reader-friendly type.

The Sans Serif Advantage.   Sans serif, too, has its advantages, chief among them the following:

- **Compressibility.** Sans serif condenses, or compresses, type better than serif does. That is, you can get more letters per inch without distorting the type.
- **Contrast.** Often, it pays to be different. If everyone else is using a serif face, at least consider the alternative. Or you may want to draw particular attention to one portion of your ad, such as a special offer.
- **Everyone else is doing it.** If everyone else advertising to your audience is using sans serif faces, try to find out why. Ask the representatives of the media where the ads run and the advertisers themselves. Better yet, run the same ad both ways and track the results. Unlike designers or authors of books, your interest isn't in typography; it's in sales. Do whatever works!
- **Reverse type.** White or light-colored type on a dark background is easier to read in sans serif than serif (although it is generally harder to read

This is 10-point Bembo Roman, often chosen for its suggestion of tradition. First designed in Italy in 1495, it was revived in 1929. *As you can see, Bembo Italic projects an image of grace and refinement.* BEMBO IS OFTEN USED WITH SMALL CAPS AND OLDSTYLE FIGURES, SUCH AS 1234567890. It is frequently employed in annual reports and publications of nonprofit organizations.

This is 10-point Garamond 3 Roman, preferred for its classic feel. It was designed in France during the sixteenth century and bears its creator's name. *Garamond 3 Italic, like Bembo Italic, is graceful and refined.* IT ALSO ENJOYS A COMPLEMENT OF SMALL CAPS AND OLDSTYLE FIGURES, SUCH AS 1234567890, IN ADDITION TO THE NORMAL 1234567890. It is frequently used in university and hospital publications that solicit contributions from alumni or philanthropists.

This is 10-point Sabon Roman, which was designed in the 1920s but is based on Garamond, with much of the same charm. *Sabon Italic differs only slightly, yet perceptibly, from Bembo Italic.* Designers often use Sabon as a substitute for Bembo or Garamond for a change of pace.

This is 10-point Bodoni Roman, classified as "modern," with its distinctive slab serifs and sharp contrasts. *Bodoni Italic is dignified and not at all flowery.* First designed during the Italian Renaissance, Bodoni was all the rage in the earlier part of this century and is now making a comeback in annual reports and high-quality newsletters.

This is 10-point ITC Berkeley Oldstyle Book, based on a 1938 design, and often selected for its elegant details. *ITC Berkeley Oldstyle Book Italic is even more detailed, as evident on the Q, & and z.* The face is sometimes used in advertising for a less subdued traditional look, and sometimes in brochures and other shorter publications.

This is 10-point Palatino Roman, a more modern serif face. Its contemporary feel comes from the taller x-height on its lowercase letters and the wider feel of its upper case. *Palatino Italic lends a touch of elegance when needed for emphasis or titles.* Palatino can be used for anything from newsletters to fine art books.

This is 10-point Futura Extra Black Condensed, often chosen for its excessive boldness. Previously thought suitable for headlines only, it is now sometimes used in text to achieve a radically modern feel. At this size, it requires additional letterspace to be readable. The face has been used in invitations to art gallery openings and nightclubs, for example.

This is 10-point Univers 55, often chosen for its sans serif simplicity and its subtle character. That subtle character differentiates it from Helvetica (not shown), whose ubiquity from train platforms to instruction manuals renders it undistinguished. Univers is less blocky than Helvetica, yet just as consistent.

Figure 2.3 Eight typefaces used by leading designers for catalogs and other advertising projects. All are 10 point in size, despite their seeming differences.

Figure 2.4 A violator.

in either typeface than standard black on white, such as what you're reading here). Use reverse type only in headlines, logos, and what ad pros call "violators" (see figure 2.4), those star-bursts, such as the one on the cover, or other shapes that highlight a very bold statement, as in the bicycle ad described earlier. No matter what your designer says *never use reverse type for an entire ad,* especially in body copy. It slows down the ability to read.

- **Overprinting.** Using sans serif definitely improves the legibility of type printed on top of ("over") a background color or illustration. However, improved does not necessarily make it good. The key is contrast between type and background. Equally important, when seniors are your target, larger type sizes are needed. Always let legibility be your guide.
- **Subheads.** Many designers use sans serif for subheads, with the rest of the ad in serif type. The authors' personal preference for subheads is a bolder (darker) version of the face used in the body of the ad.

About Type Weight

"Weight" refers to the thickness of type. Practically every face ranges from a very thick, "bold" style to a "regular" version considered the most legible for text body, to a thin or "light" design. All of these weights are also available in italic and bold, especially on more-sophisticated computerized typesetting machines, which can italicize a term or make it bold at the click of a mouse. The names given to the degrees of boldness or thinness vary from face to face and are not really comparable. One design's "black" may be darker or lighter than another design's "ultra bold." Your typesetter will have samples with the appropriate names. For desktop setting, your computer can print each version in the styles available to it.

INSIGHT 10

Use a single typeface for your ad. Variations in size and weight are almost always preferable to mixing faces. Do it!

ABOUT TYPE SIZES

Type sizes have a measuring system all their own, called points, with each point being $1/72$ of an inch. This paragraph is set in nine-point ($1/8$-inch) type, but a quick measurement will tell you that none of the letters are actually this size.

Ascenders and Descenders.   Take a good look at this paragraph. Some letters in it, such as "h" and "l," extend toward the top, and others, such as "p" and "g," extend toward the bottom. Yet despite these ascenders and descenders, none of the lines run into each other. Each letter is confined within a theoretical frame that leaves room at the top and bottom, so no matter how close (or "tight") you fit your copy, there is always space between the lowest descender and the tallest ascender. The exact size of this frame may appear larger or smaller than it actually is, according to the design of individual letters. Here are some ways to add legibility:

1. Pick the typeface you find easiest to read.
2. Place additional space, called "leading," between lines. This often is more effective than making the type larger. Spacing instructions are indicated in points. For instance, "$9/9$" means 9-point type with no extra space, "$9/10$" means one point ($1/72''$) of space between each line, "$9/11$" means two points, and so on. The type in this paragraph is $11/13$.
3. Reduce the type size, but leave the same point differential. For example, going from $10/11$ to $9/11$ often increases legibility while giving a few more letters per line. But don't set copy smaller than nine points if you can avoid it. The easier your ad is to read, the more likely it is that it actually will be read. Leave tiny type to personal classifieds.

SUMMARY

- Serif faces are easier to read than sans serif. Use serifs.
- The fewer typefaces, the better the ad. Use a single face of varied weights and sizes.
- There's no point in running ads nobody will read. Keep the smallest type for the body of your ad at $9/11$. *Reduce the amount of copy before you reduce the size of the type.*

Production Considerations for Photography and Art

If your model ad includes photography or art, you have a number of options:

1. **Do it yourself.**   Take your own photograph or draw your own illustrations. Let your conscience be your guide.
2. **Outside proessionals.**   Use a professional photographer or artist. Photographers' and artists' fees are often negotiable and the quality of their

work is seldom affected by their price. Be sure to read the section on art and photo ownership, page 126, before you order or buy.

3. **Supplier's art.** Use existing photographs or art, or use graphic materials from one of your suppliers. They may be overly familiar to you, but they'll be entirely new to your audience.

4. **Stock art.** Use stock photographs and illustrations—pictures that can be used by anyone for a set fee. There are numerous sources, Such as:

- Wonderfile. A royalty-free source. One payment for multiple uses. 888-361-9992 or www.wonderfile.com.

- Masterfile. A use-based cost. This is not necessarily a higher charge! 800-387-9010 or www.masterfile.com.

Stock Suppliers will work with you to find a picture that fits the mood or subject you specify. Usually, they will also send you a variety of pictures from which to choose. These photographs can be cropped; that is, only a portion of the photo need be used, for added impact.

Other Stock Pictures Sources

Many large cities have local creative arts resource directories. Ask the chamber of commerce, your public library, or the director of your local advertising club. Also, there's always the Yellow Pages and your very helpful media representatives. The production directors of advertising agencies are probably the best source. Ask them. They'll be able to do a favor for both you and one of their own suppliers. That's two good deeds with a single phone call. If you're neither in nor near a large city, ask your fellow advertisers what they do. Obviously, they've solved the problem already and may save you much spinning of wheels.

SUMMARY

- Use a professional photographer or illustrator when possible; otherwise get existing or stock art.
- Finding suppliers is the easy part; deciding which one to use is the hardest.

Film for Advertisements

Preparing your final ad for printing has become both much simpler and more demanding in our computer world. See Chapter 15 for the current how-to.

A Record-Keeping Hint. Underneath every ad, show the ad number, as explained in Figure 2.1, the media in which it ran, and dates when it appeared. Tell the color separator to leave that information as part of the proof. For ads that do not first go to film, do the same thing and make a good copy for yourself. Keep these record proofs in a computer file or notebooks that will not be used for any other purpose.

There's much more about film preparation, especially for color printing, in Chapter 16.

ABOUT TESTING

When time and budget permit, advertising professionals test the key elements of their ads to learn the best advertising approaches and media. You do the same, and, like them, rely on your business experience and common sense when you can't. When testing is practical, be sure to structure your ads so that you learn what you want to know.[1]

- **Testing two completely different ads** for the same product or service is fine, provided that your price and offer are the same for both. Otherwise, how will you know whether the result came from the ad, the price, or the offer?

- **In testing one key item**—a lower or higher price, headline, offer, illustration, and occasionally typeface—leave everything else exactly the same and *change the one item being tested only.* If, for instance, you change both the price and the headline, how will you know which produced the result you get? If you increased the price and sales increased, too, or even stayed the same, you won't care. But what if sales fall? Was it because of the new price or the new headline? Decide exactly what it is you want to learn, and test that without changing anything else. For example, suppose you wish to test the appeal of the same product to two different audiences. Figure 2.5 shows how this might be done. In each ad, the headline identifies the target audience. In the body of the second ad, the benefit is modified slightly from the first in accordance with the audience's needs. The rest of the copy remains the same. By placing these ads in media that provide cards for reader response, test results were achieved at very low cost. Note how adding a name at the bottom ("call Alice" for one ad, "call Jean" for the other) adds to the ease of tracking results.

Testing: The A/B Split

Many newspapers and magazines will run two different ads of the same size in every other copy of an issue, usually at a slight additional charge. This is not one ad in the first half off the press followed by a different ad in the second half. Rather, A/B means that, of the copies delivered to houses, apartments, and offices in the same block, or the copies sold at newsstands, every other one will contain ad A, with the rest having ad B. In publishing terms, that's known as a *true A/B split,* and it is just about the easiest, most effective, and least expensive way to test the appeal of two different offers, prices, headlines, and so on.

Demographic Editions

Many publications offer not only A/B splits but also *demographic editions.* When you purchase a demographic edition of a publication, you purchase a specific location and/or socioeconomic segment of the total circulation. Large-city newspers offer neighborhood editions that make it affordable for local retailers to advertise in the "big" paper. National magazines offer everything from over 100 test market

---

[1]For much more than can be covered here about testing, see John Caples *Tested Advertising Methods,* 5th edition, edited by Fred Hahn.

Figure 2.5 Produced on a computer by professional designers, these one-half-column ads (2³/8″ × 4⁷/8″) tested the appeal of the same product for two different audiences. Photography by Lucky Curtis, Chicago, IL. Copy by Hahn.

locations (*Reader's Digest*) to 1.6 million top businessmen and women (*Time*). Explore these possibilities with the media representatives, and, *if it makes economic sense for you,* weigh the factor into your final decision regarding your choice of media for your ad.

WHEN TO CHANGE AN AD

No advertisement retains its selling power forever. Even successful ads are often improved by testing different headlines, benefits, or offers—or sometimes by such a simple thing as changing and advertising new business hours. But never change a successful ad simply because you've seen it so often that you're sure that readers are tired of it. The chances are they're not. In fact, an even better chance is that they're not aware of it at all and the ad is just starting to do its best work.

One of the more counterproductive mistakes made by advertisers is to stop running successful advertising because they are bored with it. They've lived with the ad from conception through all the birth pangs, to its final arrival as a fully developed promotion. They want to move on to something new and are convinced their customers feel the same way. But their customers and prospects probably haven't seen the ad at all, and when they do, they won't pay it nearly the attention the advertiser likes to believe they will. There are only two valid business-related reasons for changing an ad:

1. The ad is no longer cost-effective.
2. A different ad or a different version of the same ad has proven more effective.

The Only Excuse for a Failed Ad

A second common—and costly—mistake made by advertisers is to invent excuses for advertising that didn't work. Of course, if you are holding a tent sale, and a tornado keeps everyone locked into their cellars, you will certainly take that into account. But if you have a proven offer, product, price, and medium, very little else, except the ad itself, is an acceptable excuse for a failed promotion. Always go back to the three ARM basics of:

1. **Attention:** Did you get readers' attention, and how might that have been done better?
2. **Retention:** Did you retain readers' interest through meaningful benefits, and how might these have been enhanced?
3. **Motivation:** Did your offer motivate the readers to act the way you had expected, and how can you improve the offer?

Learning from Success

Learning from success is much more pleasant than learning from failure, so don't forget to do that, too. Keep detailed records. Analyze them to discover what you did right, and then apply it in the future. Avoid developing new ads without feedback when feedback is available. Celebrating your successes is much more fun than being creative about excuses. And following the directions here should give you lots to celebrate. So go to it!

INSIGHT 11

Beware of the bottom-line success available through drastic reductions in or elimination of advertising. The short-run savings may all seem positive, but the long-term consequences are frequently irreversible. It costs much more to regain than to retain your customers, if it can be done at all.

SUMMARY

- Test those things most likely to matter—media, offer, audience targeting, headline, benefit emphasis, price.
- If testing the obvious motivators doesn't point you toward success, think very hard about your product or service.
- Test only one thing at a time, or test totally different promotions. Never change two aspects of the same promotion within the same test; you won't know why you got the results—no matter what they are.
- Continue to use successful ads until something else proves more cost effective.

COOPERATIVE ADVERTISING

Cooperative (co-op) advertising is an agreed-on sharing of specified advertising costs or other promotional costs among manufacturers and retailers or analogous groups. Co-op is an arrangement beneficial to both manufacturers and their business partners and an excellent way to expand advertising and promotion dollars. As Figure 2.6 shows, co-op can extend far beyond the traditional print and broadcast media; in fact, many manufacturers now allow Internet advertising under the guidelines of their co-op advertising programs. The list of eligible media continues to grow, varies by manufacturer, and will be reimbursed provided it is agreed on and specified within the manufacturer's plan.

What a Promotional Advertising Program Should Specify

- **Who pays.**   How much or what percent of the cost of the advertising the retailer and the manufacturer each pay. Written programs should clearly specify he terms and rates for reimbursement.

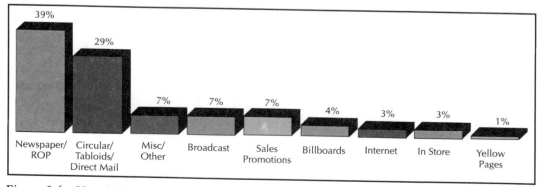

Figure 2.6   How 2001 co-op advertising was spent in the footwear industry. (Courtesy of the Advertising Checking Bureau, Inc. www.acbcoop.com.)

• **How co-op accrues.** Accruel specifies what goods or services apply to the amount or allowance that is offered by the manufacturer for the advertising, how that amount is determined, and over what period of time. By law, the accrual must be proportional for all like outlets of participants, regardless of size or volume. For instance, manufcturers may not give retailers 5 percent of sales for a 100-unit purchase and 10 percent for a larger volume purchase, thereby unfairly rewarding the larter outlets. The degree of co-op must be the same for every retailer, although it can differ or be absent for wholesalers. Co-op may also be regionalized or otherwise limited as long as it is available to *competing* users.

INSIGHT 12

Co-op accruals are "use it or lose it" amounts, not an additional discount automatically credited to everyone. Co-op is distributed for specified promotional use and is forfeited unless earned in that way.

• **What will be promoted.** This need not parallel how co-op is accrued. Often, all of the co-op earned is targeted on one or a few promotional leaders.

• **When to promote.** In planning your co-op advertising, consider any national ad campaigns scheduled by the manufacturer. Agree upon dates, seasons, or tie-in events and keep in mind the cut off date for using the current year's co-op accrual dollars. In specifying dates, consider such possibilities as using unspent Christmas co-op for January sales.

• **Where and how to promote.** National organizations tend to favor name media. However, "shoppers," "penny-savers," and similar media may be a retailer's best buy. Stay flexible. By law, not only must co-op be proportional, it must also be functionally available. That is, it may not be limited to what only the largest accruals can buy.

• **Message approvals.** Both co-op partners are responsible for claims about their products and services. Agree on who creates and who approves the advertising. To prevent conflicts, many manufacturers prepare advertisements and commercials that are easy and inexpensive for retailers to personalize. In fact, a great deal of the advertising that appears in newspapers is manufacturer-created so as to maintain the appropriate product or brand image.

• **What is not covered.** Many co-op programs exclude all creative or preparatory charges and cover only a specified percentage of the *net* cost of newspaper and magazine space or radio and television on-air time. Be sure to read the fine print of the written co-op plan to see what is eligible for reimbursement. But see Figure 2.6. With the increase in Internet advertising and the use of other alternative media, ACB has expanded verification beyond the traditional print media. Many manufacturers today have modified their co-op programs to allow the use of these media, although they will usually require that the retailer receive prior approval for advertising in selected media. The purpose of a co-op program is to promote the product or service better and sell more of it. If what will work isn't in the current agreement, attempt to add it. Just remember: put it in writing!

Auditing Co-Op: How and Why

Most companies with substantial co-op programs audit retailer or other local charge-backs through an advertising checking service such as the Advertising Checking bureau (ACB). Local advertisers submit tear sheets of their ads (the actual pages on which the ads appeared) or some other proof of promotional activity, with invoices substantiating the cost. ACB keeps a running total of advertisements that appear in many U.S. newspapers and hundreds of magazines, with their actual cost to the advertiserrs. Like other co-op advertising services, it checks charge-backs and, where necessary, corrects them to their true rate. *In most instances, the corrected charge-back is approved by the retailer.* When the original charge-backs are too high, an audit report specifies actual rates and an approved co-op amount. In case of conflict, the service, rather than the manufacturer, becomes a party to the disagreement. Thus, rather than a conflict between a supplier and a customer, you get a debate between accountants. If, as can also happen, charges are too low, notifying retailers about this can hardly be surpassed for creating goodwill.

Many co-op agreements specify that claims for co-op reimbursement will be verified by an auditing service. Such services are in every major and most secondary markets and can be found in the Yellow Pages. Most of them specilize in local and regional media. A few, such as ACB, operate nationwide. If you are the co-op provider, the incremental cost for auditing could prove to be a valuable investment in helping maintain the integrity of your program. In the evolving world of promotional advertising, manufacturers should be certain to remain current in the Federal Accounting Standards board (FASB) regulations concerning advertising documentation requirements and policies.

WARNING!

When changing your telephone number *for any reason,* several days later call Information as well as your old number to see what happens. And do it every six months even if you don't change. We repeatedly were given a nonoperating number when trying to contact ACB. It was not the first such misinformation in our experience.

SUMMARY

- Don't limit co-op to the most obvious media; instead determine what is most effective for your business and your market.
- Co-op agreements and guidelines should be clearly written and easily understood.
- Be certain that documentation requirements are followed so that co-op reimbursement can be expedited.
- Monitoring of retailer co-op advertising helps ensure that the manufacturer advertising standards, brand image, and program are upheld.

NEWSPAPER/MAGAZINE ADVERTISING CHECKLIST

Project Title _____

Project Description _____
_____

Overall Supervision By _____

Budget _____ Completion Date _____

Date _____

Project # _____

Checklist # _____

Deadline _____

Start Up Date _____

MANAGEMENT DECISIONS	ASSIGNED TO	DUE	IN	MUST APPROVE	BY DATE	IN	INFO COPY ONLY	SEE ATTACHE
1. Quotations			☐			☐		☐
2. Budget approval			☐			☐		☐
3. Project approval			☐			☐		☐
CREATIVE DECISIONS								
4. Audience Focus			☐			☐		☐
5. Message of Ad			☐			☐		☐
6. Benefits Focus			☐			☐		☐
7. Headline Focus			☐			☐		☐
8. Offer Focus			☐			☐		☐
9. Writer			☐			☐		☐
10. Designer			☐			☐		☐
11. Colors			☐			☐		☐
12. Typesetter			☐			☐		☐
13. Artist			☐			☐		☐
14. Photography			☐			☐		☐
15. New Art			☐			☐		☐
16. Material for Media			☐			☐		☐
17. Shipment to Media			☐			☐		☐
MEDIA DECISIONS								
18. Media Focus/Selection			☐			☐		☐
19. Ad Dates			☐			☐		☐
20. Ad Sizes			☐			☐		☐
21. Space Cost			☐			☐		☐
22. Media Notification			☐			☐		☐
MECHANICAL CHECKS								
23. Logo OK			☐			☐		☐
24. Address OK			☐			☐		☐
25. Phone(s), e-mail, website OK			☐			☐		☐
26. Editorial OK			☐			☐		☐
27. Legal OK			☐			☐		☐
28. Marketing OK			☐			☐		☐
29. Management OK			☐			☐		☐
30. Copy of Ad as Run			☐			☐		☐

MEDIA LIST   If checked, see back for additional media.

Newspaper or Magazine	Cover Date	Date Issued	Reservation Deadline	Deadline for Film	Size	Colors	Cost

Figure 2.7   The newspaper/magazine advertising checklist.

NOTES ON THE NEWSPAPER/MAGAZINE ADVERTISING CHECKLIST

These notes are a supplement to the material presented in this book (see Figure 2.7). They are not a self-contained substitute for that material.

1. **Quotations.** The total of all quoted and/or estimated costs accepted from outside suppliers, plus the known or estimated internal out-of-pocket costs. This is the amount given for budget approval in #2.

2. **Budget approval.** The amount either accepted from #1, or otherwise determined as a fair cost to do the project. If lower than the figure in #1, costs may have to be renegotiated with suppliers or the project modified to fit the dollar allocation.

3. **Project approval.** Once the project *can* be done for the amount in #2, a decision on whether the project is worth the cost, no matter how "fair" the individual charges may be.

4. **Target audience.** Determination of the target audience at whom the ad is focused. Usually this is done as part of a total marketing program. Everything else about this ad must then be controlled by that focus. How else will you decide the message and the media?

APPLICATION

Neither the checklist itself nor these notes are a time line. Many of the items must be done at the same time rather than sequentially. For instance, numbers 5 through 8 plus 18 are first decided, then worked on simultaneously.

---

5. **Message.** This tells the writer *what* is to be said, not *how* to say it. The actual wording is the job of the writer in #9.

6. **Benefits.** The benefits keyed to the audience in #4. If none of those benefits seem particularly suited to that group, the choice of *those* benefits and why *that* particular audience was targeted must be reconsidered.

7. **Headline.** The headline's subject, not its wording. Pick the one thing most likely to attract the target audience; usually the key benefit from #6.

8. **Offer.** Make the offer a *major* reason to get the advertised product or service *from you* and to do it *now,* especially if a competitor's options are available. As the advertiser, do not be afraid to echo your competition. If you can't do better, at least stay even. Note that the offer can appear anywhere in the ad as long as the design gives it such prominence that it can't be missed.

9. **Writer.** The checklist shows the person who *appoints* the writer.* If certain things must be said in a specific way, let the writer know before he or she begins . . . and whether this is a legal constraint or a management decision. If the latter, management should be willing to at least consider alternatives.

10. **Designer.** The person responsible for choosing the designer.* Good designers often surprise, so do not be hasty to say no to what you may not like at first sight. It is the designer's job to know how to appeal *visually* to the targeted audience. All of us, and especially the younger generation, are becoming more visually oriented. Designers are right more often than they are wrong.

11. **Colors.** The use of color in newspaper and magazine ads almost always gains readership. So does size. If dollars are set and you must choose one of the two, ask each media representative for *facts and figures* on which works better in their specific medium. If still undecided, pick color. For low-cost, striking effects, ask about "spot color," the use of any amount of a single color; just so it does not cover the entire ad.

12. **Typesetter.** For advertising that requires design skill, use professional typesetting. Limit in-house desktop typesetting to straightforward flyers, reports, and other simple-to-create projects.

13–14. **Photography/art.** Both who selects the photographer and/or artist and who gives the technical as well as the aesthetic instructions (not necessarily the same person!). Unless the person doing or given the assignment is an expert in art *reproduction* for newspapers and/or magazines, discuss this with the filmmaker in #16 before any photography or art is ordered (For instance learn about shooting photos for "contrast" or "detail" and what the disk and/or the camera can and cannot "see.") *Much* more about this is included in the Prepress Checklist.

15. **New art.** "New art," formerly called "camera ready," is the all-inclusive term for illustrations, photography, and type put into position to create the ad. Once digitized it becomes an electronic file. It is the last chance to change anything at relatively low cost. It includes *every* instruction to the disk producer or filmmaker *in writing.* If another department or an outside service or agency does this, the person who assigned the project goes over it with them. For major projects, the disk producer or the filmmaker should be present also. Everyone involved must understand the instructions and understand them *the same way.*

16. **Disk/Film.** Preparation of preprinting disk or film also includes proofs (photographic copies of what the printed ad will look like) for final approval, as well as for each publication. The proof is checked against *every* instruction on the original art to make certain it has been followed. It is literally checked off so nothing is overlooked. Equally important, the proof is examined to see whether those instructions make sense *in what is seen now.* Newspaper advertisements seldom are as "sharp" (clear) in print as on the proof. If for *any* reason the ad is hard to read on the proof, it will probably be impossible to read when printed. The original instructions must also specify how many proofs and what kind will be needed. Each medium's rate card has this information. Most ask for one proof; some want more.

---

*Here as elsewhere in these assignments, the person making the appointment and depending on skill and time available, may choose himself or herself, as well as someone else.

17. **Shipment.** Let the prepress firm ship the film to its destination—even if it is across the street from your office. That is part of *their* know-how and *their* responsibility!

18. **Media.** Does the focus of the media match the target audience focus in #4? If not, why this selection—unless it is the only paper in town? If there is no good medium for what you are advertising, use what is available . . . and work on building a mailing list.

19. **Dates.** Differentiate among the four key dates in making magazine selections:

    A. *Closing date.* The date by which ad space must be reserved (ordered) for the ad to appear in a specific issue.

    B. *Mechanical date.* When the material from which the ad will be printed—usually digitized, sometimes film, or new art—must be at the publication. If art is required, check with the publication to learn exactly what they mean by this term.

    C. *Cover date.* The date printed on the publication's cover.

    D. *Out date.* The dates on which the magazine will be mailed and when it will appear on newsstands. These may be up to a week apart.

20. **Size.** Have a reason for the size of the ad. Note that it often costs less overall to create a single larger ad and use it everywhere than to pay for the creation of smaller versions for less important *and less expensive* media.

21. **Space cost.** Dramatic discounts are possible when someone advertises fairly frequently in the same medium. Almost all publications combine "space" with "frequency" discounts to make it possible to run more advertising at lower per-ad cost. The media buyer, the person responsible for purchasing the space, should ask media representatives about "rate holders," the smallest ads accepted by a medium, and whether there are any other ways to save. Since media representatives may not be able to negotiate rates other than those given in their rate card, check with the media buying services found in major city Yellow Pages about *the possibility of negotiated rates!*

22. **Notification.** Notify or confirm orders, including telephone orders, to *each* medium by fax or mail. Use a reservation form similar to the one shown in Figure 2.8. Although reservation on a purchase order or letterhead is accepted by practically everyone, the use of a media form gives a better assurance that all pertinent instructions will be covered.

23–29. **Mechanical checks.** Someone has to be responsible for checking each of these items before anything may be printed. Make sure that the responsible person *does* check them and signs off *in writing*. In many organizations, the logo—the organization's name, address, and telephone number—is stored in its own computer file, and *must* be used from that art. It is an excellent safety measure, providing every such file is corrected when there is a change. Experience shows that practically no one really checks logos. Wise advertising directors make themselves the exception.

30. **"As run" copy.** Some *one* person must be responsible for maintaining a file of all ads "as run"; that is, as they actually appeared in each publica-

Hahn, Crane Advertising, Inc.

2035 Hawthorne Lane • Evanston, IL 60201-3002 • Phone/Fax 847-866-9009

SPACE RESERVATION

Date _____

TO THE PUBLISHER OF:

This is authorization to schedule advertising as specified in:

☐ Rate Card # _____
☐ SRDS Dated _____
☐ Other_____
Ad Size/Colors _____
Space Cost _____
Frequency Rate _____

ADVERTISER_____
Address _____
City_____ State _____ Zip _____
Telephone _____ Fax _____
Authorized Signature _____ Title _____

AGENCY _____
Address _____
City_____ State _____ Zip _____
Telephone _____ Fax _____
Authorized Signature _____ Title _____

AD ID #_____
AD HEADLINE_____
_____

ADVERTISING SCHEDULE
Date(s) _____
_____
_____

☐ Bill to advertiser
☐ Bill to agency
☐ Materials herewith
☐ Materials to follow from:
_____
_____
_____
_____

SPECIAL INSTRUCTIONS
Send 2 tear sheets of printed advertisement with billing.
_____
_____

Figure 2.8 Typical reservation form for newspaper and magazine space. For radio and television, use a Media Reservation form.

tion. The printed copies should be used for this file. Normally, only a single copy of the page on which the ad appears accompanies the invoice—even when the advertiser requests two or three. So if accounting must see the *printed* ad before a medium is paid, let them see the original as proof, thank them for their care, and leave with them a reproduced copy "for the record."

3 | Selecting Print Media

WHO READS NEWSPAPERS

The simple and truthful answer to "Who reads newspapers?" is "Just about every-one!" Though the trend in newspaper readership is downward, the majority of adult Americans, regardless of income, race, or sex, read either a daily or Sunday newspaper, and many of them read both. Furthermore, they read their paper not only for news and features but according to an *Advertising Age* study, even more intensely for the paper's advertising, including the classified section.

General Audience Newspapers

As of September 2001, 1,482 newspapers were published in the United States. Of these, 776 were morning papers, 704 were evening papers,[1] and 913 published a Sunday edition. The six-month average circulation of the daily newspapers totaled 55,859,000. Approximately 82 percent of this total, or 45 million-plus, is made up of morning papers; the remaining 18 percent, or 9 million-plus, are afternoon editions. Sunday papers, published by 913 papers, totaled 62,020,000[2] or over 6 million more than the combined morning and evening daily total.

This Sunday total is not as surprising as it might at first appear. Papers sell more copies on Sunday, and the larger-circulation papers are most likely to produce a Sunday edition. (The only papers in the top-100 group not to publish a Sunday edition are *The Wall Street Journal* and *USA Today.*) America's largest 100, make up 50 percent of the circulation of all the dailies published. Weekly papers, which are equally important in many smaller communities, add about 8 million for an overall daily/weekly total of 63 million-plus.

More than 85 percent of these papers, are delivered to homes, offices, and businesses. The rest are single-copy issues bought from newsstands, retail shops, and vending machines.

While the January 2000 circulation of general daily and Sunday papers has shrunk in the past five years, the opposite is true for target audience publications,

---

[1]Thirty-three "all-day" editions are counted twice in the morning and evening totals.

[2]All circulation figures are from *Editor & Publisher International Year Book 2002.*

Category	Publications	Paid	Free	Total
Black	125	3,538,000	2,175,000	5,713,000
Community	6,646	20,600,000	28,570,000	29,170,000
Ethnic	167	2,723,000	1,041,000	3,764,000
Gay / lesbian	49	25,000	741,000	766,000
Hispanic	146	1,209,000	5,080,000	6,289,000
Jewish	111	1,259,000	718,000	1,977,000
Military	130	117,000	1,543,000	1,660,000
Parenting	148	156,000	6,499,000	6,655,000
Real estate	91	105,000	2,649,000	2,754,000
Religious	128	4,741,000	338,000	5,079,000
Senior	129	20,743,000	5,045,000	25,788,000
Shoppers	1,413	666,000	60,430,000	61,096,000
Alternative (niche)	128	171,000	7,165,000	7,336,000
Totals	12,641	56,054,000	121,883	178,047,000

Source: Editorial Publisher Publisher International Yearbook 2002.

Figure 3.1   Special Audience Newspapers.

which match it in paid circulation and more than triple it when free circulation is included (see Figure 3.1).

Newspaper Readership

Although industry statistics on readership are best taken with a grain of salt, long experience in this field indicates that the vast majority of delivered general audience papers—75 percent seems a conservative estimate—go to homes or businesses with at least two adult readers. This gives a probable readership of about 110 million adults who have paid not only for news but also to let advertisers try to sell them their products or services!

INSIGHT 13

Advertising tends to take up 40 percent of newspaper space, yet has been and continues to be welcome in practically every home. Have you ever heard of *anyone* asking to be protected against receiving "junk advertising" in their newspapers—even if it's the same "junk" catalogs and other FSI (free standing inserts) that newspapers write editorials against if it's delivered by mail?

Who Advertises in Newspapers . . . and Why

Newspaper advertising is, overwhelmingly, used by local businesses targeted at local sales, though a surprisingly large number of these businesses have no formalized media plan. According to Direct Marketing magazine, advertising in all U.S. newspapers, including supplements, totaled over $49 billion in 2000, a 30% increase over the past five years. Of this amount, the three major categories, in thousands of dollars were:

Retail	*General*	*Classified*[3]
48%	12%	39%

Records for general advertising have not been subdivided further since 1984. But using percentages based on the ten-year averages kept from 1974 to 1983, the totals would be:

Retail	*Dept. Store*	*General*	*Auto*	*Finance*	*Classified*
51%	6.5%	6.9%	0.025%	0.035%	35%

These totals includes national advertisers, such as automotive, soft drinks, alcoholic beverages, clothing, and cosmetics. Those firms are willing to pay a higher "national" rate for three reasons:

1. To increase sales of their products in local outlets.
2. To show local retailers that they are supported by national headquarters. (A campaign I directed aimed at retailers selling the Rand McNally Road Atlas used posters on the sidewalk side of buses where retailers were most likely to see them even while inside their stores.)
3. To make certain that the national advertising message is given exactly as the corporation wants it presented.

WHO READS MAGAZINES

If we consider only those magazines that carry advertising, according to Media Research more than 90 percent of all American adults read at least one magazine per month, with the average adult reading two magazines per week and spending about one hour with each.

Magazine Categories

SRDS, a huge database to be discussed shortly, divides magazines into four broad categories:

1. Consumer
2. Agrimedia
3. Business to Business
4. Professional

---

[3]Newspaper advertising is charged by the "column inch." Classified columns almost always are narrower than the rest of the paper; therefore, more columns and more dollars per page. 2000/2001 newspaper classifieds have been lower both in percentage and dollars for economic reasons and their increasing appearance on the Internet. However, they may have rebounded by the time you read this.

Scholarly publications, a category that would add thousands of additional titles to the list, are so specialized and often of such small circulation that only those wanting to advertise to those fields concern themselves with their rates.

Unlike "scholarly" magazines, "educational" media are in the business category aimed at the preschool through university market.

HOW TO PICK PRINT MEDIA FOR ADVERTISING

The easiest way to pick media is by how well they reach your target audience(s) (TA)—the audience you want to reach. To do this, check on where other advertisers trying to reach the same targeted audience are advertising in a consistent fashion. But don't just look. Do as you did when new to setting objectives. Telephone advertisers. Explain that you are a novice and ask for anything they might tell you about the success of their ads in specific publications. Next, call advertisers who use a medium only once or a few times and ask the same questions. Ask, too, which media they would recommend that might be more effective. People love to give advice, so be sure to check whether or not they actually do advertise in the places they recommend.

WARNING! BEWARE OF "THE RULE OF TWO"

An often quoted "Rule of Two" states: "See an ad once, it's a test; see it twice, it's a success." Do *not* take this at face value in trying to evaluate where, what, how often, and, most important, why others advertise! Rather, see the "Rule of Three," which follows shortly.

Before using the Rule of Two—or any other rule like it—to evaluate a competitor's advertising schedule, consider the following three points:

1. **Response request.** Is there any response requested in the ad? If the reader is not urged, or at least asked, to do something, as in Figure 3.2, how can you know the ad's results?
   - "$1/3$-OFF" qualifies as a hint.
   - "BRING THIS COUPON TO GET $1/3$-OFF TILL WEDNESDAY!" qualifies as a test.
2. **How to quantify.** Is there an obvious or subtle way to quantify; that is, to know responses to the ad? For instance, is there a coupon or reply card that is coded to each medium and issue, or a telephone extension or name for which to ask? (See Figure 3.2.)
3. **Time to quantify.** Before assuming that good results are why the same ad was repeated, check to see whether there was enough time between issues to permit evaluation of results before the next ad was run. In a daily newspaper, that can be as little as three days. In weekly publica-

Figure 3.2 $3 OFF WITH THIS COUPON is an offer. Its expiration date and the bottom-right media code make it a tesr.

tions, rescheduling an ad even a single day after it appears can mean one to five weeks before it will run again. In most monthly magazines, the wait will be two to four months.

INSIGHT 14

Seeing the same ad over and over doesn't *prove* anything about its results. The Rule of Two is based on the action of direct marketers for whom "advertising" and "sales" are one and the same. Do *not* expect it to be the reason for most other advertisers' scheduling!

APPLICATION

"The Rule of Three"
The advertising "Rule of Three" states: "An ad must appear at least three times *in media read by the same audience* before you can expect it to be seen (paid attention to) once." This does not mean before *anyone* will see it once, but before it will be noticed at least once by *the majority* of your target market audience. *In print media, national advertisers consider a range of 3 to 10 exposures as the minimum required for effectiveness.*

The Rule of Three (or "Three Hit Theory") has primary value for longer-term "institutional" advertising targeted at brand recognition rather than the immediate response wanted by many retailers. Note that successful retailers and retail chains—from groceries to computers to autos—often do both kinds of ads.

IF YOU DON'T KNOW WHERE TO ADVERTISE

For anyone, beginner or longtime media professional, *the* guides to the full range of options on advertising to a specific audience or in a particular field are the SRDS services. The print editions are in many public libraries and practically all professional advertising media departments, which also have access to the online versions.

These huge databases, available online and in paperbound volumes, are frequently updated. They give detailed information, field by field, on practically every medium that accepts advertising. Individual SRDS guide titles,[4] as this is written, include the following:

- *Consumer Magazine Advertising Source*™
- *Business Publication Advertising Source*®
  Includes Card Decks,[5] Health Care
- *SRDS Media Planning System*™
  A new online media planning solution. Permits seamless budget, schedule, and campaign management, using SRDS consumer and Business data.
- *Newspaper Advertising Source*®
- *Community Publication Advertising Source*™
- *Circulation*
  In-depth analysis of newspaper circulation
- *TV & Cable Source*®
- *Radio Advertising Source*™
- *Direct Marketing List Source*®
- *Interactive Advertising Source*™
  Web sites that accept advertising
- *Out-of-Home Advertising Source*™
  Twenty-one away-from-home or office media such as billboards, transit, in-flight, and so on
- *The Lifestyle Market Analyst*®
- *SRDS International Media Guides*™
- *Technology Media Sources*™
- *Hispanic Media & Market Source*™

An additional SRDS service covers the mechanical aspects of production, that is, how to get each kind of ad physically ready for a specific medium. But you are unlikely to need that unless you are responsible for furnishing the materials for the ads to many advertising media. The same information is available on an individual basis from any of the media you decide to use.

Understanding SRDS Print Media Listings

Listings in SRDS follow a consistent format of subject, state, and city, ordered alphabetically within each category. Individual listings (Figure 3.3) begin with brief descriptions of the audience and editorial content of the publication. Then

---

[4]All SRDS guide titles are trademarked. SRDS guides can be purchased from SRDS, 1700 Higgins, Des Plaines, IL 60018. Call them at (847) 375-5000. Look for SRDS on the Web at http://www.SRDS.com.

[5]Card Decks are packages of postcard-size advertisements mailed on a share-the-cost cooperative basis to a specifically targeted audience. Their primary use has been in business-to-business promotions, but they are beginning to appear as a consumer medium.

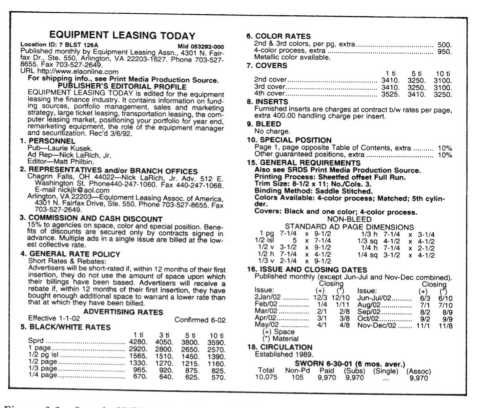

Figure 3.3 Sample SRDS listing. (As published in the August 2002 edition of *Business Publication Advertising Source*, published by SRDS.)

they go through a series of uniformly numbered segments of specific interest to advertisers. Thus, categories 4–7 always explain basic costs, and category 10 covers the availability of premium positions for advertising, such as the page opposite the table of contents. Many advertisers believe that these locations get exceptionally high readership and are willing to pay a premium to have one of their ads appear there.

If premium positions are not listed—or present on a rate card—they may be available by request on a "first-come" basis. (One of my greatest advertising coups was to get ads for a single client on all covers of all programs of their industry's most important trade show by asking and paying for the space 18 months in advance of publication. No one had ever asked before—and a special meeting of furious, and much larger, competitors foreclosed the same option for anyone, including themselves, in the future.)

Reliability of SRDS Data

SRDS does not itself research its information but uses data provided by each publication on an issue-by-issue basis. Many of the publishers supply information on circulation in a standard format that is audited by the Advertising Bureau of Circulation (ABC), an agency very much like a CPA firm.

Whether or not the information is audited is not necessarily an indication of its reliability. The auditing process is quite expensive and unaffordable by some new publications and publications with a small circulation. Other publications have a long history of satisfied advertisers and feel no need to go through auditing. Auditing is, however, a factor you should consider, especially with publications that have multiple audiences, not all of which are your potential customers.

Category 18 gives the basic statistical information about a publication and tells whether or not the information is based on audited data. If the publication is audited, an Internet link to the complete audit statement is provided. Thus, for example, in an August 2002 listing, the audited magazine *Art Business News* (see Figure 3.4), edited for art dealers and framers, tells us its territorial distribution and that of its 29,000-plus circulation, about one-third are retail galleries while the majority of the others are picture framers. If SRDS does not have this type of circulation analysis, request a media kit from the publication itself. Magazines and trade papers that sound right from their title may have substantial parts of their circulation that are not your market. For instance, without the circulation analysis, how would you know that *Art Business News* is maybe the wrong medium to promote art supplies? Don't trust luck. *Know* before you buy!

If your interest does lie in reaching galleries or framers or both, find out whether any other publications reach that audience, including those with unaudited circulation.

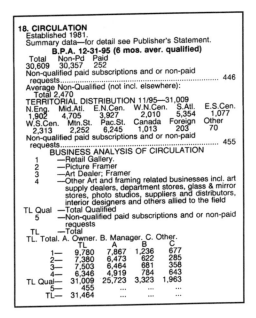

Figure 3.4   Circulation analysis supplied by *Art Business News*. From SRDS.

Before you decide on any of them, however, ask each publication *why* you should use it to reach your specific audience, and then make your evaluation as you would any other investment—including the possibility that you should switch your promotional effort to direct mail or some other medium. Don't fall into the trap of advertising just to see your name in print.

HOW TO RESEARCH A SUBJECT

Though even the SRDS services can't cover every subject, try them first. For online directories, flexible search optons are available. You can search by classification groupings, individual titles, and keyword. You can also narrow your search to just media that are audited. If you still can't find what you need, phone the SRDS Listing Locator Service at (800) 851-7737 or visit them online at www.SRDS.com.

If, as is likely, you do find your category, you can link directly to additional planning information, such as audit statements, online media kits, and media web sites. You can also communicate directly with the right media personnel using e-mail hotlinks within a listing. For printed directories, check the classification groupings near the front. If your subject is not there, turn to the index of individual titles and look for a keyword. Ask a few of your larger competitors, too. They want to keep their trade media in existence by finding additional advertisers. It is possible that no specific medium exists for your product or service. In that case, consider a more general publication that's likely to be read by your audience (the Sunday edition of the *New York Times* by college presidents, for instance, or *The Wall Street Journal* by wealthy retirees), providing your reaching them that way has at least the potential of being profitable.

If, as is likely, you do find your category, contact the appropriate media and ask for a Media Kit information package. Request several copies of each publication to get an idea of its editorial content as a "home" for your message. Each medium's representative will probably also wish to meet with you. You can arrange that at your convenience.

4 | Flyers, Brochures, Bulletins, and Invitations

FLYERS AND BROCHURES: HOW THEY DIFFER

In standard trade usage, a *flyer* is made from a single sheet of paper. Figure 4.1 shows just eight of the different formats that a flyer may assume. By contrast, a *brochure* is in booklet format. In working with outside sources, find out what distinction *they* make, so that you both speak the same language. Because different suppliers may have different definitions, keep your *internal* nomenclature consistent and "translate" as you go along.

A BRIEF MANUAL OF PROCEDURES

Procedures for creating flyers and brochures should be the same whether you do everything yourself, are part of an internal team, or supervise outside resources. The procedures apply to everything from simple do-it-yourself projects to the most sophisticated agency-produced materials. As with every promotion, creating a flyer or brochure is a five-step process:

1. Learn, or decide on, the purpose of your promotion.
2. Establish a time frame and remain within it.
3. Establish and remain within a budget.
4. Write and create the promotion.
5. Produce and distribute the promotion. This is covered as part of Chapter 6 "Direct Mail," and in greatest detail in Chapter 16.

Let's consider each of these points in more detail.

DECIDING ON A PURPOSE

The "Target" Audience

Begin by determining to whom the piece will be addressed. The type and amount of information you include should be guided by its use. For instance, senior management will require a preponderance of financial data, the engineering depart-

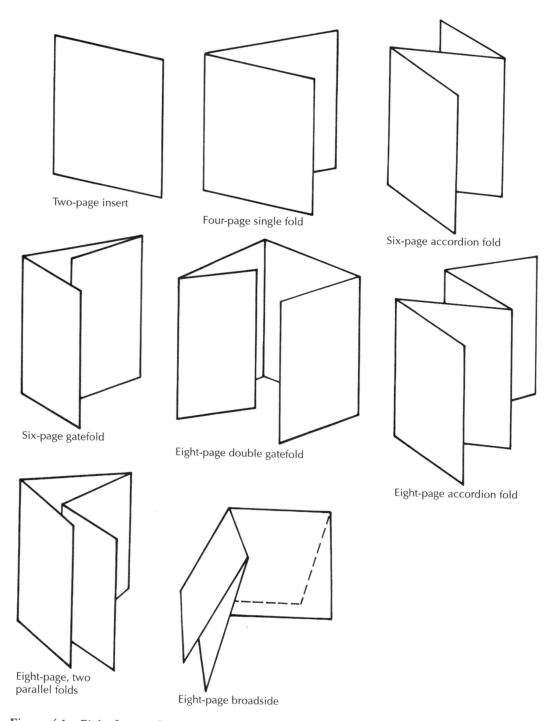

Two-page insert

Four-page single fold

Six-page accordion fold

Six-page gatefold

Eight-page double gatefold

Eight-page accordion fold

Eight-page, two parallel folds

Eight-page broadside

Figure 4.1 Eight formats for your flier. Planning a printing project requires a choice of format and paper. The most reliable way to appraise your selection is to have paper samples, called "dummies," made by your printer or paper merchant. These blank dummies give you an accurate example of how a specific paper's substance, weight, and surface qualities look and feel in the format you specify. (Formats shown courtesy of James River Premium Printing Papers. Original art for James River by Hyers/Smith Advertising, South Norwalk, CT.)

ment will demand production specifications, and an interior designer will be interested only in size and colors.

If, as is often the case, you must combine information for more than one audience within a single promotion, make it easy for each audience to find and use what it needs. Some simple ways to do this are given later in the section.

How Much to Include

Whether you're a brand-new enterprise or long established, don't just guess at how much to tell your audience about who you are and what you have to sell. If you're part of an ongoing organization, accompany several experienced sales representatives as they make their calls. Try to differentiate between sales success based on personality (I like Chuck) and that based on how goods are being sold (I like what I hear and see). If you are a member of an enterprise that is just starting up, you may have to do some or all of the selling yourself.

INSIGHT 15

Always put more detail—whether hard data or a sales pitch—into your printed promotion than into your sales call. There is no way your *readers* can question your flyer or brochure, so give them *everything* they need to make them decide your way.

An extensive guide to what and how much to write begins in a few pages. But don't jump there yet. Though writing comes first, there's a lot more to do before the actual writing begins.

Using the Promotion

Knowing how and by whom the piece you produce will be used is critical to its creation. Will it contain "high" or "low" information; that is, must it generate a sale or produce a lead? Will it be mailed? Placed on the Internet? Distributed by a sales staff? Included in packages? Posted on bulletin boards? Used at trade shows? Or all of these? Let's consider each of these options in turn.

Mailing
Mailings can be self-mailers; that is, mailed without envelopes or mailed inside of envelopes or other containers. They may go by first class or several variations of "Standard" bulk shipping. You may include a coupon or a reply form or request the recipient to write, call, or fax. These and other mailing options and decisions require a chapter all by themselves and are covered in Chapter 6.

Use by the Sales Staff
Your promotion can be a visual aid during a sales call, a leave-behind reminder, or both. It can be "Let me walk you through this flyer, which illustrates the important points about our service," or "Let me just leave you this brochure, which highlights the points we've been talking about. You can look it over with engineering, and I'll call you about an order on Tuesday."

Some "political" points must also be considered. For example, in larger organizations, how will the sales staff react if the only address shown on flyers and brochures is the home office? Conversely, how will the home office react if all the responses go to the field? As the advertising or promotion director, you may be the only person involved in the promotion who works for "the company," so resolve any such conflicts before your creative efforts begin.

Enclosures

Make sure that your promotion piece fits into the package. Is your piece the first thing you want seen or the last, and how can you be certain that it will be seen at all? Join the packaging design team first and the packaging crew later. There's no substitute for hands-on experience in this phase of promotional activities.

Distribution at Trade Shows

If you use "help yourself" literature bins at conventions, meetings, or other events, how much of the promotion piece do the bins show: the complete page, the top half, or the top few inches only? The answer will affect the design of the piece, so do let the designer know.

Internet Use

Thanks to digitized production, practically any flyer or brochure can be placed on the Internet. They can also easily be modified for the specific medium or any other medium. Think multimedia from the beginning!

ESTABLISHING A TIME FRAME AND TIME LINES

A time frame is the time allowed for the complete project. A time line details the time for each of its subprojects, such as researching, writing, designing, editing copy, typesetting, and doing artwork. For any project involving outside resources, your time frame and budget are totally interrelated. Costs are affected by time allocations, and completion dates may not be flexible. The brochure that says "Visit our booth for a special discount" will do you no good whatsoever after the exhibit closes—no matter how creative the excuses are for not getting it done.

Individual time lines are established by working backward from a targeted end date and allocating completion dates and responsibility for each of the following benchmarks:

- **End date.** When the project must be completed and what "completed" means: printed, distributed (how?), or received (by whom?).

- **Distribution.** The dates for each aspect of distribution, including mailings and warehousing of extra stock.

- **Printing and bindery work.** The time from the completion of printing film or disk to the delivery by the printer of *usable* printed pieces. For flyers and brochures, a separte bindery may be involved in collating or folding, or the print-ers may do this themselves. The time line schedules them both.

- **Copy, design, and layout.** Who will do copy, design, and layout and who must approve them are often the most flexible elements of the time line, especially if they are done by internal staff. What is sometimes forgotten is that they are also the foundation on which everything else is built. Constructing that foundation is discussed in detail almost immediately in the upcoming section "Creating the Promotion."

- **Final disk or art, prepress, and proofing.** These subjects are covered in detail in Chapter 16. Check there; schedule here.

ESTABLISHING A BUDGET

There are two types of budgets, and they must not be confused. Both are fixed, but they are based on different conditions:

1. *Administrative budget.* A specific amount is allocated, and costs must not exceed that amount.
2. *Estimate-based budget.* Costs are estimated, and projects are then approved, rejected, or changed based on the estimates.

The budget becomes a time line consideration when it must be approved by some-one other than yourself before any work may start. If this is mandated, build in time for getting estimates and quotations, as well as the approval itself.

CREATING THE PROMOTION: AN OUTLINE

The outline that follows is written as if you were the promotional supervisor of a large organization. Exactly the same procedures apply to the one-person shop or any size of organization in between.

1. **Purpose.** The purpose of the piece is the most important reason or rea-sons for preparing it; for instance: (a) to use ("walk through") during sales calls, (b) to distribute at conventions, and (c) to mail for leads and/or sales. Make an absolute limit of three. (How many can be "most" important?) *Put them in writing!*
2. **Sources.** Determine who will provide the information needed to write and design the promotion and when they will be available. Get a backup source, if possible.
3. **Check and approve.** Establish responsibility for the accuracy of infor-mation about the product, legal clearance, editorial clearance (spelling, grammar, the house style), and sales input. Determine who will edit—rather than write—review, and have final approval of the project. *Only one person can have final approval!*

4. **Concepts and presentations.** Depending on how you and your organization work, you may go through a series of concept presentations or go directly to final copy and layout. In either case, the materials must be put through the following steps, whether they be taken mentally while talking to yourself or in formal presentations to others:

A. **Organization.** Organize all your information in the order of importance to the specific audience that will see the printed piece. After it is organized, you can decide how much of the information will actually be used and the style in which it is to be presented.

B. **Emphasis.** Decide which points are to be stressed and which is the most important point of all. Make the latter into your headline.

C. **Illustrations.** Decide on photographs and other illustrations: how many there will be, what kind they should be, and where to get them.

D. **Response.** Determine what you want the reader to do and give them a reason to do it. This is the most frequently understated element in promotional literature. As advertisers, we tell the recipient everything, except why we want them to read the material.

E. **Policing.** Policing is neither proofreading nor editing, but a final check against #1, your stated purpose in producing the promotional piece. That's why we put that purpose into writing. It's very easy to get so carried away with our creativity, that we forget what we set out to do.

Once the basic concept has been developed, preliminary or "draft" copy and possible designs are produced. In organizations with several layers of management, these are the versions presented for managerial comments or approval. Note that detailed revisions may be required for draft copy and designs, as some managers can't visualize promotional materials until they see them in quite finished form. During my years as an advertising account executive, I'd reminded my clients—as gently as I knew how—that they were *paying* for all the changes they order. As employees reporting to management, you must—equally gently—give notice of impending deadlines.

INSIGHT 16

Do not show managers "rough," that is, not professionally finished, design concepts or unedited copy. Despite their insistence that they wish to eliminate the cost of "finished" presentations, in several decades of presenting to management, no manager has been happy with anything less.

SUMMARY

- Determine by whom and how your promotional pieces will be used. Make everything fit into purposes consistent with that determination. Put it in writing!
- Time frames control budgets, and vice versa. Nothing saves creative and production dollars like adequate time to do the job.
- Some deadlines must be met, and there is *not* always time to do it over, even if someone is willing to pay the extraordinary expense.
- *Know* who will be your sources for information, reviews, and approvals. Put it in writing!

A BASIC DESIGN CONCEPT

The One-Third Guide

For a one- or two-page piece (each page is one side of a sheet of paper, not the sheet itself), allow *approximately* one-third of the space for each of the following (see Figure 4.2):

- One-third for headlines and subheads, plus information about ordering or a coupon and your logo—that is, the special way you identify yourself. Frequently, your logo is also the way your name, address, phone, fax, e-mail, and website appear on your letterhead.
- One-third for illustrations, including charts, and captions.
- One-third for general copy; that is, the "body" of the ad.

For three pages or more, use the two-page guide for the first page and the last page, and then divide the remaining space so that you use half for copy and half for illustrations. Of course, these are suggested guidelines only, but they will give you a balanced approach to an inviting presentation.

Page Size Guideline

Keep your page size $8\frac{1}{2}'' \times 11''$ (letter) or $8\frac{1}{2}'' \times 14''$ (legal size). Either one will fold into a standard No. 10 business envelope and is flexible for multipurpose use.

WRITING THE MANUSCRIPT: THE IMPORTANCE OF FEATURES AND BENEFITS

The Features/Benefits basics of writing for flyers and brochures are no different from writing for general advertising described in Chapter 2. The key additions follow.

- **The offer.** Tell your readers how to order or to get whatever you have to provide. If there are options, explain them. Make it easy. This is not an IQ test for your customers. Make the information complete. Restate the offer, its benefits, and its price. Include toll-free phone, fax, and e-mail, if available. Give the address to write to. List a specific department for information if there is one. Include *anything* that will expedite a response.[1]
- **Picture captions.** Copy for picture captions must be orchestrated just as carefully as that for any other element. The illustrations are there to help get across the overall message. Like your subheads, pictures and their captions should tell your basic story all by themselves.

INSIGHT 17

Your audience is most likely to read your flyer or brochure in the following order:
1. Headline and subheads.
2. Special offer if emphasized.
3. Illustrations and captions. Put the product's name in the caption!
4. The body copy in any order that happens to interest them.

   Thus, you have three chances to sell or lose the audience, even if your general copy is never read. Use each one!

SUMMARY

- To find out the benefits of your product, base them on what your features do for customers and prospects. What sells is not what *you* put into your product or service; it's what *they* get out of it.
- Organize before you write and the manuscript will take care of itself. Brilliant copy won't help if your readers can't make out why you are writing (You want me to do *what? Why?*)

LAYOUT AND DESIGN

With the guidance offered here, you can produce your own manuscript ("copy"). But few of us are given the skill to create our own professional-quality design or layout—that is, the overall visual impression and detailed specifications that make a flyer or brochure work. Unlike newspaper and magazine advertising, for which you can find an existing model to follow, printed pieces tend to be too individualistic for that approach. So use a design studio if you can afford it. If not, you have several other options. All but one are quite inexpensive. However, the somewhat more costly one will also be the easiest for you and give you more time for other things.

- **Use the basic layouts shown in Figure 4.2.** These models were created primarily to guide you in writing, rather than layout, but they can serve both pur-

---

[1]Note the telegraphic style in this paragraph. It combines bulleted-type statements with a paragraph format. It works!

Single-page version
(Use back for mailing)

Front of two pages

Back of two pages

Figure 4.2 Sample layouts for one- or two-page fliers. Put your headline *under* the main picture. And put a selling caption under all your small pictures, too. David Ogilvy, in *Ogilvy on Advertising,* tells us you'll get 10 percent more readership at absolutely no extra cost.

poses if nothing more sophisticated—or simpler—is required. Though they are functional, they make no pretense of being superior designs.

• **Use an existing promotion as a model.** Do this with great care, as you must make certain that the model really fits your needs. Never follow competitors' highly stylized versions. Not only will your product likely be mistaken for theirs, adding to their promotional impact rather than yours, but you'll probably hear from their attorneys as well.

• **Use digitized design.** Use one of the layouts that may be built into your computer program or that are available on inexpensive disks.

• **Do your own layout.** Let your honesty about your skills guide you.

• **Use a design studio or freelance designer.** No matter where you are located, there are dozens of studios and freelancers close by, eager to work with you if only they know of your needs. For studios, check with your business association and advertisers whose ads you admire. The easiest way to find freelancers is to place a classified ad in the Help Wanted section of your local newspaper.

Tell the studios or freelancers what your project is, what your time frame is, and, if possible, your budget for design and final art. If you have no way of estimating design costs, interview a few of the designers first, and then arrive at a figure based on their quotations. Make sure to *schedule* the interviews. Tell the candidates they will have 1 hour: 20 minutes to present samples *with their charges for everything they show;* 20 minutes for you to present your project; and 20 minutes for them to ask any questions. An hour should be adequate with the likely candidates. For simpler projects, allow one week for quotations. For more complicated promotions, allow two weeks.

Cost Factors in Working with Outside Designers

Whether you work with a freelance designer, a design studio, or an advertising agency, the following factors will affect your costs:

1. **Time available to complete the project.** Begin by asking potential suppliers their normal time needs for a project such as yours. What you consider a rush project may be their regular schedule.

2. **Quality of manuscript.** Has your copy been given final approval, or will there be repeated copy changes that will require new layouts? Because *you* pay for each new version, find out how they are charged.

3. **Number of versions required.** Many clients want to see two or three (or more) designs from which to choose. For *major* projects, this is a recommended procedure, but get costs quoted in advance. For routine flyers or brochures, get a single design. It will be the one the designer considered the best of the several he or she attempted before deciding on the one you are shown.

4. **Degree of layout "finish."** This refers to how polished the layout must be. There are three generally accepted variations: "rough," "semicomprehensive," and "comprehensive." What these three terms mean varies with everyone who uses them. Have prospective designers show samples of each kind of finish and explain the difference in their costs. With most commercial art now prepared on a computer, the differences may be minimal.

5. **Preparation of disk or new[2] art.** Most designers prefer to do the new art. Let them do it. Not only will you get a better end product, but you will have a happier designer, eager to work with you again in the future.

INSIGHT 18

In giving creative or production work to outside sources, have a budget and time line agreed on in writing . . . and never change those instructions by "client's alterations" without knowing the time and dollar consequences. Ask your suppliers to recommend alternatives. There may be a better way!

---

[2]"New" art is now the preferred trade term for what was formerly called "final" or "camera ready" art.

TYPE, TYPOGRAPHY, TYPESETTING, AND DESKTOP PUBLISHING

A discussion of type, typography, typesetting, and desktop publishing, as applied to flyers and brochures, is no different from that applied to advertising beginning on page 28.

SUMMARY

If God did not make you into a designer even such lesser creatures as co-workers and employers will probably notice. For true design, use a true designer. For routine layouts, use available computer programs or modify an existing model when it is practical to do so. When it is not, get a professional.

NOTES ON THE FLYER/BROCHURE CHECKLIST

These notes are a supplement to the material presented in this chapter. They are not a self-contained substitute for the material. The checklist is presented in Figure 4.3.

APPLICATION

Neither the checklist itself nor these notes are a time line. Many of the items must be done at the same time rather than sequentially. For instance, numbers 5 through 8, plus 18, are first decided, then worked on simultaneously.

1. **Quotations.** The total of all quoted and/or estimated costs accepted from outside suppliers, plus the known or estimated internal out-of-pocket costs. This is the amount given for budget approval in #2.
2. **Budget approval.** The amount either accepted from #1, or otherwise determined as a fair cost to do the project. If lower than the figure in #1, costs may have to be renegotiated with suppliers or the project modified to fit the dollar allocation.
3. **Project approval.** Once the project *can* be done for the amount in #2, a decision on whether the project is worth the cost, no matter how "fair" the individual charges may be.
4. **Target audience.** Are you trying to force different audiences' needs and interests into a single piece? You'll probably lose more in sales than you gain in promotional savings. Do this only if you have no way to reach each group individually.
5. **Purpose.** How the item advertised will be used and which use—if there are several—is the most important. Every other item on the checklist must keep the purpose in mind.
6. **Overall focus.** What the message is to achieve as a whole. The general "feel" of the complete piece.
7. **Headline focus.** Based on the benefits keyed to the target audience in #4, the one thing you hope will make the reader stop long enough to

FLYER/BROCHURE CHECKLIST

Project Title _____

Project Description _____

Budget _____ Completion Date _____

Date _____

Project # _____

Checklist # _____

Deadline _____

Start Up Date _____

MANAGEMENT DECISIONS	ASSIGNED TO	DUE	IN	MUST APPROVE	BY DATE	IN	INFO COPY ONLY	SEE ATTACHED
1. Quotations	_____	___	☐	_____	___	☐	_____	☐
2. Budget Approval	_____	___	☐	_____	___	☐	_____	☐
3. Project Approval	_____	___	☐	_____	___	☐	_____	☐

CREATIVE DECISIONS

4. Audience	_____	___	☐	_____	___	☐	_____	☐
5. Purpose	_____	___	☐	_____	___	☐	_____	☐
6. Overall Focus	_____	___	☐	_____	___	☐	_____	☐
7. Headline Focus	_____	___	☐	_____	___	☐	_____	☐
8. Subhead(s) Focus	_____	___	☐	_____	___	☐	_____	☐
9. Desired Response	_____	___	☐	_____	___	☐	_____	☐
10. Writers	_____	___	☐	_____	___	☐	_____	☐
11. Designers	_____	___	☐	_____	___	☐	_____	☐
12. Typesetter	_____	___	☐	_____	___	☐	_____	☐
13. Artist	_____	___	☐	_____	___	☐	_____	☐
14. Photographer	_____	___	☐	_____	___	☐	_____	☐
15. Finals, Disk, or "New" Art	_____	___	☐	_____	___	☐	_____	☐
16. Prepress OK	_____	___	☐	_____	___	☐	_____	☐
17. On-Press OK	_____	___	☐	_____	___	☐	_____	☐

MECHANICAL DECISIONS

18. Page Size	_____	___	☐	_____	___	☐	_____	☐
19. Number of Pages	_____	___	☐	_____	___	☐	_____	☐
20. Color(s)	_____	___	☐	_____	___	☐	_____	☐
21. Paper Stock	_____	___	☐	_____	___	☐	_____	☐
22. Film Preparation	_____	___	☐	_____	___	☐	_____	☐
23. Printer	_____	___	☐	_____	___	☐	_____	☐
24. Distribution	_____	___	☐	_____	___	☐	_____	☐

MECHANICAL CHECKS

25. Logo OK	_____	___	☐	_____	___	☐	_____	☐
26. Address(es) OK	_____	___	☐	_____	___	☐	_____	☐
27. Phone(s) OK	_____	___	☐	_____	___	☐	_____	☐
28. Editorial OK	_____	___	☐	_____	___	☐	_____	☐
29. Legal OK	_____	___	☐	_____	___	☐	_____	☐
30. Marketing OK	_____	___	☐	_____	___	☐	_____	☐
31. Printed Samples	_____	___	☐	_____	___	☐	_____	☐

Figure 4.3   The flyer/brochure checklist.

learn more about your message. Not the words—leave that to the writer in #10—but the thought!

8. **Subhead focus.** Sell here if you can. But more important, get across the focus message from #6, even if the subheads are all that is read. If #7 and #8 are a 10-second outline that tells your story, you probably have a winner!

9. **Response.** What you hope the reader will do after reading the piece. If the answer is "nothing special," why are you producing the flyer or brochure? Make the offer a *major* reason to get the advertised product or service *from you* and to do it *now,* especially if a competitor's options are available.

10. **Writer.** The checklist shows the person who *appoints* the writer. If certain things must be said in a specific way, let the writer know before he or she begins . . . and whether this is a legal constraint or a management decision. If the latter, management should be willing to at least consider alternatives. Specify whether you want "roughs" or a best effort "finished copy" as first draft. Better yet, ask the writer to produce finished copy, but treat it as a draft. But make sure that you let the writer know you are doing this. Writers tend to get hysterical if it comes as a surprise, after they're done.

11. **Designers.** Will copy be written to fit the design, or will the design be based on the copy? If different persons do #10 and #11, make sure that they can work as a team. Good designers often surprise, so do not be hasty to say no to what you may not like at first sight. It is the designers' job to know how to appeal *visually* to the targeted audience. They are right more often than they are wrong.

12. **Typesetter.** For reasonably simple styling, turn to desktop equipment and set your own type. Give your designer samples of your in-house type faces, so the copy can be marked to match. For pieces that require design skill, use professional typesetting, now most often supplied by your designers. Be sure they understand the importance of type *legibility!* (See Figure 2.4) Too often designers sacrifice "sell" for "award." All other factors being equal, nothing heightens the appeal of your product or service like skillful professional typography!

13–14. **Photos/Art.** Determine who selects, orders, and supervises photography and art. In addition to know-how, it will probably take time. Unless the person doing or given the assignment is an expert not only in art but also in *reproduction* for commercial printing, this should be discussed with the prepress firm in #16 before any photography or art is ordered. *Much* more about this in the Prepress Checklist in Chapter 16.

15. **Final disk or "new" art.** With desktop publishing, you'll probably create simpler art and type on your computer. If you are new to desktop, find out how to make your work practical for use by your prepress firm. For outside production, this is the last chance to change anything at relatively low cost. Put *every* instruction to the prepress firm *in writing.* If another department or an outside service or agency does this the person

who assigned the project goes over it with them. The prepress firm should be present also. Everyone involved must understand the instructions and understand them *the same way.*

16. **Prepress OK.** You approve the film by checking its proof. Check everything against the instructions on the hard copy, and check the job as a whole. Better yet, if you work in an organization with film and printing specialists, turn to them for help. It's their job. Let them do it. For newer filmless printing, see Chapter 16.

17. **On-press OK.** Go to the printer for on-press approval. If not, printers will "hold the presses" for approval and take the material being printed to you—at hundreds or thousands of dollars for press and staff waiting time. But what will you do if you want more on-press changes? Wait in your office again . . . and again. *You* go to the printer!

18. **Page size.** Take the original layout to the printer as soon as it is done. Ask your printer if a small decrease or increase in the page size can make a large difference in savings. If the printer says yes, and the new size is practical, tell the designers. It's easier for everyone if they create the design with the new size in mind.

19. **Number of pages.** For ease of folding, the most economical number of pages usually is a multiple of four (4, 8, 12, and so on). Does deciding on the number of pages precede the creative effort or follow it? Why?

20. **Color(s).** Selecting colors is subjective, but it's also an art. Accordingly, have it done by an artist if possible. Just make sure that the color choices work for sales as well as aesthetics. Not too many of us can read white type inside a light blue background or light blue printed on white.

21. **Paper stock.** Where only a specific stock will do, use it. Where options are possible, check your printer or paper merchant for what they have on hand. For some projects, the use of two different papers may bring dramatic savings. Ask!

22. **Film preparation.** If someone other than your printer prepares the film, be sure that the filmmaker knows that printer's needs. Make certain that they speak *with each other,* not only through you.

23. **Printer.** Different printers have different capabilities based on equipment, experience, and expertise. Selection of a printer and prepress firm is best done by an in-house specialist, if one is available. If not, become one by asking your associates in other organizations. Visit their suppliers with them if possible. That's how we learned most of what we know . . . and that's how we continue to learn.

24. **Distribution.** Determine what "distribution" means: How many flyers or brochures will be used for mailing, shipping to staff, warehousing, and so on? Requests and orders for your pieces may come from anywhere. But for request approval and filling of orders, a single person must be in charge.

25–30. **Mechanical checks.** Someone has been assigned to check each of these items before anything may be printed. Make sure that they do check them and sign off *in writing.* In many organizations, the logo, address, and phone numbers are preprint or in an approved computer file, in a variety of styles and sizes, and *must* be used from that art, an excellent safety measure, provided that every such logo is dated and thrown out when there is a change. Experience has shown that practically no one really reads logos. Make yourself the exception.

31.   **Printed samples.** Printed samples generally get wide distribution. Set up a system that won't force you to reinvent the distribution list with every piece produced. As with newspaper and magazine ads, every piece must be coded and a permanent file maintained. I astonished a client by still having a mailing the client wanted to recreate and that the agency had done 15 years before.

BULLETINS, INVITATIONS, AND INVITATIONAL BULLETINS

Bulletins and invitations are widely—and successfully—used for business-to-business seminars to sell products and services. They are discussed together because, *for advertising and promotional purposes,* their uses are frequently the same. Bulletins are also used for two other purposes with which you may be involved as a creative resource:

1.   **Bulletins that must be posted, but that no one reads.** State and federal offices, personnel and accounting departments, and senior management (among others) issue materials that *must* be placed on bulletin boards. However, unless the information displayed has real and immediate application to the audience for whom it was written, it is simply ignored. If you ask how that audience knows it can, with impunity, ignore such bulletins, the answer is, they just do.

2.   **Bulletins that must be posted and that everyone reads.** Often issued by the same sources as in item 1, they give information on newly issued or revised mechanical, safety, or material-handling instructions, on public or private requests for assistance, and many other things. The list is endless. In this case, the audience knows what it must *not* ignore.

The preceding two categories, insofar as they require promotional expertise, can be considered flyers and handled as such. Most often, there are models that can be followed and desktop publishing that can be used to produce the disk or new art.

The Challenge of Optional Posting

A third category of bulletins is of much more concern to advertising and promotion than the foregoing two. This is the bulletin that no one is *required* to post, although everyone who sees it should *want* to . . . and want to read it, too! Usually distributed by mail, it has to jump the initial hurdle of the mail room or secretarial censor, pass its second barrier of managerial scrutiny, and, most difficult of all, crash through the stone wall of passerby indifference. Because your bulletin competes for posting with all the others received at its destination, the challenge is formidable. Your likelihood of success is directly related to a slight modification of the first insight given in this book, which said, Keep it simple . . . keep it specific . . . and you're likely to keep solvent. Apropos of bulletins, the insight would urge:

INSIGHT 19

Keep it simple . . . keep it specific . . . keep it focused on benefits . . . and you're likely to get posted.

Who Decides What's Posted?

Even if you're sure you know who controls the posting of bulletins at the places to which you mail them, call a dozen of these places at random and ask to speak with the person in charge of putting up bulletins. If the operator does not know, ask for personnel. People will tell you almost anything if asked politely, so remember what you want to learn:

- What happens when a bulletin is addressed to an individual by name?
- What happens when a bulletin is addressed to a title (say, vice president of finance) or a job description (e.g., person in charge of posting financial training bulletins)?
- Does the size of the bulletin make any difference to its being posted? Which sizes are actually used?
- Does how the bulletin is received (e.g., in an envelope, as a self-mailer, hand delivered) make any difference?
- About what percentage of bulletins received actually get posted?
- Why?

Probably the single most important insight this chapter has to offer is this.

INSIGHT 20

Take *nothing* for granted. Phone first.

The steps in the posting process will tell you how to address and how to send your mailing, as well as what message, if any, to put alongside the address. Usually, a purely informative message, such as that shown in Figure 4.4, is adequate.

The combination of the right name or title, together with an appropriate "teaser"—that is, an interest-focusing outside message—will likely get your bulletin posted. Now all you have to do is to get it read and acted on.

How to Get Your Bulletin Read

For posting on a bulletin board, get all the excitement and information on a single page. Don't force your audience to see the other side to understand your message. You are producing a kind of billboard, not a brochure!

```
┌─────────────────────────────────────────────────────────────┐
│                                               ┌──────────┐   │
│  SENDER'S IDENTIFICATION                       │          │   │
│  ADDRESS                                       │  STAMP   │   │
│                                                │          │   │
│                                               └──────────┘   │
│                                                              │
│                                                              │
│  FREE                                                        │
│  SEMINAR                                                     │
│                                                              │
│  For Employees Needing                                       │
│  Additional Training                                         │
│  in Desktop Publishing                                       │
│                                                              │
│  ─────────────                                               │
│  PLEASE POST                                                 │
│  ─────────────                                               │
│                                                              │
└─────────────────────────────────────────────────────────────┘
```

Figure 4.4   The same "teaser" copy and design can be used, as here, for an envelope or for a self-mailer.

- **Make the benefit obvious.** In Figure 4.4, "additional training" that is of interest to employers may translate into better pay, job security, a quick chance for advancement, or all three for employees. Just don't be too clever or cute. Save that for the section on invitations, which is discussed next.
- **Present the benefit in the largest, boldest, easiest-to-see type.** You want to capture the attention of the casual passerby. So make it easy to read from a reasonable distance.
- **Label everything.** Mention the time, date, place, cost, anything free, what to bring, what the reader will get to take home, how to participate, and so on.
- **Sketch a simple map.** Do this for locations away from the home, the neighborhood, or work. Give distances from known locations (e.g., "approx. 3.2 miles west of Exit 89 on State Highway 17").
- **Add a "Take One" as a reminder.** Include the map. Your printer will know a variety of ways to do this.
- **Give a destination phone number.** Do this for people like me, who get lost going around the block.

Make the information complete, but keep it as simple as possible. Bulletins often are read in passing. Make it possible to do just that. As a safety factor, place a small "Please post" request in one corner. Always tell people what you'd like them to do. Don't make them guess.

Bulletins for Fun Events

Fun events, from puppy beauty contests to the Fourth of July picnic and the Santa Claus parade, may seem exceptions to the rules for getting your bulletin posted on a bulletin board. They're not! It's the *event* that's the fun. The bulletin must still give every bit of information needed to make the event happen. It's certainly all right to lighten the mood, provided that you don't lose the message.

SUMMARY

- In the development of bulletins and invitations, be guided by the Five W's: Who, What, When, Where, Why.
- Don't create bulletins no one will post. Learn who decides what's posted and why . . . then make yours fit in.
- If it reads like a billboard . . . if it looks like a billboard . . . if it works like a billboard . . . you've got a great bulletin!

INVITATIONS

All of us have received invitations to events that made us a captive audience for a sales pitch—from the chance to meet the candidate to hearing an ex-President try to sell time-sharing condominiums. Whether it's Tupperware in your living room or executive jets at the Paris Air Show, the party proves an effective sales tool, and the one thing every party has in common is an invitation.

This section focuses on inviting people together for *business* reasons—specifically, to inform them, persuade them, or sell them—and perhaps all three. It is not concerned with purely social or personal functions, although the suggested method of structuring an invitation is practical for both. How to set up the function itself is covered in the chapter on conventions, beginning on page 272.

A Magical Word

Invitation is one of those magical words, like *free, new,* and *now,* that many prospective and current customers accept uncritically. You are "invited" in magazine and newspaper ads, by radio and television commercials, on bulletin boards, on the Internet, by fax, and in the mail. All of these take advantage of the built-in association of "invitation" and "enjoyment." It is this expectation of a pleasant experience that makes invitations such an effective sales tool and one that should be more widely used. Invitations even let you bring together fierce competitors who have nothing but you in common. Think of fitting new golf shoes to shoe retailers at a golf outing, perhaps as a surprise before teeing off. Or what about a wine-tasting session for wine merchants as they sail along on a moonlight cruise. A bit of imaginative soft sell can do wonders.

A Word about Design

Invitations permit even the least creative among us to become designers. When the event itself has a festive feel, almost anything you develop in typography and layout should work, provided that you include the eight pieces of information from the model that follows. For a more formal feel, look through any stationery store, card shop, or "quick" printer's sample book and pick a model invitation to follow.

1	**You are invited**
2	to the first public presentation
3	of a truly functional
	Solar-Powered Automobile
4	Saturday, June 24,
	10 A.M.
5	Zip-Along Racetrack
	Route 13 at Suicide Drive
6	Champagne brunch
7	Free admission and drawing
	for free test drive.
8	R.S.V.P.

Figure 4.5   A sample invitation.

Structuring Your Invitation

The basic invitation has an eight-part structure that adapts to almost any occasion. Although you may not want to use all eight parts, at least consider each one to make sure that it can be skipped. To show how this works, let's produce an invitation to attend a demonstration of a solar-powered car (see Figure 4.5).

1. **You are invited.** Invitations imply an enjoyable event. The very word "invitation" prepares the recipient to be well disposed toward what comes next, so make that word prominent and the very first thing that's seen.

2. **To the first public presentation.** Generally the single most important part of the invitation. Use your utmost inventiveness to make attending the event a *benefit.* Translate attendance into what the attendees will carry away, and then state that as a promise. For instance:
   - The most exciting test drive of your life
   - Your chance to get frank answers from . . . about . . .
   - A full month of free . . .
   - Machine tools you will never have to sharpen
   - Get richer! Get smarter! Get ahead!

3. **Of a truly functional.** Make the description of the event too valuable or appealing to ignore. If a large part of that appeal lies in a guest of honor or a presenter, let your invitation explain who the person is—even if everyone *should* know who he or she is. (For presentations, always use the best presenter rather than the person most knowledgeable on the subject if the two are different. But always have the latter there to help answer questions.)

4. **Saturday, June 24, 10 A.M.** Before setting a date and time, make certain that no conflicting activity will keep your most important guests away. Call and ask, then "confirm" later as a reminder just before the meeting date.

5. **Zip-Along Racetrack.** Make the location a benefit if possible. Glamorize it (e.g., historic, beautiful, unique), and make it a place that is easy to get to. As with bulletins, provide a map for people who drive and a telephone number for those who may get lost.

6. **Champagne brunch.** Mention food only if it's free or, for longer meetings and events, how it will be made available. Make it sound good, but don't overpromise. Let your surprises be pleasant ones.

7. **Free admission and drawing.** State the charges if there are any. For professional meetings that have a fee, be specific about what is covered and what will be provided. Be generous with the things that cost little (e.g., writing materials and note pads, outlines of presentations, tote bags, door prizes). Be equally specific about what attendees will pay for themselves (e.g., travel and lodging, specific meals, gratuities). Be mindful of possible legal problems with overly generous benefits. For example, a $500 luxury weekend for a $50 fee may raise questions later. Be prepared to document legitimate business necessities and off-season rates, or have advance approval from the appropriate attorney.

8. **R.S.V.P.** Make accepting the invitation easy. Include a reply card (and envelope for privacy). Encourage responses and questions by fax or phone. Have your reply form restate the major benefits, as well as any conditions of acceptance—especially those that favor the respondent. For example, a dieting program might read:

☐ YES! I want to get ready for fat-free gourmet cooking by attending a FREE Oil-No-More hands-on demonstration on Monday, November 9, from 2 to 4 P.M. at the Ritzy Hotel, Suite 1000. I understand that all cooking materials will be provided without charge and that I must respond before November 1 to attend.

SUMMARY

- An invitation promises something special. Keep that promise!
- In business invitations, tell those who are invited more than enough to get them to come. Your competitors, especially at conventions and trade shows, may be trying to get them, too.
- Follow up on acceptances. Confirm them by phone just before the event to let people know you *really* want them there. *Expect* about 20 percent fewer than accept . . . but *prepare* for 10 percent more.
- The how-to of actually giving a professional party is covered in Chapter 15. Don't miss it!

NOTES ON THE INVITATION/INVITATIONAL BULLETIN CHECKLIST

These notes are a supplement to the material presented in this chapter. They are not a self-contained substitute for that material. This checklist (Figure 4.6) covers the creation, printing, and mailing of invitations. It does not concern itself with who is invited or why, except insofar as that information (#6–7) must be reflected in the invitation.

1. **Event Budget OK.** Invitations generally take up only a small portion of an event's total cost. Has that complete budget been approved, and does it include the number of invitations you plan to use (#14)? If either answer is no, get written approval (#3) before you continue.

2. **Quotations.** Allow a week to get cost quotations and whatever time is required for their approval. On budgeted projects, these quotations should not have to go back to management for another round.

3. **Invitation budget.** If the budget as a whole has not been approved, can you get approval on the invitation portion? Give the decision makers absolute deadlines beyond which invitations are useless.

4. **Speaker(s).** Arrangements for speakers or other attractions or entertainment must generally be made far in advance of an event. Who decides? Who follows up? What's the last possible moment for including changes in the invitation?

5. **Free/charges.** What's free, and what costs, if any, will be charged to the participants?

6–7. **Audience.** Identify the audience to whom you are mailing the invitation and the specific focus of the invitation—the benefits, to the audience, of attending.

8–9. **Copy.** Identify the writer and designer of the invitation. Who follows whom? Who must approve the copy? When must both be done?

10. **New art.** Will there be hard copy produced by the designer or desktop publishing system?

11. **New Art OK.** Approval of final art is the last chance to make changes before the production of disk for film. Give an extra copy to those who must approve the original, for their notes and comments.

12. **Proof OK.** Approval of proofs is a combined design and advertising function, even when both are carried out by the same person. Design makes sure that the work has the quality specified on the art. Advertising makes sure that *everything* that was on the original is on the proof and that the designer's instructions still make sense when seen in print. If you do both jobs, wear one hat at a time, but be sure that both get worn.

13. **Printing OK.** For routine jobs, most printers can be left to their own devices. For large, complicated, or otherwise critical projects, be at the printer to give on-press approval. You'll be so bored that it will be the perfect time to read the entire copy one more time . . . and actually call all the telephone numbers and check on the addresses. About 10 percent

INVITATION/INVITATIONAL BULLETIN CHECKLIST

Project Title _____   Date _____

Project Description _____   Project # _____

_____   Checklist # _____

Overall Supervision By _____   Deadline _____

Budget _____ Completion Date _____   Start Up Date _____

	ASSIGNED TO	DUE	IN	MUST APPROVE	BY DATE	IN	INFO COPY ONLY	SEE ATTACHED
MANAGEMENT DECISIONS								
1. Event Budget OK	_____	___	☐	_____	___	☐	_____	☐
2. Quotation	_____	___	☐	_____	___	☐	_____	☐
3. Invitation Budget	_____	___	☐	_____	___	☐	_____	☐
4. Speaker(s)	_____	___	☐	_____	___	☐	_____	☐
5. Free/Charge	_____	___	☐	_____	___	☐	_____	☐
CREATIVE DECISIONS								
6. Audience	_____	___	☐	_____	___	☐	_____	☐
7. Focus	_____	___	☐	_____	___	☐	_____	☐
8. Copy	_____	___	☐	_____	___	☐	_____	☐
9. Design	_____	___	☐	_____	___	☐	_____	☐
10. Disk or Final Art	_____	___	☐	_____	___	☐	_____	☐
11. Disk or Final Art OK	_____	___	☐	_____	___	☐	_____	☐
12. Proof OK	_____	___	☐	_____	___	☐	_____	☐
13. Printing OK	_____	___	☐	_____	___	☐	_____	☐
MECHANICAL DECISIONS								
14. Quantity	_____	___	☐	_____	___	☐	_____	☐
15. Mailing List	_____	___	☐	_____	___	☐	_____	☐
16. Telephone List	_____	___	☐	_____	___	☐	_____	☐
17. Self-Mailer	_____	___	☐	_____	___	☐	_____	☐
18. Envelope Mailer	_____	___	☐	_____	___	☐	_____	☐
19. Components	_____	___	☐	_____	___	☐	_____	☐
20. Size(s)	_____	___	☐	_____	___	☐	_____	☐
21. Stock	_____	___	☐	_____	___	☐	_____	☐
22. Stock Colors	_____	___	☐	_____	___	☐	_____	☐
23. Printing Colors	_____	___	☐	_____	___	☐	_____	☐
24. Out Date	_____	___	☐	_____	___	☐	_____	☐
25. In Date	_____	___	☐	_____	___	☐	_____	☐
26. Phone Replies Due	_____	___	☐	_____	___	☐	_____	☐
27. Mail Class	_____	___	☐	_____	___	☐	_____	☐
28. Disk/Film Supplier	_____	___	☐	_____	___	☐	_____	☐
29. Printer	_____	___	☐	_____	___	☐	_____	☐
30. Mailing Service	_____	___	☐	_____	___	☐	_____	☐
31. Records/Reports	_____	___	☐	_____	___	☐	_____	☐
_____	_____	___	☐	_____	___	☐	_____	☐

Figure 4.6   The invitation/invitational bulletin checklist.

of the time, you'll be very glad you did! (I *twice* saved major projects by calling new toll-free numbers given to me by clients and about to be printed on every page of their catalogs, only to find them wrong.)

14. **Quantity.** The quantity is frequently more than the mailing list. Ask about nonmail distribution to staff and field workers and for last-minute follow-up.

15. **Mailing list.** Who supplies the list, contacts the sources on the list, and checks to make sure that it is reasonably accurate? When using outside lists, responses only, not the list as a whole, become your property for future use.

16. **Telephone list.** Will you phone, fax, or e-mail to issue invitations or as a reminder to those who accept? For initial invitations, what is involved in getting the phone numbers and in getting through to those you call? Test by actually trying to call a dozen potential guests before you commit yourself to getting results.

17–18. **Mail format.** If you are using a self-mailer, skip #18 and #19. If you are using an envelope, check with suppliers of envelopes regarding standard sizes and costs. It's seldom economical to customize envelopes for fewer than 10,000. Before you get *too* creative, check with the post office to make sure they'll accept the mail as designed. They almost always say yes, but check.

19. **Components.** Components include the invitation plus any other elements, such as RSVPs and reply envelopes. Don't be afraid to load up the invitation. If travel is involved, add a map. If the speaker is special, tell why. If the event is extraordinary, tell how. Use a separate invitation-size sheet for *each* of those items, and watch attendance soar!

20. **Size.** Invitation sizes are determined by the envelope. If the quantity is large so that you will use a mailing service (see Chapter 16), check with them about the practicality of inserting the invitations into the envelopes by machine. The envelope design is critical. Do this before *anything,* including the mailing list and how it will be addressed, is ordered.

21–22. **Stock/Color.** Not every paper stock comes in every color, especially when you want to match or contrast an envelope. But you can often print the stock into the color you want. It costs practically nothing extra when that color is a tint of a darker ink used on the same page. Discuss this with your prepress firm and printer. You may be pleasantly surprised.

23. **Printing colors.** Use any color paper and ink you wish—as long as the message can be read. If printed in light pink and blue or similar tones, your project may well die before the very eyes of those too nearsighted to see it.

24. **Out date.** The mailing date should be determined by considering the audience to whom you are sending the invitations. How booked up do they get for the time involved? How willing are they to commit their time far in advance? If you're not sure and can't easily find out, telephone a few invitees and ask. They will thank you for your concern!

25–26. **In date.** When *must* you have replies to permit final planning for the event? Telephone (#16) key prospects a few days before the deadline to reinvite them or to confirm their acceptance. There's nothing like an actual human voice to generate response.

27. **Mail class.** Most invitations are sent by first-class mail. Use a stamp or a printed permit that looks like a meter. For larger mailings, don't pre-

stamp the RSVP envelope. But just to play safe, test your level of response by adding a stamp to every tenth reply envelope. Let results guide future invitations.

28. **Film supplier.** For routine mailing pieces, your printer may wish to supply the film. Whether you agree or use a prepress firm, the proofing process (#12) is the same and is a production responsibility rather than an advertising decision. Where the two jobs are handled separately, thank those involved, and let them do their job.

29. **Printer.** Printing is also a production function. For major projects, insist on being kept informed. For others, let those doing the job do it without your help. If you are a printing novice, ask them to help you learn. Don't pretend to expertise you don't have: You do not have to know how to fix something to insist on its being done right.

30. **Mailing service.** Your direct mail production company works on a schedule, too. Don't surprise them with projects out of the blue, or you may be blue indeed when you get the bill. Usually, anything can be done if you are willing to spend the money. Just remember . . . it is *your* money. Plan, stay on schedule, and save.

31. **Records/Reports.** What records must be kept? By whom? What analyses of results done? What reports made and to whom?

5 | Direct Mail and Database Direct Marketing

DIRECT MARKETING METHODS

Direct magazine's 2002 analysis shows 19 methods to persuade or sell your prospects and customers through direct marketing. Though not all are in this chapter, they all are covered in this book.

- Card packs
- Catalogs
- CD-ROM marketing
- Co-op mailings
- Direct mail (noncatalog)
- Direct response promotions
- Direct response radio advertising
- Direct response TV
- E-mail to prospects
- E-mail to customers
- Fax marketing outbound
- Freestanding inserts
- Inbound telemarketing (including toll-free)
- Interactive TV
- Internet[1]
- Outbound telemarketing/teleservicing
- Package inserts
- Point of purchase
- Self-mailers
- Trackable coupons

DIRECT MAIL

> ### INSIGHT 21
>
> Do not confuse "selling by direct mail" with some simple, magical profit generator called "Starting a Direct Mail Business." Selling by mail has all the risks, expenses, and probably all the costs of any other way of selling.

This chapter has three goals:

1. To help you create your own direct response mailings.
2. To guide you in the supervision of mailings done by staff or outside experts.
3. To give you the basic rules and cautions for doing both.

---

[1]Not on *Direct's* list.

The chapter begins with some basic rules and cautions about what is likely to work—and what isn't—in selling by mail. It continues with specific guidance on how to create a direct mail promotion—always keeping in mind those basic rules and cautions. Four of these will be absolutely critical to your success:

1. The single most important factor in selling by mail is the list.
2. Test whenever possible. Treat every mailing as a retest.
3. Believe the numbers.
4. Know the value of a customer, not just of the order.

Help Abounds

Practically every major city in the United States has a direct marketing association that is able and eager to help you. Check the Yellow Pages. If you are unable to locate the association by this means, check the Direct Marketing Association. Web site at www.the_dma.org. Then join your local association. They will help you, even if you're not a member, but the continuing contacts alone are worth the price of admission.

In addition, there is the excellent how-to magazine, *Direct Marketing,* published monthly by Hoke Communications. Call the company toll-free at (800) 229–6700. On a more managerial level, *Direct* magazine is published monthly by Primedia, (888) 892–3613. For up-to-the-minute news, there's the weekly *DM News,* published by BPA International, (847) 588–0675; or www.submag.com/sub/du. Read several issues of each one. Subscribe to all that are helpful. Lots of additional publications exist. As member of a direct marketing club, you'll get information about them, as well as the many new online sources.

Figure 5.1 Basic must-know law for direct marketers.

WHAT YOU NEED TO KNOW ABOUT DIRECT MARKETING LAW

Although it cannot take the place of your attorney, the *Business Checklist for Direct Marketers* (see Figure 5.1) is an excellent place to begin. The brief, pamphlet-form *Checklist* is described as "written for mail, telephone, fax, and computer order merchandisers to give them an overview of rules or statutes that the Federal Trade Commission enforces." Note that each of the 50 states has its own laws and rules, which this pamphlet does not cover! Produced by DMA, the Direct Marketing Association, in cooperation with the Federal Trade Commission, the pamphlet is available without charge from DMA at 1120 Avenue of the Americas, New York, NY 10036–6700, or by calling (212) 768–7277.

TO CREATE OR SUPERVISE: WHEN TO DO EACH

Of course, *any* project may be supervised rather than self-produced, depending on the time, budget, and talent available for it. If you have no skill for doing designs or layouts, employ others for those tasks, no matter how simple the project or how much time is available. Whether you do it yourself or supervise, here are some basic rules any design should follow:

- Show and tell the readers what you are selling. If what you say and picture isn't absolutely clear, they won't guess. They won't buy!
- Use type that's easy to read. The less sans serif, the easier it will be to read.
- Keep it simple. The fancier the design, the more costly it will be to print it well.
- "Flow-channel" your reader; that is, make sure that the mailing as a whole, and *every piece in it,* flows from an attention-grabbing beginning to an action-doing end.

These and other such "rules" are found throughout this chapter. Use them when you do the job yourself. But equally important, insist on them when you turn work over to others. Do this *before they begin,* as part of your directions, not as expensive, time-consuming client's alterations after they've completed their initial copy and design. Make the rules part of your own checklist if they're not already included in the ones presented here.

What You *Must Not* Do Yourself

Two kinds of mailings must be created by direct mail professionals and should never be attempted as do-it-yourself "gifted amateur" projects:

1. A project, no matter how seemingly simple, that determines the survival of your business. (Of course you'll go to a specialist for a heart transplant, but will you try your own simple appendectomy?)
2. True direct mail "packages," such as multicomponent sweepstakes, giant "bedsheet" folded and refolded self-mailers, pop-up or other multidimensional projects. On any mailing that will cost more than $15,000, allow 20 percent for copy and design, and you'll probably be ahead in dollars and results. Good management includes learning to recognize the difference between getting something done exactly as you would do it yourself and having it done competently in some other way.

Doing Your Own Mailings

Help with creating your own mailings begins on page 90, but don't go there yet. The basics of lists, testing, and numbers that you must know for success, hold true no matter who does the mailing or what it costs. The next few pages explain them and how to apply them to what you write, design, and mail.

SUMMARY

- Focus each mailing to generate leads, sell, or keep customers sold on you and your product or service. Decide on one of these goals before you start. Let the others happen.
- Selling by mail is sales, not advertising. Budget accordingly.
- If you can't average at least $20 per response, you probably can't do mailings and stay in business.
- If you can't charge *four times* the cost of manufacturing or service time, don't sell by mail.
- When *everything* hinges on a successful mailing, use a professional. If everything hinges on a single, untested mailing, reconsider your options. What if the mailing doesn't work?

MAILING LISTS

The single most important factor in selling by mail is the mailing list. According to a Dun & Bradstreet online report, other factors being equal, the list contributes 60 percent to the success of your mailing. Offer is given 20 percent; copy, 15 percent; and format (design, envelope, art treatment, etc.), 5 percent. The art and science of selecting lists lie in our ability to match the recipient with the offer—to mail only to those most likely to buy. No matter what we are selling—no matter how appealing the offer—if the recipient is not in the market for our products, nothing else matters. We're not going to sell dog food to cat fanciers; we're not going to sell chain saws to apartment-dwelling couch potatoes. From the *marketers'* standpoint, a mailing—as well as any other promotion—becomes junk when it is targeted at the wrong audience or when the quality of the mailing gives the wrong image of the sender. Note that the wrong image may be too rich as well as too poor!

There is no better prospect than a satisfied customer. The most responsive mailing list is almost always made up of your present customers and clients, provided that such a list exists and that they have been well served in the past. That is why so many businesses use such ingenuity to gain your name and address when you pay by cash. You're their best prospect for mail order, too. When, however even your customer list *seems* to contain little useful information, some basic research is in order.

People with like lifestyles tend to purchase alike. The key to selling is to determine which lifestyles match what you are offering. There are thousands of mailing lists available through list companies and brokers. (Chicago's business-to-business Yellow Pages list about 100 such companies.) The more we know about the meaningful characteristics of our current customers or clients, the easier it will be to find likely prospects by matching their customer profiles to ours. What's meaningful may not be a matter of common sense, so discuss with several mailing list professionals how they propose to help you find out and what they charge for their service. Then check the advice you get in a test mailing.

- Fewer than 5,000 names is not a statistically valid test. No matter how large the list, a 10,000-name test is almost always adequate.
- For consumer lists, services exist that can match addresses with socioeconomic census data. Use the nth-name system of every 20th, 50th, or 500th name, depending on the size of your list, for a test mailing. You'll get a wealth of information on these people's lifestyles.
- For business and professional lists, existing directories can tell you everything you need to know—from an individual's specialization, age, income, family, and automobiles owned to a corporation's history, profits, officers, and credit rating. If a certain piece of information seems pertinent, it's there for the matching.
- A mailing list specialist, preferably experienced with your type of business, can help you analyze your lists. *Before* you request such help, get firm, written cost quotations and current references. Check them out!

For New Businesses

When your business is new, without customers or clients, there are four possibilities regarding mailing lists:

1. Lists exist to fill your needs. Your market is so well defined that available lists are all you need to get started.
2. Your market is hidden within a larger audience for which there are lists.
3. Lists exist, but they are not available to you.
4. No known list exists that will fill your needs.

Let's consider each of these in more detail.

Lists That Fit

With lists that fit, your most important decision may seem to be whether to use the list as a whole or to start in with a test. But before you do either of these, check on the percentage of previous *mail order buyers* in that list, no matter what they have bought or what you are selling.[2] Have the sources of the list give you those proven direct mail buyers only. (Forced subscriptions to association magazines and newsletters don't count.) It's almost always easier to sell such buyers a second time than to sell nonbuyers the first. If no list of previous buyers exists—and you feel that you must sell by mail—test!

Lists That Hide

Let's assume that you have a special racket for overweight, left-handed tennis players, but no mailing list exists for such individuals. A broader "umbrella" list of all tennis players, however, is available. Should you try to sell your submarket within it?

The answer involves the same analysis you should do before any other mailing. Do as little blind guessing as possible. Do a market breakdown; that is, work

---

[2]The most successful initial list for the University of Michigan modern history series was mail-order buyers of Swiss Army knives, according to its then sales manager, Henry Fujii.

with what you know or can learn—for instance, the percentage of left-handers in the general population and the degree of overweight seen at local tennis courts and clubs. Although this type of "knowing" is far from certain, it's better than sheer guesswork, and it lets you go to the next step: the calculation of testing costs and the application of test results as a predictor of complete mailings. A number of easy-to-use formulas exist for this purpose (see pages 105–107).

Lists That Remain Private

Many mailing lists are so valuable to their owners that they are never made available to anyone else. This is especially true of business customers and prospects, such as Collectibles for whom their list is their most valuable promotion property. General consumer lists tend to be less jealously guarded, for two reasons:

1. Increased use of a mailing list tends to build a larger universe of frequent buyers. As different kinds of products and services are offered, more recipients get into the habit of ordering by mail, making the list increasingly valuable as a source of proven mail-order buyers.
2. For many owners of a list, the income from renting the list is a major factor in their profitability. Suppose a list of 200,000 names generates net rental revenues of $25 per thousand 15 times a year. How much of the product would have to be sold to produce the same number of dollars in net income?

The fact that some lists are not generally available tells you that people have been able to build them for themselves. If you have a list of your own, perhaps you can trade, rather than rent. If not, perhaps you can build your own list, too.

When No List Exists

Even when no list exists for a particular market, it's probable that the names are there if only you can find a way to get at them. It is possible that no one else has previously wanted just those names badly enough to create a list. But it's more likely that gathering the list would have been too difficult or costly. When no list exists, test using other media, including the Internet, to generate leads or sell. When no list exists, think very hard about the *practicality* of making direct mail the key to your selling effort.

Things to Know about Using Lists

Eliminate Duplicate Mailings Where Practical

When using more than one list, the possibility of duplicate mailings becomes increasingly likely. Through a computerized system called merge/purge, most of this duplication can be eliminated. But before deciding to use this program, discuss the *process and costs* with both a mailing list expert and a mailing service. Cost alone—lists, printing, mail handling, postage—may not be the key factor: Recipients may become so annoyed at receiving multiple copies of the same thing that they will consider it junk mail and pay no attention to it. Testing here, as elsewhere, will be the best way to discover what, if any, increase in response is achieved—at what cost—by merge/purge. *Much* more about this is in Chapter 16.

Some Legal Limitations on the Use of Mailing Lists
When using a list other than your own, the rental agreement almost always calls for *one-time mailing use only.* You may *not* copy the list or any part of it, or use it for any other purpose, unless agreed to in writing by the owner of the list. After testing, consider negotiating for multiple use of the most successful lists at reduced cost. Do not, however, pay for such multiple use in advance. First make sure the full mailing lives up to the promise of the test return.

Rental lists are "seeded," that is, they include a few names specifically added to discover unauthorized use. *Any response* to your mailing, however, whether it is an order, an inquiry, the acceptance of a premium, or anything else, makes the respondent's name yours to use in the future. With many mailings, you justify their cost by gaining repeat customers, rather than one-time selling of a product or service.

SUMMARY

- Nothing else is as important as your mailing list.
- Your best prospect is a satisfied customer.
- Your best noncustomer prospects are selected from previous mail order buyers with the same buying "profile" in the same price range.
- Predetermine what *you* are buying—customers or one-time sales, or both—and what each is worth.
- Lists abound. They are often very price competitive. Check them out.
- List selection is critical. Get professional help.

Customer or One-Time Buyer
Know what you need to gain from mailing—one-time sales or long-term customers—and evaluate the results accordingly. But beware of paying for customers and then giving them a product or service that reduces them to one-time buyers, or budgeting for customers while having nothing more to sell. Direct response may be the one way of doing business where you *can* sometimes lose a little bit on each sale and then make it up in volume—but only if you also know how to play *that* tune. Know what business you are in and your capabilities!

THE ABSOLUTE NECESSITY FOR TESTING

In direct mail, or any other kind of direct response advertising, the likelihood of getting things just right and most cost-effective on the very first try is quite small. We can, of course, and often do produce profitable mailings on just one try. But *most* cost-effective is most often the result of testing—*a process that never stops* in many direct mail organizations.

INSIGHT 22

Before performing any test, decide which category will determine the outcome. Will it be percentage of response? Average order? Quantity of response?[3] Cost per response? Quality of response? Something else? No matter which you pick, be sure to record and analyze all of these, especially the Q Concepts; that is, the relationship of quality to quantity of the response. Just because we don't get the answer we want doesn't mean that another answer isn't better.

In testing, the version ("package") that does best is called the control. Everything thereafter is controlled by (evaluated against) this package. Most of us tend to use "control" synonymously with "success." Its actual meaning is "the best results *thus far*," which are subject to change with every mailing.

WARNING!

A *word of caution:* When a test shows an extraordinary improvement over the existing control, do a retest with a larger portion of your list, if possible. Don't hesitate to change to a package that works better. Believe the numbers; just make sure that they aren't a one-time fluke.

Test One Thing Only

Changing one or more factors in your mailings may give you a better response, but it may also have no effect or decrease returns. Even an increased response may have to be balanced against higher mailing costs, and lower costs may have to be balanced against fewer sales. It is quite common to test totally different mailing packages against each other—one or more quite expensive and the others somewhat plainer and less costly. But when testing to see whether *a specific package* can be made more effective, *change only one thing if you wish to understand the results.*

Structuring a Test

Suppose that you have a reasonably successful package printed in full color (four colors) and offering a specific product at a specified price. You wish to find out if any of the following will be more cost effective:

---

[3]One of my mailings, at $9,000 cost, produced only a single order from 6,000 prospects. That order totaled $500,000, from the A&P supermarket chain. The client did not object to the paucity of responses. Another client wanted to fire our agency because we'd far exceeded the long-term $3.50 maximum they allowed per lead. When I pointed out that the $3.50 was established for a popular $300 product and not for their new $37,000 limited edition item, the client said, "We've never thought of that."

Type of Offer	Test Package	Test Price and Number of Pieces		
		$12.95	$15.95	$22.50
Offer A	4-color	5,000	5,000	5,000
Offer A	2-color	5,000	5,000	5,000
Offer B	4-color	5,000	5,000	5,000
Offer B	2-color	5,000	5,000	5,000

Figure 5.2   Why a three-factor test requires 12 mailings.

- Changing the offer.
- Changing the price.
- Changing to a less costly two-color mailing package.

Because it takes a mailing of 5,000[4] pieces to generate fairly predictable results, you will need 12 different mailings totaling 60,000 pieces for your test. The reason we need so many, as Figure 5.2 shows, is that we are testing one specific factor in each mailing, yet testing that one factor against all the other 11:

- Each of the prices is tested against all combinations of offers and colors.
- Each of the color arrangements is tested against all combinations of offers and prices.
- Each offer is tested against all combinations of colors and prices.

Should one of the offers be tested at random—for instance, the four-color offer A at $15.95 against the two-color offer B at $22.50—one will probably sell better than the other. But you have no way of knowing why—whether it was the offer or the price or the color that was responsible for the increased sales. Nor will you know which factor(s) you might change for even better results. You seem to need to perform all 12 tests to get your answer! But don't give up on testing as being too complicated and costly. Help is on the way immediately after the next paragraph.

When to Stop Testing

As you see in Figure 5.2, testing one more price will add 20,000 units for four more packages. Testing envelopes against self-mailers, or first-class postage against third-class postage, however, will double the number of units needed—from 60,000 to 120,000. You'll run out of names or money or both before you run out of tests, so let's take another look at testing.

Five Ways to Approach Testing

1. **Test everything.** Test your product or service in exactly the way that was described in the last few pages. It's what the largest, most successful mailers do.

---

[4]Many direct mail experts are convinced that it takes at least 10,000 names, especially for business mailing. When using more than one list and duplicates are eliminated by merge/purge, it is the net quantity that counts—what comes out, not what goes in! (See Chapter 16)

2. **Decide what might really make a difference, and test just that.** For instance, of the 12 options in Figure 5.2, test only the four-color offers A and B at $15.95. If one is successful, or close to successful, test the other two prices for the same package. Now test what has become your control against that same package in two colors. The result is that you've mailed 5 sets rather than 12. In other words, you've mailed 35,000 fewer pieces and saved at least $6,000 just in postage ($3,000 at nonprofit rates). For mailings where four colors might be perceived as an extravagance—to nonprofit organizations, charities, hospitals, and so on—test two colors or one color first. But do try four colors also. Don't assume; test.

3. **Test fewer than 5,000 names.** When you really need to test how a large number of changes will influence results, and restrictions on budget, time, or names make testing 5,000 names impossible, test 2,000 names instead. Then take the top two or three results, and do a "real" test of 5,000 each. If you can possibly avoid it, don't go from a 2,000-name test to a "rollout"—a mailing of a much larger portion of your list or a complete mailing of the entire list. If you do not have time for a real test and results are important, either don't mail, or use a professional—and pray!

4. **Use telemarketing to test before you mail.** If your primary concern is your offer or price, give serious consideration to a telemarketing premailing test. Properly structured, it's fast, accurate, and the way to find out why someone doesn't buy, as well as why they do. (See Chapter 9 for a more detailed discussion of telemarketing for premail testing.)

5. **Use print media to test before you mail.** Find print media—magazines, newspapers, and newsletters—that go to the audience you want to reach. Check with each one to learn whether it accepts preprinted advertisements on postcard-weight stock. You want the best results from your test, and a reply card almost always increases response. That card, in combination with a toll-free number, should give you the best results. If card stock is not acceptable but regular paper inserts are, consider an order form similar to what is used in most catalogs, preaddressed and, *if publication policy permits,* postage free.

How to Prepare Your Print Media Test

Let's use the 12 variables shown in Figure 5.2. Do the following:

- Use a freestanding insert for your test.
- Check with each publication on the size, format, and delivery date for your insert. Newspapers will probably accept $8\frac{1}{2}'' \times 11''$. Magazines not only vary in page size but usually require extra paper for trim. If unsure how to handle all this, get help from a printer experienced in this field or a print media production pro.
- Prepare each test as an insert with all of the four-color or all of the two-color offers printed together. If you are printing on postcard-weight stock, for easy removal, have the card edges perforated.

- Use a department number to code each reply form. Use the same department codes for telephone response and add "M" for mail and "T" for telephone. Keep the system simple. If you're not staffed to handle telephone orders, see telemarketing services in Chapter 9.
- After printing, have the 12 versions separated by your printer or bindery and collated sequentially, that is, into the order 1, 2, 3, 4 . . . 12. This gives you random, valid testing. What you must not permit is using all the #1's first, then all the #2's, and so on.

Testing Just Two Variables

If only two variables are to be tested, discuss, with each publication, the practicality and cost of running an A/B split advertisement with a reply card. (See page 35). This format, especially when also used with a toll-free number, gives statistically valid results. If you do not have a toll-free number, check with a telemarketing company that offers this service. They're in the Yellow Pages.

INSIGHT 23

Do not expect the percentage of response from a print media test that you would get from direct mail. If print gives you a clear winner and time and budget permit, test the winner in the mail against the two runners-up. Otherwise, use only the winner for the complete mailing. The least that you want to learn is the reliability of your print media testing.

A word of warning: Many professional publications build their circulation by sending multiple copies to the same destination, although not often to the same person. Persons within the same organization will thus get different versions of your offer! If they compare and contact you about the differences, *tell them you are running a test.* They'll understand.

INSIGHT 24

Various laws permit you to test different offers in the same mailing or advertisement. Check with the post office concerning current restrictions—if there are any—before testing. *It is good business practice to fill all test responses at the lowest price being tested, no matter what the final price turns out to be.* If that should be one of the higher prices, write the respondents who purchased with the lower prices in mind a thank-you note, and mention the price at which you will fill their orders in the future. If a lower price wins, congratulate those who purchased at the higher prices on recognizing value. Explain that the large volume of orders now permits a cost saving . . . *and would they like to order some more at the unexpected saving!*

Code Everything!

Create a letter or number code for every variation in response. You want to know where, when, and in what quantity it was used. Change the code for *every* variation, including tests and rollouts, to check on the influence of mailing dates. It is a critical part of evaluating direct response success. Analyze all results (professionals call this *back-end analysis*), and get professional guidance if you are not sure how to do this.

SUMMARY

- Rented lists permit onetime use only, but responses are yours . . . forever.
- Test! Wouldn't you rather be 98 percent sure *before* you mail?
- Tests are expensive. Use them for what's really likely to make a difference: the list, the offer, the copy, the format—*in that order!*
- For responses to have predictive power, limit each test to one thing only.
- Believe the numbers, but have an adequate statistical universe on which to base your further actions. If not, validate the test results.

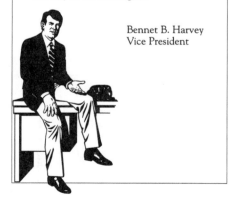

From the Desk of
Bennet B. Harvey

Dear Buyer:

The enclosed brochure offers the biggest single discounts we have ever been able to give you on our children's books. Don't pass up this extraordinary profit opportunity. It expires on September 1st and may never come again.

Bennet B. Harvey
Vice President

Figure 5.3   The effectiveness of a simple letter. Testing has repeatedly shown the effectiveness of including a letter in mailings. Above is a simple one-paragraph letter. It worked!

CREATING YOUR OWN MAILINGS: THE LETTER

Chapter 4 covered the creation of the flyers or brochures you might include in your mailings. Chapter 6 will concentrate on letters. Just as the list is the most important external factor in determining whether direct mail will be successful, the letter is almost always the most important internal element within the mailing itself. In our experience, which ranges from self-mailers to catalogs to elaborate multicomponent mail "packages," *every* test has shown the cost-effectiveness of including a letter. Most of the letter/nonletter tests were used to convince clients who were new to direct response selling. But the most convincing test of all was caused by an accident. It involved a simple, one-paragraph memorandum something like that shown in Figure 5.3.

A mailing prepared by me for Rand McNally offered, in the largest type that would fit on the envelope and cover of the brochure, the biggest discount that company had ever offered on its children's books. The mailing, to those on the publisher's regular customer and prospective customer list, was a resounding flop. Practically no one ordered. Then the mailing service called. Its staff had just discovered the 5,000 letters that were supposed to be included in the mailing and realized that the mailing had gone out without them! Would Rand permit them to duplicate the mailing at their expense, but this time including the memo? Rand McNally agreed. The result was as dramatic a success as the incomplete predecessor had been a failure.

"High" and "low" information. Choice can also depend on what is being tested. For instance, I used postcards to test offers and mailing lists for the *Cricket* children's magazine. While none of the card mailings would have paid for themselves, as *tests,* the "winning" offers and lists produced excellent results from a letter/brochure package. Postcards were used to explore lists for which the publisher had "low" (little) information. The much more expensive mailing became justified when "high" (tested) results were available.

SUMMARY

- Letters work!
- Practically everyone likes to get mail.
- Most everyone looks at the letter first. Take advantage of that fact.

Writing the Direct Mail Letter

Practically anyone can write a good sales letter, provided that they follow the same two-step approach used by most professionals:

1. Decide what you want the recipient to do.
2. Decide what's most likely to get the recipient to do it.

The writing itself is often the easiest part. Where most of us go wrong is that we try so hard to make our letters sound businesslike and professional, that they seem forced and no longer believable. So if you're not yet a direct mail pro, don't write to the person who will actually get the letter. Rather, write to a friend, real or imaginary, who knows *just a little bit less* about the subject than your real audience. The friendship will provide the warmth in tone. The little bit less will keep you from leaving out anything important. Often we're so afraid of insulting our recipients' intelligence that we leave out those "obvious" facts that show we know what we're talking about!

The Two-List Approach to Letters

Start out with two short lists that you keep pinned on the wall, in front of your eyes.

List One
- What, exactly, you want the recipient to do.
- How, exactly, the recipient is to do it.

- How, exactly, you will fulfill your end of the deal, especially if the mailing is more of a success than you expect.

Based on a consideration of these three points, you may need to restructure your response to the mailing, especially as the proliferation of response media becomes more important to the sales effort. For instance, are you structured to take orders over the Internet, by e-mail, by phone? Do you wish to be? Test! In case you can't believe that success can be more of a problem than failure, be warned by the following "success story."

My own worst direct mail disaster involved a business-to-business promotion that promised to "give you the world for 14 minutes of your time." It also promised to deliver the world—a handsome desk-size globe—through a personal visit from a sales representative. The sales manager, who had no faith in premium-induced response, agreed to the mailing only to humor my agency. There were 28,000 names on the mailing list, 14 company reps . . . and a 31 percent response. That meant an average of 620 visits per rep with a like number of globes to be delivered. It was the agency's first mailing for that client and the last one where they had to plead for permission to test for results.

List Two

- The benefits and features used to create the brochure, now to be used in the letter. If no such list exists, because there is no brochure or because you don't plan to use one, see page 20 and create that list now.
- The three most important benefits from the list. For each of them, find at least three reasons why that specific benefit is more important than the other two.
- A comparison of the benefits, with their supporting reasons, together with a statement of the combination that offers the most *for the audience to whom you are writing the letter.* If you can't decide which combination is best, it may not make any difference, but more likely, you need to learn more about your audience and how *it* benefits from what you are trying to sell.

You now have *the* benefit about which you tell the recipients and at least three reasons they should act to get that benefit *now.* With both of the aforementioned lists at hand, you are ready to write (or supervise the writing of) your letter.

The Three "Tells"

In writing your letter, do not try to emulate the pros, with their cascading cornucopias of compelling reasons for complying with your offer. Keep it simple. Use the "what, why, how" technique:

What: *Tell* your audience *what* you want it to do. Translate that into a benefit *for them,* not for you.

Why: *Tell* them *why* they should do it. Use the reasons you found to be the strongest *for them.*

How: *Tell* them *how* to do it—*how* easy, *how* fast, *how* safe, and *how* resounding the benefit is if they act *now.*

The sample letter shown in Figure 5.5 can serve as a model for applying this technique. It was written not for this book but to help solve a very real business problem faced by one of my clients. Some background information is needed to understand the approach.

Background

For two decades, the Lectro-Stik hand waxer grew in annual unit sales. Throughout this time, the manufacturer had sold through retail outlets only. Now, for the first time, unit sales did not exceed the previous year's sales for the same period. The decline was not attributed to competition, because, although a number of competitors had recently appeared on the scene, their much higher retail price and less sophisticated electronics were felt to keep them out of contention.

Assignment

The agency's assignment was to discover the reason for the decline in sales and return Lectro-Stik to its previous growth pattern.

Approach

It took them four weeks to come up with the plan you have probably already formed just from reading the background. It took another month to convince Lectro-Stik to act on the suggested approach—to *increase* the price, thereby giving retailers the same high profit they were getting from selling the competitors' models.

Because of the industrywide change from "paste-ups" to computer-generated desktop art and film, the need for handheld waxers was lessening every day. With a shrinking market, retailers were attracted to the higher profits from the competitors' higher-priced models. At the old price, there was no *economic* advantage to the retailer in recommending Lectro-Stik over the other brands and every economic interest in switching the customer to someone else.

The new plan was as follows:

- **The strategy.** Give retailers and wholesalers an economic reason to push aside the competition and recommend Lectro-Stik.
- **The tactic.** Let them stock up at the current lower $45 cost and then sell at the new $59 price, which basically marched the competition. The $14 difference between the old and the new price was theirs . . . an unexpected profit bonanza—if they acted *now!*
- **The test.** Because the total mailing was less than 5,000, Lectro-Stik tested 10 percent of the list.

The test was a success, as was the mailing that followed. The notes explain why the letter was written as it was. Figure 5.4 shows the envelope in which the letter was mailed.

LECTRO-STIK CORPORATION

NOW...
MAKE $14 MORE
ON HAND WAXERS—

$1 MORE ON WAX REFILLS

Special Early-Bird Notice for Long-Range Planners

Figure 5.4   The envelope for the Lectro-Stik letter.

INSIGHT 25

In a direct response, make your main point at least three times in *each* major part of the promotion—in the letter *and* in the brochure, as well as in other pieces that might be included. The *words* don't have to be the same; the *meaning* does.

Notes on the Letter for Waxer Mailing

1. Use this box device, called a "Johnson box," in one of two ways: (a) When you have a single point you wish to emphasize—in this case, the extraordinary profit opportunity—but you want more than just a few words with which to do it. The box focuses your readers' attention and tells them instantly whether or not the rest of the letter must be read. (b) When you can use a statement from someone other than the person signing the letter—for example, a note from the CEO of your company telling how important this letter is to the reader, or a plea from a local relief worker hoping we'll listen to the national appeal.

2. All three of your "tell them" reasons are in these three lines:
    *   *What* you want is that dealers recommend the Lectro-Stik product rather than the competitions'. In this case, that can be implied rather than stated. Retailers and wholesalers aren't stupid; they know their profit on the waxer won't increase unless they do just that.
    *   *Why* they should do it—in addition to profits—is detailed later on. Here, we concentrate on the single most important reason: profits!
    *   *How* to gain the benefit is made simple and easy: Order *now!*

3. Personalize the letter—that is, address the dealers individually by name if that is practical. If it is not, note the welcome variation from "Dear dealer."

Lectro-Stik
CORPORATION

3721 BROADWAY ● CHICAGO, ILLINOIS 60613 ● PHONE (312) 528-8860

FAX 312/528-2874

(Date)

①

> **MAKE $14 MORE** on every Lectro-Stik Waxer, **PLUS**
> **MAKE $1 MORE** on every box of Lectro-Stik Wax
> . . .you order now and sell after September 1! ②

③

To Our Valued Dealers :

For the first time in over eight years, inflation has forced us to increase the price of the Lectro-Stik Waxer and Wax. Effective September 1, 1991, the nationally advertised price of the Waxer will be $59 and the 10-oz. box of wax will be $4.50. ④

Order now for shipment *before* September 1st and we will fill your order at the price of $45 per Waxer and $3.50 per box of wax. That's a mammoth increase in your profits now. . .and a huge on-going larger profit from now on. ⑤

YOUR CUSTOMERS WILL PROFIT TOO ⑥
By featuring Lectro-Stik, you give your customers much the best on the market—by far! No other hand waxer gives them more than 2 of these 6 state-of-the-art features. . . *All standard on Lectro-Stik!* ⑦

1. **LEAKPROOF**

2. **TRULY HANDY**. Rolls on an economical strip 1-1/4'' wide vs. bulky waxers that lay down strips up to 3'' wide.

3. **NEW TIRES** These should last the life of the waxer.

4. **SEE-THROUGH BODY** for instant wax visibility. A Lectro-Stik exclusive!

5. **ELECTRONIC HEATING** for precise control and long life. Won't burn out or fluctuate. . .as do some competitors' thermostats.

6. **"TACKIFIER"** is **NOT NEEDED** and **NOT USED** in Lectro-Stik Wax. Sticky tackifiers make it harder to position the bits and pieces that go into pasteups. . . negating the very advantage wax is designed to give!

⑧ Write, FAX, or phone your order *before* September 1st and let us know when you want delivery (before September 1). It's the profit bonanza of the decade! Do it now. ⑨

Cordially yours,

Bill Taylor

P.S. TO HELP YOU SELL EVEN MORE, WE'LL BE RUNNING ADS — AS ENCLOSED. Get FREE reprints with room to overprint or rubber stamp *your name.* Just write or call with quantity and whether to fold. ⑩

Figure 5.5 Letter to prospects not familiar with the product.

4.   One of the oldest rules in direct mail selling is to make your most important point(s) at least three times. The theme is profits, but though raising prices and profits to match the competition has to be announced, that alone gives dealers no particular reason to favor Lectro-Stik. It removes the lower profit negative, but what's needed now is a jump-start to the positive.

5.   That jump is here, a reiteration and amplification of point 2. In writing direct mail letters, all the rules are working at the same time—especially the ones that say to keep it simple . . . make it easy . . . and make one point at a time; but where possible, make it in multibenefit fashion. In three short paragraphs, readers have learned (in points 2, 4, and 5) what you want them to do, what's in it for them (especially in 2 and 5), and how to gain this benefit (also in 2 and 5). Everything else in the letter will reinforce what you have already said.

6.   When possible, use a key word loaded with benefits to add even more value to your message. Dozens of words might have substituted for *profit,* such as "benefit" and "value." But if profit is the theme, be as generous with the term as clearly understood meaning permits. *Don't become cute,* however: Very few businesses find what they do funny.

7.   The six features that follow grew out of a feature-benefit analysis like the one explained on pages 20–23. Notice how they let dealers justify—to themselves and their customers—their recommendation of Lectro-Stik without any mention of price. Note, too, that every point gives both the feature (presenting the dealer as expert) and the benefit (presenting the dealer as the customer's friend), in language that does not demand great technical expertise. When—as sometimes does happen—a feature and benefit are exactly the same, leave them that way. We seldom gain from making things more complicated than need be!

8.   A repetition of the "how to take advantage" information. Always put it just before the signature, no matter how often it's mentioned elsewhere. That's where your readers will look for it. Don't disappoint them.

9.   In the final version of this letter, one sentence was added immediately before this call to action. It said, "A preaddressed order form is enclosed." And don't think you are insulting your readers by statements like "Do it now." Repeated tests have shown that they will; or worse yet, if the exhortation is left out . . . that they won't!

10. Postscripts (P.S.s) tend to be the best-read portions of letters, so they are often used to give one more repetition of the writer's single most important point. In this instance, the news of a national advertising campaign was felt to be even more important. The additional offer of free reprints is well understood by the industry and needed no further explanation.

Post Office Clearance

For your mailings, get *written* clearance from the post office as a first step, not as the last. Show those in charge at the post office a layout of the envelope or self-mailer with the key words in place, and request approval for mailing the items. They will date, indicate "OK," and sign that layout. If they refuse, find out why. The reason may be an easily changed technical detail, not the mailing itself. When they approve, ask whether there is any way to make postal charges less costly—from changing the size of the self-mailer or envelope to changing the way it is addressed. Legal clearance is next. But keep in mind that there's little point in asking—and paying for—legal guidance before you've taken advantage of the *free* and generally very able assistance from your postal staff.

Always remember you are *legally bound* to any commitment promised by your mailing. Make certain that you know the implications of what you are offering and what you must do to make good on the promise. Don't guess. Know!

When planning a look-alike simulation, such as a window envelope's see-through "check" or a seeming legal or governmental notice, consider both the percentage you anticipate will respond and the percentage you anticipate will have a negative reaction because they have been "fooled." John Dewey's warning that we are responsible for the foreseeable consequences of our actions applies to business as well as morals. Fortunately, in direct mail, it's easier to foresee the consequences. Test!

SUMMARY

- Include a letter in any mailing you do. It's what transforms mass mail into personal communication.
- Be absolutely clear about what you want the recipients to do . . . and that you can handle the response if they agree to do it.
- Translate your self-interest into benefits for your prospective customers. Don't tell them about your wonderful seeds, tell them about *their* glorious garden.

ENVELOPES AND TEASERS

The "teaser" is the message—actual or implied—by which you, the sender, gets someone to open an envelope or to look through a self-mailer. Like the headline in our ads, its job is to capture their attention—to separate a particular piece of mail from all the others and get them to explore it a bit further. The majority of teasers, especially in business-to-business mailings, can be do-it-yourself projects. Others should be attempted only by professionals, with you responsible for overall supervision.

```
SENDER'S IDENTIFICATION
ADDRESS                                                          ┌──────────┐
                                                                │  STAMP   │
                                                                └──────────┘

YOU
MAY HAVE
ALREADY
WON
$10,000,000!

Check Your Personal Entry Number and Other Details Inside
```

Figure 5.6   Sample of type of envelope "teaser" best left for pros. Note how much stronger the message is without the ".00" before the exclamation mark. Try it and see.

For Professional Pens Only

Some mailings tease us with offers we cannot refuse, in giant type right on the envelope or the front of the self-mailer. Figure 5.6 is of this variety.

Other mailings tease with the look of important documents, legal forms, or checks, and the simple request:

POSTMASTER: Dated material. Please expedite.

The Other 90 Percent

Set aside the mailings you'll assign to the pros: anything to do with insurance, finance, and banking; contests, games, and sweepstakes; clubs (for books, foods, or records), continuity programs, and negative options; fund raising and politics, and almost all consumer direct response. That still leaves 90 percent to get done. Most are business-to-business mailings, and you *can* do those yourself by applying some businesslike techniques.

If you are writing the mailing yourself and are not a direct mail professional, leave the envelope blank. No teaser is almost always better than *any* teaser that is poorly done. Would *you* throw away a plain envelope without any teaser—without even looking inside? Well, neither will your recipients.

If you do decide to use a teaser, here are some guidelines:

• **Make your message instantly compelling.** In larger companies, it's likely that it will be screened by a mail clerk, secretary, and administrative assistant. That doesn't mean it will be dumped. It does mean that the teaser message must offer a benefit *worth investigating* by the person to whom it is addressed. If there's more than a single major benefit, or more than one way to sell it, don't guess. Test!

• **Relate the teaser to what comes next.** Or relate what comes next to the teaser. When your readers open the envelope or self-mailer, continue the message of the teaser. Before you go on to anything else, expand on, expound on, and solidify the benefit hinted at or promised in the teaser. The fastest way to lose your audience is to remove the reason you gave them for paying attention.

• **Make it easy to read.** Be as creative as your imagination and skills permit, but relate the message to your audience. Be aware that art directors and interstate trucking firms *may* require a different approach, but don't take that for granted. Prepare several versions, make copies, and ask a dozen members of the group to whom you are mailing your promotion which version they like best. Then, after they have told you, ask them why they like it best. There is no *statistical* validity in the responses, but you should at least learn whether you are totally off base. You're not trying to eliminate the test; you just want to zero in on *what* to test.

The Response: More Than Just a BRC

Busy readers, especially in the business community, often go directly from the teaser to the BRC—the business reply card or coupon. Before spending time learning all the details, they want to discover what the offer is going to cost them—in dollars, time, effort, or some other commitment. So many of us now do this from force of habit, that mailers load the BRC with the key benefits. Usually, it echoes the offer, the guarantee, and the conditions, as in Figure 5.7.

The BRC is so important that many direct marketing copywriters do the response card or order form first. It forces them to summarize the offer and turn it into benefits that sell the target audience. Once you can do that, you've solved a major part of the direct response problem.

Lectro-Stik LIMITED TIME OFFER * Expires September 1

☐ YES! We want to get **an additional $14 profit** on every Lectro-Stik waxer and **additional $1** on each box of Lectro-Stik wax! Fill the order below at the current $45 price for waxers and $3.50 for wax, and ship at our regular discount before September 1. We understand that the nationally advertised price will increase to $59 and $4.50 after that date and that our orders will be filled at these new prices thereafter.

Figure 5.7   Load your reply card with benefits.

To Card . . . or Not to Card

The format and media you choose for your customer's reply, whether a card, an order form, an Internet address or something else, will depend on what you can get your readers to do and the impression you want them to have about you. For many business mailings, practically no one uses the response form you enclose; they use their own purchase orders instead. But don't eliminate the BRC. It's what gets sent to the purchasing department with instructions to "order this." The more complicated the offer, the more important it is that there's fully spelled-out agreement for your recipients to copy or to return. Make it easy. Let them fax—toll-free:

• **Use a reply card** when the offer is simple and there's no need for privacy or confidential information, such as credit card or personal phone numbers. An increasing number of businesses ask us to give our credit card numbers and signature on the back of a reply card. You have an obligation to protect a customer who might not know better, so *don't do this* in mailings you prepare.

• **Use an order form** when the offer is complicated, there is a need for privacy, or confidential information is requested.

• **Use the order form** also to survey customers and prospects. (Yes, even nonordering prospects will respond, if properly motivated.) This is delicate customer relations. Get professional help.

• **Include a postage prepaid envelope** when asking for payment by credit card number, check, or money order; or when multiple pieces or order forms need to be returned.

• **With multiple-product mailings,** especially if the items being sold are similar, illustrate them on the order form when possible. (As advertising manager for Rand McNally, I dramatically increased sales of premium atlases by picturing similar-sounding atlases on the order form. Being new to the company, I could not immediately connect product names with the stock numbers then used as the only way to identify them on order forms. Pictures made the connection instantly obvious. My assumption that some buyers might have the same difficulty, especially when a sales representative was not present to assist in ordering, proved correct.)

• **As a multiple-product (or service) supplier doing a single-product mailing,** list other products on the order form, too. Doing so can have astonishingly positive results. Feature the subject of the mailing by framing it within a Johnson box, used in the letter shown in Figure 5.5 then list as many other items as you wish. Use very short descriptions if names are not self-explanatory. Thus, if you are a manufacturer of bicycles introducing a new model, you might also list other models and peripheral equipment, such as helmets, pumps, and tool kits. If you have not done this before . . . test! In our experience with a variety of companies, the results have been positive, but each distinctly grouped "universe" of mail recipients is different. Always remember that with direct mail, you do not have to take anything for granted. Test!

Toll-Free Ordering

Give *all* the options you have available. If you do not have toll-free or Internet order taking capability, use a teleservice firm (Chapter 9) for a test. Encourage toll-free phone—and fax—ordering, especially if your competitors don't and, even more important, if they do. The fear that you'll be faxed lots of advertising literature is largely unfounded. Most advertisers are too smart to make *you* pay toll-free line charges for something *they're* trying to sell. For outside handling of toll-free orders, check with your direct response association or see the Yellow Pages. Suppliers are becoming increasingly competitive in price and service. Shop before you buy. Put your agreement in writing.

SELF-MAILERS AND REPLY CARDS

Think of your self-mailer as a large sheet of paper on which you print and then cut out an envelope, a letter, a brochure, and a coupon or reply form. But instead of cutting them apart, you fold the sheet in such a way that, when unfolded, they present your message in a logical fashion. Figures 5.8 through 5.12 show a few examples.

Figure 5.8 uses a basic page size of $8\frac{1}{2}'' \times 11''$ or $9'' \times 12''$. Almost any printer can run and fold the double gate fold format economically. Use this as a self-mailer or as the flyer in a multipiece envelope mailing.

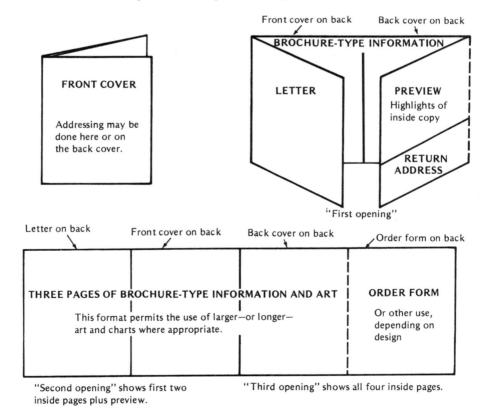

Figure 5.8 Double gate fold format. Use this as a self-mailer or as the flyer in a multi-piece envelope mailing.

Figure 5.9 shows the single fold with return flap. It can be a self-mailer, a newspaper or magazine insert, or enclosed in an envelope as part of a multiunit mailing. If the paper stock is less than minimum postcard weight, the flap is removed and folded for mailing. The front cover can be folded as shown (it can even fold down to business letter size) or be used in its full $8\frac{1}{2}'' \times 11''$. The advantage of this format is that the first opening goes to a letter and the second opening to two facing pages—what printers call a spread.

The third opening is a four-inch flap that can be used as a reply form when folded in the middle. Be sure to get the latest postal specifications on the size and minimum weight of the paper used for the flap.

Self-Mailer Advantages and Disadvantages

The advantages of the self-mailer are its lower cost, the immediacy of its message, and its ability to "stand out in the crowd" of recipients' business mail. *The disadvantages* are that it may be less response efficient than a "standard" mailing and that it is often perceived as junk mail. Do not take any of these for granted, however. Test if possible!

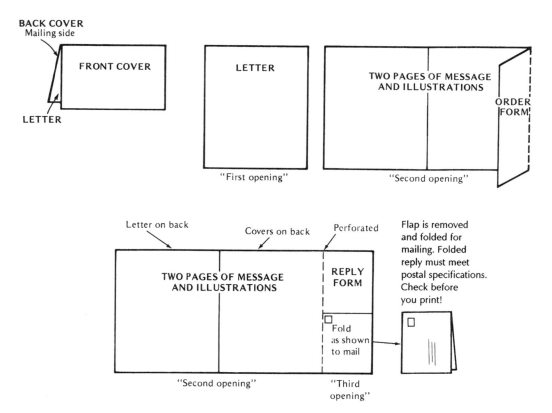

Figure 5.9   Single-fold format with return flap.

The Triple Postcard

An interesting variation of the single fold with flap is the triple postcard—in my experience, consistently one of those formats with "the most bang for the buck." To make a "dummy," or sample (see Figure 5.10), take an $8\frac{1}{2}'' \times 11''$ sheet of paper, fold it horizontally into thirds, and cut along the fold. Tape the shorter ends together to make a single strip. Cut $\frac{1}{16}''$ from one end. Then fold as shown in the figure.

A teaser or brief note can go on the front cover addressing side (A). Currently, postal regulations do not require that this card be sealed, but check for the latest rulings before every mailing.

The back cover (B) may be used for your letter or other supporting materials—professional evaluations, testimonials, or any favorable printed comments. Many recipients look at the back before they check the inside, so use benefit-laden headlines or subheads to create and hold interest.

For easy folding, the reply card (C) is slightly shorter than the other two sections. Note that you do not have to use the entire panel for the reply. Postal regulations give you the option of creating a smaller card (check the latest regulations for exact sizes) with the remaining space—section BB—available for other purposes. When using the "postage-free" reply format, note that there are severe restrictions on what, other than the address, may appear on a postage prepaid return address side (C). With the smaller format for the reply card, area BB can emphasize telephone, fax, and/or Internet ordering service; deadlines, savings, guarantees, and so forth.

Figure 5.11 shows the second opening of the triple postcard. The messages on all three cards are now visible. Note that area EE may be used for optional mes-

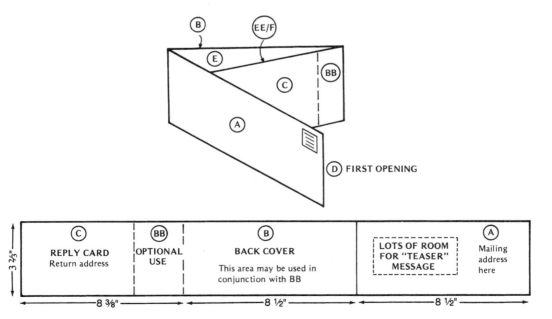

Figure 5.10 "Dummy" of triple postcard, front and back. (A) Front cover, addressing side. (B) Back cover. (C) Reply card. For easy folding, the reply card is slightly shorter than the other two sections.

Figure 5.11   Second opening of triple postcard.

sages even if the ordering side is extended to its full size *and* you use the prepaid return format shown in section C of Figure 5.12.

Use the space in portions D, E, and EE in any way you wish. It does not have to divide neatly into thirds. Let your message create the format!

In designing the triple postcard, it is generally preferable to use panel C for the return address and panel F for ordering or other response information. As the card is opened, the recipient has all the necessary information in one straight-line communication, following our very first insight: Keep it simple.

Additional Triple Postcard Suggestions

Your triple card does not have to have a removable reply card. Design it to be returned with section C on the outside (Figure 5.12), and two, or all three, of the sections are returned to you. Make certain that the card will refold easily. *Very few optional messages* may appear on side C, the return address side. Check with the post office regarding regulations on such self-mailers. Two advantages of the triple card format are:

• **Questionnaire and other research answers seem less formidable in the triple card format.** For ease of processing, limit answers to the D-E-F interior only. This has proven particularly successful when accompanied by a short explanatory letter and sent in an envelope. It has, however, also worked as a self-mailer. As always . . . test.

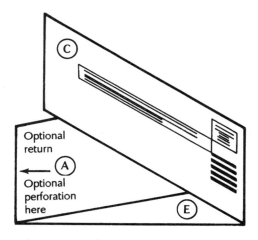

Figure 5.12   Triple postcard refolded to place return address (C) on outside.

• **Lower-cost paper, rather that card-weight stock, can be used for the two- or three-section reply.** Consider allocating the same dollars as for card stock, but purchasing a finer, rather "heavy" paper for first impression impact. Before you decide, test the paper stock in the mail. Get paper samples from your printer, make dummy copies to size, and send them to yourself. Better yet, send a dozen to people you know across the country and have them returned.

• **To make it stand out, use an oversize card.** Have the card size somewhat larger than the standard formats. Discuss with your printer the practical aspects of fitting a larger design onto regular paper or card stocks. Take both a standard size and a dummy of the oversized card, prepared on the proposed paper stock (or stocks), to the post office. Find out the difference in mailing rates, outgoing and incoming, caused by the larger size and its increased weight. If either, or both, are a factor, find out the maximum size or weight that will not cause an increase in cost.

THE MAILING COST/TESTING AND BUDGETING FORMULA

All calculations for the following formula (Figure 5.13) must be based on firm quotations. The cumulative cost of all test mailings or other premail tests is included as part of the total cost when estimating profitability. Some companies and organizations charge mailing tests to advertising and final mailing to sales. The formula will let you do it either way.

INSIGHT 26

Your pretesting estimates are used to calculate the likely profit from a complete mailing—tests plus rollout. But once that testing is completed, only the profits it predicts from the rollout—*without including the cost of the tests*—should control further action. The money spent on testing is gone, no matter what its results! That is why some firms budget testing as "advertising" and rollouts as "sales." The dollars are the same, but management tends to feel better.

The $20 Rule Applied

Earlier in this chapter, it was suggested that profitable selling by mail required a $20 minimum order. To see why, let's apply the formula given in Step 2 of the three-step calculation shown and assume a $20 selling price with $4 cost of goods including overhead, a $2 (10 percent) profit requirement, and a 50¢ per unit mailing cost. The formula now looks like this:

$$\frac{100 \times 50¢}{\$20 - \$4 - \$2} = \frac{\$50}{\$14} = 3.5714$$

That translates into 3.57+ orders per 100 mailed to break even. Increase the price to $25 and break-even becomes 2.63 percent; lower mailing costs to 40¢ or

MAILING COST/TESTING & BUDGETING FORMULA

Project Title _____ **Date** _____

Project Description _____ **Project #** _____

_____ **Deadline** _____

Overall Supervision by _____ **Start Up Date** _____

Test Quantity _____ **Rollout Quantity** _____

Budget _____ **Completion Date** _____

		TEST	ROLLOUT	
A.	**PRE-FILM**			✔*These calculations are*
	• Creative Supervision	$_____	$	*required for EACH test*
	• Concept	_____		*or rollout with*
	• Design/Layout	_____		*differences in out-of-*
	• Copy	_____		*pocket costs. Note that*
	• Editorial Supervision	_____		*final art or disk is*
	• Type	_____		*prepared for the test (A)*
	• Photography	_____		*and has no charges for*
	• Illustration(s)	_____		*rollout. New film may be*
	• New Art/Disk	_____		*needed. Multiple*
				suppliers are less likely
B.	**FILM**	_____	_____	*for a DMPC, but check*
				it out!
C.	**PRINTING/BINDERY**			
	• All Printing	_____	_____	
	• Special Folds/Die Cuts	_____	_____	
	• Bindery	_____	_____	
	• Other _____	_____	_____	

VALUE OF THE NEW CUSTOMER!
In evaluating returns, do not neglect the dollar value of gaining a new customer. It is a vital part of any evaluation in which getting customers as well as one-time buyers is your goal.

		TEST	ROLLOUT
D.	**ENVELOPES/CONTAINERS**	_____	_____
E.	**MAILING LIST(S)**	_____	_____
F.	**DIRECT MAIL PRODUCTION COMPANY (DMPC)**		
	• Merge/Purge, if used	_____	_____
	• Inserting all elements into envelope or container; seal & mail	_____	_____
	• DMPC/mailing service, in addition to the above	_____	_____
	• Postage	_____	_____
	TOTAL	$_____	$_____
G.	**COST OF GOODS PER UNIT & OVERHEAD**	$_____	$_____
H.	**MINIMUM ACCEPTABLE PROFIT**	_____	_____
I.	**SALES PRICE PER UNIT**	_____	_____

THE 3-STEP CALCULATION

STEP 1.

$$\frac{A + B + C + D + E + F}{\text{Quantity Mailed}} \times 100 = \text{Cost per 100 mailed} \quad \$_____ \quad \text{(Eliminate "A" for Rollout)}$$

STEP 2.

$$\frac{\text{Mailing Cost per 100}}{\text{I (including G + H)}} = \text{Percentage of return needed for minimum acceptable profit. If more than 3\%, check with expert about likely success.}$$

STEP 3. Based on the likely percentage of return needed to justify mailing, modify "I" and/or test various options before deciding on any rollout.

Figure 5.13   The mailing cost/testing and budgeting formula.

increase the price to $30 and break-even is reduced to 2+ percent. Many mailings produce the 2 percent return; few achieve 3.57. Calculate as you plan. Adjust your costs where possible. Test!

NOTES ON THE DIRECT MAIL *CREATIVE* CHECKLIST

These notes are a supplement to the material presented in this chapter. They are not a self-contained substitute for that material. See Figure 5.14 for the checklist.

1. **Purpose.** What the mailing is to achieve. This can include immediate sales, finding long-term customers, building a base on which to sell through personal, telephone, or additional mail follow-up, information gathering, and so on. If more than a single purpose is selected, pick one as key. Where else in life would you devote exactly the same effort to every objective?

2. **Budget.** The budget for direct mail *creative* stops with design (#10) plus internal and outside charges for #11 to #14. How the total project is budgeted and what must be approved before creative design may begin are decided here. Note that #15 and #16 are for *approvals only*.

3. **Test(s).** What, if anything, is to be tested. Schedule not only the time allocated for the tests themselves but also for analyzing and following up on them. #4 must have this information to build a workable time line.

4. **Time line.** The specific time line for the creative process and how it relates to testing, plus the time required to satisfy all the other check-lists noted at the bottom of this checklist.

5. **Supervision.** Supervision for the creative processes, if such supervision is different from the overall supervision. If several supervisors are involved, decide who may and who may not override whom. Only one person can be in charge.

6. **Audience.** All we can learn about our obvious target audience(s) and, possibly, new prospects we had not realized were there. (In regard to the latter, the evil of "B.O." (body odor), was invented by an agency to find a need for a strong-smelling soap practically no one had known they wanted.)

7. **Focus.** The specific focus (approach) of each test in attempting to achieve the purpose in #1. Most often, this is done by giving the copy-writers and designers broad guidelines on which to use their personal creativity.

8. **Research.** If research is wanted or needed, what will it cost? How long will it take? Who will do it? Who must approve? Most important, what actions will you take on the basis of the research results? Start with the last point first. If the answer is "none," go directly from #7 to #9.

9. **Writer.** If you are the writer and are new to writing, do just one approach from beginning to end before going on to the next. Then base the second approach on the first, the third on the second, and so on. Now go back and redo the first—and probably the others, too. You'll be

DIRECT MAIL CREATIVE CHECKLIST

Project Title _____   Date _____
Project Description _____   Project # _____
_____   Checklist # _____
Overall Supervision By _____   Deadline _____
Budget _____ Completion Date _____   Start Up Date _____

MANAGEMENT DECISIONS	ASSIGNED TO	DUE	IN	MUST APPROVE	BY DATE	IN	INFO COPY ONLY	SEE ATTACHED
1. Purpose	_____	___	☐	_____	___	☐	_____	☐
2. Budget	_____	___	☐	_____	___	☐	_____	☐
3. Test(s)	_____	___	☐	_____	___	☐	_____	☐
4. Time Line	_____	___	☐	_____	___	☐	_____	☐
5. Supervision	_____	___	☐	_____	___	☐	_____	☐
CREATIVE DECISIONS								
6. Audience(s)	_____	___	☐	_____	___	☐	_____	☐
7. Focus	_____	___	☐	_____	___	☐	_____	☐
8. Research	_____	___	☐	_____	___	☐	_____	☐
9. Writer(s)	_____	___	☐	_____	___	☐	_____	☐
10. Designer(s)	_____	___	☐	_____	___	☐	_____	☐
11. Typesetter(s)	_____	___	☐	_____	___	☐	_____	☐
12. Photography	_____	___	☐	_____	___	☐	_____	☐
13. Art	_____	___	☐	_____	___	☐	_____	☐
14. New Art	_____	___	☐	_____	___	☐	_____	☐
15. Disk/Film/Proofs OK	_____	___	☐	_____	___	☐	_____	☐
16. On-Press OK	_____	___	☐	_____	___	☐	_____	☐
17. Test Analysis	_____	___	☐	_____	___	☐	_____	☐
MECHANICAL CHECKS								
18. Editorial OK	_____	___	☐	_____	___	☐	_____	☐
19. Legal OK	_____	___	☐	_____	___	☐	_____	☐
20. Postal OK	_____	___	☐	_____	___	☐	_____	☐
21. Lettershop OK	_____	___	☐	_____	___	☐	_____	☐
22. Logo	_____	___	☐	_____	___	☐	_____	☐
_____	_____	___	☐	_____	___	☐	_____	☐
_____	_____	___	☐	_____	___	☐	_____	☐
_____	_____	___	☐	_____	___	☐	_____	☐
_____	_____	___	☐	_____	___	☐	_____	☐
_____	_____	___	☐	_____	___	☐	_____	☐

Separate checklists cover testing & budgeting, disk/film & proofing, printing & bindery, and DMPC mailing service.

© 2003, Fred Hahn

Figure 5.14   The direct mail *creative* checklist.

astonished by how much you've learned and how fast you've learned it. This chapter gives you a step-by-step approach. Use it *every time.*

10. **Designer.** Direct mail design is a specialized art, so find and use a specialist, especially if you are a beginner.

11. **Typesetter.** For simpler projects, try desktop publishing—but only if your in-house setting meets professional standards. Professional quality typesetting, generally provided by the designer, tends to be the least expensive of outside costs.

12–13. **Photo/Art.** Not just a nice illustration, but a picture that does something—that moves the viewer to share your objective. Would the Sistine Chapel be nearly as much of an attraction if the finger of God were closed into His fist? Generally, use art for emotion and photography for fact. If in doubt, test . . . and always be ready to be pleasantly surprised.

14. **New art.** Who prepares it? Who approves it? Who reviews it with the filmmaker? Who, if anyone, may change it, based on the film-maker's suggestions?

15. **Film proofs OK.** If the designers (#10) are not the only approval required, the designers should at least be consulted . . . and listened to. They'll be the only ones to catch the "obvious" *design* mistakes no one else sees.

16. **On-press OK.** This is often a time-consuming process, but it is absolutely essential. If possible, send two persons: a print production expert who knows how—and when—to give on-press approval and one to learn how to do it. There's much more to this part of the job than meets the untrained eye. (See Chapter 6 for my near disastrous introduction to the approval process.)

17. **Test analysis.** "Back-end" testing and analysis affect everything the creative people will do if they are given the opportunity to learn about it. Accordingly, share the results, no matter what they are. Be specific: It's hard to do better next time if all they are told is, "It failed." It's even hard to do as well if all they know is, "It's great!"

18. **Editorial OK.** This is the final authority on the mechanics of language, the house style, and the technical accuracy of the text, including stock numbers and prices. The editorial person or department sees and has final approval of the *final manuscript* and checks the *final type* against it, whenever that is ready. Make no changes in either one without editorial approval. Remember, there can be only one final version!

19. **Legal OK.** Direct mail and other direct response advertising are regulated by federal, state, and even local laws. (Sales tax collection is just one of the legal issues.) Make yourself knowledgeable, and if in-house legal expertise is not available, use your direct marketing association to lead you to where it is.

20. **Postal OK.** Your post office approved your design in writing, including any message you plan to put on the outside of your package. Right?

21. **Lettershop OK.** Your mailing service saw dummy samples of your package, told you they could do it, and quoted a price in writing. And the mailing package hasn't changed without their knowing it.

22. **Logo.** Someone has actually looked at *and checked* every logo, every address, and every contact number on the mailings. And so have you.

MAIL ORDER, DIRECT MARKETING, AND DATABASE DIRECT MARKETING

Database marketing is based on two criteria: (1) the existence, availability, and use of pertinent information on which you can base your marketing decisions and (2) the modification of that marketing effort as new data become available.

Database *direct* marketing involves exactly the same things. Its only difference is in the way it sells—directly rather than through others. For example, a mailing that urges you to buy by mail and makes it practical to do so is a basic part of mail-order direct marketing. Exactly the same mailing that urges you to make the purchase in a retail outlet is mail advertising. Quite a bit more than nomenclature is involved in this difference.

Marketing concerns itself with "the four p's,"—product, price, place (distribution), and promotion, explained in more detail starting on page 112. In direct response, what we normally think of as promotion is actually sales—our advertisement and method of selling are one and the same. Promotion, therefore, is best budgeted and utilized for research to find better ways to make sales work. The distinction is arbitrary, but of value in (1) selling the absolute need for advertising to management and (2) keeping the research budget from skewing ultimate sales costs.

Establishing Your Database

Imagine that you are a sales representative with 25 key accounts. In your customer database, or old-fashioned notebook, you keep the names of your clients with, as far as you can learn, their business reasons for dealing with you—price, delivery, quality, and so on—as well as such things as their birthdays and favorite places to eat. You'll note others on the staff who are important to the purchasing decision, and you'll note the "politics" involved in the decision. You'll try to discover the key competitors' approach to luring your business away and how you might react to it. This database is for clients or customers. You have an analogous file for prospects. Both of these information-laden resources are your database. The database is invaluable, but only as long as you continually *both* update your information *and* act on it.

Now, expand this example to thousands or millions of names. The process still holds. But now your data are on a computer, and a whole new set of considerations is required:

• Which department "owns" the computer: Accounting? Order processing? Estimating? Direct marketing? What is the pecking order? Most systems generate data through order entry. Access to that information and to computer time for its analysis is critical to databased marketing.

• What can the computer do? That is, what is its capacity for receiving, analyzing, and acting on each piece of information? If your sales efforts involve 1,000 different items, how much time and capacity are involved if you want access to everyone who ordered any single item? Any one of 100 different categories? Twenty-five categories? Can the computer do the same for prices? Frequency of orders? Any combination of these? Can it add, remove, and correct data quickly and easily? Can it protect data? What are its limitations, and how does it fit into today's state of the art? Note that *your* computer is not involved with lists you purchase for mailing but only with supplying in-house lists and handling responses. Purchased lists go directly to a mailing service.

• **A Note on Style:** Go back and reread the preceding two paragraphs—not for content but for style. Note the many short sentences and sentence fragments. See how question marks emphasize the need for answers and action. Mentally remove those question marks, and substitute commas. You'll have an instant demonstration of the need to *keep it simple.*

What You Really Have to Know

INSIGHT 27

Limit your data to information you are likely to use. Robert Kestnbaum's widely accepted FRAT formulation suggests Frequency, Recency, Amount of purchase, and Type of merchandise or service as the key components. For psychographic components, consult professional help . . . but get a firm price quotation before you begin.

Determine what you must know, store, and be able to manipulate by computer to improve sales. What would you do with different kinds of information if you had it? Differentiate between "nice to know" and "vital for improved performance." Your computer will, if instructed, endlessly store expensively gathered information you thought you wanted but didn't know what to do with once it arrived. *Before* you ask for it . . .

1. Determine what will be done with *any* information once you have it.
2. Be open to and welcome unasked-for information, unwelcome information, and inconclusive information. They can be as important to your marketing as actual sales. Believe the numbers . . . but in addition to getting just the facts, consider whether it makes any difference to also know "why."

Database Direct Marketing and the Four P's

1. *About the Product (or Service)*

    -   Research for customer needs before anything is produced.[5] Research further when you get conflicting answers. (Yes, we want the lowest price. No, we don't have time for comparison shopping.)
    -   Research for satisfaction after the product or service has been delivered. (Is it what you expected? Are you satisfied? How might it be better?)
    -   Modify the product or service based on what you learn, providing it is practical, cost effective, and in your long-term interest to do so. And remember . . .
    -   Your concern as a marketer is *not* with profit but with customer satisfaction.

APPLICATION

"No firm is going to find the future first if it waits around to get direction from existing customers.

"The goal is not simply to be led by customers' expressed needs; responsiveness is not enough. The objective is to amaze customers by anticipating and fulfilling their unarticulated needs. . . . Companies that create the future are companies that are constantly searching for ways to apply their competencies in novel ways to meet basic customer needs."

---

2. *About Price*

    -   Database analysis lets you produce a "best" price before more than your test is put into print, on the air, on the Internet, or is used in telemarketing.
    -   You determine that price based on *your audience's criteria.* It is the audience that makes the buy/no buy decisions.

3. *About Place (Distribution)*

    Determine how the order will be solicited, how it will be received, and how it will be filled.

    -   Will you use only mail? Newspaper or magazine print advertising? Radio and TV? The Internet? Telemarketing? Package inserts? Out-of-home? Sampling? Or some combination of these?
    -   Will orders be received by mail only? By phone (including a toll-free number)? By fax (including a toll-free number)? By computer? Or by some combination of these?
    -   Will everything be shipped from a single location or from regional centers? Which will be faster? Which will produce lower shipping costs?

---

[5]For this different-from-the-usual approach to learning and satisfying customer "needs," see Gary Hamel and C. K. Prahalad's brilliant book, *Competing for the Future,* Harvard Business School Press.

- How will you control drop shipments sent directly from manufacturers or wholesalers rather than by you?
- Should you do direct response only? Establish your own retail outlets? Sell through others? Use your promotions to help you answer these questions!

4. *About Promotion*
    - Test your product, price, and sales approaches as requested by those in charge of each. Note that this testing is *not* limited to mail but may—and often does—include telemarketing, focus groups, and other types of research.
    - Assist the people in charge of the product, price, and sales in evaluating test results.
    - Apply specified results in test promotions to validate research.
    - Test direct mail or other direct response media continually, from minor revisions to totally new online approaches.
    - Believe the numbers.

INSIGHT 28

Analyze every direct response effort as if it were a test.

---

6 | Catalogs
A Project for Creative Nitpickers

Producing a catalog is different from any other promotional project you are likely to undertake. It permits (but does not demand) copious creative flair, combined with meticulous mastery of mountains of minutiae, expertise in a half-dozen technical specializations, financial acumen to match that of a dedicated auditor, the human relations rapport of a soother of egos, and the management skills of a mover of mountains. Few experienced catalog producers claim to be able to juggle all of those at the same time during the actual production of a catalog. If you can possibly avoid trying, neither should you.

This chapter guides you, step by step, through the creation, production, and distribution of a *printed* catalog. Digitized versions follow analogous creative steps, using much of the same hardware, software, and skills. Your major "creative" decision may well be whether to go from your print version copy to online or vice versa. My suggestion is to do the print version first. It forces you to focus on what is most important; what benefits and features do the real selling. Then transfer and expand that onto the Internet, where everything you add is a selling bonus. Unlike some of the other chapters, it concentrates less on creativity and more on procedures that let your creativity have maximum impact. It tells you *how* to achieve superior copy and design, nor *what* to write or draw. It assumes that *you* are the soother of egos and mover of mountains. If, in addition to that, you could take on additional roles, ask yourself whether you really should. In any major catalog with which we have been involved, just those two functions alone have been a full-time job. Where staff is available, assign what you can and do only what you must. What you must do is assume responsibility for the job as a whole. Management is unlikely to accept as an excuse or explanation that you were too swamped with detail to supervise. No matter how much better you could do it than the person assigned to the details . . . don't! Your function is to manage. Do it!

INSIGHT 29

If you are new to management, it will be hard not to insist that everything be done exactly as if you had done it yourself. But few of us do our best as clones. Force yourself to recognize when proposed solutions, although different from your own, will work. That's what makes you a good manager—and a great soother of egos, too.

DECIDING ON GOALS AND CONSTRAINTS

Management

In most organizations that use a catalog, its budget and overall purpose must have management approval. Automobile dealers and department stores, as well as other retail outlets that have a sales force, are in a different position from vitamin manufacturers, food-of-the-month clubs, and giftware importers that sell *only* by mail and/or the Internet. What is the purpose of the gift catalog issued by your local art museum? Very much like a magazine competing for readers' interest and subscription dollars, the "mission" of each of these catalogs must be defined at the highest level and then produced with that goal in mind.

Marketing

Marketing is the overall activity that encompasses the creation and production of your company's product or service, its pricing, its product/service distribution, and its promotion. Advertising, including the production of catalogs, is only one—albeit important—part of the total marketing mission, which, like the management mission, must be incorporated into your decisions relating to the catalog. The function of the catalog in the sales plan is of vital importance. That is, is it business-to-business or consumer, traffic-building, mail order, or, if some of each, how much? It must be defined *in writing,* to avoid later "retroactive omniscience."

Editorial Matters

Someone must have final approval over the *technical accuracy* of the features and benefits presented in the catalog—that is, over *what* is said rather than *how* it is said. The exact authority of this person and who, if anyone, can override it, must be defined in writing.

Legal Matters

The law is quite clear. You are responsible for anything you claim, promise, and generally say in your catalog and other promotions. Other laws specify how fast you must ship paid or charge orders, or get customer approval for delay. Get legal clearance while the catalog is still in its manuscript stage, not when it is printed and ready to mail! Learn and keep up-to-date on the rules through your direct marketing club and association news.

Copy

Copy is the preparation of *every word* of the manuscript, no matter who writes it. Assign specific responsibilities for information on ordering and your policy on returns, as well as for product descriptions—for the nuts and bolts as well as for the glamour.

Design

Design is a rendering of the visual impression given by the catalog. The design concept may be presented for approval in rough form or with as much detail and finish as the designer wishes. In either case, it must be finished enough to show how the major elements that make up the catalog merge into a synergetic whole. Among those elements are the catalog's covers, type, descriptions, illustrations, ordering information, and outer envelope; if one is used.

Layout

Layout is a detailed rendering of how each page of the catalog and every other element of the catalog package reflect the design concept. The layout may be prepared by the designer, but it is frequently done by a specialist in turning design into a practical blueprint for writers, typesetters, artists, and photographers. Approval of the layout—not the design—is the signal for the start of the physical production of the catalog.

Production

Everything begins with agreement on a production schedule. This schedule is controlled by the approval process, which follows in the next section, and how that process fits into the catalog checklist. The process and checklist may differ from what is suggested here, but both are needed and best put into writing.

A SYSTEM FOR INTERNAL APPROVALS

The approval process is unique to each organization. Fight, if you must, to organize and limit the number of approvals required. Nothing is as frustrating as waiting for approvals from managers who assign deadlines and then do not find time to meet them themselves.

The approval steps in creating and producing the catalog constitute a process rather than a specific number of persons. Whether you do it all yourself or have a staff, the procedure is the same. No matter how large the staff, the project manager should be the person with the most advertising expertise. Assign this function first, to let that person play a key role in filling the other slots.

Figure 6.1 shows the steps involved in the approval process, from creation to printing of the catalog.

PRODUCING YOUR CATALOG

The production of a catalog involves three sets of activities:

1. Preproduction activities
2. Physical production of the catalog
3. Postproduction activities

Catalog Printing Approval Process

Step	Assigned To:	Approvals By:	Conflict Resolution By:
1. Initial discussion/assignments	___	___	___
2. Creative suppliers: design, copy, photo, art	___	___	___
3. Production suppliers: type, new art or disk, film, printing, die cutting, etc.	___	___	___
4. Design presentation	___	___	___
5. Copy: concept presentation	___	___	___
6. Complete layouts	___	___	___
7. Complete draft manuscript	___	___	___
8. Editorial oversight, proofing	___	___	___
9. Manuscript/Editorial reconciliation	___	___	___
10. Art/photography approval	___	___	___
11. Prepress approval	___	___	___
12. Proof approval	___	___	___
13. On-press (printing) approval	___	___	___

Figure 6.1   Approval process for printed materials—creation to printing.

Preproduction Activities

Probably the single most important preproduction decision is agreement on the dare when the catalog must be ready to mail or otherwise be distributed. Every other decision will be driven by that date and the inflexibility of the printing and distribution schedules.

Meetings

The number of meetings required for producing a catalog—or for any other promotional project—depends on the role of advertising and the degree of independence assigned to advertising by management and sales. In most organizations, this is management's decision to make. It reflects the importance of the project, the specifics of the sales message, the amount of time available for their supervision, and, probably most important, the degree of autonomy earned by the promotion department through its own performance.

Approvals

A number of signed approvals are almost always required to start production of the catalog. These include the approvals of management, finance (the budget OK), marketing, sales, and advertising. Other departmental OKs may be involved later on and are designated when the catalog is first discussed.

First General Meeting

Call an initial meeting of all interested parties, including the in-house design, print production, and editorial departments if they exist in your organization.

In the memorandum calling for the meeting, specify what is to be discussed and the decisions required, together with a *brief* outline of data that will help in making the decisions. The meeting should cover at least the following subjects:

- **Budget.** Give the cost of the entire project. Show costs for the most recent similar catalog. Outline reasons why the cost of the new one may be higher, lower, or the same.
- **Objective.** Will the catalog be used for direct sales, by a sales staff, for convention and meeting distribution, for public relations aimed at employees, stockholders, and so on? Other? If more than one of these, rate their level of importance as a percentage.
- **Theme.** Get agreement on the overall sales or marketing themes the catalog must reflect and their order of importance. For instance: Contemporary . . . New . . . Updated . . . Safe . . . Faster . . . Cheaper . . . More personal online help . . . Single source . . . and so on. This is *not* an attempt to coin a slogan but to get direction.
- **Physical specifications.** Specify any general or special considerations that must be followed. Among the possibilities are fewer or more products to be shown, modification of the physical size of the catalog to permit its broader use, and the inclusion of more or fewer order forms or enclosures.
- **Due date.** Set the date of the first use of the catalog. Answer the following questions: What use? Where? When? How many?
- **Mail date.** Set the date when catalog is to be *received* (rather than sent out).
- **Special instructions.** Get specific instructions from management, marketing, and sales for items not already covered. Make sure to differentiate between instructions and suggestions. Get the instructions in writing.
- **Approval process.** Determine who must see and approve the items covered on the catalog checklist if this is not already established procedure. In what order? Who has *final* sign-off?

INSIGHT 30

For meetings at which senior managers are to be present, ask them to call the meeting. Attendance will jump.

Let us consider six of these subjects in a bit more detail.

Budgeting

You will be starting on either a new creative effort or a revision of an existing catalog. Where only minor revisions are needed, such as updating prices and getting a new cover design, a budget is easy to specify. Even when a major new creative effort is called for, a budget can be estimated. Where similar work was done during the past three years, use that figure, adding 5 percent per year for inflation, except for postage. Get exact current postal rates and use that amount. (Figure 16.1 shows their range. If not knowledgeable about this, get help from your post office or a mailing service.) Where no comparable recent costs are available, ask likely suppliers to give you "ballpark" estimates. Add 5 percent to those, too. Present both options at the first meeting. Management appreciates—and rewards—that kind of foresight!

Objective

If your catalog is to be available on the Internet, do you have the internal know-how to produce—or even supervise—that version and to handle the response? As this is written, few consumer online catalogs are profitable, though many are successful in distributing product and service information. How important is it for you to be there? How much are you willing to invest in learning the medium? See Chapter 11 for more.

Theme

One of the major purposes of the initial meeting is to come to agreement on a theme for the catalog, though *not* on how the theme is to be implemented. The latter is the responsibility of the advertising people.

Every catalog has a theme—that is, it conveys a message to its recipients, whether or not its sender intended to put that message into its pages or web site. The theme can range from "We are better at what we do than anyone else" to "We don't know what we're doing" . . . from "Nobody beats our service!" to "Service? Beat it!" Obviously, some of these themes are implicit rather than explicit and not what the producer deliberately planned. *Some* theme is going to be there, so be sure it conveys what you *want* to say. Do not permit its accidental creation by inattention to *any* detail!

Physical Specifications

The concerns of senior management with the details of physical specification are likely to reflect the importance of the catalog in the marketing plan. The more critical the catalog is to sales, the more intense will be the pressure for direct involvement from the sales department. Unlike some of our colleagues in advertising, we try very hard to not find that frustrating. As we point out to our advertising associates: "If sales doesn't sell . . . *nobody* gets paid." The salespeople may actually *know* something that can help. Ask them, and see how quickly they change from inter-departmental adversaries to cooperative friends!

Other Considerations

The other four subjects—due date, mail date, special instructions, and the approval process—are likely to be routine. They are covered at the initial meeting to make certain that the advertising people can proceed without getting caught in unforeseen booby traps, for example, an earlier than expected due date, special instructions you didn't get because you didn't ask, or a new link in the approval chain that you "should" have known about.

The Approval Ladder

Only one person (please, not a committee) can have *final* authority for any aspect of the production of a catalog. If your organizational meeting does nothing else, have it create an approval ladder to determine who must approve each step and who must resolve or dictate solutions to conflicts. In multilevel organizations, keep senior managers out of these conflicts. That's why the rest of us are around. Do, however, keep senior managers informed—not about the problems but about their solutions!

SUMMARY

- Begin planning for the catalog with a proposed schedule and budget estimates. Conclude all meetings with a review of the decisions made.
- Issue your own meeting report. Spell out every decision as *you* understand it.
- Have everyone who must approve anything sign off on *your* meeting report.
- Do not begin the catalog until approval is granted or your report is officially corrected in writing.

PHYSICAL PRODUCTION OF THE CATALOG

"Producing" a catalog and catalog "production" have somewhat different meanings. *Producing* is all inclusive. It goes from the first discussion of the project to "back-end" analyses of results and what they mean for future efforts. *Production,* on the other hand, refers specifically to the period from the initial copy and design through printing and distribution.

Assignment and Scheduling

Catalog production involves nine major areas:

- Writing copy
- Design and layout
- Art and photography
- Typesetting
- New art (hard copy) and/or "film-ready" computer disk
- Film preparation or direct-to-plate, and proofing (Chapter 16)
- Printing and binding
- Distribution and mailing
- Back-end analysis

Some or all of these will be assigned to outside suppliers. The first order of business will be to find and approve these suppliers and to agree on a schedule for the work to be supplied. In working with either an inside or an outside supplier, the following insight should be your guide:

INSIGHT 31

The Laws of Outside Services
Law 1: Everything takes longer than it takes.
Law 2: Everything costs more than it costs.

Writing Copy

If your products or services require specialized understanding, at least the first draft should be written in-house. Outside writers can and do add their own special touch. Let them provide the sell that dramatizes your data.

The Function of Copy
The function of catalog copy will be to make a direct response or in-store sale, generate a lead, and/or reinforce other promotions; that is, one or more of the following:

1. To sell the reader who is unfamiliar with your product or service (the new order).
2. To sell the reader who is familiar with your product or service (the reorder).
3. To generate a lead by persuading the reader to ask for samples or an in-person presentation (major industrial purchases, computer or phone systems, educational programs, etc.).
4. To reinforce the sales message the reader has gained from a presentation or examination of the product (the auto dealership, trade shows, etc.).

For 1 and 2, the function of catalog copy is, at a minimum, to give enough information to let the purchaser order. This information probably includes an order number, price, and basic hard data, such as sizes, colors, and materials. In addition, guided by space and policy, there will be descriptions, illustrations, and, sometimes, special inducements to get the reader to buy.

INSIGHT 32

Your audiences remember less from presentations than the sales force likes to believe. They also remember less of the written message than writers like to acknowledge. Therefore, for catalogs that reinforce a presentation, let the written message echo the spoken one, in emphasis if not in exact wording. By reinforcing each other, the messages make the whole become greater than the sum of the parts.

Show Rather Than Tell

For all four functions of catalog copy, show, rather than tell, the reader if at all possible. Today's audience is more likely to be visual and oral, instead of literary. This does *not* mean that the copy must be exceptionally brief; rather, it must be as succinct as you can make it and still do its job.

Train yourself to read your own copy with the mind-set of your most likely audience. Pretend that you have never heard of the product:

- Would you understand the message?
- Would you want to learn more about the product?
- Is there a practical way to give that information—in text or picture—right in the catalog? (Here the Internet can have the great advantage of letting the "reader" ask for and immediately get more information.)

Your readers are busy and frequently impatient. Make their lives as easy as you can. Efficiency and consideration always reflect well on your company.

Now read the copy with the mind-set of an audience that has been to a presentation. Have you attended such a presentation yourself within the past six months? Have you videotaped several of them—especially the audiences' positive and negative reactions to the points being made? They may not be at all the points you would assume just from *reading* the presentation back at your office. Nonetheless, the positive reactions are the high points your catalog should echo. The negative are the points your catalog must try to overcome *before they are raised.*

Finally, review your checklist of catalog imperatives. Do you have the correct stock numbers, prices, quantities, colors sizes, materials, special offers, conditions of sale, and so on? Now look at your copy as a whole, and ask yourself the following questions:

- Does your copy sell the uninformed reader?
- Does your copy confirm the partially committed reader?
- Does your copy make it easy and practical to order?

If the answers to these questions are yes, you've done your job. If the answer is no to even one of them, continue to work on your manuscript until all the answers *are* yes. When it comes to copy, don't settle until you have it in writing!

An Approach to Getting Manuscripts Approved

Throughout the production of printed materials, getting manuscripts approved offers endless opportunities for confusion, delay, and ill will. If more than a single person is involved, the following suggestions will help alleviate all three problems.

1. **Appoint a single *final* approver.** A final authority is needed for each different aspect of the catalog—the factual accuracy of descriptions, numbers and prices, the promotional approach, grammar and spelling, the house style, and legal clearance. Determine who must, and who may, comment on each specific point and

who, in case of conflict, will rule. Designate a final authority for resolution of conflicts.

2. **Circulate suggested draft copy.** Circulate the draft copy of the catalog to all designated parties, *except those in charge of grammar and spelling.* Their time-intensive editorial expertise should not be requested until all other revisions have been agreed on.

3. **Negotiate . . . and settle.** Where conflicting suggestions or instructions are given about the same subject (for instance, differences in promotional approach), have the suggesters negotiate a resolution among themselves. But don't let the process drag on. That's why there's an authority in charge of resolving conflicts.

4. **Create a single master manuscript.** After, and only after, it is agreed on, clearly marked, and dated, send it to the editorial people. There are likely to be conflicts between what they know is correct and what the promotion people consider necessary. Here, too, negotiation should be attempted, but in most instances, promotion will win. Of course, you do not wish to appear illiterate, but your copy must sell. Editors are not blind to this need; they often have excellent suggestions for resolving promotion and editorial problems. Ask them. Then thank them!

INSIGHT 33

A single master manuscript, as ultimately corrected and approved, becomes the original against which everything else is checked. Only one "master" may exist, though clearly marked copies may be circulated. Subsequent changes to the master must have appropriate authorization noted. While copies of the master may be used, proofing is done against the final master.

Design and Layout

Design and layout are not the same thing. The *design* of the catalog is the overall visual and aesthetic concept underlying the material presented. The design develops reader flow and gives your catalog sales impact just from its appearance and 'feel.' The *layout* is the arrangement of words and illustrations within the overall design. The design is analogous to an architect's sketch for a building, with the layout the later detailed blueprints for the construction crew.

Design Sources and Costs
The creation of design concepts is often assigned to an outside source. For important projects, such as producing a catalog, several sources may be commissioned, with the understanding that just one will be selected to complete the project. *Each of these designers is paid an agreed-on amount for his or her work!*

When assigning this or any other project to a designer, be clear about what the designer is to achieve. Get agreement *in advance* from concerned in-house managers about the goals for the catalog. Because debate inevitably occurs on questions of design,[1] agree on a final arbiter for both the design goals and the results achieved.

When there is more than a single designer, give *exactly* the same guidelines to each. If, as often happens in discussing a project with a designer, you modify your instructions or add to them, inform your other designers of these changes. Keep the playing field level, but remember who could help you think, as well as do.

Whatever the final instructions, you will want to see at least the following:

- The front and back covers or the cover "wraparound" where the front and back are one
- The inside front cover and page 1—the first thing the recipient is likely to turn to
- The typical treatment of a single item on a page or facing pages "spread"
- The typical treatment of multiple items on a page or spread
- A one-of-a-kind page, such as the page containing the ordering information, an index, or a table of contents
- The order form or other reply device

These items should be presented in fairly detailed renderings, with major headlines shown in their suggested typefaces and colors clearly indicated. Have your more important projects evaluated by one or more focus groups of typical recipients. This is generally done by a professional focus group research organization. For a less costly and quite effective approach, bring together 10 to 12 typical catalog recipients or users for a social event and have the competing catalog designs simply lying around. Observe your guests' reactions. If you have an obvious winner—and you usually do—you've saved yourself thousands of dollars and rewarded all concerned with a grand party!

The other pages may be presented in rough "thumbnail" sketches, usually one-quarter of the final page size, to show that the designer has resolved the major visual problems without any obvious oversights. To return to the analogy with an architect, you want to be sure that there are windows and bathrooms in your house, as well as a stairway to the second floor.

Bidding the complete job.   Most designers will want to bid on the complete job, from original concept through supervision of proofing and printing. Let them do so, but get their bid to specify each of the following, even when the "package" is bid as a whole. *You* want the cost of each component for your own information and for future comparative shopping.

Costs included in the designer's bid
1.   Original designs.
2.   Page-by-page layouts, including type specifications and necessary instructions to artists and photographers.
3.   Art and photography.

---

[1]Such as debates between authors and publishers about book covers, which authors always lose.

4. Supervision of art and photography.
5. Typesetting.
6. All art, including digitized production or instructions for disk or film preparation.
7. Supervision of film and proofing.
8. Printing supervision.
9. Hourly or a full project rate for revisions and client meetings.

A note about profits. Outside sources cannot work for you unless they earn a profit on your projects. It is important for them to know that you understand this. If their billing structure is such that they make a small profit on each aspect of the total job—from initial concept through printing supervision—and you want less than this from them, be certain that they know this *before* they accept the job. They can then adjust their cost structure to permit a profit. Otherwise, they will adjust their level of commitment to give you "what you paid for."

INSIGHT 34

Once a catalog or other promotion project is well under way with an outside source, there is little opportunity to change suppliers. Think of yourself as a marriage broker who has to make both parties happy with each other for a long time.

SUMMARY

- Differentiate between design and layout before deciding on the same supplier for both.
- Before assigning multiple components to a single source, find out how much the supplier will charge for *each* component if, *for any reason,* you pull (remove) the job. Get the costs in writing.
- Remember the supplier's pledge: "My clients are my friends, and I'll do *anything* for my friends—except work for nothing."

Art and Photography

WARNING!

Artists and photographers frequently have different charges for outright purchase of their work versus a one-time or specified limited use. Decide whether you will need more than a single use. It is the least expensive of their charges. For multiple or unlimited use, get written agreement. *Artists and photographers* may, of course, show examples of their own work for presentation. Get *everything* in writing!

The conventional wisdom states that for catalogs, photography is better than art. There are some exceptions, however:

- Use art for highly styled treatment when impression is more important than reality.
- Use art where it's better at showing necessary detail, for example, for certain hardware, colorless products, or the interior workings of closed systems, such as pumps and people.
- Use art for dreams that have not yet been realized. Unbuilt homes are a typical example.
- Talented artists are comparatively rare and expensive. They do, however, create a "feel" that few photos or computer designs can create.

Unless you are an advertiser who uses art as a personalized signature, use photography for everything else. It gives a psychological as well as a visual perception of a "real" product.

What to Specify on Your Purchase Order for Art

- **The cost of the initial concepts.** If, for *any* reason, the project is canceled or the final art is not assigned to a certain artist, you still have to pay the artist for his or her work. Not liking the concept does not release you from payment; after all, that's why a "concept" is ordered.
- **The cost of final art. Specify an outright purchase.** If that price seems too high, check on the cost of one-time or limited use—if that is practical. Negotiate!
- **The time allowed for delivery** of the concept and for final art after approval of the concept.
- **Any penalties for late delivery.**
- **Any penalties for delivery of final art that does not meet the agreed-on concept.**
- **Put everything in writing** and have the agreement signed by the supplier. Your verbal instructions alone are not proof that they were received. Very little else focuses attention like writing one's name on a contract.

The Photographer
There is an astonishingly large number of excellent photographers, though not all of them are equally good at the same thing. Check their samples for the *type* of photography you hope to achieve, rather than expecting to find an exact sample. Selecting a photographer is very much like selecting an artist, except that you will want to work with someone whose studio is fairly close to where you work or live. It's common practice for the client to be present while the photographer works. No one else is as likely to know the products and to keep the photographer from making "obvious" mistakes in what is combined for each scene or shot.

Finding your photographer. If you have not already established a source of photographers, ask your corporate art director, your designer, or other advertising people to make a recommendation. Visit photographers' studios to get a feel for how you might work together. Ask those with whom you might wish to work to give you their costs on a daily rate, a half-day rate, and a minimum per-shot rate for repetitive photography needing little setup time. Get references and check them, especially for meeting deadlines.

How to order.   Give the catalog layout to each photographer you have selected as probably qualified. Have each quote a price for the total job, including an estimate for the additional cost of film and processing. This quotation is for *complete owner-ship by you* of all photography, including "outtakes" of film and pictures shot but not used. Specify that the photographer may use any of the pictures in a personal portfolio of samples.

If several photographers meet your criteria, have each one do the same picture for the catalog. Keep the picture simple. You'll be able to tell the difference among them. After reviewing their work with your art director and production director, make a decision on whom to use.

What to specify on your purchase order for photography
- **The cost of the entire project,** including photography, film, and processing.
- **The cost of a photographer-supplied art director or stylist.** You may wish to supply such a person yourself or have one supplied by your design studio. If the latter, get the studio's cost of the charges before giving the assignment.
- **The cost of any props or outside purchases made by the photographer.**
- **The time required to complete the job.** Specify the start-up time and the finishing time, not just the number of workdays. Specify what happens if *you* are not able to start on time or supply materials, as well as if the photographer causes delays.
- **Specify whether photos are to be shot for contrast or detail.** But first, discuss this with your filmmaker and printer.
- **Specify your outright ownership of all photography, including pictures not used.**
- **Put everything in writing.** Have everyone sign before you buy.

INSIGHT 35

There is nothing better than involvement from the beginning to give the feeling of project responsibility and ownership.

Getting Your Production Manager and Art Director Involved

On any project that will involve the purchase of design, art, photography, film separation, and/or printing, go over the project with your organization's art director and production director before it is assigned to the outside sources. Also, go over it with them before the completed art is actually approved. Their contributions can save you much frustration and, frequently, much money. Have the art and production directors:

- Review your *instructions* to suppliers. They will recognize when you've asked for too much . . . as well as when you've requested too little.
- Review quotations from suppliers, as well as their concepts and production layouts. They will know which prices are negotiable without losing quality. They will also alert you to problems a design may cause in the production of film or in printing or binding. You may elect not to follow their suggestions, but you will be wise to obtain them!
- Review the art and photography for their *reproduction* quality, as well as purely aesthetic considerations. Listen to their warnings!
- Accompany you to the printer when major jobs are produced. They will be much more demanding—and get better results at the same cost and within the promised time!

Finally, recognize the contribution of the art and production directors publicly. They will have earned it!

SUMMARY

- To show products, use photography rather than art, unless you have a special reason to do otherwise.
- Artists and photographers get paid whether you like their work or not, so specify what you need . . . in writing.
- Get your experts involved early before work is assigned. It's easier and cheaper to avoid problems than to fix them.

Typesetting and Desktop Publishing

Desktop publishing, the ability to produce layouts and high-quality typesetting from a desktop computer, has revolutionized much of the production of catalogs. It is now *possible* to do a great deal of typesetting in-house. But before deciding to do it yourself, the following must be considered.

Design Quality

When in-house typesetting fails to meet promotional needs, it is most often because it lacks the qualities a trained typographer adds to typesetting. Some of this lack results from the use of less sophisticated equipment; some is caused by a lack of training. Likely problem areas include the following:

- **Line spacing.** How much room should you leave between each line and between paragraphs? This will vary, depending on the size, density (a lighter or darker version of the same type), style (sans serif or with serifs), and characteristics of each typeface.
- **Letter and word spacing.** How much room should you leave between each letter in a word and between words in a sentence? This will vary for the same reasons mentioned in regard to line spacing, as well as because one has to make a subjective judgment about legibility. Contemporary

typography tends to leave little such room; that is, it is "set tight." Your older, 50-plus reader will find a "looser" setting easier to read. Know your audience and act accordingly.

- **Flexibility.** Find the style you want within a given typeface—ultralight to ultrabold, regular, italics, small and large capitals, and so on. With true computer-generated typesetting, this is unlikely to be a problem; most so-called desktop systems, on the other hand, are quite limited. Figure 2.4 shows and explains eight professionally set typefaces used by leading designers for catalogs and other advertising projects.

- **Staffing.** Who can take over when trained in-house personnel are on vacation, ill, absent for some other reason, get fired, or quit in the middle of a rush project?

Some Typesetting Considerations

The more important the project, the more critical is the first impression of its product. Therefore, lean toward outside, professional typesetting.

WARNING!

Today's technology permits almost anyone to proclaim themselves a typesetter/typographer. Before using an unfamiliar outside source, ask about their employees' training and ask for references and samples. You want a *typographer,* the typesetting equivalent of an art director or designer. Typesetting without typography can now be done in-house.

Your less important projects have a cumulative impact that is just as great and just as profit or result sensitive as your most important ones. *Everything* that bears your name represents *you* and is the only messenger of that moment.

- ✔ Less important? Yes.
- ✔ Unimportant? Never!

Typefaces

Try to limit the number of typefaces used *in the body* of the catalog to one or two. There are so many variations available *within* each face, that creativity won't suffer. In addition to the obvious changes in the size of the type and the use of standard italics or boldface, computer typesetting systems give you practically unlimited degrees of boldness and styles that can have dramatic impact. Changing the amount of space between lines and between paragraphs, indenting or not indenting paragraphs, making all lines of uniform length ("justified") or letting the margins fall where they may (ragged right; very seldom, ragged left), and the use of capitals for *short* headlines are useful devices.

Serif versus Sans Serif Type

Sans serif (square) type is harder for most adults to read than type with serifs (the little flourishes at the ends of each letter, as in the type in this book). The more sans serif type there is in a document, the more difficult it is to read. Hundreds of studies on the legibility of type verify this rule, and—to my knowledge—not a single study contradicts it. Many *designers* suggest sans serif because of its design-like, chiseled look. Let what you learn in this chapter guide you before you agree.

Costs

To give quotations on typesetting, your typographer/typesetter must have from you a reasonable estimate of both the length of the manuscript and its degree of difficulty. For catalogs, it is best to wait until you have a completed layout that shows both of these. If you must estimate in advance, find the cost of a similar project and add 10 percent (last year's catalog price, plus 10 percent), plus an estimate for any additional length or difficulty.

Typesetters estimate original setting costs based on the number of lines and the number of changes in typeface and style within a copy block (another reason for keeping it simple!). After the type has been set, they charge for client-ordered changes on either an hourly rate or a rate reflecting the number of lines corrected. There is always a minimum cost just to put the job into production. That cost is there whether you change just one comma to a semicolon or whether you change every other word on the page. Typesetters do not charge for their own mistakes, called typos or PEs (printer's errors), only for *client* changes and alterations.

In getting quotations for lengthy typesetting jobs, get the costs for setting with no client changes and the formulas for changes in 5 percent and 10 percent of the lines (i.e., 32 pages times 35 lines per page, or 1,120 lines, with 56 lines corrected for 5 percent), and so forth. Because you will probably have two or three sets of corrections, estimate those costs also. Get the agreed-on pricing structure in writing before you assign the work.

Chapter 2 also presented a discussion of typesetting beginning on page 29.

SUMMARY

- Typeset in-house only if you have the right equipment and personnel. Either one alone is not enough.
- Find and use a typographer you trust, whether you set in-house or out. (It's allright to battle with your typographers, but usually they should win.)
- Get estimates that include more changes than you know you're going to make. You'll still be too low.

Disk or New Art, Film Separation, and Proofing

Information on film separation and proofing, including a checklist, is given in Chapter 16.

INSIGHT 36

Discuss the capabilities—and limitations—of their separation process with your "color separator" film supplier before art or photography is assigned. It's a lot easier and cheaper than crying to "fix" the material after it's delivered!

INSIGHT 37

Accidents can happen anytime anyone works with film. So don't just check your own corrections—check *everything*. But don't change anything unless *absolutely* necessary. Correcting film is costly and requires equally careful rechecking every time.

Printing and Binding

Printing and binding is covered in detail in Chapter 16. It is a process in which original materials—the hard copy and/or computer file—are scanned or photographed and separated onto film or directly onto the printing plate. If film, each holds one of the colors used in printing. The image is transferred from film onto a printing place and then printed.

The best advice that can be given about working with printers and binderies is to know what you want to achieve, but never to tell them how to do it.

Things You Can Do

1. Get a firm quotation, as well as samples of paper to be used, based on actual layouts and specifications. An excellent safety measure is to show the potential printer a copy of the designer's concept and ask whether printing it will present difficulties. Then act accordingly.

2. Any unusual folds or combinations of materials or sizes may cause difficulties and increase costs. Check these aspects for possible problems as early as possible—certainly early enough to change them to something more practical if need be.

3. Anything unusual in shape or size must be checked with the post office for mailing approval, as well as for special handling charges. Make an exact sample (called a *dummy*), and have someone in the post office permits section *approve it and sign the approval.*

4. If the catalog, or any other mailing, will be sent by standard (bulk rate) and you mail fewer than 100,000 pieces, a fractional ounce of additional weight should not create budgeting problems, but check for the latest postal rates to make sure. If, however, you will be mailing any materials first class, have your printer give you an exact dummy made from all of the different papers that you expect to use (Figure 6.2). If you are close to any whole ounce in weight, do something to make

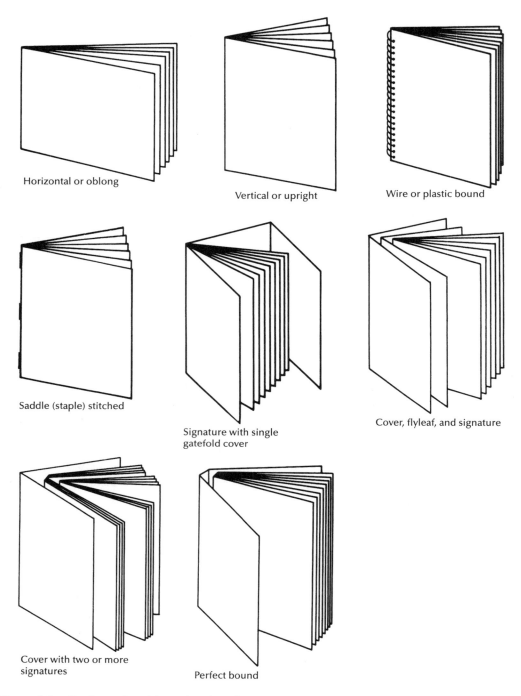

Horizontal or oblong

Vertical or upright

Wire or plastic bound

Saddle (staple) stitched

Signature with single
gatefold cover

Cover, flyleaf, and signature

Cover with two or more
signatures

Perfect bound

Figure 6.2 Catalog and multipage brochure formats. Planning a catalog or brochure requires a choice of format and one or more papers. The most reliable way to evaluate tentative selections is to have paper dummies made by your printer or paper merchant. These blank dummies will give you an accurate way of judging how a paper's substance, weight, and surface qualities look and feel in each of the formats you are considering and how much each of them will cost to mail. (Formats shown courtesy of James River Premium Printing Papers. Original art for James River by Hyers/Smith Advertising, South Norwalk, CT.)

the project lighter. *The chances are that adding ink to the paper will be enough to put you into the next ounce and a higher postage rate.* Consider making your project: $\frac{1}{32}''$ smaller on one side. That's generally enough to compensate for the weight of the ink. But check with your printer and your mailing service to make sure.

5. Deal with printers and binderies through your print production department. Its staff are the experts in these areas. Ask them to explain what they are doing and why they are doing it. Your job is to *know,* not necessarily to *do.* So join them at the printer and bindery when your projects are being produced. Ask about anything you do not know or understand . . . but remember to insist on what you want to achieve. Questions about "more red" or "less blue" or "heavier black" are turned over to the production or art staff. If you are the only one at the printer or bindery, point to the proof and repeat the magic words:

"That's what we want. I wouldn't begin to try to tell *you* how to get it." Resist the temptation to claim more expertise than you have.

SUMMARY

- Printers know how to print. Don't try to help, even when they ask.
- The proof is your bible. Remain a printing fundamentalist.
- The press run won't get better after you leave. Stay until you are satisfied with what you see.

Additional information on printing, including a printing/bindery checklist, is given in Chapter 16.

Distribution and Mailing

Distribution refers to catalogs sent in bulk to outlets and sales staff, to company offices and departments, to the warehouse for bulk storage, and to the mailing facility for handling. *Mailing* refers specifically to those catalogs mailed to customers, prospects, and any other groups and individuals specified by management.

Determining Who Handles the Mailing
Postage costs will be exactly the same and the delivery time will be approximately the same, no matter who handles the mailing. Your mailing service should therefore be chosen for the following reasons:

- **Distance from bindery.** What will it cost to ship the bound catalogs to the mailing service? A bindery that has its own mailing department is preferred over one that does not, *other factors being equal.*
- **Cost of service.** Cost is based on the size and weight of the catalogs. Get a written quotation. Be sure the potential mailing service staff sees a layout of the mailing side of the catalog—usually the back cover—while there is still time to make changes. Their equipment may make it

impossible to put the address where your layout indicates. That's generally an "easy fix" for you, given adequate warning; it may be an impossible fix for them.

- **Reliability of service.** If you are planning to use a supplier for the first time, get references *and check them.*

Seeding the Mailing List

When using outside mailing lists, ask the list suppliers if they can, at little or no cost to you, add ("seed") the lists with the names and addresses of some of your fellow employees (in different parts of the country if possible), as well as yourself and other in-house staff. Then ask these people to let you know *exactly* when they receive the catalog. This will give you a record of when catalogs are received in various parts of the country and whether there are any likely problems in the mail handling. Do this with *every* mailing, whether you use an outside list or your own.

INSIGHT 38

Do *not* let your printer rush a sample *of anything* to your employer, the chairman of the board, or anyone else. Invariably, it will be one with a glaring mistake, such as a page printed upside down that they later corrected but were saving to show how helpful they were to fix your oversights. *You* deliver the sample, checking it very carefully first. It's *your* project. You do the showing off!

SUMMARY

- Get *exact,* complete dummy samples from the printer as soon as designs are approved. You'll need them to learn the cost of postage and to make final postage-related adjustments. Your post office will help.
- Seed the mailing lists with the names of some people who'll tell you when the catalog arrives. Add your name, too.

Much more detailed information on lettershop mailing services, including postage rates and a lettershop/distribution checklist, is given in Chapter 16.

IT ISN'T OVER UNTIL . . .

Postproduction Activities

Here's a way to close out the current catalog before the next one comes due: Use the items applicable to your situation, modify where necessary . . . and celebrate when done!

- **What to return.** Get all products used for photography and return them to stock. Make sure that your department is credited with their return, because you were surely charged when they went out. Gather any other materials (such as original art or photo props) that were borrowed for the project, and return them as promised. Anything of value must be insured and return delivery signed for.

- **What to store.** Store the complete catalog and disk files.

    Save photos and transparencies, and file them in the advertising/promotion department. You will want instant access to them for other projects. These photos should be noted "best" and filed with any backup shots.

    Save all price quotations, purchase orders, and advisory or instructional memoranda in a permanent project file.

- **What to throw away.** Thirty days after the catalog has been distributed, notify management and departments that you will dispose of "all manuscripts, proofs, and incidental paperwork" concerning the project, unless they instruct you to the contrary by a certain date (say, seven days hence). Unless you are ordered to save any of these materials, throw them out!

Recordkeeping and Reporting

The following detailed records must be kept and reported:

- The actual cost of the project versus the estimated or quoted costs and reasons for any discrepancy. This report is issued as soon as all invoices have been received.

- The response to the mailing. If possible, a detailed record of responses should be kept for at least 90 days after the first response is received. This is especially important if the catalog is used to test lists or the viability of products or a promotional effort. A report on the response is issued at the conclusion of a specified period. Where comparisons to previous similar efforts are practical and pertinent, they are, of course, included. Back-end analysis is a specialty all its own. Get professional help if it is needed.

NOTES ON THE CATALOG CHECKLIST

These notes are a supplement to the material presented in this chapter. They are not a substitute for that material. The checklist is shown in Figure 6.3.

1. **Schedule.** For scheduling purposes, the most important management decision is the date the catalog must be completed and what "completed" means. If meeting the deadline is impossible under normal time or budgeting constraints, management must decide whether or not to authorize the impossible. (Do *not* present management with an on-time delivery at a cost that is significantly over budget because you "knew" they wanted it that way. Even if they did, it is *their* decision. Some of our best friends have been fired for not understanding this difference.)

CATALOG CHECKLIST

Project Title _____   Date _____
Project Description _____   Project # _____
_____   Checklist # _____
Overall Supervision By _____   Deadline _____
Budget _____ Completion Date _____   Start Up Date _____

MANAGEMENT DECISIONS	ASSIGNED TO	DUE	IN	MUST APPROVE	BY DATE	IN	INFO COPY ONLY	SEE ATTACHED
1. Schedule	_____	__	☐	_____	__	☐	_____	☐
2. Quantity	_____	__	☐	_____	__	☐	_____	☐
3. Budget	_____	__	☐	_____	__	☐	_____	☐
4. Theme	_____	__	☐	_____	__	☐	_____	☐
5. Audience	_____	__	☐	_____	__	☐	_____	☐
6. Report(s)	_____	__	☐	_____	__	☐	_____	☐
7. Project Manager	_____	__	☐	_____	__	☐	_____	☐

CREATIVE DECISIONS

	ASSIGNED TO	DUE	IN	MUST APPROVE	BY DATE	IN	INFO COPY ONLY	SEE ATTACHED
8. Design Concept	_____	__	☐	_____	__	☐	_____	☐
9. Layout	_____	__	☐	_____	__	☐	_____	☐
10. Copy	_____	__	☐	_____	__	☐	_____	☐
11. Typesetting	_____	__	☐	_____	__	☐	_____	☐
12. Cover Subjects	_____	__	☐	_____	__	☐	_____	☐
13. Photographer(s)	_____	__	☐	_____	__	☐	_____	☐
14. Artist(s)	_____	__	☐	_____	__	☐	_____	☐
15. Insert(s)	_____	__	☐	_____	__	☐	_____	☐
16. Order Form(s)	_____	__	☐	_____	__	☐	_____	☐
17. Envelope	_____	__	☐	_____	__	☐	_____	☐

MECHANICAL DECISIONS

	ASSIGNED TO	DUE	IN	MUST APPROVE	BY DATE	IN	INFO COPY ONLY	SEE ATTACHED
18. Disk/New Art: Cover(s)	_____	__	☐	_____	__	☐	_____	☐
19. Disk/New Art: Body	_____	__	☐	_____	__	☐	_____	☐
20. Disk/New Art: _____	_____	__	☐	_____	__	☐	_____	☐
21. Film: Cover(s)*	_____	__	☐	_____	__	☐	_____	☐
22. Film: Body	_____	__	☐	_____	__	☐	_____	☐
23. Film: _____	_____	__	☐	_____	__	☐	_____	☐
24. Print: Cover(s)*	_____	__	☐	_____	__	☐	_____	☐
25. Print: Body	_____	__	☐	_____	__	☐	_____	☐
26. Print: _____	_____	__	☐	_____	__	☐	_____	☐
27. Bindery	_____	__	☐	_____	__	☐	_____	☐
28. Mailing Service*	_____	__	☐	_____	__	☐	_____	☐
29. Postage Check(s)	_____	__	☐	_____	__	☐	_____	☐
_____	_____	__	☐	_____	__	☐	_____	☐
_____	_____	__	☐	_____	__	☐	_____	☐

* **Separate checklists are included in Chapter 16 for film work, printing, and mailing service.**

Figure 6.3   The catalog checklist.

2. **Quantity.** If the needed quantity becomes a budget problem, here are a few ways to get more catalogs for the same dollars:

   - Use less expensive paper. Often a slightly lighter-weight paper, a somewhat smaller size, or both will save enough on postage to make up the difference.

   - Use fewer (or more!) pages, provided that they give you the least expensive printing. Adding just 4 pages to a 32-page catalog adds appreciably more than one-eighth the cost. The same or even higher costs may be true when printing "only" 28 pages on presses designed for 32. Discuss with your printer the most economical ways to get the job done. If you are unfamiliar with purchasing print, make sure that you learn the whys involved.

   - Give your printer a needed quantity and the budget decided on. If the printer can't meet it, shop around for another.

3. **Budget.** In estimating budgets, make sure that the suppliers know when the services will be needed. If there are likely increases in union rates, nonunion shops will probably have similar raises. Check with the post office for possible changes in regulations as well as postage. As always, try to keep management's surprises pleasant.

4. **Theme.** Try to keep managers from becoming copywriters. Good luck!

5. **Audience.** "Audience" relates directly to #2, the quantity needed, and #3, the cost of getting catalogs to each recipient. Remind management of this interrelationship, and, where budgets are limited, get the priorities or some other guidance.

6. **Report(s).** Is there a report needed or wanted beyond the budget, costs, and results? Discuss the practicality of each request if getting the information is not already built into your system. Much of this kind of data is nice to know, but what will be done with it after it's been gathered?

7. **Project manager.** The project manager, if different from the overall supervisor, will be *directly* responsible for the supervision of points 8–28. She or he most often appoints as well as supervises the persons involved.

8–9. **Design/layout.** Who will do each? In some instances, the layout can be done internally, even if a design is purchased outside.

10. **Copy.** How much does the writer have to know about your product or service to do the job? Write technical copy inside, and then give it to an outside writer for review. In accuracy versus sell, settle for accuracy every time.

11. **Typesetting.** Discuss with your designed typesetter the practicality of your producing the manuscript on disk, then having them prepare the typographically designed version for printing or web site use. This is often the best solution when the copy is other than standard English or there are numerous last-second changes in numbers, prices, or other data.

12. **Covers.** Who decides? Who assigns? Who approves final art?

13–14. **Photo/art.** Commercial artists and photographers tend to do best at specific kinds of projects. Get samples. Negotiate for prices. Get a *signed* agreement. Try to give "the kid" a chance.

15. **Insert(s).** Inserts are a practical way to address specific audiences without adding everything to the main catalog. Use them also for testing, as described on pages 85–90. In using different inserts for different parts of your mailing, discuss controls with your mailing service *before* mailing lists are ordered or anything is printed. Identification codes will be required on each part. Find out where to place them!

16. **Order form(s).** It often pays huge dividends to have more than a single order form in catalogs that have a fairly long life. Test.

17. **Envelope.** Few catalogs are mailed in envelopes, unless they are accompanied by a variety of loose materials. Often the latter can be bound in. Check, Save!

18–23. **Proofs.** Be sure to build in adequate time for in-house review. Everyone who sees anything will want to suggest changes, so ask for corrections and comments from the fewest number of persons safety allows. Nothing gets reviewers more furious than being asked for comments and then being ignored!

24–26. **Printing OK.** Use in-house expertise if available; get the designer involved if not. On-press approval tends to be a *very* lengthy job. Allow for that in scheduling and budgeting.

27–28. **Bindery/mailing.** Two excellent ways to let beginners learn the importance of nitpicking detail is to supervise the bindery and to supervise the mailing operation. Little is likely to go wrong. But everything must be checked—continually—to keep it that way.

29. **Postage.** The postal service will not accept a mailing without payment in hand. In organizations where payment is sometimes slow, get management to set up a system that won't delay the mail.

7 | Out-of-Home Advertising and Promotion

This chapter has been brought up to date with the help of **Steven H. Mueller,** president, and **Stephen Faso,** director of Strategic Planning, Outdoor Services, Inc., the national planning and buying agency for out-of-home guidance and information (www.OutdoorServices.com).

This chapter describes and gives advice on using the major "out-of-home" media, from billboards to in-store advertising. Few of these are literally do-it-yourself projects in the sense of doing your own ads or direct mail—you'd hardly paint your own billboard or put up your own bus cards! Like the chapters on audiovisual communication (Chapter 13) and information on convention display construction (Chapter 15), we offer guidance to buying, supervising, and using the media, as well as a reminder of the many effective ways you have to advertise out-of-home if someone just calls them to your attention.

For maximum success (and why would you settle for less?), the use of these media demands the integrated marketing approach to your advertising and promotion that we urge throughout this book. As one example, Figure 7.1 shows how

Effect of Adding Out-of-Home Media to a Media Mix
(Medium-Sized Market; Target Audience: W 25–54; Schedule: 4 Weeks; 30-Sheet Posters)

	Without O-H-M	With O-H-M
Budget	$54,104	$54,104
Television	100%	85%
% Out-of-Home	—	15%
GRP's	500	795 (+59%)
Cost/Rating Point (Prime Access)	$108	$68 (-37%)
% Reach	45.3%	88.1% (+17%)
Average Frequency	6.6 times	9.0 times (+36%)

Source: OAAA

Out-of-Home Advertising Source

Figure 7.1 How a 15 percent out-of-home budget share gained 59 percent in gross rating point prospect awareness.

a medium-sized 2001 market had a 59 percent increase in message reach when just 15 percent of an original TV budget was switched to out-of-home media.

The major out-of-home media, listed alphabetically within the major categories, follow.

TRADITIONAL OUTDOOR MEDIA

- Aerial/inflatable advertising
- Bus bench advertising
- Bus shelter advertising
- Mobile advertising
- Outdoor advertising
- Taxi advertising
- Transit advertising

PLACE-BASED MEDIA

- Airport advertising
- High school/college campus advertising
- Hotel advertising
- In-flight advertising
- In-store advertising
- Movie/theater advertising
- Shopping mall food court advertising
- Sports/fitness/leisure facility advertising
- Stadium/arena/sports team advertising
- Truck stop advertising

EVENT MARKETING

- Event advertising and promotion

PLANNING AND BUYING TRADITIONAL OUTDOOR MEDIA

Traditional outdoor media range from spectacular 48-foot-long lighted "displays"[1] to 46-inch overhead terminal clocks and 21-inch interior rail cards. Many out-of-home media have industrywide specifications that will let you work in a uniform size no matter where they will be used. Others, such as cold-air inflatables, can be practically any shape or size you want.

The Yellow Pages, SRDS, and Your Sanity

Suppliers for out-of-home media are in major city and some smaller community Yellow Pages "Advertising—Outdoors" listing. But unless you are *very* familiar

---

[1]What everyone not in the trade calls billboards.

with a specific medium and market, check the *SRDS Out-of-Home Advertising Source™* directory[2] before you do anything else. Not only will you find national and local suppliers, but you'll see pricing structures (inclusive of discounts) for practically every size community or occasion. Although pricing may or may not be negotiable, at least you'll know the "ballpark" before you decide to play.

Constructing Your Own

Many desirable out-of-home locations are under long-term contract. If the one you want is not available, consider constructing your own. For instance, offer to pay for surprisingly inexpensive bus-stop benches and to even pay rent for its ad. For placements on private land, talk to the property owners, from airports to farmland to zoos, about your need. Given the abundance of unused parcels of property available, you will find very receptive owners who are entrepreneurial in nature and more than willing to lease or sell for the right price. Then talk to a local outdoor company about zoning and the cost of construction, maintenance, and the message itself.

Zoning Restrictions

Out-of-home media are controlled or restricted by local zoning laws as to size, placement, lighting, and content—such as advertising alcohol or tobacco in certain locations. Before ordering any outdoor advertising, discuss zoning clearance with your supplier. Whether the responsibility is theirs or yours, get clearance, *in writing,* from the appropriate community zoning and engineering departments. If in doubt, work through your attorney.

BILLBOARD OUTDOOR DISPLAYS

Outdoor advertising, dominated by but not limited to billboards, works for local and national advertisers by selling goods and services to travelers, commuters, and those living in the local communities.

INSIGHT 39

In outdoor advertising, it is critically important to decide on the 3 W's—who, when, and what—when dealing with your local or national representative:
1. *Who* you are trying to reach with your advertising
2. *When* you want to reach them (timing)
3. *What* you will spend to reach them (budget)

---

[2]SRDS Directories, 1700 Higgins Road, Des Plaines, IL 60018. Phone: (800) 851-7737, Fax: (847) 375-5001. For additional SRDS Directories, see pp. 50–51.

How to Get the Billboard You Want

Billboards are owned or represented by hundreds of different local and national companies, many of which have groups of billboards in specific markets. For local use, if just a few of these companies are listed in your Yellow Pages, have each one give you a map or tour of their board locations. If that proves unworkable, scout the area holding the boards you want. You'll find the name of the leasing agent, as shown in Figure 7.2, at the bottom center, hoping to be seen by potential buyers like you.

Billboards and Their Cost

Outdoor companies offer programs in showing levels, from a single panel to 100 percent of the GRP (gross rating point) potential audience. Common showing sizes include #25, #50, #75, and #100 with the number of display pannels relating directly to a market. For instance:

#50 Showing Market	30-Sheet Size # of panels
Los Angeles	240
Chicago	197
San Francisco	136
Denver	39

In smaller communities, local suppliers may need comparatively few panels to offer a high-frequency audience "100 percent showing"; that is, a billboard on

Figure 7.2   For ease of contact, the name of the leasing agent is centered underneath the billboard. Lamar (www.lamar.com) is the leader in the outdoor industry, with the largest number of billboards.

```
┌─────────────────────────────────────────────────────┐
│              2001 Average Cost per Thousand           │
│                      Adults 18+                       │
│  Outdoor (Top 100 Markets)                            │
│      Eight-Sheet Posters #50 Showing        $    97   │
│      30-Sheet Posters #50 Showing               2.05  │
│      Rotary Bulletins #10 Showing               4.04  │
│      Transportation, other shelters #50 showing 1.48  │
│                                                       │
│  Radio (Top 100 Markets)                              │
│      60-second Drive-Time Commercial            8.61  │
│                                                       │
│  Television (Top 100 Markets)                         │
│      30-second Local Prime-Time Spot           17.78  │
│      30-second Prime-Time Network              12.77  │
│                                                       │
│  Magazines (23 Publications)                          │
│      One 4/C Page                               9.35  │
│                                                       │
│  Newspapers (Top 100 Markets)                         │
│      1/3 Page B/W                              22.95  │
│                                                       │
│  2001 Sources:                                        │
│      Outdoor Planning Systems—Harris Donovan, Inc.    │
│      Squad, Spring 2001                               │
│      Media Dynamics                                   │
│      NAA-NPA                                          │
└─────────────────────────────────────────────────────┘
```

Figure 7.3   Comparative cost of using outdoor media compared with print and electronic advertising.

the major roads entering and leaving all four sides of town, with a "50 percent showing" being half of that.

Many businesses that use outdoor advertising are comparatively small and local, with the fastest-growing group of advertisers involved in travel and tourism, automotive, retail, real estate and insurance, and business products and services. As shown in Figure 7.3, outdoor advertising is highly competitive on a CPM (cost per thousand) basis compared with other media targeted at adults age 18 and up. Market by market, it is surprisingly inexpensive. In any community, less traveled locations and smaller billboards are much cheaper. Many locations require multiple-month leasing. Others are available for a single month or for special events of a few days or weeks. Considering the impossibility of economically reaching the majority of the billboard audiences in any other way, that's quite a buy!

Production Costs

The cost of producing the visual ad is often included in the space rental. When it is not, production of some of the largest expressway displays, which are either vinyl printed or, increasingly, computerized, ranges from $1,500 to $2,500. Displays that require elaborate three-dimensional construction may, of course, cost much more. The smaller displays are usually lithographed (printed) or silk-screened and vary in price depending on the complexity of the artwork.

On Billboard Design

Many outdoor placement and production companies offer free guidance in billboard design.[3] Take it! The key to successful billboard design is a message that is seen, is understood, and *motivates* after no more than a quick glance. Here's an example.

A Case Study

Rand McNally had promoted a new line of school maps to be introduced at that year's most important buyers convention. Unfortunately for the promotion plan, world politics brought last-minute changes in geographical names and boundaries. Revised maps could not be produced in time.

The solution, as in many similar cases, was to pass the problem to advertising.

A visit by the advertising manager to the convention city discovered five billboards on the main roadway leading to the convention center. Incredibly, all five were available! Soon all five had the same message:

DON'T BUY MAPS
UNTIL YOUR SEE THE REP FROM RAND McNALLY
IN BOOTH 535!

There are two sequels to this story:

Sequel 1.   Company president Andrew McNally received calls from his major competitors, chiding him for use of the negative "Don't buy maps" theme.

"Negative?" he responded. "It was the most successful convention we ever had!"

Sequel 2.   Jack Heimerdinger, the Rand McNally advertising manager who created the billboard theme, got calls from the next three occupants of Booth 535. They told him his message was still there and though *they* had nothing to do with maps, they'd never had the kind of traffic—and business—the billboards created.

Basic Billboard Formats

Outdoor billboard advertising has three basic formats:

- *Bulletins.* These huge vinyl displays, 48 feet long by 14 feet high, deliver impact in size, placement, color, and lighting.
- *30-sheet posters.* "30 Sheet" refers to the number of printed sheets it originally took to fill this 123-inch by 273-inch space.
- *8-sheet poster.* This much smaller 130-inch by 130-inch billboard is most frequently used in neighborhoods such as those with local ethnic populations that are hard to reach economically through other print media. In

---

[3]OutdoorServices.com, the leading agent for billboard rental, publishes an excellent guide to practical—and creative—outdoor design and production, including the use of computer-generated art. Additional information at Outdoor Advertising Association of America (OAAA.com). Check both!

advertising to this audience, be sure you use a creative source that figuratively and literally speaks your target market's language.

About Vinyl Printing

The development of full-color, billboard-sized printing on vinyl is rapidly replacing hand-painted poster art. Even the huge 48-foot bulletins can now be preprinted this way. The finished vinyl is fastened to ratchets on all four sides of the display, then stretched tight. Unlike paper or hand-painted posters, vinyl is practically weatherproof and takes a fraction of the time to install. Unlike hand painting, it is absolutely uniform in color and design, no matter where, when, or by whom installed, and can be stored for future use and shipped to other markets.

Three Kinds of Mobile Billboards

1. Truck Advertising

Three distinctly different kinds of truck "billboards" are in use:

- *Special events billboards.* These special event promotions, quite literally billboards-on-wheels, take attention-catching, brightly lit messages where ordinary billboards would not be permitted. Many can change messages electronically, within minutes, as often as desired.
- *Mobile billboards.* Billboard posters, similar to 50-sheet in size, are attached to commercial trucks on regular routes. Other trucks use actual artwork. Excellent for markets that restrict conventional outdoor advertising.
- *Truck self-advertising.* Though all large trucks are painted, few carry a real billboard-type selling message as is done by McDonald's. The selection of specific routes and technology that permits truck-message tracking makes this a medium waiting to be discovered . . . and used.

2. Taxi Advertising

Taxis are increasingly becoming carriers of exterior and interior advertising messages. Depending on local rulings, many have lighted signs; some with computer animation and/or LEDs (like TV stock tickers), great for news and sports add-on. An excellent medium for restaurants, lodging, entertainment.

3. Painted Cars

A localized phenomenon in some markets. The personal car-billboard, painted in attention-grabbing psychedelic colors and designs, has sales message impact on a younger audience. Ask the driver how he or she became the mobile message, then follow their lead to the medium source.

TRANSIT AND BUS DISPLAYS

To ease production problems, the transit industry has adopted a system of uniform sizing for exterior "posters" and interior display "cards." Because placement can be ordered for specific routes or lines, these offer a superb medium for socioeconomic and ethnic targeting, with "take-one" cards as an inexpensive—and underused—method of testing promotional appeals. For instance, use six different headlines—one on every sixth display card—and see which brings in the best response.

Production Considerations

Transit advertising materials have rigid production specifications. See the Yellow Pages under "Advertising—Transit & Transportation" for placement services and for the placement companies' recommendations on printing. Get references from both. Check them out!

Nine different formats are available for buses, transit buses, and subway stations and cars. These are all miniature billboards! Limit the copy to what can be absorbed at a glance.

Bus and Station Formats

1. *Super king size.* On street side of the bus. 240 inches long by 30 inches high. Produced in four sections.
2. *King size.* On both curb and street side. Just under 30-inch by 144-inch display produced in three sections.
3. *Queen size.* Just under 30 inches by 88 inches. Produced in two or three sections.
4. *Front and rear displays.* A variety of size specifications depending on placement. Sizes are not interchangeable!
5. *Interior subway and bus cards.* Mounted in frames, they are from approximately 11 inches by 21 inches to 11 inches by 48 inches.
6. *Interior rail car cards.* Available in two sizes: 21 inches long by 22 inches high or 21 inches long by 33 inches high.
7. *Subway and bus station displays.* Available in three sizes: 30 inches long by 46 inches high, 5 feet long by 46 inches high (the most widely used), and 42 inches long by 84 inches high.
8. *Domination displays.* All advertising in a station. This may or may not include vehicles.
9. *Bus and train wrap.* Vinyl "wraps" with tiny holes by windows give visibility from inside.

OTHER TRAVEL-RELATED DISPLAYS

Bench Displays

These "mini-billboards," often within feet of a bus stop, are seen by bus passengers, auto traffic, and pedestrians. Although most are contracted for by local businesses, often for years at a time, some are available for special events, such as a farewell message with which students surprised a retiring teacher at her regular bus stop. For locations and costs, see "Advertising—Outdoors" in the Yellow Pages or check an advertising bench for the name of the display company.

In-Station Displays

Many displays within rail stations, airports, and bus terminals are controlled by national companies; others by the local transportation authority. These displays include interior backlit dioramas and islands, clocks, and exterior bus shelters. For availability and costs, check the SRDS directory, the Yellow Pages, or contact the airport or train station management, or the rapid transit or bus line.

AERIAL/INFLATABLE ADVERTISING

Most—perhaps all—aerial messages are vanity or show-off advertising aimed as much at publicity or public relations as sales accountability. Consider it a short-term aerial billboard aimed at a known target. Employees see their company name overhead as they sit in a stadium. A political or religious group is identified by a banner towed by a small plane. "Cecilia, Will You Marry Me?" floats across the sky as she hopes the one to whom she's saying yes—probably on the local TV news—is really Chuck! Aerial banners, balloons, blimps, and depending on wind conditions, sky writing is used at sporting, political, religious, and other outdoor events. For night advertising, some blimps are now available in a backlit format that glows as an eye-catcher. It's all great fun and, with the exception of the true multicrew blimp, surprisingly inexpensive.

Other aerial promotions. Preformed aerial devices, with or without advertising messages, include smaller blimps, life-size and oversize animals and story characters, and helium-filled, regular-sized balloons that lend a festive feeling to any occasion.

Where to Find Suppliers and What It Costs

Flyovers

It is possible to do full-color graphics/murals that can be pulled behind planes or low-flying helicopters as was done for some major beverage companies during spring break activities in Florida. Many aerial suppliers give national services. Look in the Yellow Pages under "Advertising—Aerial" or in the SRDS directory to find the help you need.[4]

Costs

Expect to pay from $300 to $500, including creation of the message, for a banner flyover. For the most expensive of aerial advertising, a manned blimp, you'll pay about $200,000 per month. To turn a commercial passenger jet into a flying billboard, check the appropriate airline. It's a great stunt, but who will actually see it?[5]

---

[4]However, after the terrorist attacks of September 11, 2001, and the resulting limitations on flight, this option may not be widely considered or even available.

[5]*A case history.* Air France transformed a Zurich–Paris jet into a striking black-and-white promotion for *Phantom of the Opera.* Because passengers had to walk at ground level from the terminal to the plane, it got more undivided attention than most roadside billboards.

Inflatable "Cold Air" Advertising

Inflatables, also known as "cold air advertising," are three-dimensional plastic creations that are filled with air or gas. They include large rooftop or ground balloons and children's holiday and seasonal favorites such as dinosaurs, Santa Claus, and Uncle Sam. Inflatables can be custom-made to practically any shape and size for special events. See Figure 7.4 for a sample rate card.

Locating Suppliers

Many suppliers give national service. Look in the Yellow Pages under "Advertising—Aerial" or in the SRDS directory to find the help you need.

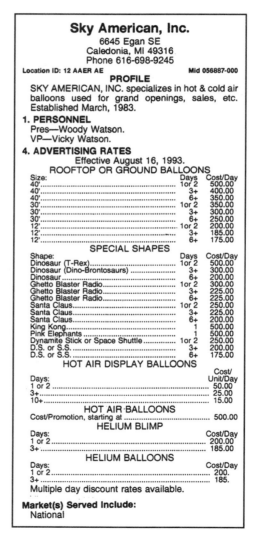

Figure 7.4 A typical range of "cold air" and "hot air" services and products and their costs. *2002 SRDS Out-of-Home Advertising Source.* (There has been no increase in Sky American costs since 1997.)

Costs

Costs for rental of standard, preformed shapes are for days, rather than the fly-by minutes or hours. They range, as seen in Figure 7.4, from less than $200 to $500 and up. Custom-made shapes are more, of course, but also give you ownership of the shapes for future use.

AIRPORT ADVERTISING

Located in airport terminals and their parking lots, these displays include an ever-expanding family of media, including waiting-area television, backlit structures (dioramas), murals, wall posters, phone boards, clocks, luggage carts and carousels, and so on.

Advantages of Airport Advertising

Few media buys offer so large a captive audience that is frequently bored with waiting or desperate for local information, or both. Use the billboard approach to give them a *benefit-filled* reason to react to your message and you have a winner.

Placement, Production, and Costs

Advertising in more than 90 U.S. airports is handled by Clear Chanel.com/outdoor and J.C. Decaux.com. Check them first. Check other airports to learn whether they handle their own or use one of J.C. Decauxs competitors. Pricing seems to have little relationship to passenger traffic but much more to "all the traffic will bear." That does *not* mean you will be cheated. It does mean—as in all advertising—that you must build in a way of documenting and evaluating what you get from your buy.

IN-FLIGHT ADVERTISING

In-flight advertising, which began as the airlines' magazines, soon expanded to direct response catalogs. It now includes television, movie, and audio commercials and product sampling. Think of it, too, for destination premiums such as entertainment, dining, auto rental, and lodging discounts, especially for business travelers who use the same suppliers from force of habit. Contact any airline's marketing department for current programs and a discussion of innovative new approaches.

SHOPPING MALL AND FOOD COURT ADVERTISING

Don't limit your thinking to posters, signage, and displays in windows and free-standing structures. Think about inside for on-screen showings of each department's fashions . . . to explain the advantages among different model bicycles . . . or to let diners table-top screen show the chef prepare their meals. Put the electronic screens in your display windows and see how live action draws a crowd and, almost always, perks up sales.

Computerize Your Mall Directory

Create an interactive mall directory—in effect, a mall catalog—for in-mall as well as web site use. Younger shoppers especially will love it. Give specific directions to who . . . where . . . when, but also give each mall location a chance to promote themselves. More about this in Chapter 11.

SPORTS/FITNESS/LEISURE FACILITY ADVERTISING

From ski resorts to roller rinks, from health clubs to race tracks, from golf courses to amateur and semi-pro sports facilities, there are local, regional, and national advertising opportunities. Think, too, about tie-in promotions with sports bars and eating and drinking places near sports facilities. For industrywide or other large-scale advertising, see the SRDS directory. For local promotion, this demands one-on-one contact and persuasion. Begin by creating a benefit *they* will want and your selling job will take care of itself.

HIGH SCHOOL AND COLLEGE ADVERTISING

For the small to medium-sized company, advertising opportunities include posters on gym boards and other news and information station bulletin boards, ads in college papers, and messages on newspaper distribution racks. More ambitious efforts include preprinted book covers and class schedule booklets, even custom publications, often tailored to and given free for use in specific courses.

With the exception of college publication advertising, in-school and on-campus promotions probably require permission, or at least following the rules, as to size, length of time, and so on. For just a few locations, call to find the appropriate school officers, then check with them as to clearance procedure. For more ambitious distribution, contact service organizations, such as those described in the SRDS directory. Get *and check* references with both their clients and schools.

MOVIE, CONCERT, AND THEATER ADVERTISING

Theater and Concert Programs

Programs are one of the underused advertising media. They give you a captive audience, almost all of whom will read the program. Furthermore, depending on who is performing and what is presented, the socioeconomics of your audience is known. Theater audiences are new for each performance. For musical occasions other than one-shot extravaganza events, be mindful of seasonal or other repeat attendance ticket holders. Check with each organization's business manager on advertising opportunities and costs.

Movie Advertising

Many movie theaters begin their show with on-screen ads or commercials, often for local businesses. If interested in just one or two theaters, discuss it with their managers. For broader distribution, contact one of the firms listed in the SRDS directory. These are not "TV" commercials, so for production, use someone who knows the medium. Let Chapter 13, "Media Creativity and Production," be your guide.

HAVE YOU THOUGHT ABOUT . . .

Only our imagination—and pocketbook—limits our use of out-of-home advertising. Here are three more ideas to start your thinking.

Floor Graphics

One of the newest point-of-sale devices. Any image can be placed on the floor: an oversize product picture, a slogan or offer, a follow-the-footsteps theme . . . *anything.* You'll stop prospects in their tracks, or lead them where you want them to go. Some companies produce images on adhesive, easy-to-remove film. Others use graphics floor tiles that temporarily replace the regular floor. Depending on zoning, you may be able to create outside graphics, too.

A case history. In a floor graphics 20-store test of a new Trident gum and an existing Nestlé chocolate bar, both showed excellent results. Ten stores used standard point-of-sale graphics, 10 others used floor graphics.

Results[6] showed that in stores using the floor graphics, sales of Trident brand gum rose 19.2 percent during an initial test period and over 21 percent during a second test. Sales of the Nestlé bar increased even more, 24.8 and 23.6 percent, respectively. Even more important, not only did the floor graphics increase immediate sales, they maintained high sale increases over time.

Painted Walls

Housed in a drab building? Use it as a canvas to paint or vinyl wrap to make it the striking structure you'd like it to be! Of course, zoning permitting, you can use a blank wall as a billboard, but why not make it something your prospects and customers will not only notice but thank you for, too! Don't forget to advertise on scaffolding. Everyone looks up there. Sell them something.

County Fairgrounds, Picnic Grounds, and County Stadiums

Practically every county has public facilities that are busy year-round. Whether it's a stock show or trailer swap, a true old-fashioned fair or a real modern art exhibit, a Fourth of July political picnic or Thanksgiving pumpkin pie contest—everyone is there for a good time. With that in mind, create an on-site advertisement that promises to make their good times even better. Of course, that benefit approach isn't limited to out-of-home promotions, but it's a great place to start!

---

[6]Reported in *Sales And Marketing Strategy & News.*

NOTES ON THE OUT-OF-HOME CHECKLIST

These notes are a supplement to the material presented in this chapter. They are not a self-contained substitute for that material. The World Outdoor Services media and management company provided much of the information on which this checklist is based. The checklist appears in Figure 7.5.

1. **Purpose.** What is the *one* thing your message is to do? Give directions? Make it simple and exact (Next Exit. Left $\frac{1}{4}$ miles) . . . Emphasize a price? Add a benefit (Unconditional 2-Year Guarantee! Only $99.95) . . . Create a product image? Assure a long-term commitment?

2. **Client image.** Every out-of-home message shows a "picture" of the advertiser. Make certain it's the brand image you want portrayed.

3. **Budget.** If out-of-home is part of another advertising or promotion budget, how is each element determined? What has priority?

4. **Testing.** If out-of-home is only a part of the total advertising package, consider testing some of the program without it. Or try out-of-home without the rest. Both together, *use the same TOTAL dollars* and allocate at least 15 percent for out-of-home.

5. **Project supervision.** Out-of-home needs special know-how. Give supervision to someone who has it . . . or is willing to learn!

6. **Time line.** Make this step one! Base creative time on your experience with other ads, or on guaranteed art supplier delivery. Rules-of-thumb scheduling exists for production. Check with Outdoor Services or other industry guides to make sure your time line works in your overall integrated promotion plan. If not, ask your suppliers for suggestions. Budget permitting, the impossible becomes routine.

7. **Audience.** Keep the focus as narrow as practical. Don't try to attract everyone. Do aim for the vast majority of those you really want.

8. **Copy.** Clever wins awards. Direct sells.

9. **Design.** From type selection to colors to word count, you can find out what works best in out-of-home advertising. Ask your creative or production source for the industry association's *documented* guidelines. Follow them!

10. **Mechanical art.** Mechanical art specifications, from giant bulletins to overhead platform clocks to in-flight film commercials, vary with each production company. Do not assume that your creative resource knows what production needs—even when the creative is you. Check to make sure there have been no overnight changes!

11. **Client approval.** Out-of-home advertising will be seen by everyone on the client's staff. But unless they are also the prospects at whom the message is aimed, keep them out of the approval process. Do not make out-of-home a committee project. Make some one person responsible. Let him or her decide!

12. **Physical production.** A three-step process: (A) The physical producer chosen. (B) The reproduction process agreed on. (C) The schedule fixed.

OUT-OF-HOME CHECKLIST

Project Title _____ Date _____
Project Description _____ Project # _____
_____ Checklist # _____
Overall Supervision By _____ Deadline _____
Budget _____ Completion Date _____ Start Up Date _____

MANAGEMENT DECISIONS	ASSIGNED TO	DUE	IN	MUST APPROVE	BY DATE	IN	INFO COPY ONLY	SEE ATTACHED
1. Purpose	_____	___	☐	_____	___	☐	_____	☐
2. Client Image	_____	___	☐	_____	___	☐	_____	☐
3. Budget	_____	___	☐	_____	___	☐	_____	☐
4. Testing	_____	___	☐	_____	___	☐		
5. Project Supervision	_____	___	☐	_____	___	☐		
							_____	☐
CREATIVE/PRODUCTION							_____	☐
6. Timeline	_____	___	☐	_____	___	☐	_____	☐
7. Audience	_____	___	☐	_____	___	☐	_____	☐
8. Copy	_____	___	☐	_____	___	☐	_____	☐
9. Design	_____	___	☐	_____	___	☐	_____	☐
10. Mechanical Art	_____	___	☐	_____	___	☐	_____	☐
11. Client Approval	_____	___	☐	_____	___	☐	_____	☐
12. Physical Production	_____	___	☐	_____	___	☐	_____	☐
13. Media Sizes	_____	___	☐	_____	___	☐	_____	☐
14. Format	_____	___	☐	_____	___	☐	_____	☐
15. Duration	_____	___	☐	_____	___	☐	_____	☐
16. Quantities	_____	___	☐	_____	___	☐	_____	☐
17. Shipping Instructions	_____	___	☐	_____	___	☐	_____	☐
18. Media Notification	_____	___	☐	_____	___	☐	_____	☐
19. Records & Samples	_____	___	☐	_____	___	☐	_____	☐
20. Evaluation	_____	___	☐	_____	___	☐	_____	☐
21. Report	_____	___	☐	_____	___	☐	_____	☐
MECHANICAL CHECKS								
22. Editorial OK	_____	___	☐	_____	___	☐	_____	☐
23. Legal OK	_____	___	☐	_____	___	☐	_____	☐
24. Marketing OK	_____	___	☐	_____	___	☐	_____	☐
25. Management OK	_____	___	☐	_____	___	☐	_____	☐
26. Copy As Used	_____	___	☐	_____	___	☐	_____	☐

Figure 7.5 The out-of-home checklist.

13. **Media sizes.** Make sure sizes are determined by both market and medium; that is, billboards as well as bus exterior and interior signs can vary in sizes.

14. **Format.** If the same art is used for more than one format, is approval required for each? For the record, code every change in every item!

15. **Duration.** What are the posting dates and the duration of postings? The coding used in point 14 makes a visual record easy to create and maintain.

16. **Quantities.** Almost all media require some extra. Check requirements with each.

17. **Shipping instructions.** If unfamiliar with shipping options and terminology, have both explained ("Best way" versus "Fastest" versus "Least expensive to arrive by . . ." etc.). Give shipping instructions to the producer *in a mutually agreed on format.* Be sure method of shipping and drop-dead due date are included.

18. **Media notification.** Notification to media company(ies) of what is being shipped—including design—tells how, how many, when, and by whom.

19. **Records and samples.** Samples of audiovisual, if practical. Picture or photo of each design, with product code and record of use.

20. **Evaluation.** Results, insofar as they are known, of total integrated promotion with out-of-home contribution.

21. **Report.** Presentation of #20 evaluation as required or scheduled.

22. **Editorial OK.** The final authority on the mechanics of language, house style, and technical accuracy of text and art.

23. **Legal OK.** Out-of-home is regulated by federal, state, and local laws and rules. Work with an organization that is knowledgeable in the specifics of what you want to do. Don't guess and hope for the best!

24. **Marketing OK.** The final sign off—in writing—from the marketing person or department. Make sure your creative solution still fits the overall marketing plan.

25. **Management OK.** Get this approval if required . . . or if politics suggests you should.

26. **Copy/sample as used.** Some *one* person must maintain a permanent file of photographs, samples, disks . . . and an index of where *anything* can be found.

8 | Successful Yellow Pages Advertising

This chapter by **Tom Davis**, the nation's leading Yellow Pages consultant, has been modified, with his approval, to fit the format of our book. For more information about Yellow Pages advertising and his book, *The Truth about Yellow Pages*, contact Davis at (407) 647–5990 or by e-mail at truthyp@aol.com.

ECONOMICS OF YELLOW PAGES ADVERTISING

There are three keys to making your Yellow Pages (YP) ad creative and to making buying decisions:

1. You are not looking for customers, clients, or patients. They are doing the looking for someone to fill their needs.
2. You are unlikely to get a second chance at attracting an individual YP user. You either get that response from your Yellow Pages ad or you don't.
3. Whatever you decide about YP advertising, you will have to live with that decision for a year.

Extent of Yellow Pages Usage

To help in making your creative/buying decisions, you must know the how, when, why, and extent of how the Yellow Pages is used. That is the secret to profitable ad buying. If you truly understand to what extent Yellow Pages is used by your potential customers, clients, or patients, you will have the right foundation to build your Yellow Pages strategy.

A Look at Yellow Pages Usage

Yellow Pages is *driven by usage.* You are not buying an ad on a piece of paper. You are buying exposure to the usage of your heading(s) and the directory(ies) you are considering. Proof of a specific directory's usage is its continued financial support from its advertisers. There is a simple rule of thumb: "If an ad pays it stays, year after year." So if the directory you are considering has been around for some time, go to your likely heading for the past five years and check for consistent support from its advertisers, especially its largest ones. But don't just assume that being there proves profitable usage. Speak with the advertisers. Ask them (diplomatically) how they know. We'll tell you how shortly.

Take Advantage of Usage Demand

YP "usage" is driven by *demand* for the various products and services offered by a directory's advertisers. You know the demand for the various products and services *you* offer. Analyze that demand. The demand for some of them is growing; for others it may be relatively steady; and for still others it may be declining. Adjust the content of your Yellow Pages ads in relation to the overall demand for each product and service you offer and changes year to year as demand changes.

Adjust for Situational Reality

In making your Yellow Pages buying analysis, recognize that demand often is *situational*. That is, different people needing the same product or service are in different situations that will affect their buying decisions. You also know what those situations are. Some have all the time in the world to make their decisions; others need something in a relative hurry. Some have needs outside of normal business hours, others don't. Some will look for the product or service as close to them as possible, others will travel a longer distance to get what they need, the way they need it, and when they need it. Some are very price conscious, whereas others are more concerned with quality, and so forth.

Be Your Own Yellow Pages Guinea Pig

Before deciding on YP advertising, think about how *you* use the Yellow Pages. When you are looking for something and there are many ads and listings, chances are you don't contact every one. In some way, you select those you contact. That is what Yellow Pages usage is, a *selection process*. That is the name of the game: to be selected as often as possible for the money you are going to spend for the advertising. If you understand what you need to do to be selected more frequently, you will make good Yellow Pages buying decisions and get a better return on your investment as a result.

Again, consider your own usage of Yellow Pages. As you are looking at ads and/or listings in your selection process, you eliminate some. Than means usage is also the process of elimination. The better you understand what might cause a YP user to eliminate you from their selection process the better decisions you will make in ad creation, a subject discussed in detail beginning on page 164.

As you can see, Yellow Pages usage is more complicated than most Yellow Pages advertisers realize. But not to worry. The remainder of this chapter will simplify it for you.

SUMMARY

- Yellow Pages usage is driven by demand for products and services.
- Analyze the demand for your product or service, and create your copy accordingly.
- Match the Yellow Pages message to the reality of customers you are trying to attract.

YELLOW PAGES AS A *"MIRROR OF A MARKET"*

You can know how much usage there is by the people needing your products and services by studying your Yellow Pages as "a mirror of a market." For that is just what YP is, and it mirrors a market in many ways.

Looking at the Size of "the Mirror"

Yellow Pages mirrors the market by the very size of the directory. That gives you a clear idea about the population covered by the directory. Some directories only have two columns on a page; others have three; most have four; some even have five. In a few cases, they are so large they are split into two alphabetical parts like A through L and M through Z. The directory size also gives you a good comparative idea of how much the ads will cost. Obviously, you would expect a quarter-page ad in the Chicago Yellow Pages to cost considerably more than a quarter-page ad in the Peoria version.

The number and size of the ads *in your heading* also mirrors the amount of income it produces for advertisers like you. Like any worthwhile advertising, it must make more money for its advertisers than it costs. That means *you* must have a way to determine how much your Yellow Pages advertising makes and increase or decrease your YP budget accordingly. Most YP advertisers are more concerned with the cost of the ads than they are with the income they are trying to derive from that form of advertising—probably because they haven't figured out how to find out. *You* don't have to be in that position, as you'll learn below!

How to Calculate Yellow Pages Ad Results

The "100 Checks" Check

To focus on income rather than cost, look at the last 100 checks written by your business or practice. (If you have a huge organization, make it 500 or 1,000.) Separate out all those that produce your *profitable income.* They will include rent if location is a major factor in drawing customers to your business. They may be checks you wrote for your radio, TV, direct mail, or other types of advertising. If you have a commissioned sales force, they are certainly your commission checks. In truth these income-producing checks were just a relative few out of the 100 checks you wrote. The problem is that they go on the same side of your ledger as all those other checks—the "E" side of the ledger—as an "Expense." That is a leading factor that causes advertising buying decisions based on how much it will cost.

Your income-producing checks should not be treated that way. If your commission "expense" doubles, you'll hardly cut your sales force in half to save money or move to a cheaper location at the danger of losing your bricks-and-mortar customers. Yet Yellow Pages and other advertising expenses often are treated as if they had no consequences, even when they become some of the few ways to actually keep business afloat and create new customers!

So carefully examine the checks that are supposed to produce revenue for you. Only if they are not profitable are they "costs." But if they are doing what they should, ask yourself it they could do even more. Make your buying decisions to produce income, not just to save money.

Look Inside "the Mirror"

Looking inside a YP directory tells more about the market it covers than is told by any other medium. It does so because more businesses and professional practices advertise in their Yellow Pages than any other local medium. Users expect to find *all* of the businesses and professional practices in their area in their local directory; for the most part they can.

Market Quality and Size

"The mirror" also tells about the *quality* and *size* of a market. For instance, West Palm Beach, Florida's "Automobile Dealers—New Cars" heading lists many more names of luxury cars than the same heading in Okeechobee, Florida, just 50 miles to the west. The population numbers are not in control, the market "action" is.

Relative Usage: Who Uses the Directory and for What

What's true of luxury cars may not be true of discount stores and vice versa. "The mirror" tells about the *relative* usage of each heading in a directory. Most advertisers tend to look at it as the number of people using the directory. A better measurement is the amount of dollars that flow to the advertisers through the heading. The more dollars of income to the advertisers, the more advertisers you will find under a heading and the larger their ads will be. The majority of headings have no display ads. The usual reason is the income produced by those headings does not justify advertisers buying display ads. But there are exceptions. When you find a heading *in your field* that contains display ads in most other directories, but not locally, that heading probably is underadvertised and you've found a real buying opportunity.

"The Mirror" as Yellow Pages Spending Guide

"The mirror" also tells you how much you should consider spending. There is a reason why the "Attorneys" heading contains full-page and frequently two-page and three-page ads (known as double-trucks and triple-trucks) in directories all across the country. It also tells us that much of the income flowing through that heading goes to personal injury attorneys as they buy more space because of the potential profit compared to others in their profession. (Of course there are some very profitable legal specialties that do not advertise.)

There must be a reason why plumbing contractors and building materials suppliers spend a large amount on Yellow Pages (see Figures 8.1 and 8.2, page 169) and notary publics don't. When you see a lot of money being spent under your heading(s), you know that being selected as frequently as possible from that group can mean much more income for you.

The Exception, Not the Rule

Though "the mirror" says there is money to be made, it does not necessarily mean that Yellow Pages advertising *by itself* will be the key to your financial success. In most cases your other sources of income are even more or just as important as the income you can get from YP advertising. What it does mean is that a certain portion of your market buys through using the Yellow Pages. You must do your best to find out who those buyers are and how your YP advertising can influence them. Although Yellow Pages cannot produce the same income at the same time as your other sources, your other sources cannot produce the same income at the same time as Yellow Pages! In other words, you can only get those Yellow Pages users through Yellow Pages advertising. Your issues are how much usage there is, whether you want to profit from it, and what you have to do to be "selected" most frequently for the Yellow Pages dollars you spend. The rest of this chapter gives you the keys to the answers.

"The Mirror" as Profit Forecast

To a great extent, "the mirror" tells you how much money there is to be made from a given heading in a given directory. If you are a plumber, an auto insurance agency, or personal injury attorney, the money that is spent under your heading in directories across the country is a clear indication of the value of that heading. At that same time, in practically every business or profession, there are additional sources of income as well. Plumbers frequently get a large amount of business in new construction from general contractors. Real estate firms and auto insurance agencies are location businesses; their physical locations draw in a significant number of customers/clients. Plastic surgeons frequently advertise on TV and in magazines, whereas the big personal injury firms use a wide range of advertising in addition to or instead of Yellow Pages.

Yellow Pages can bring you only a piece of your total market. It is important that you examine the other advertising and marketing methods covered in this book to determine what they, too, can add to your business or professional practice.

RETURN ON INVESTMENT

Your marketing plan must factor in a return on investment (ROI) from *all* of your advertising. Unless you are a politician, you do not advertise to keep your name in front of the public. You advertise to get income. Properly done, the process of *profitable* advertising will help you gain name recognition as well.

Measuring Yellow Pages Return on Investment

To measure the return on your Yellow Pages investment,[1] the following four-step formula has proven its success.

YELLOW PAGES ROI FORMULA

1. **Incoming calls.** The number of incoming telephone calls it takes to produce an order.
2. **Actual profit.** The average gross profit per average Yellow Pages order.
3. **YP cost.** The cost of your Yellow Pages.
4. **Expected profit.** Percentage of expected profit from your ad.[2]

---

1. Incoming Calls

First, estimate what percentage of your Yellow Pages calls you can reasonably expect to sell. Unless you are in the pizza or other take-out business, most advertisers tend to overestimate their success. Some will be from customers checking on an order. Some will be from people trying to sell you something and are using Yellow Pages as a search for business. For now, assume you will sell one out of five, so it will take you five calls to get one sale.

2. Average Sale

Next you need to know your *average* invoice. Most advertisers use their most frequent sale amount and call that their average. To find a true average, take your last month's invoices, add them, and divide the total by the number of invoices. That will give you a true *average* sale.

Take the average sale and estimate its tangible costs, including commissions to salespeople (if any) and other labor costs. Do not, however, include "special overhead." Thus, if you are a florist, your stylist gets paid whether she works on the average order or not, and your restaurant pays its pastry chef, even if everyone orders ice cream. Use only what it costs you to create an additional average order. When you deduct those costs from your average sale, you will have its gross profit. (Using the gross profit figure will be explained in the next section.)

3. Yellow Pages Cost

The monthly cost of the ad you are considering.

4. Determining Your Yellow Pages Advertising Expected Profit

Be reasonable about the percentage of profit you expect from your Yellow Pages ads. Surely you don't expect a 100 percent return on your other expenditures. So

---

[1]An investment, not an expense.

[2]These four steps make up the formula used by Davis in his consulting work.

what is wrong with a 20 percent or 25 percent return on your Yellow Pages? Consider this example.

A BICYCLE DEALER'S CASE HISTORY

- Three calls to get one order
- $40 average gross profit per sale
- $200 per month Yellow Pages ad cost
- 20 percent return on YP investment expected
- $240/month profit needed from $200/month YP advertising
- Six orders needed at $40 gross profit each
- 18 calls per month needed and reached to achieve 20 percent return

---

INSIGHT 40

- Look at Yellow Pages as an investment, not an expense.
- Calculate your ad's ROI.
  1. Number of calls to make a sale
  2. Average gross profit per order.
  3. Cost of ad being considered.
  4. Percentage of profit expected from Yellow Pages ad.

THE OCCUPANCY THEORY

In some ways, all businesses and professional practices are occupancy businesses. Examples are hotels, air lines, and cruise ships. The hotel industry actually judges itself by its occupancy percentage. They know *exactly* what percentage of rooms they must rent to reach the break-even point of covering all of their fixed and variable expenses. Once reached, every room rented above that level is almost clear profit. In addition they can quantify the value of their vacancies. If a hotel is at break-even, yet has 30 vacant rooms with a potential gross profit of $100 each, it has $3,000 in vacancies. That's $3,000 available to *net* profit. Should such a hotel average 30 vacant rooms 150 nights per year, it has $450,000 worth of vacancies. The key is to determine what additional advertising can fill some of those vacancies. Even if it cost the hotel $100,000 per year to fill just half, its bottom line would still be improved by $125,000!

Translating "Vacancies" to Your Business

Four Questions for You to Answer:
- Do you have "vacancies"?
- What are they?
- What is the profit value if you filled them?
- What more can you do to fill those vacancies *profitably?*

Assuming your business or professional practice is above its break-even point, every additional sale becomes all profit, reduced only by the cost of providing the product or service and the additional advertising or promotion. The more cost-effective you are at filling your vacancies, the more profitable your business or professional practice will become.

You grow a business or professional practice by creating vacancies and then filling them. That means that it is not enough to merely fill your existing vacancies. You must also plan for how you are going to increase the demand for your products and services so you can add capacity and fill those new vacancies as well. Location-oriented businesses, such as restaurant and retail chains, understand this concept. They know the key to their growth is in adding profitable locations. Every new profitable location increases their total profits. If you are truly going to have a successful business and not just a job, you will need to build your business so that most of your income comes from the work of others. That means you had better know how to fill vacancies! To do that, two of your marketing questions are:

1. Can Yellow Pages advertising help you fill some of those vacancies?
2. What do you have to do in the way of Yellow Pages ads to fill those vacancies?

You can see how filling vacancies with additional money spent in Yellow Pages or any other form of advertising is a key to your total profitability. Better yet, that advertising continues to produce profits even after you stop paying for it. Some of the customers or clients the advertising brings to you will continue to spend money with you, often for years to come. In addition, satisfied customers and clients often generate no-cost referral income. Effective advertising continues the building process you set in place for your business as you continue it over the years.

INSIGHT 41

- Determine what kind of vacancies you have.
- Quantify the value of those vacancies in terms of gross profit.
- Determine what you can do more of now, and what you can do in addition, to fill vacancies.
- Add capacity and fill those vacancies to grow your business.

THE DECISION-MAKING PROCESS

Once you have identified the number of new customers or clients you need, you can determine the amount of Yellow Pages (or any other) advertising you should consider. The ROI formula on page 160 tells you how many new customers or clients an ad must bring to get your desired ROI. Obviously the more you want from your YP advertising, the more you need to consider spending to achieve that goal. That means larger ads, more ads, or a combination of both.

Getting More Bang for Your Yellow Pages Bucks

Though there are some additional keys to getting more bang for your Yellow Pages buck, nothing can truly substitute for ad size. Larger ads produce more calls than smaller ads. It is that simple. They draw more attention and therefore have more people looking at them. Returning to the beginning definition of Yellow Pages usage, you have to be seen to have a chance to be selected. Larger ads also enable you to give a more complete sales message about your products and services. The more useful information you give to people looking at your ad, the less likely a user will eliminate you and the more likely you will be selected.

INSIGHT 42

Yellow Pages display ads are positioned according to size, the biggest first, the others follow. Where size is the same, when you originally bought that size ad under that heading determines your position.

INSIGHT 43

No single Yellow Pages ad can produce the income of another ad under a different heading or that an ad in another directory can produce. You must make your decision one directory and one heading at a time.

HOW TO PROVE THAT MORE YELLOW PAGES ADVERTISING PAYS

You probably will never do *everything* in Yellow Pages that could be profitable for your business or professional practice. Practically no one does. But there are some practical, simple, and inexpensive ways to prove to yourself that size pays. Then, the more profitable you find your Yellow Pages advertising, the more you should consider investing additional YP dollars in the future.

Dominate Somewhere

You must buy a reasonably dominant ad to test the selling power of Yellow Pages advertising. Most advertisers do not have ads large enough to grab the users' attention. They don't try very hard to be selected. If that is true of competitors in your major heading, so much the better *for you*. If others already dominate and you can't get yourself to go head-to-head with them, try these other options.

A Major Directory Strategy

Buy a big enough ad to be one of the largest under a smaller heading that applies to you in your *major* directory.

A Smaller Directory Strategy

Buy an ad under your major heading in a smaller directory that covers part of your market. It will cost you less to be relatively dominant under the heading. Once you find that domination pays, consider competing aggressively under you main heading in your major directory.

LAYOUT AND DESIGN

In-Column Advertising

Most headings in a directory are made up of listings and do not contain display ads. These headings are much easier to dominate in terms of the amount of dollars you will have to spend to attain that dominance. But don't try a small in-column ad. To find out what works, make it big enough to really dominate! Get your local directory and look at the ads that appear alphabetically under the headings. This will give you a good idea of the kinds and sizes of ads and listings for you to consider. It will also help you see how some advertisers dominate in this way while most under the same heading do not.

You dominate in-column through ad size and potentially through the use of color. For the most part, there is not a great deal of freedom in the use of art in in-column representation. But you *can* make your ad stand out by making it bigger, by using larger and bolder type, and by using color.

Display Advertising

Large display ads (see Figure 8.3, page 170) usually are the most difficult to convince yourself to buy. They cost more than in-column advertising, and, as stated earlier, most advertisers make buying decisions primarily by ad cost rather than the income they want the ad to produce. Let's make these decisions a little easier for you.

•   The majority of headings do not contain display ads. That means you should *not* consider buying a *small* display ad under those that relate to your field. Rather, dominate by a relatively large in-column ad under those headings. There probably is a good reason why they do not contain display ads. But that also gives you the chance to dominate.

•   When you see several or even many display ads under a heading you are considering, there is a reason for that also. The more and the larger the ads, the more you need to consider advertising under such a heading. To get maximum or near maximum results, make the ad large enough to get the attention of a high percentage of the users looking on its page. We cannot stress it enough, other factors being equal, *the size of the ad is the most important factor of your Yellow Pages buying decisions.*

Ad Copy

Although ad size is important, what you say in the ad will eventually determine how often you are selected. Too many Yellow Pages advertisers are concerned that they are saying too much. They believe Yellow Pages users will not take the time to read a lot of copy. As a result, most of their ads are weak sales tools. The sale a Yellow Pages ad must make is to cause users to select *and contact* the advertiser. Most YP advertisers would fire a sales representatives who, on a sales call, said only what the advertisers say in their Yellow Pages ads.

How to Write a Great Yellow Pages Ad

The key is to writing great ads is to identify and differentiate among what you *could* say, what you *don't want* to say, and what you *definitely do want* to say. Do this by a Yellow Pages copy study. (For much more on copy writing, see Chapter 3.)

The Yellow Pages Copy Study
- In your local Yellow Pages directory, look at all of the ads under your heading.
- In smaller communities, go to the library to get access to some major city directories to learn other things being said by advertisers under your heading.
- Make a list of every copy point.
- Highlight the points used in your current ad.
- Cross out all of the points you can't say or don't want to say.
- Now, from the copy points that are left, identify the most important that you have not used. These, along with any already used, are the ones around which you will build your ad content.

Headlines as Bait
Use what you consider the most important point as the headline in your ad. Though in-column ads are placed alphabetically and require your name to be at the top, use a strong headline immediately below, specifically aimed at the segment of the market you are trying to attract.

INSIGHT 44

Focus *totally* on the various needs of the user of the heading. Give every reason that you can fit into the ad why *they* should buy/contact/call. Use a copy study!

Display ads do not require your name at the top, but many advertisers put their names there anyway. Use a headline instead! You can still have your name prominently placed elsewhere in the ad. With display ads, you are advertising to attract the users who are not specifically looking for *you* but for *the help* you can provide.

For *your* success, tell them what *they* are most likely to need to make a decision: location, ease of ordering, hours of service, and so on. You will find plumbing contractors emphasizing "24 Hour Emergency Service—7 Days A Week." You will find many attorneys with large ads using headlines like "Personal Injury and Medical Malpractice" or "Criminal Law—DUI—DWI." You will also find auto insurance advertisers with headlines such as "Low, Low Rates" or "We Can Cover Anyone."

Study the largest advertisers in your directory. Most use headlines rather than their names at the top of their ads. This is not a time to think outside the box.

A CASE HISTORY

The best headline I have ever been associated with is: "RUSH ORDERS DON'T UPSET US!" I originally used this headline in an ad for a florist. It does several things for this advertiser. First, it attracts a segment of the market that is much more service-focused than cost-focused. Second, it appeals to a specific situation many users find themselves in when they have looked under the "Florists" heading. It also helps the advertiser know when a call is coming from the Yellow Pages ad because frequently the caller will say, "You say rush orders don't upset you. Can you, will you, and by the way how much?" This headline also works well for printers, advertising specialty companies and formal wear shops, just to name a few.

TRACKING YOUR YELLOW PAGES ROI

The more money you spend, the more important it is to know how many calls you are getting from your advertising. Yet most advertisers cannot track accurately the number of calls their Yellow Pages dollars produce. Some use rather elaborate reports from their employees trying to track the source of all of their customers or clients. These are never truly accurate for a combination of reasons. Some employees are more conscientious than others. Often an employee has another call to answer or another customer waiting and doesn't take the time to get the information. Sometimes the wrong question is asked in the first place. For example, "How did you hear about us?" frequently will get a different answer than "Where did you get our telephone number?"

How to Track Calls

To track calls accurately, use what are called remote call forwarded telephone numbers. Most phone companies offer them, although they may call them something else, such as a "market extension line." Whatever they are called, they are special phone numbers that you put into your ad to track the calls that come directly from that ad. If you use several ads, you can get a trackable number for each one. When someone uses that number, it is forwarded to your main number. In the process the phone company tracks the calls that are placed through the tracking number and, in most cases, can give you a monthly report on the number and duration of calls. If you have done the Yellow Pages ROI computation suggested on page 160, you can compare the profit objective you set in the computation.

INSIGHT 45

Your Yellow Pages ad can also produce walk-in, fax, e-mail, and Internet business. Put *all* your options in the message.

A Toll-Free Tracking Option

Should your local phone company not provide call information on their bill, you can still get one of these tracking lines and forward it to a toll-free number. Although this is somewhat more expensive, it will give you even more detailed information. It will detail each call, tell you the time and day it was placed, and the number of minutes it lasted. Usually a toll-free number will cost about $10 per month plus a per-minute charge for each call. However, the information is so valuable that if you are considering spending a considerable amount of money for the ad, the additional cost of toll-free tracking is negligible. Once you have sufficient data that proves the ad is profitable (or not), you can always contact the phone company to have them stop forwarding the calls through the toll-free number and forward them to your main phone number.

MULTIPLE DIRECTORIES IN A MARKET

Telephone Company Directories

Most areas have more than one directory. Some local phone companies distribute a directory covering a large metropolitan market and also have smaller directories to geographical segments of the larger area. Frequently, other publishers also enter a market to compete with the local phone company directory. There is no single answer to making your decisions in these situations. Smaller directories offer you the opportunity to pay for less coverage and get a larger ad for your money. Sometimes this is your best buy. This also can be the best way for you to test the ability of a Yellow Pages ad to produce profitable income. Once you have learned that from a smaller directory, it will be easier to spend even more to have the same ad in the larger directory.

INSIGHT 46

The larger directories most frequently used by your targeted audience always produce the most total income for their advertisers! Draw your response from the larger directories' total coverage, use it aggressively, and it will make you the most money.

Independent Directories

The use of independent publishers in your market needs special business consideration.

- Just because someone decides to publish a directory does not mean they will do so profitably and therefore continue to be in a given market.
- Additional directories do not produce additional Yellow Pages users, they just divide up the usage.

Usually an independent publisher is not able to get to the same level of usage as the local phone directories with which they compete. Consider these independent directories very carefully and look at them over time before you decide to put money into them. Check how much advertiser support they have compared to their phone company counterparts. Is this support growing, staying the same, or declining? Have they been in existence for at least two years?

The Power of Independents

In some markets, it is difficult to dismiss independent publishers. Only they can deliver their users to you. Some independent publishers have gained a substantial share of the Yellow Pages usage, to the point of getting 20 to 30 percent of their markets. So consider advertising in them *and tracking the ROI results,* just like with the phone company directories. In most markets, the local phone directory can deliver the most income to you, but many independents can also produce profitable results for their advertisers. Test!

BUYING AT A DISCOUNT

Most Yellow Pages publishers offer incentives for you to buy an ad for the first time or increase what you are spending with them. Surprisingly, many advertisers are suspicious of such offers, concerned that the ad may cost them more when they renew it the following year. Although that is usually the case, the incentives not only are a smart way to save but give you a discount year to check on Yellow Pages ROI. Full-price or not, make your decisions one year at a time and buy at a discount as often as you can.

SUMMARY

This chapter has given you a quick summary of how to make your Yellow Pages advertising decisions. Much of what it says applies to the other advertising you may do. The main difference is Yellow Pages advertising is a place where you have to "out-advertise" your competition right in front of them. Each advertising medium has this characteristic to some extent, but none of them have you competing with essentially *all* of your competition at the same time! That is why you must find ways to set yourself apart. There is no better way than the size of your ads and to load them with more information, the two most critical secrets to more profitable Yellow Pages advertising.

THREE STEPS TO YELLOW PAGES SUCCESS

Basic Single-Column, Two-Inch Ad

AFFORDABLE PLUMBING

QUALITY & PROFESSIONAL
WORKMANSHIP

- Repairs & Remodel
- Drain Cleaning
- Dual & City Water Hook Up
- Water Heaters

Lic. # CFC 1000401

277-1331

·····················277-1331

AFFORDABLE PLUMBING

QUALITY & PROFESSIONAL
WORKMANSHIP

- Repairs & Remodel
- Drain Cleaning
- Dual & City Water Hook Up
- Water Heaters

Lic. # CFC 1000401

277-1331

·····················277-1331

AFFORDABLE PLUMBING

QUALITY & PROFESSIONAL
WORKMANSHIP

- Repairs & Remodel
- Faucets • Sinks • Toilets & Disposals
- Dual & City Water Hook Up
- Water Heaters • Drain Cleaning
- Commercial & Residential
- Free Estimates • All Work Guaranteed

Lic # CFC 1000401

277-1331

·····················277-1331

Figure 8.1 A single-column, two-inch Yellow Pages ad. *Note:* This format always has advertiser name at top and address and phone at bottom. *Left.* So "clean" it gives practically no information. Yellow Pages advertising is *not* the medium for white space design! *Center.* Addition of eye-appeal with the use of a standard cut. Although this will attract more of your audience, it fails to give any additional information once you have them. *Right.* Keeps the illustration and doubles the information that's likely to produce an order. Note the same easily readable type in all three ads with the third having the most information for the reader.

Basic Display Ad

Figure 8.2 A basic Yellow Pages display ad. *Note:* All three ads are same size. All three cost the same to run. *Left.* A great deal of information, though the name of the business is used as the headline. In Yellow Pages ads, rather than listings, readers are looking for what you do and where you are. Make that your key, too. *Center.* The same ad as above, but note the strength added by heavy border with *rounded* corners. *Right.* Exactly the same content, but redesigned to feature what sells the reader. A strong benefit headline with two subheads framed for emphasis. An attractive logo and use of shading give the entire ad the effectiveness of an illustration. The far right panels of Figures 8.1 and 8.2 both show how to improve your ad without spending any more money!

Major Quarter-Page Ad

T.G.D.

Auto Air Conditioning & Electric Service

- Climate Control
- Manual A/C Systems
- Complete Auto Repair

Fast Courteous Service
Long Convenient Hours
Open 6 days
Monday-Saturday 7:30 AM - 7:30 PM

647-3990

101 MARINER WAY
WWW.TGDAIR.COM

Figure 8.3A Like the leftmost ads in Figures 8.1 and 8.2, it lacks any immediate eye appeal and uses white space, rather than selling copy, something that does not sell in Yellow Pages advertising.

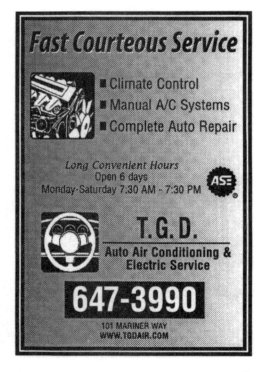

Figure 8.3B Much improvement in appearance plus the use of a real headline and two illustrations, but no more information than the ad at top left.

Figure 8.3 A quarter-page Yellow Pages ad. *Note:* Figures 8.3A, B, and C are the same size and cost the same to run.

Figure 8.3C Loaded with eye appeal *and* information. Use of reverse box to highlight two headlines, with subhead between illustrations. Over double the services listed, including credit cards pictured. Like the rightmost examples in Figures 8.1 and 8.2, this also shows how to improve your ads without spending any more money!

Figure 8.3 *(Continued)*

NOTES ON YELLOW PAGES ADVERTISING CHECKLIST

These notes are a supplement to the material presented in this chapter. They are not a self-contained substitute for that material. The checklist appears in Figure 8.4.

1. **Quotations.** Total of all quoted and/or estimated costs on proposed project.
2. **Budget approval.** If lower than the amount in item 1, determine how the project is to be modified to fit the dollar allocation.
3. **Project approval.** Once it is determined that the project can be done for the amount in item 2, decide on whether it's worth the cost.
4. **Target audience.** When more than one Yellow Pages heading relates to your audience, check each for its amount of display advertising. Often you are better off dominating in a less advertised group than as an also-ran where everyone is competing.

YELLOW PAGES ADVERTISING CHECKLIST

Project Title _____   Date _____
Project Description _____   Project # _____
_____   Checklist # _____
Overall Supervision By _____   Deadline _____
Budget _____ Completion Date _____   Start Up Date _____

MANAGEMENT DECISIONS	ASSIGNED TO	DUE	IN	MUST APPROVE	BY DATE	IN	INFO COPY ONLY	SEE ATTACHED
1. Quotations	_____	__	☐	_____	__	☐	_____	☐
2. Budget Approval	_____	__	☐	_____	__	☐	_____	☐
3. Project	_____	__	☐	_____	__	☐	_____	☐

CREATIVE DECISIONS

4. Target Audience	_____	__	☐	_____	__	☐	_____	☐
5. Message	_____	__	☐	_____	__	☐	_____	☐
6. Benefits	_____	__	☐	_____	__	☐	_____	☐
7. Headline	_____	__	☐	_____	__	☐	_____	☐
8. Location	_____	__	☐	_____	__	☐	_____	☐
9. Phone Number	_____	__	☐	_____	__	☐	_____	☐
10. Offer	_____	__	☐	_____	__	☐	_____	☐
11. Design	_____	__	☐	_____	__	☐	_____	☐
12. Colors	_____	__	☐	_____	__	☐	_____	☐
13. Typesetting	_____	__	☐	_____	__	☐	_____	☐
14. Art/Photography	_____	__	☐	_____	__	☐	_____	☐
15. Production	_____	__	☐	_____	__	☐	_____	☐

DIRECTORY DECISIONS

16. Directory Selection	_____	__	☐	_____	__	☐	_____	☐
17. Dates	_____	__	☐	_____	__	☐	_____	☐
18. Ad Size	_____	__	☐	_____	__	☐	_____	☐
19. Space Cost	_____	__	☐	_____	__	☐	_____	☐
20. YP Notification	_____	__	☐	_____	__	☐	_____	☐

SAFETY CHECKS

21. Logo	_____	__	☐	_____	__	☐	_____	☐
22. Address	_____	__	☐	_____	__	☐	_____	☐
23. Phone	_____	__	☐	_____	__	☐	_____	☐
24. Mechanical Checks	_____	__	☐	_____	__	☐	_____	☐
25. Printed Samples	_____	__	☐	_____	__	☐	_____	☐

Figure 8.4   The Yellow Pages advertising checklist.

5. **Message.** After completing copy study, select as many important points as room permits. Yellow Pages is not for white (blank) space design.

6. **Benefits.** Not general or vague, but keyed to the heading under which your ad appears. This is absolutely necessary for your ad to succeed!

7. **Headline.** Use the key copy point from #6 as your headline. Be sure it relates to the #4 target audience. Stay focused throughout the ad.

8. **Location.** This is often the first thing looked for by your audience. If your location is not obvious to practically everyone, relate it to someplace they know (Two blocks north of Main and Evans). If you are a service company, consider using multiple phone numbers (local area codes) targeting areas that you serve to increase calls from your ad.

9. **Phone number.** The second thing everyone looks for. Make it prominent, right by your address. Again, consider using multiple numbers for ads. Where necessary, especially for business-to-business, add e-mail and Web site in less prominent type.

10. **Offer.** Remember, your Yellow Pages ad runs for a long time. Don't promise offers you might not want to keep for months to come. Individual publishers have different restrictions as to what kinds of "offers" you can make. Check before you begin writing.

11. **Design.** Much Yellow Pages advertising is designed by the Yellow Pages company at no extra cost. But don't just let them do it. Go to our examples, or look through various Yellow Pages publications, and have them follow an ad you think particularly effective.

12. **Colors.** Check your advertising competition. Colors cost extra. Printing on white paper rather than yellow (dropping the yellow background), costs even more. If your competitors on the page all use color, spend the money to increase the ad size. Above all, you want to dominate your listing.

13. **Typesetting.** Typesetting is handled by the Yellow Pages company at no extra cost.

14. **Art/Photography.** Nothing too fancy. Yellow Pages printing is limited to basics.

15. **Production.** There is no industry-wide standard for Yellow Pages production, so Yellow Pages companies prefer to do it themselves, even when designed by an outside agency. There is no extra charge for this, so let them.

16. **Directory selection.** When more than a single Yellow Pages exists for your target audience, media selection depends on what you sell. Be realistic about how far your audience will go to shop. Sometimes smaller local directories will be your best buy. The larger your geographical market, the better buy larger directories become.

17. **Dates.** Differentiate among the key dates:

    A. *Closing date.* When ad space must be ordered and copy submitted.

    B. *Proof date.* When ad must be submitted to get a proof before publication.

    C. *Delivery date.* The date on which the Yellow Pages will be distributed and calling will start.

18. **Ad size.** A critical decision. The larger the size of your display ad, the closer to the front of the heading and the more space to get across your message. In Yellow Pages, nothing else succeeds like ad-size domination.

19. **Space cost.** Look for ways to buy at a discount whenever possible. Have your Yellow Pages representative explain pricing options to you. Prices may not be negotiable, but they can be remarkably flexible.

20. **Yellow Pages notification.** Get a written copy of your order with rates.

21. **Logo.** Make your name clearly legible. Save fancy logos for fancy media. Some logos become difficult to read when reduced in smaller adds.

22. **Address.** Assume everyone is a first-time visitor and needs directions. (See #8 above.)

23. **Phone.** Your number, of course. If you have a different number for evening or Sunday calls, identify them as such to become a 24/7 concern.

24. **Mechanical checks.** Someone has to be responsible for checking items 21–23 in all your other ads. Do it for here, too. Your Yellow Pages advertising lives much longer than most others.

25. **"As run" copy.** Some *one* person must be responsible for maintaining a file of all ads "as run"; that is, as they actually appeared in each publication.

9 | From Telemarketing to Teleservicing

> This chapter has been brought up to date with the help of **Molly J. Cashman**, director, Corporate Communications, APAC Customer Services, Inc., Deerfield, IL. One of the leading companies in its field, APAC handles both inbound and outbound teleservicing accounts. (www.Apaccustomerservices.com, (800) OUTSOURCE).

Telemarketing is the planned use of telecommunications equipment with a set business purpose or goal. What it is *not* is simply picking up the phone—whether to answer or call out—with no set directions as to what is to follow. Like media communication (see Chapter 13), telemarketing is expensive and easily done wrong, with its success depending as much on management commitment as on in-house or outside expertise. Teleservices is the new industry term for telemarketing, shedding its practice and image of those outbound sales calls to unsuspecting customers. Teleservicing embraces all the new customer interactive tools available today, including self-service Interactive Voice Response (IVR), e-mail, web chat, and inbound services. It has become increasingly more complex as advanced technology improves contact handling capabilities and the trend toward data warehousing of customer preferences turns simple order entry calls into large-scale revenue improvement opportunities. What is required for success is what this chapter is all about.

SCOPE OF TELESERVICES

Excluding the brief dot-com bubble, teleservicing was the fastest-growing (see Figure 9.1) legitimate economic activity of the 1980s and 1990s and the industry shows every sign of continuing its growth into the twenty-first century. Just how its impact should be counted is one of the more pleasant industry debates. (For example, do you rank the impact of the phone call that ordered the Boeing 747, the same as the one that ordered the 79¢ ballpoint pen that signed the confirmation?)

Teleservices Expenditures
Teleservices *expenditures* grew from $54 billion to more than $76 billion in just five years—from 1996 to 2001—and are expected to reach $105 billion by the year 2006.[1]

---

[1] Data from the Direct Marketing Association, June 2001.

VOLUME OF U.S. DM-DRIVEN SALES (*Billions of Dollars)				
	1996 (Actual)	2001 (Actual)	2002 (Estimate)	2006 (Forecast)
Telephone Marketing	**$404.1**	**$661.8**	**$719.5**	**$990.6**
Business-to-Business	223.0	387.6	424.3	587.8
Consumer	181.1	252.7	295.3	402.8
Direct Mail	**$364.7**	**$582.5**	**$636.7**	**$880.2**
Business-to-Business	132.8	223.4	246.0	347.2
Consumer	232.8	359.1	390.7	532.7

Figure 9.1   Growth of U.S. teleservices and direct mail–driven sales. Source: Direct Marketing Association's 2000–2001: "Economic Impact: U.S. Direct Marketing Today." PLEASE NOTE—The five-year DMA forecast published in our 2nd Edition was astonishingly correct: within 1% for Telemarketing and 3% for Direct Mail!

Teleservices Employment

According to industry statistics, employment in teleservices grew from 4.5 million in 1996 to 6 million in 2001, with 7.4 million predicted by 2006.

Status Report

- Telephone marketing, at 35 percent, is the largest category of all direct marketing.
- At $387 billion-plus in 2001, *business-to-business* advertisers spend more on teleservices than any other medium.
- Business-to-business teleservices accounts for approximately 65 percent of all telemarketing sales.[2]

Teleservicing as Today's Way to Telemarketing Success

The change from telemarketing to teleservicing is more than a difference in name, it is a change in mind set as important as the change from direct mail to direct marketing. Because of market saturation, legislation, and increased competition, the new focus of toll-free numbers is on customer service and loyalty, and sometimes cross-selling opportunities. The original Internet hope of "build it and they will come" may have faded, but for teleservicing, it has become the engine of growth.

By 2010, traditional telemarketing will see significant decline in use as a major business sales tool, to be replaced by the exponential increase in teleservicing.

---

[2]Based on Direct Marketing Association research.

1. **Non-sales teleservicing that offers a benefit to the consumer;** for instance:
   - The call from the cell phone company a week after you bought their product to ask if you haven't used it because you need help understanding how it works. With these calls, thousands of phones about to be returned became keepers.
   - The auto insurance company that checks on satisfaction with their claim service and the quality of the repair work.
   - The local lawn mower service firm calling in August to suggest that now—not December—is the best time to tune up your snow-blower.
   - The doctor whose office calls to check on possible side effects a few weeks after starting a new prescription.

2. **Concentrating nontelephone media on generating incoming calls.** Many business-to-business, business-to-consumer, and nonprofit organizations are focused on generating incoming rather than outgoing calls. Business-to-consumer is faced with increasing regulation by states and, in 2003, by proposed national do-not-call legislation. Their customers and prospects have neither time nor patience for calls that do not offer an obvious benefit *to them.* To reach their goals, even nonprofit groups have to learn what "benefits" contributors derive from their giving. So forget telemarketing. Start teleservicing for success!

INSIGHT 47

Verisimilitude. Though it is true of all advertising and promotion, verisimilitude, the quality of not only *being* true but also of *appearing* to be true, is critical to teleservicing. You have only a very few seconds to convince someone to listen to the rest of your story. Make everything—words, voice, time—work for you.

Integrate Your Customer Communications to Create More Sales/Service Opportunities

Your customers want versatility of ordering—by phone today, e-mail or fax tomorrow, a self-service use of your Web site the day after. To succeed, you must have compatible platforms that wed data originating from older mainframes to the latest state of art CRM solutions. No matter what the customer's technology, you must get the information you need from them, then back to your database, so you both can function effectively. Fortunately, such platforms now exist. Once integrated, they not only tell what customers have bought but can give a predictive evaluation of what they are likely to buy. Thus, if a woman calls who has bought black skirts for the past year, you can tell her about great new styles or values in black and offer to show them on your Web site, send a descriptive brochure, or invite her into your store. What works for business-to-consumer is equally true for business-to-business and nonprofit. Every communication becomes a personalized sales and service opportunity.

INSIGHT 48

5 ASPECTS OF TELESERVICE
IN ORDER OF IMPORTANCE

1. **Understanding the customer:** 50%. As everywhere else in selling, knowiny-our customer is most important.
2. **The script:** 20%. This is definitely not for amateur dramatists!
3 and 4. **The teleservicer and the offer:** 20%. If the list and the script are not good, the teleservicer and offer can't help!
5. The **product or service:** 10%. Placed last because you are not going to try *any* marketing unless the product or service are first rate.

TECHNICAL AND PRACTICAL FACTORS

To Achieve your Goals

Under the broad categories of "inbound" and "outbound" teleservicing, there are at least a dozen kinds of activities. Before exploring them in detail, let us consider the technical and practical factors that apply to them. After setting your goals, these *must* be agreed on before any teleservicing project is begun. Often, they also control the decision to work in-house or go to an outside firm.

Teleservicing Goals

To achieve success, think carefully about setting your goals. Plan a customer contact relationship of phone, fax, e-mail, Internet, and even personal contact. Experience suggests changing from a total focus on lead generation and sales to customer retention by satisfying your callers' needs and guaranteeing *their* satisfaction. Set that as your clear goal for each touch point (type of contact) and type of customer. It's as important in teleservicing as anywhere else in your marketing program. With access to your database, current technology lets you differentiate among prospects, new customers, repeat buyers, or long-lapsed customers, then decide on order taking, plus-selling, and/or customer service. Without goals against which to measure, how will you establish success?

INSIGHT 49

Establish maximum cost criteria for *every* program *before* you begin. Decide what you need for any or all of these options with a stop point, if they are not met.
- Are you selling a thing?
- Are you selling (reselling, retaining, regaining) a customer?
- Are you buying a new customer? What is the lifetime value?

- **Time line.** When will the project begin? How long will it continue? How many calls will you get or make? How much time is allowed per call? Beware of confusing quantity with success! Would you really rather get 10 calls per hour at $15 in sales each as opposed to 6 calls averaging $45?
- **Personnel.** How will teleservicers *and clerical staff* be acquired, trained, and supervised? How many workers will you need for peak hours? For regular and slow periods? How much will you pay? To whom? On what basis?
- **Labor costs.** The available labor pool and local wage rate are critical, because labor will cost more than 60 percent of ongoing operations. On a practical basis, location and unemployment in an area will affect how much you must pay. Look for your labor staffing and restaffing potential, especially for inbound calling, for which you often cannot predict daily or hourly receipts. Don't ignore college and high school students who want or need part-time jobs and can supply an effective on-call workforce. The use of an outside (outsourced) teleservicing firm has the advantage of their being able to locate staff where wages are low. Thus, companies in a higher-priced labor market may place/receive calls in a low-wage college town a thousand miles away.
- **Skill definition.** What skills must personnel have to make an effective call or answer incoming ones? In general business service, personnel can be trained on the job. However, some specialized industries must have licensed or highly trained professionals, such as licensed insurance agents or security brokers. For example, some drug store chains use a teleservicing firms' licensed pharmacists to check on drug interactions.
- **Connectivity and automation.** Connectivity is the access to your customers' purchasing history. Only by the willingness *and ability* to share this database for analysis with your in-house or outsourced teleservicers can you get high-end, focused calls. Teleservicing is much too costly for a mass mailing approach where a 5 percent return is a big success. Once your customer base is analyzed for teleservice success, the most likely prospects are targeted. Then, through teleservicing automation, this system places several calls at a time, automatically skips recorded messages, and as soon as one is answered, connects to available representatives. This nearly eliminates the costly labor time of waiting for a real person to answer.

INSIGHT 50

Success in teleservicing does not just happen. It demands, from management, a commitment to a plan that permits the costs of learning. It works best—and often works only—when it is integrated into the marketing plan from the very beginning. It is seldom successful as desperate first aid when everything else has failed.

- **Location for in-house operation.** Is your location safe before and after standard office hours? Teleservicing often its a 24-hour service. Is there public transportation nearby? Parking? A place to purchase food? Where will staff work, rest, eat, have their coffee breaks, and use toilets?

- **Mechanical.** What equipment must be acquired, installed, and maintained? For how long? At what cost? By whom? If its use is short-term, can it be leased? If not, can it be resold? For how much?

WHAT TELESERVICERS DO

Standard Teleservices Firms

Standard teleservicers are "standard" only in that they have a variety of different specialties. The services they provide can sometimes be bought individually, as well as in combinations or as packages. They include the following:

- **Consultation at the marketing plan stage.** What is feasible by teleservicing? What are some alternatives? How long it will take to plan, test, and do, and what will it cost? These are best discussed before a marketing plan is even begun, not after it is set. Many teleservicers will meet for this discussion without charge. Some will have a fee if they do not get the project. Ask!

- **Consulting on what the project is to produce.** Shall the teleservicers do nothing but take the order? Deliver a message? Answer a question? What else, if anything, is practical and affordable? What can you get from the person on the line, once they are there?

- **Scripting, testing, and training.** Writing for teleservicing is an art in itself. But successful scripting is more than that. It is testing to see whether the script works, modifying where necessary, and then training a staff to be suitable for a particular project. In teleservices, the importance of *how* something is said, as well as *what* is said, is a fact of life. It's also a continuously changing fact that only monitoring and testing will keep current.

- **Serendipitous supervision.** Some teleservicing operators are better than others. Sometimes it's innate talent. Often it's subtle improvements in the script that the individual operator is not even aware that he or she is making. But *supervisors have to know* that something good has happened, test it with others, and if it works for them, too, give credit to its originator. That is the kind of supervision you search for in building your in-house abilities, as well as evaluating outside services.

- **Continuing evaluation and reports.** Every teleservicing project will become more and more proficient as its operators become more comfortable and efficient with their assignments. Especially with in-bound evaluations and reports, begin with the first call. On an agreed-on (often daily) basis, they should tell the following:
  - Number of operators involved, and for how long.
  - Number of calls made or received.

- Average time per call per operator.
- Results.
- Operators' comments, both impressions and "hard" facts.
- Teleservice firm's or departmental evaluation and recommendations.

- **Standard teleservices firm technologies.** To process calls, the most important technologies are predictive dialing, call handling via an ACD (automatic call distributor), and on-screen script and database viewing. In addition, the firms should accept multiple forms of incoming client data (magnetic disk, cartridge, or electronic data transfer) and offer various output methods. They should also be able to offer remote monitoring, bridge and transfer capability, order verification (tape-recorded or digitized), quality assurance technologies, and extensive information management capabilities. Also look for fault-tolerant systems, backup systems for uninterrupted power, and expandable/flexible technologies that readily accommodate clients' needs.

A firm should not only *have* these technologies, but management should be able to *utilize, manage,* and *apply* them *to your specific project.*

How Teleservicers Charge

Teleservices, in-house or from an outside firm, has three sets of costs. For outside organizations, these usually require partial payment in advance to help cover up-front expenses. Because teleservicing programs can be—and often are—canceled before even the first call is made, specified cancellation fees are included in most agreements. The three costs are for the following services:

1. **Planning and consultation.** Know exactly what you wish to discuss, have a written agenda, and make sure that every point is covered. Once a firm has been selected, it charges for planning and consultation meetings. If there's a per-person rate for visiting you, ask their charge for your visiting them instead. Even if that won't be practical for you, it will make them aware of *your* budget concerns.

2. **Writing, testing, and training.** Preparing scripts, testing, revising, and retesting them, and training operators all precede the first call. Just as with preparation of copy and layout for an ad, 90 percent of the planning and creative thinking will have been done and will be charged for, even if the actual program is canceled.

3. **Calling, refining, reporting, evaluating, and recommending.** Most teleservicers charge for their inbound and outbound calling by the hour. The success or completion rate, especially on outbound service, practically demands honor-system billing, with frequent, detailed supporting documentation. If your initial evaluation of a teleservicing service makes you uncomfortable about this, consider other teleservicers until you find the right match. Evaluating, refining, reporting, and giving recommendations on the ongoing projects are usually (but not always) included in the hourly rate. Make sure.

TYPES OF TELESERVICING

There are several types of teleservicing with which you're most likely to be involved. All can, of course, be given to outside firms. We emphasize the opportunities and problems each brings the do-it-yourselfer.

Inbound Teleservicing

In inbound teleservices, the inquiries and orders received by phone/fax, e-mail, or Web, are increasingly important to direct response selling. Where speed in fulfilling orders is *vital* to business success, the toll-free telephone—and, increasingly, the Internet and toll-free fax—have practically replaced ordering by mail.

Simple Product Ordering
Taking orders by phone has always been the most widely used of all teleservices activities. Simple product ordering, whether from a print on Internet catalog with thousands of items or in response to a television commercial offering a product that is "not available in retail stores!" *can* be handled in-house. Whether they *should* be depends largely on traffic flow. Although you might be able to handle gigantic bursts of phone activity economically for two weeks every two months, how would you staff for such a contingency? Outside help is unlikely to wait the other month and a half without seeking more dependable employment. Here are some approaches that work:

• **Stagger your promotions, where practical.** For instance, mail, advertise, broadcast, or release your products via the Internet. Do this for one quarter of your audience two weeks apart. You'll need only a fraction of the staff to handle the responses, and you'll be able to give them all full-time work and decrease turnover, with its recruiting and training costs.

• **Promote the products more often to the same audience.** Even the most successful of promotions leaves the vast majority unsold on *that* item at *that* time. If you can't find new products or services, use what worked before. Run exactly the same promotion twice and even three times. But, of course, test first!

• **Use an outside teleservices firm.** These organizations *are* staffed to handle sudden bursts of activity with trained teleservicers who'll learn and remember your ordering system the next time it comes on line.

A catalog or other promotion may bring orders for years. Many firms can continue to handle these orders as well as in-house personnel could, throughout that time. Through a system known as automatic phone distribution, callers are given to specific teleservicers who know a particular product line and have become even better at selling it as time goes by.

After-Hours Business
Telephone activity does not stop after normal business hours, especially not for toll-free, e-mail, and Web-generated calling. Many outside firms can handle this for you.

Relationship Selling

This is not the illegal "bait and switch," but legitimate and often appreciated "cross-selling" and even "up-selling." Relationship selling works best when the selections are comparatively limited (say, an 80-item catalog rather than an 800-item one) and the conversation is presumed to be with an expert in the field. Thus, a skilled teleservicer might suggest the scarf or glove shown on page 12 to go with the jacket ordered from page 17 . . . brushes or cleaning fluid to go with a specific paint . . . or an additional fall flowering plant when one is ordered for spring.

Supervise relationship selling as if your life depended on it. If potential customers are turned off by it, your business life may cease as well.

Free Information

In offering telephone information about a product or service, a number of factors have to be evaluated on an ongoing basis:

- **How the call will be charged.** Options include a local, regional, or national toll-free service, to accept collect calls, or to have the caller pay.[3]
- **Who will get the initial call** and to whom it will be transferred if the first teleservicer can't answer the question?
- **When will phone help be available,** especially to do-it-yourselfers and for products likely to be used evenings or weekends?
- **Limits on types of telephone information** regarding how to *use* a product, rather than the physical product or service itself. This involves both the time you need to spend and possible legal ramifications (for example, telling a caller how to use battery jump cables to start a car). Check your insurance for appropriate coverage.

INSIGHT 51

Whether using an outside or in-house teleservicer, the *quality* of service is equally critical. Customers and prospects assume the caller is *you*.

Charges for Information and Other Online Services

Fees for giving immediate teleservices—though not for information on products—are becoming common. The development of 900-number systems has made it possible to charge practically any amount—from pennies to dollars—to the telephone from which a call originates. Thus, a technical service bureau can charge just enough to keep nuisance calls within manageable limits, a legal or accounting service can

---

[3]One of my hardest selling jobs, while speaking at a major electrical supplies wholesaler convention, was to convince them to install inbound toll-free fax. They were convinced they'd be flooded with junk advertising charged to their numbers. I argued that few (if any) advertisers were that stupid and that many of their customers did their ordering after hours and the chance to fax those orders—toll-free—for next day delivery would more than pay for itself. Several of them called some months later. Those who'd followed my suggestion were happy to report that I'd been right.

cover the cost of an initial telephone consultation, and a children's storyteller (or adult sexual fantasizer) can charge whatever the traffic will bear. The fact that tele-servicing can do all this does not, of course, mean that all of it *should* be done. Consider the long-term consequences before joining either side. Your power to turn off *their* messages may well be their right to turn off *yours!*

Outbound Teleservicing

Outbound teleservicing can simply mean making your calls in a routine or mechanical fashion. For this, live operators and computer-generated dialing can deliver the same *message*. But very few of the simpler automated dialers have any built-in judgment. Many of these call programs are operated from a one-person office or a home. The costs are comparatively modest and allow the system's owner to be away, handling leads or projects the calls have brought. But this type of auto-mated dialing has led to annoyances and even dangers; for instance, the tying up of lines by calling every number in a hospital, police, or industrial network. Such automatic dialers have now been outlawed in many communities and some states. More sophisticated—and expensive—systems call specific numbers only and are an important part of traditional telemarketing.

In Case of Failure

Today's teleservicing outbound program is much more than mechanical or routine calling. It includes ongoing database analysis on which actions are based. The true teleservicer knows what is being said on both ends of the line—not only what message is sent, but how it is received and responded to. Together with ongoing changes and improvements in communication, this knowledge is key to much of teleservicing's success. It also can—and indeed, at times, must—signal failure. When teleservicing will not work—at least, not on a cost-effective basis—the tele-servicer must recognize this and be willing to stop the operation. Teleservicing must be used as a self-monitoring tool!

Outbound Sales Calls

Placed as "cold calls," without preparing the prospect, outbound sales calls are the most difficult of all teleservicing efforts. Cold calling requires knowledgeable guidance and continuous, positive reinforcement. When these three factors are kept in mind, it will succeed in many instances. However, don't expect results without professional help.

Requests for Donations

INSIGHT 52

In the vast majority of cases for nonprofit fund raising, future giving will be the same as the first amount. Don't work so hard trying to get the $25 giver to increase to $50 once a year. Ask four times a year and get $100.[4]

---

[4]"Direct Marketing for NonProfits Seminar," Chicago Association of Direct Marketing, May 2002.

Even when placed cold, requests for donations for community, religious, fraternal, or educational organizations imply a common interest and usually get a friendly hearing. But take care in using professional service bureaus for such efforts. Their fees often absorb the lion's share of what is raised. A volunteer effort may not produce the gross that an outside firm would, but it will probably vastly increase the net amount. Get a pro to help with the message; let dedicated amateurs make the calls.

INSIGHT 53

Make fund-raising efforts and other telephone requests for donations a group effort, if at all possible. The group will cheer each other up and on during the inevitable "dry spells" that might cause volunteers at home to give up calling.

Warm-Up Calls for Mailings
Do *not* use warm-up calls unless the offer is truly special. It's a very expensive way to have your audience disregard your subsequent mailings.

Qualifying Leads
It is imperative to have agreement on the desired results, but also to be flexible on how they are to be achieved. To that end, begin by defining:

- What *exactly* it will take to qualify a lead.
- What *exactly* follows when someone does—or doesn't—qualify.
- How you will handle overwhelming success—or failure.

Qualifying the Qualifications
Allow for all possible responses, especially if you are new to teleservicing. Your actual follow-up will show very quickly whether your identification of those who qualified is valid. But don't leave it at that. Give a random selection of nonqualifiers the same positive selling effort. Experienced teleservicers will insist on this as a check on their *real* success. Take nothing for granted. Learn at least *what* works, even if you can't tell *why*. Build a file that can be used as a database. A decade from now you want 10 years' experience, not 1 years's 10 times!

Pretesting Mail
Teleservicing is *not* direct mail. What works *and is affordable* in the one may not work in the other. But the advantages of using teleservicing to *present* direct mail offers is proving its worth to many direct marketers.

- Testing by mail gives only yes and no answers. Teleservicing can tell you *why*—both why they are *not* ordering and why they *are*. The latter especially may not be at all what you expect. It can turn a merely good mail response into a bonanza.
- Testing by mail can take months, from concepts and copy to production, printing, and mailing and then waiting for and analyzing the response. Skillful teleservicers can get their results in weeks . . . or days!

INSIGHT 54

Consider testing by teleservicing as giving you an expanded instant focus group. It won't work for color or taste, but for many options, it gives a hundredfold increase in participants for about the same cost.

- Skillful teleservicers can change their trial script right in the middle of a message. Properly trained and supervised, they can refine or reposition the offer instantly. Immediate feedback and response can help discover the best target markets, the most likely lists to reach it, and the most persuasive offer to convince it—almost while you wait!

Surveys and Other Research

Many *business* surveys can be do-it-yourself projects. Decide what you need to learn, decide who can give you the answer, get a statistically valid list of names, and call. Here are a few things to help bring do-it-yourself success:

- **Have a written script** of the entire conversation, not just the questions. If not, after about the tenth call you'll forget your own name!
- **Tell them immediately the reason for your call** and about how long it will take. (For example, "Good morning. I'm Charlene McCarthy from the Scofield corporation, and I'd appreciate just three minutes of your time to ask about your likely need of toothpaste in the next six months.")
- **When calling competitors** who are unlikely to share information, give the project to some graduate students, who can honestly say. "I'm a graduate student at ZLU, and I'm doing a survey of . . ."
- **Establish an in-house research arm** with an identity, address, and telephone that is different from yours. The more important the statistical validity of the responses, the more you will need experience or help in teleservicing, setting up surveys, and analyzing data. For just a general "feel of the situation," do it yourself.

Legal Constraints

As of spring 2003, approximately half the states have their own laws concerning outbound telemarketing with national legislation under consideration. If you call only within a state without such restrictions, these laws need not concern you. But for a smaller firm calling other states, a professional teleservicing firm that is staffed to keep track of legal requirements, including state-by-state licensing, and the automated equipment to follow these laws, is usually best.

FINDING THE HELP YOU NEED FOR IN-HOUSE OPERATIONS

Setting up in-house, whether business-to-business, business-to-consumer, or inbound consumer-to-business, *must* begin with a teleservicer experienced in *successful start-up operations of that kind.* Just knowing how to run a program is not enough. Starting up is the key! This telemarketer is not necessarily the person who can or will run the ongoing operation, so consider a consultant. Here's how to find one.

• **Check with local direct marketing associations.** If you are unfamiliar with where they are, the Direct Marketing Association will tell you. Write Direct Marketing Association, Dept. DM Clubs, *Associations Networks.* 1120 Avenue of the Americas, New York, NY 10036–8096. Or call (212) 768–7277. If you write, enclose a self-addressed, stamped envelope. Then join your local direct marketing club. It will help you even if you're not a member, but the continuing contacts alone are worth the price of admission!

• **Check with local or regional telemarketing/teleservicing firms.** Some may recommend themselves. All will know appropriate consultants. None will want to see you—and telemarketing—fail!

INSIGHT 55

Consider starting up with an outside firm, even if you plan to go in-house. It will give you instant professional telemarketing, plus invaluable research on your work flow and staff needs, while your own facilities and personnel are put into place.

• **Check with telemarketing users, including your competitors.** Every start-up operation needed help. Teleservicing is still growing so fast that they may well remember where they got their initial help or know of other sources you can use.

• **Check professional magazines.** Several industrial publications include annual directories of telemarketing products and services. As a comparative novice, subscribe to several. The resulting flood of mail, and (we hope) calls, will keep you alert to everything new in the field. The *Bacon's Magazine Directory,* (800) 621–0561, lists and describes dozens of telecommunications publications. For specific needs, check there, too.

• **Find a mentor.** Search for someone whom you can call for advice when disaster strikes—or who can warn you before it happens. Practically everyone loves to find a new audience to hear about *their* pitfalls and how *they* solved them. Your business, direct marketing, and advertising associations are ideal sources. Join. Participate. Learn.

FINDING THE HELP YOU NEED FOR OUTSOURCING

Finding the Right Firm

The process of finding a firm is the same as that just discussed for finding a consultant. The problem isn't in the finding; it's deciding on what you need to find. Begin, as always, with a list. Figure 9.2 is an example.

TELESERVICE BUREAU EVALUATION

Date: _____

ABOUT US

☐ What teleservicer must know or learn about us: _____

☐ Our outbound need(s): _____
☐ Size/source of lists: _____
☐ Our inbound needs: _____
☐ Source of calls: _____

ABOUT THE TELESERVICER

☐ Teleservicer Bureau: _____
☐ Web site: _____ e-mail: _____
☐ Account executive:_____
☐ AE experience with similar lists: _____
☐ Bureau experience with similar lists: _____

☐ Bureau's years of continuous teleservicing:_____
☐ Legal history: Ask teleservices. Check (use) DMA/Better Business Bureau. Check annual reports for public companies
☐ Service bureau specialization
_____ % business to business
_____ % business to consumer
_____ % incoming for each
_____ % other (Non-profit, political, etc.)
☐ Maximum number of work stations: _____
☐ Maximum number of operators for our project: _____
☐ _____ Years pertinent experience of our account executive
Number of accounts that AE will handle
☐ $ _____ guarantee to service bureau. $ _____ advance
☐ Hourly rates: For whom and for what $ _____
_____

☐ Additional costs explained: $ _____
☐ References: _____
_____

EVALUATION COMMENTS: _____
_____
_____
_____

By: _____ Date: _____

Figure 9.2 A teleservice bureau evaluation.

A million names on an outbound lead-list is wholly different from inbound responses to a million catalogs. The first may be completed in 30 days and you risk comparatively little in working with start-up teleservicers who will go all out to prove their worth. The second may bring inquiries and orders for 30 months. For inbound service, longevity is all important. Your toll-free number, e-mail, and Web site once published, take on a life of their own. Consider also what happens when the initial rush of calls tapers off. Can and will the service bureau handle a few calls as well as many? How? For how long? At what cost?

Few (if any) teleservicers can do everything. Define what you need, and then hunt for it with a rifle, rather than a shotgun.

Testing Teleservicers

Elsewhere in this book—for convention displays, catalogs, and major direct mail projects—we suggested a contest among possible suppliers, *with everyone paid for their work.* Teleservicers also seems to lend itself to direct head-to-head testing, but first, consider the following:

•   What is the size of the sample you will test and what percentage of contact gives you an adequate response? Teleservicers consider 1,000 *completed* outbound calls a reasonable test to learn what percentage will actually buy. If 15 of those called can be contacted per hour, that is 73 hours for which you will be charged—*in addition to precalling set-up costs.* Should you want to test the 5,000 to 10,000 names used in testing direct mail, your hours charged will jump five- or tenfold. That's true for each competing firm, so stick with 1,000 calls. If there is going to be a significant difference in the rate of contact or positive responses, it will show in the smaller quantities. That will save significant dollars and let you use (rollout) your entire list much earlier.

•   Key to evaluating a test is the type of analysis provided. Is it both quantitative and qualitative? Are the firms making any recommendations as to the market? The product or service? The offer? Or are they simply calling? You really shouldn't do any testing unless you want to learn as well as sell. Teleservicing has the ability to gather vastly more information, and do it more quickly and cheaply, than testing by mail. Determine what you hope to learn. Make a list. Give it to each of the service bureaus being tested. Let *them* decide what's practical. After all, it is a test.

•   Where significant differences in success appear, use the winner. More likely, the competitors will be evenly matched. In my experience, even that result has made a decision quite easy. Working with any outside service means forming a partnership toward a common goal. When all other factors seem equal, select the partner who you are convinced has the most to contribute and is willing to give that as part of your relationship.

TELESERVICES CHECKLIST

Project Title _____ **Date** _____

Project Description _____ **Project #** _____

_____ **Checklist #** _____

Overall Supervision By _____ **Deadline** _____

Budget _____ **Completion Date** _____ **Start Up Date** _____

MANAGEMENT DECISIONS	ASSIGNED TO	DUE	IN	MUST APPROVE	BY DATE	IN	INFO COPY ONLY	SEE ATTACHED
1. Purpose	_____	___	☐	_____	___	☐	_____	☐
2. Budget	_____	___	☐	_____	___	☐	_____	☐
3. Time Line	_____	___	☐	_____	___	☐	_____	☐
4. In-House/Outside	_____	___	☐	_____	___	☐	_____	☐
5. Project Manager(s)	_____	___	☐	_____	___	☐	_____	☐
INBOUND								
6. Types & Purposes	_____	___	☐	_____	___	☐	_____	☐
7. Toll-free number(s)	_____	___	☐	_____	___	☐	_____	☐
8. 900 number(s)	_____	___	☐	_____	___	☐	_____	☐
9. Regular	_____	___	☐	_____	___	☐	_____	☐
OUTBOUND								
10. Types & Services	_____	___	☐	_____	___	☐	_____	☐
11. Phone Lists	_____	___	☐	_____	___	☐	_____	☐
IN-HOUSE								
12. Location(s)	_____	___	☐	_____	___	☐	_____	☐
13. Personnel	_____	___	☐	_____	___	☐	_____	☐
14. Equipment	_____	___	☐	_____	___	☐	_____	☐
15. Training	_____	___	☐	_____	___	☐	_____	☐
16. Budget	_____	___	☐	_____	___	☐	_____	☐
OUTSIDE FIRM								
17. Selection	_____	___	☐	_____	___	☐	_____	☐
18. Script Approval	_____	___	☐	_____	___	☐	_____	☐
19. Schedule	_____	___	☐	_____	___	☐	_____	☐
20. Reporting System	_____	___	☐	_____	___	☐	_____	☐
21. Billing System	_____	___	☐	_____	___	☐	_____	☐
22. Cancellation Option	_____	___	☐	_____	___	☐	_____	☐
23. Budget	_____	___	☐	_____	___	☐	_____	☐
INBOUND/OUTBOUND								
24. Database Records	_____	___	☐	_____	___	☐	_____	☐
25. Evaluation(s)	_____	___	☐	_____	___	☐	_____	☐
26. Reports/Actions	_____	___	☐	_____	___	☐	_____	☐

Figure 9.3 The teleservices checklist.

NOTES ON THE TELESERVICES CHECKLIST

These notes are a supplement to the material presented in this chapter. They are not a substitute for that material. The checklist is shown in Figure 9.3.

1. **Purpose.** Before deciding on the purpose, suggest a brief professional updating on what the state of the art makes possible. Don't let management limit its options by not having that first.

2. **Budget.** Set specific, though generous, budgets, especially for getting started. Definitely get outside guidance if you are new to this medium.

3. **Timeline.** Be specific about dates. Set time lines for management as well as staff: Specify when testing must be done, reported, and evaluated. No "ASAP"![5] Specify when after-the-test decisions must be made, with agreement as to what that involves and on the budget to make it possible.

4. **In-house/Outside.** This is not necessarily an either- or decision. Often, both are required, at least for getting started.

5. **Project manager.** Consider separate managers if *major* in-house staff and a service firm are both required. Teleservicing—even its supervision—is a time-intensive job!

6. **Types and purposes.** Have *written* agreement on why the inbound services are established and what they are to achieve. Spell out the details against which evaluations can be matched.

7–9. **Call payment.** Decide who pays for each type of call. If different types of calls (routine orders, requests for technical data, simpler how-to questions) require different personnel, will they be available when callers are likely to phone? Who monitors what actually happens? Who's authorized to make it all work?

10–11. **Outbound how-to.** What outbound sales calls are to accomplish and the data available to help make it happen. Do *not* count on getting usable teleservices data from *any* computer—especially your own—without first seeing it happen. Don't settle for assurances or promises. Demand a demonstration. For new equipment or software, demand a guarantee.

12. **Location.** Consult your phone company teleservicing expert—there is one!—before setting up in house. Teleservicing experts may even have solutions to which you have not yet discovered the problems.

13. **Personnel.** Don't start up without a *teleservicing start-up specialist* who's been through it all before . . . several times. This is critical to everything you'll do, from finding people to write the scripts and answer the phones to figuring out who works where with whom on what. Think of them as test pilots . . . there to get you safely launched.

14–15. **Equipment/training.** Match equipment and training to what you need now. Allow for future expansion in long-range planning, but concentrate on making the present successful first if you want that future to arrive.

---

[5]See Insight 2.

16. **Budget.** Do as was suggested for direct mail. Separate budgeting for start-up, testing, and ongoing telemarketing. Start-up is probably a capital cost. Testing is advertising. Ongoing teleservicing is sales. Money for start-up and testing is spent no matter what else you do. Don't let it distort posttesting success or failure. Analyze, too, the effect on budgets of changing from in-house to an outside firm or vice versa. Keeping within budget is seldom the only reason for such a decision, but it is certainly a major one.

17. **Selection.** Personal rapport is vital in your working relationship with the account executive, especially during start-up. Let management set parameters for the decision on which firm to choose. Let the actual choice be made by the project manager.

18. **Script approval.** Read scripts for what they say, not the details of how they say it. Don't try to do the teleservicer's job. It's why you went to an outside service.

19. **Schedule.** Allow for the learning of what works best that can be achieved only on the phone. Discuss needs and scheduling with the firm before promising results to management.

20. **Reporting system.** The frequency and detail of reports, evaluations, and recommendations from the firm. Who must see everything? Summaries? Only decisions?

21. **Billing system.** Have a *written* agreement on how the firm bills. What work—if any—they do before payment is made. What adjustments—if any—must take place in your system, as well as theirs.

22. **Cancellation option.** Get an unmistakable written agreement. (*Unmistakable* means that both parties understand the same thing the same way.) Establish routine checkpoints for continuation of the service. Set an automatic halt for review if specified goals are not met. Include an option for instant cancellation, with a basis for calculating costs incurred.

23. **Budget.** Most of a firm's charges are established as standard costs. Totals are easily estimated for purposes of budgeting.

24. **Database records.** Build customers as well as sales. Meet with data-processing personnel to learn whether and how a database is being built. Take the same precautions as in #10 and #11. Check!

25. **Evaluations.** Much of teleservices is a team effort. It's teleservices *plus* mailing . . . *plus* space and electronic advertising . . . *plus* selling in person . . . *plus* more and different prospect/suspect/customer contacts. Differentiate here and elsewhere between "prospects" on whom you spend more effort and dollars and "suspects" who are not worthy of that much attention. Relate all this to evaluation, where appropriate.

26. **Reports/actions.** Note especially what has been learned that may apply to future efforts. Check later to make sure the learning is actually passed on . . . and applied.

10 | Fax and Broadcast Fax

> This chapter has been brought up to date with the help of **David Shaub,** vice president, Absolute Communication Solution, a leader in service and functionality for the enhanced fax and e-mail communications industry. (www.absolutecs.net, (888) 387–9741)

THREE NEW MEDIA

The 1990s saw something unique in the history of communication—the use and acceptance of *three* new media for advertising: broadcast fax, e-mail, and the Internet. Of these, fax has become astonishingly undervalued and underused. Sent and delivered overnight, it is the message most likely to be placed on the recipient's desk and read. It guarantees privacy and is opened without fear of virus and systemwide contamination. Whether you fax to one person or "broadcast" to a thousand, this medium is more effective than ever, because so few of your competitors recognize its worth!

WHEN TO BROADCAST YOUR FAX

If you're a travel agent or use one, you've received messages from tour groups offering huge discounts for not-quite-sold-out travel packages.[1] Experience with broadcast fax has taught them they can still earn a commission the last practical moment offering the empty berths.

Given the right list—we'll get to lists in a moment—almost any special (and even not-so-special) event profits from the same kind of broadcast fax use. For instance:

---

[1]If it's a Monday departure, call Friday afternoon and offer to pay 50 percent for the best cabin. The ship leaves whether it's full or not, and 50 percent is better than nothing. Prepare to negotiate!

- Announcement of overstocked inventory or older merchandise *suitable for the audience receiving the message*
- Newsletters (industry updates)
- Publications (renewals, introductions)
- Business and professional association meeting reminders
- Convention or trade show inducements to visit a specific booth or social event
- Favorable reviews of artistic, musical, and other cultural events sent to likely ticket buyers, especially if they have asked for the information
- Publicity releases to electronic and print media (much more about this in the chapter on publicity and public relations)

Here are somewhat different ways to use broadcast fax:

- Invitation to a seminar or other self-improvement event important to the person being addressed.
- *Fast* individualized follow-up (see Figure 10.2A, page 197) to everyone who attended the event. Thank them and offer an action-generating benefit that reinforces the main sales message of your meeting. Always remember that broadcast fax is a *personalized* medium. You're sending one individual message to one man or woman.
- For exhibit booth follow-up, use the same kind of benefit-filled fax. Be sure to give your convention-site visitors a reason to leave their own fax numbers (much more about this in the chapter on conventions and trade shows).

INSIGHT 56

Do not think of broadcast fax as "advertising." It is the most *personal* of *business* promotional media. Business expects to get "advertised at" in person, in print, by phone, on the Internet, and by mail. But not by fax! That is reserved for immediate *business* communication. Make sure your message meets this standard. And make it *personal,* too!

FINDING BROADCAST FAX FIRMS

Broadcast fax is listed in the Yellow Pages under "Fax Transmission Services" and "Fax Information and Service Bureaus." A highly technical medium, it is best obtained from one of the companies that specialize in this field, rather that the major long-distance carriers, which consider it a side line.

BUILDING YOUR DATABASE

WARNING!

For likely marketing success, fax only to persons and companies who have *directly* given you permission or their fax number. Beware of using a list from fax service transmitters that sell or provide fax numbers. Many of these companies obtain their numbers through speed dialing and have not been given permission. Furthermore, because they have a fax number only, they cannot create a meaningful target audience. Fax is too expensive for pie-in-the-sky spamming.

Someday, hopefully quite soon, every business will have its fax as well as its regular telephone number in the Yellow Pages. Until then, you must gather, collect, store, and keep current your own database. Fortunately, that's easy to do.

- Many business, professional, and membership directories include fax numbers. Some will provide the listing on a disk. Others can be copied from the directories.

When Fax Numbers Are Not Easily Available

- For a small list, call each regular phone number and say, "May I please have your (name or department) fax number?" Few will refuse.
- For larger lists, send the missing fax-number destinations a double, postage prepaid card as in Figure 10.1 requesting the number. Two weeks after receiving the first response, you'll have 90 percent of the likely mail answers. Use a teleservice firm to contact the rest. To increase response, put an offer on the postcard.

PERSONALIZING BROADCAST FAX

Broadcast fax can be personalized with an unlimited number of fields, anywhere in your documents, using different type sizes and fonts (type styles) for emphasis. For letters, as in Figure 10.2A, stick to a single "business" type face! It can add a name or phrase to personalize within the body of a message.

Some Guidance in Personalization

Maury Kauffman, a broadcast fax pioneer,[2] suggests 12 tricks of the trade to make your fax broadcasting more successful and more cost-effective. They are so

---

[2]Now a larger-company fax technology and services consultant, he can be contacted at Maury@KauffmanGroup.com.

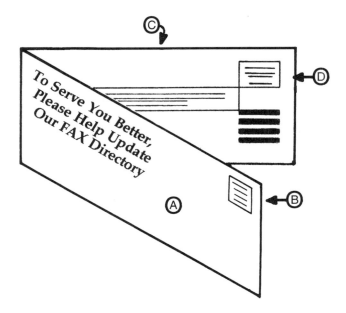

Figure 10.1 A double postcard serves as an excellent, inexpensive way to request—and get—fax numbers and e-mail addresses from a large list. (A) Front cover addressing side. (B) Brief message about use you will make of fax number. Make this a benefit to customer or prospect! (C) Room for fax number fill-in and, possibly, some free offers of "How we can help you with this additional information," described in Checklist point 14. Show small illustration of double card refolded for mailing back. (D) Prepaid return address. You can use much lighter and less expensive stock than having a single card separated and returned.

valuable, we have made them a special Kauffman's Dozen part of this chapter's Broadcast Fax Checklist!

SUMMARY

- Almost any event can profit from a broadcast fax push.
- Broadcast fax is a personalized medium. Do *not* make your message an ad! Keep it focused on the recipient.
- Add a simple way to respond to your message. For instance, "Sign and fax back" or "Call toll-free."
- When checking a fax transmission service, check on equipment, personnel, and service. Don't settle for two out of three!

NOTES ON THE BROADCAST FAX CHECKLIST

These notes are a supplement to the material presented in this chapter. They are not a substitute for that material. The checklist is presented in Figure 10.3.

A

B

C

Figure 10.2 (Copy at 200% for easy legibility.) A full-page cover certainly adds "class" but is seldom worth the extra cost. The simple "To" personalization in Figure 10.2B works just as well. If immediate sender identification is important, use a regular or modified letterhead as in the newsletter in Figure 10.2C. If you broadcast fax a newsletter, keep it brief and make sure it contains news that offers a benefit to the recipient as well as you. For self-puffery, stick to the mail.

1. **Quotations.** The total of all quoted and/or estimated costs accepted from outside suppliers, plus the known or estimated internal out-of-pocket costs. This is the amount given for budget approval in #2.

2. **Budget approval.** The amount either accepted from #1, or otherwise determined as a fair cost to do the project. If lower than the figure in #1, costs may have to be renegotiated with suppliers or the project modified to fit the dollar allocation.

3. **Project approval.** Once the project *can* be done for the amount in #2, a decision on whether the project is worth the cost, no matter how "fair" the individual charges may be.

4. **Target audience.** Determination of the target audience at whom the fax is focused. Everything else about this fax must then be controlled by

BROADCAST FAX CHECKLIST

Project Title _____   **Date** _____

Project Description _____   **Project #** _____

_____   **Checklist #** _____

Overall Supervision By _____   **Deadline** _____

Budget _____ **Completion Date** _____   **Start Up Date** _____

	ASSIGNED TO	DUE	IN	MUST APPROVE	BY DATE	IN	INFO COPY ONLY	SEE ATTACHED
MANAGEMENT DECISIONS								
1. Quotations	_____	___	☐	_____	___	☐	_____	☐
2. Budget approval	_____	___	☐	_____	___	☐	_____	☐
3. Project approval	_____	___	☐	_____	___	☐	_____	☐
CREATIVE DECISIONS								
4. Target Audience	_____	___	☐	_____	___	☐	_____	☐
5. Message & Results	_____	___	☐	_____	___	☐	_____	☐
6. Benefits	_____	___	☐	_____	___	☐	_____	☐
7. Headline	_____	___	☐	_____	___	☐	_____	☐
8. Offer	_____	___	☐	_____	___	☐	_____	☐
9. Writer	_____	___	☐	_____	___	☐	_____	☐
10. Design	_____	___	☐	_____	___	☐	_____	☐
11. Transmission Service	_____	___	☐	_____	___	☐	_____	☐
KAUFFMAN'S DOZEN								
12. Personalization	_____	___	☐	_____	___	☐	_____	☐
13. Response	_____	___	☐	_____	___	☐	_____	☐
14. Interactive Fax	_____	___	☐	_____	___	☐	_____	☐
15. Graphics	_____	___	☐	_____	___	☐	_____	☐
16. Frequency	_____	___	☐	_____	___	☐	_____	☐
17. Legal Limits	_____	___	☐	_____	___	☐	_____	☐
18. Budgeting	_____	___	☐	_____	___	☐	_____	☐
19. Cover Page	_____	___	☐	_____	___	☐	_____	☐
20. Off-peak	_____	___	☐	_____	___	☐	_____	☐
21. Length	_____	___	☐	_____	___	☐	_____	☐
22. Database	_____	___	☐	_____	___	☐	_____	☐
23. Multiple Faxing	_____	___	☐	_____	___	☐	_____	☐
MECHANICAL CHECKS								
24. Record Code	_____	___	☐	_____	___	☐	_____	☐
25. Editorial OK	_____	___	☐	_____	___	☐	_____	☐
26. Legal OK	_____	___	☐	_____	___	☐	_____	☐
27. Marketing OK	_____	___	☐	_____	___	☐	_____	☐
28. Management OK	_____	___	☐	_____	___	☐	_____	☐
29. Hard Copy File	_____	___	☐	_____	___	☐	_____	☐

© 2003, Fred Hahn

Figure 10.3 The broadcast fax checklist.

that focus. Do *not* use fax broadcasting for shotgun marketing or for prospecting. *Do* use it to market to your existing customer base or enclosed groups like tour organizations to travel agents or associations to their members.

5. **Message and results.** Give the reason for the message and the results it is to produce. This tells the writer *what* is to be said, not *how* to say it. The actual wording is the job of the writer in #9.

6. **Benefits.** The benefits offered in the message, keyed to the audience in #4. If none of those benefits seem particularly suited to that group, the choice of *those* benefits and why *that* particular audience was targeted must be reconsidered.

7. **Headline.** The headline's subject, not its wording. Pick the one thing most likely to attract the target audience; usually the key benefit from #6.

8. **Offer.** Give the recipient a *major* reason to respond *now!*

9. **Writer.** The checklist shows the person who *appoints* the writer. If certain things must be said in a specific way, let the writer know before he or she begins . . . and whether this is a legal constraint or a management decision. If the latter, management should be willing to at least consider alternatives.

10. **Design.** The person responsible for choosing the designer. This is a fax. Keep it simple and legible!

11. **Transmission service.** Before hiring your fax transmission service, get references for the quantity of work you need done. Don't just ask for references. Check them!

Kauffman's Dozen

12. **Personalization.** Fax personalization is critical. Name, company, and ID numbers can all be added to a personalized fax. If your database has a field, it can, as in Figure 10.2, be put practically anywhere on the fax.

13. **Response.** Add a response mechanism to your fax. "To get more information (or order), sign here and fax back" is just one example.

14. **Interactive fax response (IFR).** IFR, also known as fax on demand and document on demand, is usually handled by a broadcast fax company. It lets the fax recipient fax or call a toll-free number for frequently requested information. Callers can—*usually within minutes, around the clock*—get a return fax with up-to-the-minute information on product availability and price, order forms, product instructions, training materials, and so on.

15. **Graphics.** Keep the medium in mind when creating a fax. Photos and detailed graphics never fax well. Even fine lines may be a problem.

16. **Frequency.** Do not overuse the fax as a promotional tool. These documents have a sense of urgency that will lose their impact if you send everything by fax.

17. **Legal limits.** Know the limitations placed on fax broadcasting by the Telephone Consumer Protection Act. Find an attorney who specializes in this field.

18. **Budgeting.** Allocate 5 percent of your advertising budget to test broadcast fax. Programmed faxing should cost no more—and often less!—than a comparable document send by mail . . . and be delivered in hours, rather than days. Get knowledgeable help. Believe the results.

19. **Cover page.** Whenever possible, limit the use of a full-page cover page. Use a "headline" or Post-it™ note format.

20. **Off-peak hours.** Transmit during off-peak lowest-cost hours when possible, especially when sending multiple faxes.

21. **Length.** Send as few pages as possible. A single page is most likely to get read. Single-space most documents. Cut down on white space, but don't jam so much onto a page it becomes uninviting to the eye or hard to read. If you use a typesetting format, make the text at least 12 points in size.

22. **Database.** Establish a system to keep your database up to date. Use it!

23. **Multiple faxing.** Use a broadcast fax service bureau with the staff and equipment to do the job right. You'll save countless headaches and countable money.

24–28. **Mechanical checks.** Someone has to be responsible for checking each of these items before anything may be sent. Make sure that they *do* check them and sign off *in writing.*

29. **Hard copy file.** Some *one* person must be responsible for maintaining a hard copy file of all fax "as broadcast"; that is, as they actually appeared.

11 | Basic Internet Advertising
It Doesn't Have to Start on the Internet

> This chapter was written in collaboration with **Ken Magill**. Magill, a frequent speaker to business groups, is Internet-Marketing editor of the weekly *DM News,* found online at www. dmnews.com.

WHAT YOU WILL FIND IN CHAPTER 11

As a beginning Internet marketer, don't you wish you could consult a knowledgeable mentor who could guide you from e-commerce ignorance to insight? Wouldn't it be great to spend an afternoon chatting with that expert about the very things you most need to know? Well, you're in luck, because this chapter is precisely that experience.

Think Small!

The first thing to do, if you are a small business, is to remember to think small. You must not begin by deciding to put everything involving your small business on a Web site. That is the absolute opposite of the tack you should take because you can advertise and sell on the Internet today without needing a Web site and make it begin to work for you. Whether you are a retailer, a manufacturer, or service provider, it is practical for just about any kind of business. You can take advantage of Internet marketing in ways you never thought possible, because whatever goods or services you sell, you can get on the Web simply by collecting people's e-mail addresses. That is the first step for a small business: Start by collecting people's e-addresses.

How to Collect E-Mail Addresses

Ask people for their e-mail address at every point of contact. It is important to realize that e-mail is not the prospecting vehicle everyone seems to envision it to be. You can't just send e-mail to people you don't know and expect them to buy from you. We've all known for years that the best way to increase our profits is to get more business from our best customers. E-mail is a beautiful medium for that.

So what you do every time someone comes in or phones is to ask for their e-mail addresses.

Start with a Plan!

Because they will want to know what you'll do with their e-mail address, you need a plan before you begin. Are you going to start a weekly or monthly e-mail special? Will they get the first chance at new items of special interest to them or at the savings when you close out older inventory? Whatever your plan, make the reason something that will benefit them. Be completely honest Deliver what you promise.

AN E-PLAN CASE HISTORY

A bar owner asked his customers to give him their e-mail addresses if they smoked cigars and would like a Friday after-work "smoker." In a few months he had a substantial list. But he had planned more than just inviting them in to drink and smoke. Before his first e-mail message was send, he had learned about cigars and gotten a license to sell them. His e-mail now tells them about the unusual or special brands these aficionados can buy and try at each week's gathering. If they like something well enough, it becomes regular stock. Occasionally he also announces a Monday evening (his slowest night of the week) for drink tastings or specials. Both were a social and financial success from their first e-mail message.

Special Interests: Your List for Success

Depending on the variety of what you plan to offer, you will want a single master list or separate smaller lists by recipients' specific interests. True, your online fee probably pays for "unlimited" e-mail usage, but if you repeatedly send to thousands of addresses, at some point your Internet service provider (ISP) will cancel your services unless you arrange for such heavy volume in advance. Even more critical from your point of view is the importance of not irritating the recipients by sending messages they do not want. Think of them as individuals whose e-mail boxes are filled with dozens of messages they do not need—the same daily joke forwarded by 14 acquaintances, phony "warnings" about things that aren't true, chain letters, "spam" (junk e-mail) offers (about which more later), and so on. Hidden in all of this are the messages they really want, hopefully including yours, if only your message can get them to recognize it as such.

The Business-to-Business Application

What is true about consumer e-mail is even more important for recipient-focused, business-to-business messages. When you get someone's e-mail location for a smaller businesses, it is often both their personal and work e-mail address, so that 100 or 150 e-messages per day is not unusual. Not only do they get the e-mail garbage sent to their home, they get it at work too, all in the same virtual mailbox.

Cutting through the E-Mail Glut

To cut through all that, whether as a consumer or business-to-business firm, you must make sure that the e-mail you send is instantly recognizable as having value to the recipient. Like in every other medium, a value that is of benefit to the specific prospect or customer is what sells. That is why, no matter how much customer and prospect information you collect, you want to divide it into specialized lists that make sense to the recipient.

The Importance of "You"

The e-mail headline is its *subject line.* What that means for you as an e-mail sender is the need to make each headline such an obvious benefit to the recipients they will open the full message. To do this, you must make both your headline and message totally "you"-focused. One of the most powerful selling words in the English language is "you"; one of the least powerful is "I."

Importance of the Subject Line Benefit

Put the benefit to the recipients in the subject line. Tell what's in it for them. Practically everyone looks at the subject line and sender ID first; after all, like the teaser on an envelope, it's the only thing they see. Like that envelope, if your e-mail teaser appears to be of no use, it won't be opened either. They'll simply delete it. To avoid this, remember these three important factors:

1. In the subject-line "headline" you have only 35 characters (including spacing) to get your point across. The full line may be longer, but the first 35 characters is probably all they will see.
2. E-mail readers are no different than you. Most of them read only the first two lines of the body message before they decide to read on or toss it. So get to the point!
3. Experiment with your messages. Try a variety of approaches as explained in more detail throughout this book.

The No-Secret "Secrets"

No matter what you sell, how big or small your business, the two "secrets" of e-selling success are the same:

- Give the recipients a reason to shop from you, rather than from a dozen other possibilities.
- Give them a reason to shop now, rather than next week or next month.

Make It Easy to Get Off Your List, Too

To keep your e-mail recipients happy, provide clear "opt-out" instructions from the very first message. Many times people change their minds about being on a list or have forgotten they signed up. Sometimes people will sign up others as a joke.

For all those reasons, it is important that your message makes it clear from whom the message is coming. Use an e-mail format like this:

Dear Ms. Consumer,

Recently you signed up for news about the weekly specials from Kilgora's Dress Shop.

Here are today's sales items available only this weekend and only to people on this list . . . .

[Description of specials]

If you would like to be removed from this e-mail list, just click on the reply button and type "remove" in the subject line.

Although it may seem a poor business practice to let people off the hook so easily, studies have shown that when people know it is easy to get off an e-mail list, they are less likely to ask to be removed.

A Retailing Example

Assume you sell shoes and have customers who have small feet, or especially large ones, or who want the very latest fashions. Collect all the information that might make sense to them. Then think of some benefit you can offer through this fast new medium that they will recognize could not be offered to them in any other way. For instance, men and women with especially small feet shop everywhere they suspect their size might be available. You could e-mail that group to tell them what has just come in and that you won't put it on general sale for a week. Be sure to include your phone number so they can call and put some pairs on one- or two-day hold. Of course they could reply by e-mail, but a phone conversation lets you (and them) narrow down what they're most likely to want.

Prepare for Instant Results

With e-mail advertising, you will find out almost instantly how well your list and your message worked. Better yet, if you are a bricks-and-mortar merchant, not only will they order the particular product you advertised, many of them will visit and find other things to buy. This is the critical factor small businesses must not forget or ignore. The continuing success of small business comes from building first-time buyers into regular customers, and there is no better way to do that than by providing more and better service than the competition. Add to this the fact that if treated right, your best customers will also be your best word-of-mouth advertising. If not treated right, you invite the negative word of mouth at your peril.

GETTING YOUR SITE KNOWN

How to Get the Existing Business Front Line Involved

In adding e-commerce to your business, you must get your front line involved. Your clerks, your sales force, your phone order and service personnel are all critical to your success. They must be trained not only to ask for e-mail addresses (which they may consider an extra pain) but to make the asking a service to the customer. To make this easier, have a short written form that your personnel can follow or the customers can fill out. Be helpful here, too. In addition to some specific interest options, ask customers what else they would like to be notified about. Explain that if they want to be removed from the list at any time, their name will be removed with no hassle. You'll be wise to get help from a public relations person to create that message. Be sure that PR person spends time at your business to learn about your employees and your customers. Here, as elsewhere in your e-mail messaging, empathy is everything!

Fish Bowl Do's and Don'ts

Many businesses and organizations have a prominently displayed "fish bowl" with a sign something like this:

> Drop your business card with e-mail address here
> for our weekly drawing for a *free* [whatever].

The e-mail list from that bowl is essentially worthless as an advertising medium. Practically no one drops in their card because they want your future e-mails; they want a chance at your *free* whatever. So do something like this:

> ## JULY SPECIAL!
> Drop your business card with e-mail address here
> to get our monthly list of overstock specials.

Give them a reason to want to hear from you, something that offers a self-selected benefit, and you will have a golden winner. To discover what that is, change the offer monthly to learn what customers consider worthwhile. As in all direct response, you can't know what works best until you test the options. Periodically repeat the benefit—which may change over time—but not so often visitors will stop checking your offer.

The Importance of Blind "Carbon Copies"

Blind carbon copy (BCC) systems let you send the same *personalized* note to any or all of the e-mail addresses without their knowing who else got your message. Without such a system, every message will include the entire list, no matter how long! What is the likelihood of your ever opening that person's or company's message in the future? There are many such systems. Check out a few and see which works best for you.

Some Fundamental Rules When Going after New Business

Every business is a neighborhood concern, whether that "neighborhood" is within a few blocks, a few miles, or a few continents. In advertising terminology, your business neighborhood is the universe that contains your customers and prospects. For consumer businesses, if you are not getting business across town without e-mail, you are unlikely to get business from there with e-mail. Even if you might do so, usually it is too costly and too much work. Almost always, the small business is better off adding value for the 20 percent of the customers who make up 80 percent of the sales. Nevertheless, getting sales from outside your universe is possible, but has to be weighed against at least four factors:

1. Your cost for the additional advertising and promotion.
2. Your cost for the benefits that gets customers to you.
3. Your cost for providing the goods and services, if those must be delivered.
4. The cost of the first three against your cost for doing nothing, should competition threaten your present sales universe.

E-Mail as a Customer Service Tool

There may be companies and businesses that do not need a Web site, but everyone can profit from having e-mail. In addition to its use in selling, e-mail can be unequaled as a customer service tool. Think of the person trying to assemble a tent . . . a machine . . . a bridge at 2 A.M. If you are not there to provide answers, they can send an e-mail, explain the problem, and ask when to expect the solution. Respond at the first possible moment and tell them what to do or how long it will take you to send the answer. Most important, whatever you promise, be sure it's done, and better and faster, if possible. Make all your surprises pleasant ones. There is no faster way to lose a prospect or customer that the failure to live up to your promise. Of course having a Web site is an even better customer service tool, and we will turn to that shortly.

E-MAIL SUMMARY

Five "Secrets" of Successful E-Mail

The secrets of successful e-mail are essentially the same as they are for successful faxes:

1. Give recipients an immediate reason to read it. Make the subject headline a benefit to the recipient—preferably in six words or fewer.
2. Remember, your headline has only 35 characters. So keep it short.
3. When making more than one point, as in this section, use bulleted or number copy. It makes transitions easy and obvious.
4. No misspellings. No glaring errors in grammar. How can prospective customers trust you to deliver what you promise when you can't even deliver a short, literate message?

5.   Note this major difference from other direct response: Do not use *"free"* in the subject headline.

Why Not to Use *"Free"* in Your E-Mail Headline

E-mail recipients won't believe the word "free." They know nothing is really free. Save that for the message itself, where you can explain the conditions.

There have been so many phony free or get-rich-quick spam campaigns that many ISPs will not send a message using those words in the subject line, though they may be used in the text. Check your ISP for other forbidden headline words and phrases.

MOVING ONTO THE WORLD WIDE WEB

The mechanics of getting on and using the World Wide Web are covered in the instructions that are built into your computer and in literally thousands of books, articles, and community college classes. But before you start, you will want an Internet plan detailing why you want a Web site and what to do with it once you have it.

What to Put in Your Internet Plan

A surprisingly large number of business and nonbusiness men and women now search on the Internet, rather than use the printed Yellow Pages. That is reason enough to establish a Web presence. In fact, for many businesses, their Web site is exactly like a Yellow Pages ad, limited to a home page telling who they are and giving contact information. Frequently this approach results from someone having applied for a site, then not having the least idea how to make it work effectively. You are not going to do that!

Your Home Page "Billboard"

The first thing anyone sees when they reach your site is your home page, the most critical billboard for the small and medium-size business. As with a highway billboard, you have a very few seconds to get attention and move to action. Nationally known businesses and organizations with established brand recognition may get away with poor home pages—as many of them have proven. You can't afford this. So be sure to put all of the following in an easy-to-use, "click here" home page index, as shown in Figure 11.1.

Your Seven-Point Web Site Index

1.   **Home.** An immediate point-and-click way to jump from anywhere in your Web site and return to your home page.
2.   **About us.** When detailed information about your business is of interest to the buyer, put it here. But always remember that the most important word in direct marketing is "you," rather than "I."

Figure 11.1 An example home page. Note the index at the bottom right that appears somewhere on every page.

3. **Contact information.** How to reach you on-site, by phone, fax, mail, and in person. If you are not available 24 hours a day, 7 days a week, be sure to list business hours. Customers and prospects who may want to visit should be able to find a map with exact directions, including mileage and landmarks in case street or highway signs are covered with snow or lost in the fog.

4. **Feedback.** The place customers and prospects can ask questions or tell you how you are doing. Make it easy for your audience to do both.

5. **News.** Put this on your site only if you have news important to the site visitors. If it isn't worth a mention in the trade press, it probably isn't to them either.

6. **Promotions.** Promotions can be important for business-to-business commerce. For consumer sites, use something like "February Specials" or "New Shipments," or whatever is of most likely interest to the site visitor. If you're not sure, test by changing the teaser daily or weekly to see what works.

7. **Q&A.** One of the most valuable uses of your site, for you, your prospects, and customer is its ability at Q&A—to answer the most frequently asked questions without tying up customer service personnel. Invariably, most of the questions are about the same things and can be answered right there, on the site. If visitors don't find the answers they need, do not let them leave in frustration. Refer them back to Contact Information and your customer service personnel for the really tough stuff. They will like it better and so will your customers.

How to Collect Most Frequently Asked Questions

• *For established businesses.* Have everyone with customer contact keep track of product, service, and policy questions and the answers. Prepare a Q&A form employees must use and turn in each day. Assure them they are not being judged on literary ability. Give them some examples in brief outline format.

• *For new businesses.* Put in what you suspect will be the most likely questions and answers. As actual questions arrive, you can add and subtract from your list.

• *For old and new.* Limit yourself to frequently asked questions. Consider a second list of less frequently asked question. Make it a link, possibly labeled "Click here for things not covered."

No "People-less" Revolution

Do not begin your online marketing initiative in the belief that the Internet will revolutionize the way to do business. The Internet does not eliminate the need for people. Quite the opposite! To succeed on the Web, you must provide customer service, and that requires people—lots of people—who know the answers and do not make your customers feel that they are stupid for asking; you'll need workers who can answer not only on the Web but also with snailmail or e-mail, by phone, or by fax. Do not limit the way a prospect or client can get in touch with you to your Web site. That may "save" costs on phone and personnel, but you are losing more—probably much more—in business.

Learn from the old-school direct mailers and catalog sellers. They not only give their phone, e-mail, and Web addresses but many also put their phone number—usually toll-free—on *every* page. When someone wants to reach them they can, instantly. Do the same with your Web site. No matter where visitors are on your site, make the how to reach you information just a click away!

TECHNOLOGY AND MARKETING RESPONSE

The "Online" and "Catalog" Difference

When you fly anywhere in the world, you can use your computer to learn about departure times and costs, local hotels and weather, and order your ticket and reserve your room, then and there. Your prospects, customers, and clients want the same kind of help from you. No matter how sophisticated the technology, the way to Internet success is to understand and use proven marketing techniques.

Unlike TV, practically no one turns on the Internet to see what's on. Despite everything you read and hear about Internet "browsing," most people do not go online to browse, they go online to do something. They have a specific task in mind. Though they have a "browser" in hand, they do not browse as if the Net were a catalog. Be useful. Save people time. Make it easy. Make it practical. Do that, and as a by-product, you'll probably make it easier for yourself, too.

> ## INSIGHT 57
>
> For prospects and customers—especially to businesspeople—the Internet is a tool. For Internet success, rather than set up a Web site to make it easier for *you* to do business, you must set it up to make it easier for *your customers* to do business!

Finding Your Web Site Designer

One of the leading misconception about Web design, especially for smaller businesses, is to think that one must find and employ some young techno wiz to start an Internet strategy. Our advice is the exact opposite. You obviously have to understand what the technology can do, but *not* how it does it. Much more important is to find someone who understands both business and marketing. Those two are the critical issues.

Just about anyone—including you—can learn to design a basic Web sites. But do not do this yourself. There are excellent off-the-shelf Web site packages. However, should you, like most Web site owners, wish a more customized and optimized approach, many other options are available. If at all possible, use a local designer, someone you can work with on a daily basis. No matter where you live, there are people nearby hanging out their shingles as Web design firms. See what they have done. During your interview, try to make certain of the following three critical factors:

1. They come off as communicators.
2. They like people.
3. They have respect for their clients' customers and want to learn about them.

Note that we have not mentioned technology once! Today, technology is secondary. If you ask someone to do a TV commercial, you don't talk about how cameras work. You talk about creative skills and their ability to sell. Web design needs the same approach. Understanding the technology is a given. The hard part is finding the right communicators for your needs who will empathize with your audience. They must be marketers who understand basic human selling psychology. No matter what the medium, that need will never change. The selling values of hyping the benefits have remained true through the ages. They are not going to change on the Internet.

The Empathy Factor

Beyond Web site design, one of the biggest failures of much e-commerce is its inability to empathize with the audience, to be "you"-conscious rather than "us"-centered. The fact that 28 percent of online shopping attempts were thwarted during a Christmas season shows a lack of customer empathy by owners and managers who never try to place an order on their own site.[1] The same is true of buttons, and banners, and e-mail campaigns.

The Marketing Factor

Before you employ any designers, check if they are marketing conscious:

- Do they ask "What do *your customers* want, and can we work to find out?" as well as "What do *you* want?"
- Do they insist on learning about your business before they do anything else? Marketers begin with that!
- Have they ever done a Web or e-mail campaign before? How many and for whom?
- Check the sites they have done for others. If there are things that alarm you, think again. You will probably get the same. Perhaps most important, get references and check them out.

In design firms, if your designers do not understand basic business and marketing, their supervisor must have that know how. Otherwise, you will get really stupid things. They might bury your contact information. They might insist on sans serif type, though hundreds of tests have shown "reader type," such as in that used in this book, is easier to read. Then, adding insult to injury, the type might be too small to be comfortable for reading for anyone over 25 years of age. It will look beautiful, a really smashing design, but unless you are selling primarily to age-25s and younger, it will not do the job for you. In fact, even if you are selling to the younger group, you will lose the parents, who might do most of the buying.

From Web Site Designer to Web Campaign

Many advertising agencies, consultants, freelance designers, and other specialists now not only do Web designs but also promise to do whole e-campaigns. Not only will they design your site, they will place it online and negotiate your costs for preferred listing in search engines and other Internet tools. However, before you give all of this to anyone, get references of proven, *successful* experience. Then check them! Though the Web has seen a blurring of who does what, these nondesign activities require very specialized know-how.

The "No More Need for Phone Reps" Fallacy
(It's Not Always the Web Site Designer's Fault!)

Despite the caveats we have said about some Web site designers, many are not at fault for the design problems. Often, those are forced on them by a company that

---

[1]Report by the Boston Consulting Group of 1999, fourth-quarter e-shopping attempts. *DM News,* March 13, 2000.

hopes to have the Internet replace costly telemarketing sales and service. Do not make that mistake! If a prospect or customer wants to contact you by phone, fax, or e-mail, make it easy to do so. They want a live person with whom to communicate and do not want to figure out anything on the Internet alone. They may well be using the Web as a substitute for Yellow Pages and nothing more. If you do not want to drive customers to your competitors, put a "How to reach us" button on your home page, then make sure that they can!

The Internet without "Experts"?!

Although is seems all-pervasive today, it has only been a decade or so since the online revolution began to explode before us. There were only 50 sites in 1995. By 2000, there were 2 million and growing by thousands more per day. No one in those few years has become a true Web advertising expert. No one "knows" everything that works. Everyone is still learning. For instance, some experienced site designers are now convinced that people react best when given between five and nine "click here" choices on a site, as in Figure 11.1. Certain patterns are emerging, and it is important to work with people who have learned what is known so far because they can help avoid common mistakes. But what you, the business owner or manager, must insist on is that the rules of business and marketing have not changed. Without pretending hardware or software expertise, insist that basic marketing be applied to any work done for you. After all, it is your money at risk.

Guiding through Goals

To guide both your design suppliers and yourself, you must have specific goals for what each part of your Internet strategy is to accomplish. You do not have to be an Internet expert to know that in addition to being your online advertisement or catalog, your presence must achieve all four of the following:

1. Speeds announcements of special offers or opportunities to the most interested audience in a timely manner.
2. Speeds people getting in touch with you and giving them your answers.
3. Speeds communication about who you are and what you do.
4. Speeds responding to competition.

The fact that you are doing this on the Web, in addition to the old-fashioned ways, does not change *what* has to be done. Do not let anyone tell you differently.

The Need for Experimentation

Without losing sight of your marketing goals, do not hesitate to experiment with what you put on the Web. The industry is so new that everyone is still experimenting. No one, whether Microsoft, Amazon.com, or the local cigar bar has won the how-to contest. The important thing is to have specific goals that can be quantified and evaluated, whether you do it yourself or use outsource help. If you do the latter, find someone whose expectations and vision matches yours and make sure that vision stays within basic marketing fundamentals.

The Critical Importance of Testing

Whatever your site design, make provisions for testing. The beauty of Internet response is that it happens very fast. You will learn what works practically overnight. If you have a local customer universe, plan to run different tests for a week or two to see what happens. If you are a more broad-based firm, you can test changes by diverting a certain number of site visitors to a different Web page; that is, every 10th response goes to the test site and your computer tells you what response you got from each. Talk to your ISP to get details, options, and costs. Here are things you will want to learn from testing.

Six Areas for Web Site Testing

1. As we emphasize for all visual communication, the most important parts of your message are the headline (like e-mail), illustration(s), offer, and price. Your Web site is the perfect medium for testing all four!
2. Your home page illustration must reinforce your main benefit message. If not, find one that does and test it against any other. Sometimes you do better without a picture. Test!
3. Is your type too small (a frequent mistake), or perhaps too large? Try to use nothing smaller than what your computer calls 12-point size. The size you are looking at now is 11. Very large type for things other than headlines and subheads can be harder to read and may hurt response. Test!
4. Does serif type, such as you are reading here, bring better response than sans serif? Practically every newspaper, magazine, and book uses such serif faces, yet many designer prefer sans serif for its artistic quality. Don't let them! Your site's job is to communicate, not to make reading a challenge.
5. Long lines of reading matter are uncomfortable for reading. Shorter is better. When in doubt, test!
6. Experiment until you have the right "click here" labeling for your audience. Is "Q&A" better than "FAQ" (frequently asked questions)? Does it help to spell them out rather than use initials? How will you know, if you don't test?

No Design Committee, Please!

A Web site designed by committee may not be a Mars probe, but for all the difficulty in getting it approved and launched, it might as well be. After final agreement on what to send out into the Internet, the committee pulls the big red switch, sees it appear on their screen, and applauds the wonder they have wrought. All too often, there it remains, untested, because any change requires the same committee's approval, and no one wants to go through all that again. That is no way to design your site and certainly no way to keep it effective

Assigning Responsibility to Get Results

Producing an effective Web site, like putting together a successful catalog, is very hard. Things constantly change in the customers' world and yours. It is unlikely you will get everything right the 2nd or even 22nd time. Continual testing and instant application of the test results is vital to sales success, something almost impossible within the standard corporate structure and committee supervision. Every member has to prove his or her expertise by offering mutually contradictory instructions—all of which must be carried out, then anointed by management so that they can't be changed without again going through the same procedure. Rather than that, let a top marketer make the decisions. Perhaps pay him or her by results, such as the number of site visits, the number of contact requests, or the number of sales. But begin with reasonably modest goals. We are all still in the learning stage and do not know what to expect. In any case, give your marketer a big raise after a year or find someone else.

INSIGHT 58

Unlike catalog marketing, the Internet produces a response practically overnight. That is why the slower hierarchical and committee supervision of Web creation and function is an invitation to disaster. Instead, appoint your best marketer to the project and make that person responsible for agreed-on goals.

Why Testing the Message Is Not Enough

The study that showed a 28 percent failure of Web shopping attempts—customers actually trying to make a purchase—also showed that they were thwarted by something on the Web site. Here are three steps you can take to avoid that fiasco:

1. Have your Web site designers use the site to learn its efficiency and suggest improvements. Daily use is best; weekly is the minimum. Get weekly or monthly reports. Of course you will have to pay for them, but if that's not worth it, you have picked the wrong design group.
2. Use the site yourself. Have staff do it also. Get immediate reports of any problem.
3. Do not accept "hardware" as an excuse for systems failure. Although that can be the case, especially when a site becomes overwhelmed with visitors, it is unlikely to happen to a smaller business. Almost invariably, it's the design. So be a do-it-yourself design checker. "Doing business" on your Web site is no different from doing business in any other way. You won't know the problems with systems and personnel unless you use the product or service. We promise you'll be surprised, sometimes happily.

What a Good Site Is All About

In many ways, a good Web site is like the old time neighborhood butcher: He recognized you by name, knew what you liked, made sensible suggestions about what to buy, and kept you coming back as a satisfied customer. As far as your budget permits, have your Web site do the same. No matter how you feel about Amazon.com, you will be wise to order from their site at least occasionally to see all the things they do right.

- The site makes personal recommendations.
- It recognizes customers when they come back.
- Customer service is consistently top-notch.

For instance, when a customer orders more than a single copy of an item, Amazon's program asks if one is a gift. Then, if you want it shipped by them, you enter the address right there and add the message for a gift card without going back to the beginning.

All the things direct marketers learned before the Internet was developed apply even more so on the Web. If your site does not make it easy, fast, and simple, your Web visitors will leave with clicking speed. Just as much as your site needs a designer, you need the Web marketer for success.

How Online Marketing Response Differs from Direct Mail

Although direct mail experience is invaluable in its application to e-commerce, the differences are equally important. In direct mail, the results usually follow a predictable bell curve. Typically, by the fourth day of responses you expect 20 percent of the orders and plan ahead another week for the peak before responses curve down. There is time to stock up for likely winners. On the Internet, a successful promotion brings immediate response. The majority of sales come within a single day. You do not have time for anything except the filling of orders, which must, by law, be done within a very few days. Often the success or failure of your online advertising is apparent within a few hours, something direct marketers love because it gives them an immediate opportunity to fix what isn't working, then apply what does work to the next thing they do.

The Consumer Is in Control, but So Are You

Always keep in mind that e-commerce puts your consumer totally in control as never before. They can instantly go somewhere else. Though they are unlikely to "shop" through a hundred choices, they are likely to visit a few other sites because they don't have to walk or drive. The saving factor for the Internet merchant is that practically no one wants to spend hours sitting there, waiting for downloading, new instructions, and gathering merchants' information. Give them a benefit reason to go to you and stay with you by making it easy to find the products and the service they want. Do that and you are likely to keep them right there, especially for repeat visits.

Requests for More Information

Give your Web visitors a variety of "Send me more information" options. If possible, design your site to give the information online. But no matter how explicit you have made that information, make it easy for someone to ask for more. Probably the information was right there on the site, but lots of people are still more comfortable with something written, rather than on a screen. So if you don't have more than what is on the site, make a hard copy and fax or mail it with your phone number, in case they still need help.

How to Get Repeat and Add-On Sales

Whatever your business or its size, whether you lease heavy equipment to construction companies, supply popcorn to movie theaters, or are a neighborhood retailer, there are purchasing patterns you know and others only a computer record will reveal to you.

Smaller businesses as well as large can have this major advantages of e-commerce—the individual customer's sales history. It can also let you know immediately who your best customers are. If you wish, it can even be programmed to tell—from your sales patterns—the often surprising things customers and prospects are likely to appreciate knowing about in addition to what they have asked about or bought.

When limited to Web site sales, many computer programs can do this automatically. However, integrating e-commerce, telemarketing, mail, personal sales, and customer service into a customer's record and then applying all that to inventory control requires the much more sophisticated "portal" technology, such as that offered by Aspect Communications (www.aspect.com). Fortunately for smaller businesses, this formerly expensive technology is becoming more accessible and cheaper and should certainly be explored.

The Cost of Doing Internet Advertising and Business

A direct marketer's rule of thumb tells us that it costs just as much to sell by mail or phone as it costs to do it in bricks-and-mortar outlets or with an in-person sales staff. The secret of sales success has been (and still is) to use any or all of these in whatever combination works best for selling your customers.

Online marketing is sometimes is the only good way to advertise and sell. More often, it as one of several media to be tested and used as long as they are cost-effective. But in most cases, Internet marketing will not be a cost saver. As more people are learning every day, whatever online marketing saves on handling paper work, the costs for media charges and people usually equal the savings. Learning how to use Internet advertising as all or part of your marketing mix reinforces four more of direct marketing's oldest rules of thumb:

1. You "know" nothing until you test.
2. Keep meticulous records.
3. Believe the numbers, but know what the numbers mean.
4. Act on what you learn

No "Friction-Free" Commerce

Many would-be entrepreneurs entered Internet marketing because they believed that the Net provided "friction-free commerce," that it was a medium where the customer would do most of the work to find the seller, rather than the opposite. In a few cases that has proven to be true, as witness the loss of business for travel agents. But as the number of Web sites increase literally by the thousands per day, making yourself known as a small to medium-size enterprise demands more than the Web. It needs all the tools listed at the beginning of Chapter 5 and a few more we will cover shortly.

No "People-less" Revolution

People are social beings. Many enjoy shopping where there are other people and the Internet is not going to take them away to sit at home or in an office in front of a computer screen. For most businesses and manufacturers, it is a valuable additional way of doing business and getting that extra sale. Certainly the biggest share of retail is still—and will continue to be—the bricks-and-mortar establishment, even as much of it adds a "brick and click" component. The Internet is not the death knell of retailing, telemarketing, or direct mail. That is not going to change!

Will Internet-Only Commerce Survive?

As we write in 2002, some analysts predict that few Internet-only firms are going to survive. We doubt that is true. By and large, they are operated by a very smart group of men and women who will learn how to make the transition from use of the Internet as their only marketing tool to its use as one of several. If not, perhaps they can gain new wisdom from our book and start again.

Alternatives to Getting Your Own Web Site

If you do not want to go through all the design and business needs of establishing your own Web site, there are numerous alternative. Many established, reputable concerns have templates for you to use and most basic small business needs figured out so you can have an Internet presence. You won't have your own URL, but with an address such as Amazon.com or Yahoo/store/*your name,* as opposed to www.*your name.*com, you may gain credibility rather than losing identity. An even simpler option is Yahoostore.com. For a small charge, you can put a certain number of products in this "Web store" to be on a Web site without putting it up yourself.

Finding the Right Web Site for You to Advertise

As in other forms of advertising, ask those in related businesses or professions about their experience. Your direct competitors may not wish to tell you or give you helpful information, but you can check their Web sites and ask their ISPs how long they have been advertising and what format they have been using. Most media sales representatives sell by pointing to related businesses/professions/ services using their medium, so you are not asking for forbidden knowledge. "We really like the Blank Blanket Bundles site and we're thinking of doing something like that. Can you tell me how long they've been on and what formats they're using?" If you are not a direct competitor—and sometimes even if you are—you'll probably get the information.

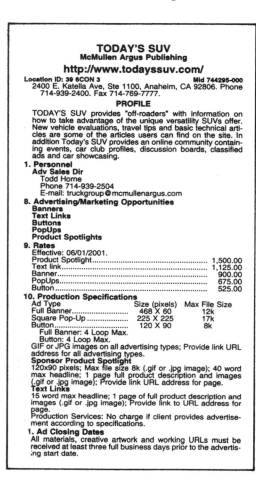

Figure 11.2   SRDS listing for SUV fanciers (left) and SRDS reports on outdoor services (right).

Industrywide Information

For industrywide information, the *Interactive Advertising Source,* one of the many SRDS guides listed on page 51, gives detailed information on thousands of Web sites that accept advertising. As you can see in Figure 11.2, some offer opportunities available nowhere else, while others have sites you can compare to print, radio, and TV media. If unfamiliar with Internet advertising, its terminology, opportunities, contacts, or costs (many of which are negotiable), this is the place to start.

The Need to Find the Right Bank for Credit Sales

If you are a small business offering credit sales, you may want a third party to manage the financial aspects of online sales for you. Many banks have a working relationship with ISPs to handle this, have knowledgeable legal help, and include programs to detect attempted frauds and other scams. A bank offering e-commerce credit service is more likely to spot fraud attempts on Internet and telephone sales. Find out if your current bank can handle those transactions and give advice. If not, ask your ISP to recommend one. Some banks even have Web design services. Of course, there are costs involved, but as we have said before, most often the Internet is not a cheaper way of doing business, it's just a different way.

As of October 2002, some major credit card companies guarantee payment of Internet sales. Check with them to see if restrictions apply.

SUMMARY

Four Small Business Advantages

INSIGHT 59

In the land of infinite online shopping choices, the best advantage and best hope for small business success is to become both the most trusted resource as well as the one with which it is easiest to do busines.

---

1. You can—and must—be the most customer-focused: from your advertising, through your sales, to your customer service.
2. You do not necessarily have to offer the best price as long as it is within reason.
3. You can—and must—be the one that is most reliable in having the product or service the customer wants, that keep your promises about delivery, and has a computer system that makes it easy to purchase!
4. You can make immediate decisions. Whatever your computer tells you about your online customer activity, you can do something about it without having to go through channels. Do it!

Setting Your Strategy

People do not go online to see what is on. They have a specific purpose in mind, whether it be chatting, shopping, or information gathering. Your entire goal—while setting your e-mail and Web strategy—is to find and work with persons who understand your needs. You and they must always keep in mind that you want people to think about your company *before* they turn to their computer. You want to be the reason they turn it on. Here, too, there are no new "how-to" discoveries. You do it with the same old way, by giving people a benefit valuable enough to take them to your Web site.

Instead of thinking of e-mail as "here is how I can do things more cheaply," think of it as "here is how I can show my best customers how much I appreciate their business by offering them benefits no one else gets." In addition, and this is a difficult leap for entrepreneurs to make, you need to think of not selling occasionally. For instance, if you are a manufacturer of safety signs required by OSHA, use e-mail to keep those customers up to the moment on local, state, and federal regulations. Make sure you have the right e-mail address for those who need the data.

Offer the information on your Web site to noncustomers, too. In business-to-business applications you can help people who are swamped with data by pointing out what really matters and let them know where to find the details. Use it for industry convention updates. Warn them of pending price changes if they are going to increase. Surprise them with the good news if prices go down.

Make Your Goals Reachable

Set goals reachable for your business and your budget. Certainly you want an Internet presence. It will answer frequently asked questions so you can reduce—not eliminate—phone time. It should add some incremental sales. Properly installed and used, it can cut order processing costs from dollars to pennies.

Using e-mail lets you serve customers with computers even better by giving them special treatment, such as a note from you—one more personal than direct mail. As the company president, you can communicate individually with your best customers and make them feel the way they should feel—special! They are the people who pay your bills, pay your mortgage, maybe pay for a pool in your back yard, and should be treated as such.

Be Easy to Find

Make sure you are easy to find. You want a Web address that differentiates you from others. But be very careful of what careless customer spelling can do, as Publicsports learned from irate (and a few grateful) customers. Some X-rated and soft-core sites chose names that are frequent misspellings of the most popular Web addresses.

NOTES ON THE BASIC INTERNET ADVERTISING CHECKLIST

These notes are a supplement to the material presented in this chapter. They are not a self-contained substitute for that material. The checklist appears in Figure 11.3.

E-mail Things to Do

1. **Written plan.** Have a *written* plan that begins with what you expect to achieve, then lists, step by step, how you are going to achieve it, including staffing and costs. Remember: Everything costs more than it costs and takes longer than it takes!

INSIGHT 60

Nothing focuses the mind like putting a plan in writing.

---

2. **Prospects/customers.** List, in *writing,* the reasons your customers and/or prospects want to hear from you—by e-mail. Make a separate list that tells how you know. No fair beginning with, "I won't know until I try."

BASIC INTERNET ADVERTISING CHECKLIST

Project Title _____   Date _____
Project Description _____   Project # _____
_____   Checklist # _____
Overall Supervision By _____   Deadline _____
Budget _____   Completion Date _____   Start Up Date _____

E-MAIL THINGS TO DO	ASSIGNED TO	DUE	IN	MUST APPROVE	BY DATE	IN	INFO COPY ONLY	SEE ATTACHED
1. Written Plan	_____	___	☐	_____	___	☐	_____	☐
2. Prospects/Customers	_____	___	☐	_____	___	☐	_____	☐
3. Address Collection	_____	___	☐	_____	___	☐	_____	☐
4. Type of List(s)	_____	___	☐	_____	___	☐	_____	☐
5. List Coding	_____	___	☐	_____	___	☐	_____	☐
6. Customer Service e-mail	_____	___	☐	_____	___	☐	_____	☐
7. Front Line Staff	_____	___	☐	_____	___	☐	_____	☐
8. Staff Job Fears	_____	___	☐	_____	___	☐	_____	☐

INTERNET THINGS TO DO								
9. Written Plan	_____	___	☐	_____	___	☐	_____	☐
10. Web Marketing Supervisor	_____	___	☐	_____	___	☐	_____	☐
11. Staff Addition/Training	_____	___	☐	_____	___	☐	_____	☐
12. Web Designer Interviews	_____	___	☐	_____	___	☐	_____	☐
13. Website Test Plan	_____	___	☐	_____	___	☐	_____	☐
14. Internet Advertising	_____	___	☐	_____	___	☐	_____	☐
15. Banking Partner	_____	___	☐	_____	___	☐	_____	☐

© 2003, Fred Hahn

Figure 11.3   The basic internet advertising checklist.

3. **Address collection.** What will systematically permit the collection of e-mail addresses of value to you, and even more important, to those receiving your messages? The key word here is *permit.*

4. **Type of list(s).** Will you begin with a with a single list and, as it grows, divide it into special interests later? How many special interests are likely? Do they have enough in common to make a single-page message work for all?

5. **List coding.** Assume you want to have specialized lists from the beginning. Can you code them in a way that is practical for your e-mail system to personalize and for you to retrieve any or all? Who is going to do all this?

6. **Customer service e-mail.** Check Chapter 9 about the transformation of telemarketing to teleservicing. The same is true of e-mail and other Internet communication. Often it's what changes buyers into long-term customers.

7. **Front line staff.** Front line, the staff that has direct contact with your customers and prospects, need help not only in learning their e-mail functions but in wanting to do them well. Include incentives to do both from the very beginning.

8. **Staff job fears.** Be realistic about job loss fears. Explain that the e-mail effort is part of advertising/marketing and not a plan to cut other jobs. It helps if this is true.

Internet Things to Do

9. **Written plan.** Whether expanding from e-mail or starting with full use of the Internet, begin with a *written* plan. List your goals, then outline how you'll reach them. Put time and dollars for every step. Most businesses do not make money on the Internet, so be sure why you're there.

10. **Web marketing supervisor.** If you're thinking of doing this yourself, who will do the rest of your job?

11. **Staff addition/training.** Train your staff—especially if it's yourself—well in advance. You won't turn prospects into customers or customers into buyers by rewarding them with Web site use frustration or unhelpful customer services responses.

12. **Web designer interviews.** Verify your prospective Web designer's credentials two ways. Speak with the clients for whom he or she has worked. Even more important, *use* the Web site(s) he or she produced. Some clients are satisfied with less than you need.

13. **Web site test plan.** Before design begins, insist that testing be built in as an ongoing part of your site. So learn what is possible—and practical—for you. Hire a consultant, if necessary. Consultants get paid in advance, so check those credentials the same way!

14. **Internet advertising.** In all probability, there are Web sites, often by the dozen, whose users specialize exactly in what you have to offer. Test advertising there to see who'll switch over to you and then apply what you learn to improving your own site.

15. **Banking partner.** Leave Web site billing and collection for comparatively low-cost goods or services to someone else. Find a bank that specializes in this. Use it. Its fee will be less that becoming your own collection agency. (But just in case, get a *complete* fee schedule, in *writing.*)

12 | Publicity and Public Relations

This chapter has been revised and updated with the assistance of **Kelly Hughes,** president of DeChant/Hughes, Inc. This leading Midwest agency specializing in publicity and public relations for the publishing industry can be contacted at (312) 280–8126.

This chapter aims at helping you generate and disseminate good public relations (PR) for yourself and counteracting any bad PR you may receive. It does not cover the generation of bad publicity about your competitors or opponents—whether they deserve it or not.

INSIGHT 61

Media wastepaper baskets are filled with PR from sources that equate "free" with "too cheap to invest in doing right." Publicity and public relations are *not* "free"! The effort, knowledge, skill, experience, time, and budget needed to prepare effective PR are every bit as great as required for paid advertising. To get such PR, management must understand this and commit the resources that make it possible, because without those resources and that commitment, it won't get it.

Throughout this chapter, certain words and phrases are used repeatedly. Their definitions, as given here, will usually be assumed by your audience. However, it is always safer to confirm such an understanding, rather than take it for granted. Point out that "there are so many ways I've heard (fill in the appropriate term here) used lately, that I'd feel a lot safer if we agreed on a definition in advance." Doing this will save endless grief, without forcing anyone to admit to ignorance.[1]

PR: Abbreviation for "public relations." "Publicity" is generally understood to be part of the total public relations function.

---

[1]Do not confuse "ignorance" with "stupidity." Ignorance means we don't know something . . . yet. Stupidity means we're too dumb to learn it . . . ever.

Medium (plural, media): Any method of communication for getting PR made public. Newspapers, radio talk shows, TV, the Internet, and word-of-mouth are all media.

The press: Newspaper and magazine reporters and feature writers; sometimes, depending on the context, the term includes radio and television reporters also.

Electronic media: Radio and television. Sometimes the Internet.

Print media: Newspapers, magazines, and newsletters.

Published: Made public by print media. Sometimes the Internet.

Broadcast: Made public by electronic media.

Aired: A synonym for "broadcast."

INSIGHT 62

For internal communication, don't fight about what something's called, only about what it is to accomplish and how to get it done. For external communication, you must use generally accepted nomenclature to get across what you wish to communicate.

ABOUT PR ON THE INTERNET

Little PR material is picked up by traditional media from the Internet. Specific Web sites are quite effective in forming single-issue groups to contact legislators or suggest other types of combined action. But the media that are the targets of "business" PR rely on known or trusted sources rather than searching a screen for messages of unknown origin and validity. This is *not* to imply that any of the Internet material lacks validity. It *is* to tell you that PR media expect *you* to do the work. Get the message to them; don't expect them to hunt in the Web for ways to publicize you!

PUBLICITY AND PUBLIC RELATIONS

How They Differ and Why It Matters

PR professionals can and do write and speak endlessly about the differences between publicity and public relations. But, for our purposes, an arbitrary distinction is appropriate.

Publicity: Do good and let the world know. A good product, good cause, good film, or good deed all meet this criterion.

Public relations: Limit harm when it strikes and, where possible, neutralize harm or turn it into good.

This chapter has three goals that relate to these definitions:

1. To help you formulate publicity and public relations procedures agreed upon by every level of management.

2. To guide you in doing your own publicity.
3. To urge you to use professional help—from internal or external resources—in major publicity campaigns and in all public relations.

Your Relationship with the Press

The press and electronic news media are in the business of presenting news and otherwise useful information, not of giving favorable free coverage to whoever requests it. The best way to establish an excellent relationship with the print and electronic press is to make yourself a resource for news and to present your stories or story ideas to them in a "news" or "feature" context. How to do this is shown in the pages that follow. Of course, the more news or features you provide to the press, the more valuable you will become, and the more likely it will be that even your lesser stories will get favorable attention. You may even become a source that the press will contact for interesting filler materials when the "hard" news is "light" (sparse).[2] Much more important, you will want the press to know you as a reachable and especially *honest* source of fact and opinion about your organization. That's an invaluable reputation to have earned when raw news, without interpretation, can be harmful to your interests. The opportunity to present your side, in context, when a story *first* appears, is immeasurably more valuable than a dozen after-the-fact correctives (as targets of "dirty politics" have learned to their sorrow).

An Opportunity

Downsizing of in-house news staff at practically every medium makes news- and feature-worthy PR more welcome than ever. But the old rule still applies: The more professional the PR, the more likely its acceptance. Fit the presentation to the standards of the media. Don't expect them to do lots of work to fix it when it's so easy to leave it out.

Be a Pro!

There is absolutely nothing wrong with having your relationship with the media on a personal, first-name basis . . . *provided that it also remains on a professional level.* That media people respect and believe you is much more important than that they like you, although it certainly helps if they do both.

Deciding Who's in Charge

Whether publicity and public relations are assigned to the advertising department or to a separate public relations department depends on both the workload and the experience and PR expertise the departments have. Advertising involves compara-

---

[2]There are many columnists and feature writers whose coverage is as important as news is to companies and organizations. These writers and electronic commentators live on a constant supply of publicity-type information. It takes a long while to build this type of relationship, but once established, it becomes a very nice bonus for both sides.

tively little direct contact with reporters, on-air personnel, or editorial staffs. As an advertiser, your contact is more likely to be with a sales representative. Your advertising concern is *where* and *when* the advertisement is placed—in which section and on what page of the newspaper or magazine it appears and at what time and in which segment of a series of commercials it runs. You're paying, and your fiddle calls the tune. The ad will appear exactly as agreed on.

Publicity and public relations operate under quite different rules. Unlike paid-for advertising, their goal is favorable coverage by media without payment for space or time. The PR/publicity purpose is threefold. Deciding who will be in charge must be based on who can accomplish all three purposes:

1. Favorable public notice for what you *do* want publicized.
2. The opportunity to present your point of view on what would otherwise be presented only in a negative fashion. Your hope is to neutralize, in whole or in part, the *approach* to a story, not the story itself.
3. The ability to get instant public notice for certain kinds of news, no matter what the negative consequences to your organization. Tampering with products in a way that may endanger the lives of buyers is a familiar example for which you would want such instant public notice.

SUMMARY

- Your best chance to get published or to get air time is to give the media *news*.
- Your best chance to get trusted is to give the media *truth*.
- The best person to handle publicity and PR is the one who can best do both of these, unhindered by persons or departments who do not understand the preceding two points.

THE NEED FOR AGREED-ON PR PROCEDURES

As the PR person charged with spreading the news, you'll likely get more help than you really want. Everyone wants to spread good news and be the first to pass off blame for the bad. Where news is widely known or suspected, both of these are bound to happen. Here's an example from my own experience. When I was a young account executive for a public relations agency, I learned from a client's infuriated PR director that it was not *my* job to reveal the agency's new publicity campaign to the company president whom I happened to meet in the hallway, thereby depriving the director of her moment of glory. Fortunately, my apologetic realization that inexperience doesn't excuse stupidity saved the account.

I never repeated the error, but it's probably impossible to get that kind of self-discipline from nonadministrative employees. They'll spread your news, good and bad, and any attempt to stop them may well be counterproductive. After all, why would you want to hide the story of *their* success and *your* failure? Are you trying to steal all the credit or shift all the blame?

Is It Really a Problem?

The problem with having your news become published through unofficial, word-of-mouth sources is that even when it's reported accurately, you are unlikely to gain the full advantages good news can generate. While bad news can expect ongoing and practically unlimited attention, good news most often gets only a single mention, unless the press is given specific reasons for continuing its coverage. A manufacturing contract presented without an interesting explanation of its civic and human advantages will likely appear on page 37 of the newspaper; a lawsuit will surely be featured on page 1. You may not be able to change that placement, but your PR efforts should get either story to reflect your point of view. The rest of this chapter is a guide both to doing just that yourself and to recognizing whether the PR work done for you by others is likely to get the results you want.

Convincing Management

The first impulse of most people contacted by the media is to feel so important that they tell more than they know. The second impulse is to be so fearful of saying something wrong as to say nothing at all. An agreed-on, *written guide to media contacts* will guard against both of these extremes.

Because reporters usually try to contact the more senior personnel in an organization, management, too, must agree to follow your procedures for them to do their jobs. Here, as in just about every other aspect of organizational life, senior management sets the tone. If the CEO not only signs off on your plan but actually follows it thereafter, your organization's media problems will be simplified. Since the majority of CEOs reached their position by recognizing the obvious, getting their agreement should present little difficulty. Here's the agreement:

1. **Designate an official spokesperson for PR.** This has the advantage of letting everyone else point to one person as having *all* the facts when, in fact, some of the facts are still in doubt. This becomes especially important when questions contain totally new "information" to which you are asked to react. "(Name) is going to find that out and get back to you immediately" is a perfectly acceptable answer, whether from the president of the United States or the vice president of the local garden society. If your spokesperson is not a well-grounded PR pro, put him or her through a media rehearsal run by professionals and with video playback. Many PR agencies will do this on a fee basis. *Always* do this before known TV or other major coverage. Make your blunders during rehearsal, not during interviews or on the air!

2. **Preplan whenever possible.** Good news is seldom a total surprise—although it may sometimes not be equally good for everyone concerned. "How to Maximize Good News," a few pages on, alerts you to some of the problems, as well as the opportunities, that good news offers. Whether such problems exist or not, discuss your story options at the senior level, and then put the approved approaches *in writing.* Note that what you are putting on paper is *not* "how we can fool our audience into thinking we're better than we are." It *is* "the very real benefits our audience will gain from this event." Make your media guide something you'd feel comfortable about having "leaked" to the press, and structure it accordingly.

3. **When good news does come as a total surprise.** Occasionally, good news does come as a total surprise. A telephone call from a reporter will ask your reaction to something almost too good to be true—as quite often it is. Be honest. Tell the reporter that it's the first you've heard of the event, that you want to double-check to get all the details, and that the reporter will be the very first to get your reaction the moment the news is confirmed. Now check the facts. If the story is true, put your media plan into place exactly as if the story were preplanned, and then contact the reporter who broke it to you. If it is untrue, report that even faster. When it comes to *pleasant* surprises, there is nothing wrong with telling the media that you need some time to check out all the great ramifications. But when it is only a myth, do your best to stop it before it can raise expectations that won't be met.

4. **When bad news strikes.** Where possible, leave the handling of bad news to the professionals. When that proves impossible, do as they would. Whether the event is preplanned, such as a reduction in the workforce, or totally unexpected, such as a fire or explosion, the possible legal as well as PR consequences are not for off-the-cuff handling. If management is asked to comment before a PR plan is in place, ask what the media's deadline is and promise to get back to them before then. Whatever that deadline is, keep it! Emphasize that you are trying to get at the facts. Until you do, uninformed comments might mislead the public and unnecessarily jeopardize your organization. Getting the help you need is covered in this chapter.

SUMMARY

- Designate an official PR spokesperson.
- Preplan your media approach whenever your news, good or bad, can be predicted . . . and then follow the plan.
- When good news is a pleasant surprise, admit the fact . . . but check it before you comment.
- Bad news may have unsuspected negative consequences. Leave the handling of bad news to professionals, unless you really have the experience, qualifications, and authority to respond for your organization.

INSIGHT 63

In announcing what you consider good news, be alert to the possibility that it may be less than welcome to some part of your audience. Your news should be worded with that fact very much in mind!

HOW TO MAXIMIZE GOOD NEWS

1. List every audience to whom news about your company or organization may be of interest. Be sure to include the specialized interest groups or "publics" you wish to influence or inform.

2. Imagine yourself in the place of each group that, on hearing your news, asks, "What's in it for *me?*" Try to make your news into a benefit specific to that group, especially if the group's first reaction may be more negative than you would wish. The chances are that by practicing this type of empathy, you not only will foresee the negatives but also will be able to translate them into something positive. *Do not, under any circumstances, lie!* In almost every instance, you will be found out, with consequences more dire than those you face for telling an unwelcome truth.

INSIGHT 64

It is extraordinarily difficult for any person or group to think beyond self-interest. Nevertheless, this is the job of the PR person: to get the company or organization to think that way and to tailor the message to the *media's* needs and interests. Management is no better, or worse, about this than employees; the writers of news than its readers. PR has the challenge of understanding and satisfying them all.

---

3. After deciding how each of your interest groups is likely to react to your news, you can draw some reasonable conclusions to guide further action. Here are some points you'll want to consider:

- **Should there be any official notice at all?** Your news can be announced by a media release, a news conference, or some other official notice. Or it may simply be permitted to happen. Many—probably most—events aren't worth the time and effort needed to make them into a story that's likely to get published. So concentrate on your best bets—the ones that affect the most people or that concern your audience in a very direct way.

- **Who tells your employees?** Decide how, by whom, and to whom to spread the news. Anything that benefits employees should be told to them at the earliest possible moment. To avoid distortion, put it in writing. Place it on bulletin boards and mail it to their homes. You want good news shared with the entire family, to help build goodwill toward the employer.

INSIGHT 65

Make the immediate supervisor the first spreader of good news. Resist the temptation so prevalent in politics to have everything good come from the top and everything unpleasant from below. Use the "Army system." The same sergeant who had us dig the latrine also gave us a weekend pass!

- **What to do when it affects the community.** When your news will have a positive impact on the community (whether it's the neighborhood or the whole state), share that fact *in advance* with the political leadership. Invite the politicos to share in the goodwill the news can generate. If it is important enough, suggest a joint news conference for the announcement. If you're not experienced at gathering the media, they are! Be sure to have a news or media release (see next section) ready for the event. Just as in communicating with your employees, you want to make certain the story reflects your point of view.

If the political leadership is otherwise occupied, find out whether you can gather the press on your own. Offer a personal interview, but don't be hurt if the press doesn't desire it.

Just because a very limited news staff can't pay a personal visit does not mean that your story will be ignored. Get it to them in some other way. Mail and messenger are always welcome. Don't, however, fax or e-mail without making sure that this method is equally well received. Your attorney and accountant will give you the legal requirements concerning what you *must* tell. Your publicity/PR director will tell you what you *should* tell in addition and how to do it.

- **Investors love good news. Give it to them!** If you are a large enough organization to issue public stock or bonds, you are large enough to use professional help for your communication. Smaller organizations, whether financed by family, financial institutions, or venture capitalists, will want to keep their investors informed, too. As with the giants, the advice, consent, and continuing support of these investors largely depends on what *you* tell them. But their wrath at being misled is likely to be even more fierce than that of the public investment community. In financial matters, while the truth may not make you free, the untruth may well send you to prison. Unlike our possible amusement at the politicians' spin control, your investors insistence on financial veracity is likely to be unforgiving and with a very long, very accurate memory!

SUMMARY

- Aim your news to influence a specific audience.
- Put yourself in the place of that audience, and consider how your news will be received. If the answer isn't "Great!" why are you sending it?
- Let your employees know when good news happens. The rumors they hear are usually the opposite.
- Let the political leadership share in your goodwill. You need them even more than they need you.
- Keep your investors informed. Be happy when you can share good news with them and prompt to tell them the bad. Reluctance to share any financial data is a dangerous stance!

THE MEDIA RELEASE OR NEWS ADVISORY

A media release is a story that you (a) hope will be newsworthy or otherwise worthy of attention and (b) want to make public. Notice that being newsworthy is the more important criterion. In most instances, print and electronic media get many more stories than they can use. The importance and interest of each story *to the medium's particular audience* will largely decide what gets published or aired. That's why the news must be in the very first paragraph, reinforced and emphasized by a suggested headline.

What Not to Do

Do not begin your release with something like "President Jane Jones of Acme Motors announces . . ." A great many releases do begin that way because so many companies and organizations think that *that's* the "news" or the most important words. *The media* never begin *any* story that way—unless it's with the words "President Bush announced . . ."

INSIGHT 66

News media are swamped with requests for coverage. They don't have the time nor personnel to study long press releases to discover whether each one truly contains some news. So put the heart of your news into the first paragraph, preferably into the very first sentence. If you don't catch them there, you're unlikely to keep them looking.

The news advisory or release (Figure 12.1) is the basic tool in your publicity campaign. It's also a tool you should have no difficulty in learning how to use. By way of example, let's create a release about the same senior citizen bicycle invented in the chapter on advertising:

22 Ways to Get Your Story Printed

There are 22 points highlighted in this story:

1. Make your corporate or association identification clear. Many of us are so used to identifying ourselves with divisions or departments, that we forget the publicity power of our parent organization.

2. "NEWS" is what your recipients want. Promise it with the largest type on the page. Use "Media News Release" when including electronic media.

3. No one wants to publish old news, so make the date of your release absolutely current. If the same release is used for more than a single day, fill in the dates as they are used.

Use word processor–style type for the entire release. Double-space! Make sure that it's a typeface you can match for filling in the date and the recipient's name if your releases are preprinted before being personalized.

E-Z-Ryder Bike Factory * 123 East Fourth * Wakenaw, KY (1)

NEWS RELEASE (2)

March 22, 199x (3)
To
Charles Smith (4)
Sports Editor
Wakenaw Daily Bugle

For additional information, contact (5)
Jeanette Miranda O'Keefe
Information Director
E-Z Ryder
789-001-0002

Release date: FOR IMMEDIATE RELEASE (6)

**New bike for seniors hailed by
50-plus test riders (7)**

Warrensville, KY. (8) Twenty-nine volunteers, ranging in age from 50 to 81, today test drove the new E-Z Ryder bicycles especially designed for seniors to give them more mobility for both entertainment and basic transportation. While only 5 said that they currently use bicycles regularly, 27 said that they might do so in the future because of the **E-Z Ryder's special features**. (9)

"I drove the bike around town for over an hour," reported the most senior of the group, retired Warrensville fireman Chuck Quinzley. (10) "I don't know how they made it so easy," he said, "but that's the most biking I've done all at once in the past 10 years."

Ladies version pleases, too (11)
The 11 women test drivers, who were not asked to volunteer their ages, (12) were equally pleased with their bikes. "They must have done something special with the gears to make riding this easy," suggested former science teacher Mrs. Lisa Spengler. (13)
"I think it made all of us feel a lot younger to be biking around town just like the high schoolers I used to teach."

New patent to Ryder Company (14)
"Mrs. Spengler is absolutely correct," said Edwyn Ryder, President of E-Z-Ryder, (15) when told about her remark. "The gears have just been granted a patent, and we're going to tool up for a major increase in production right here in Warrensville, (16) though that won't be ready for about another year. (17) Right now, we're going to sponsor some Sensible Junior/Senior Cycling races in which you have to be over 50 or under 15 to compete. (18) Not only are we going to let us seniors (19) feel like kids again," concluded Ryder with a laugh, "we're going to beat them at their own game!"

-30- (20)

Photograph herewith. (21)

Broadcast-quality video available. (22)
Contact J. O'Keefe for details.

Figure 12.1 Example of professional-style press release with the 22 reasons that make it work.

4. There is nothing more direct and personal than an individual's name and title, even when the recipient knows that it's all done by computer. You will, of course, have identified the most likely sources for publication through personal contacts or phone conversations. If you're not sure whom to address in larger news organizations, ask the editor most likely to be in charge. (We'll tell how to find them, shortly.) Not only will you get a name, but you may also interest the editor!

5. Give your recipients a specific person to contact, if possible with a phone number that cuts through the growing computerized switchboard maze. You're hoping for free in-print and on-air publicity, so don't make contacting you a challenge. Your recipients may not have the time or patience to be so challenged.

6. Your story will usually be held—that is, not published or aired—until the date specified by you. (There are occasional violations of hold dates when the news is "hot" enough.) Most stories are distributed "for immediate release." Others have specific release dates, usually to give weekly or monthly publications the chance to break the news at the same time as the daily media. This is especially important when a key writer won't mention your story once it has appeared elsewhere.

In some media, specific individuals are so widely read that they won't consider a story, unless it's given to them before anyone else. When such an "exclusive" is offered, be sure to give it a time limit. Rather than "for immediate release," indicate something like "Exclusive for (name) to (date)." Indicate release after the specified date on all other copies. An exclusive is valuable and should get you a bit more than routine attention in return.

7. Your headline will help determine the kind of attention each medium gives to your story. In this example, we've given the story a human interest rather than a business emphasis. When used, such emphasis should be a well-thought-out part of your overall plan. Note that you can supply several stories with different emphases as part of a media kit and then add another story that summarizes all of them. Add a contents page, and not only will the media be grateful, but you're less likely to omit something.

8. This tells where the story takes place, not necessarily where it was written. When a particular local context is important, tell the story from that point of view. A Kansas wheat grower teaching Eastern Europeans how to use an Illinois-built combine typifies both the challenges and opportunities PR faces every day.

9. Note how packed with information the first paragraph is. Make *your* first paragraph tell the story in such a way that if nothing else is published, you will still have made your main point. You'll be happy to find that many releases are printed in their entirety, exactly as they are written, especially by smaller publications with limited editorial and rewriting staffs. But most media will use only a portion of the release. Under the "all the news that fits" rule, stories are written to be cut (shortened) from back to front, so load the beginning. Readers, too, pay more attention to initial paragraphs. Whether they are consciously aware of it or not,

they know that scanning just the headlines and first paragraphs will give them the overview that determines whether reading more is worth their time.

Everything after the first paragraph is an expansion on what's just been read. It's our job to make this material so enticing or important that the reader can't resist learning more.

INSIGHT 67

In writing the first paragraph of a news story or feature item, picture an individual whom you most want to inform or influence. Within the format of the media that will get your release, write the initial paragraph so *that* individual will want to know more. Relate your story or feature to the specific interests, wants, and needs of that special reader and you will also capture the much broader audience for whom you are looking. You may hope that what you write will be read (or heard or seen) by vast numbers of groups, but groups don't read—individuals do. You'll succeed when you make it worth the while of each separate reader.

---

10. Take the story from the abstract to the personal as soon as possible. Chuck is someone to whom readers, as well as a radio or television audience, can relate. And note how he gives the product a believable testimonial, a fact that will be reinforced a bit later in the story. Remember that you are writing *news,* not advertising. Keep the plugs for the product soft sell!

11. Your headline and subheads serve two purposes:
   • To "highlight" the main points of your story
   • To let the readers spot their own specific interests. No one has time to read everything. Use subheads to make it easy for readers with different interests to find the parts of the story that are important to them.

12. Beware of sexism. Beware doubly of humor. That the female test drivers were not asked to reveal their age may bring a chuckle to some readers, but it would be resented and found not at all funny by many women. It's placed here as a warning of things to avoid, rather than to include. Attempts at humor, unless quoted or put into a totally humorous context, are best left to the professionals.

13. Featuring women and minority groups in a positive manner is permitted and often encouraged. (Be careful, however, not to create resentment by appearing condescending—"Why do you have to point out that *we're* just as good as others?") A photograph usually works well in this regard. Provide a picture that shows the science teacher and gear-guru as African American or Hispanic and you've made your point—without saying a word. Religious affiliations, unless absolutely required by the story, are best left unmentioned.

14. This subhead and the text that follows could easily have been the major focus of the story. They are put here to show how a subhead can signal a change in the direc-

tion of the story, even as it downplays the content that follows, by placing it last. It's a handy device for forestalling wild rumors through your own official version.

15. The introduction of the senior corporate officer's testimony signals a change to a more serious emphasis.

16. Note the calming of fears about a possible negative local impact, placed here to minimize the likelihood of such fears. The president *immediately* answers the universal questions, "What's in it—positive or negative—for me?"

17. When promising good things for the future, leave some flexibility as to specific dates. "About another year" is a good deal safer than "One year from today." Notice also that this statement invites an ongoing series of progress reports, with continuing interest and excitement for everyone involved.

18. The story can stop after the previous sentence or continue with a return to the lighter tone with which it began. The media using the story will make that decision.

19. Ryder's identification of himself as a fellow senior—the group to which the major headline is addressed—is an effective way of returning the story to the human interest tone with which it began. It is generally better to maintain one tone throughout a story. However, if, as in this story, you do switch, it is best to return to the tone with which you began, very much as in a symphony or sonata, where the opening and concluding themes most frequently echo each other and a middle section is given more freedom to wander—though not to get lost.

20. The notation "-30-" is a standard way of showing the conclusion of a story and signals that the writer is in the know about even the trivia of his or her craft.

21. When including a photograph with your release, it may be in color or in black and white. The important things are its degree of contrast and its degree of detail. A photograph or other illustration that you hope to have shown in color must, of course, be that way in the original. Standard size for the originals is 8 inches by 10 inches, a format photographic duplication services are set up to handle economically. When ordering duplicates, note that it is customary to give the horizontal size first. Make sure that here, as elsewhere, you and your suppliers are speaking the same language.

When sending photos, have a suggested caption on a regular sheet of paper, and tape that sheet to the back of the photo. Have the caption include the name of the product! Be sure that both the caption and the illustration can be seen at the same time, as shown in Figure 12.2. For shipping, fold the caption over the photograph.

22. Consider the creation of television-quality video only if TV coverage seems assured and worth the considerable investment. You may, of course, gain even more important advantages from your video in financial, zoning, and other face-to-face presentations. A more detailed discussion of electronic media is presented in Chapter 13.

Fold over like this
before mailing.

Your caption here.

Figure 12.2   Captioning a photo. Tape the caption to the back of your photograph. Make sure the message and picture can both be seen at the same time. (Photo by Shellie Rounds.)

MEDIA KITS

A media kit (see Figures 12.3 and 12.4) is a package of materials that both includes and expands on your news release. It *may* contain an expanded news story or feature article. It *will* contain photographs, charts, and other pertinent illustrative materials for print media. Less often, it also holds audio and video materials for radio and television. It may contain a variety of background materials about your organization, including human interest stories about the people you want mentioned.

INSIGHT 68

Do not load your media kit just to impress the media with the importance of the sender.[3] More likely, you'll simply try the patience of the recipient. Check for and take out material that duplicates anything else or that is not essentially tied to the story. Your problem, as always, is to get attention and interest, so make the kit complete but concise. The media will contact you for more background when they do a story that needs it.

HOW TO GAIN LOCAL COVERAGE

For the majority of us, gaining truly national attention, through, for example, an article in *Business Week,* the *Wall Street Journal,* or *Time,* is unlikely. But don't despair. Send your *major* news releases to them anyway. They may surprise you! More likely coverage, however, lies in your local media—including major cities' neighborhood newspapers—*INC.* magazine, and your regional or national professional and trade publications. They not only want your news; they need it!

---

[3]The term *media kit* is used in two ways: In public relations, for the package in which you send information to media. In advertising, for the package in which media send information about themselves to you.

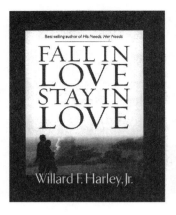

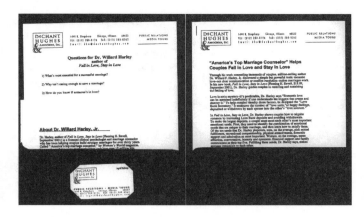

Figure 12.3   Using publicity to sell. A DeChant-Hughes media kit formatted with some special attention-getting features. The striking book jacket serves as cover on a simple pocket folder. When this cover says "Open me!" half the PR battle is won. Once opened, the kit includes enough author and book information to serve as a standard review. Even more important, it includes a series of question that radio and television hosts—who are flooded with dozens such interview requests—can ask the author without having to read all those books. Here, as elsewhere in publicity, the building of a trust relationship between the book's representative and the media is all important. For ongoing success, PR must know what's important and not waste the media's time.

In larger communities, such as New York, Chicago, Denver, or Seattle, news of local interest competes for publication with all the news in the world. In smaller communities, including big cities' neighborhoods, you *are* the world. When I was growing up in Chicago, the neighborhood *Hyde Park Herald* told what was really important—in local schools, local politics, and the local business community. I now live in Evanston, a city of 70,000 bordering directly on Chicago. Here, too, as far as the community's 120-page weekly newspaper is concerned, the world at

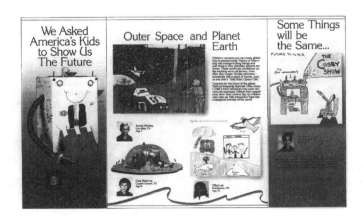

Figure 12.4   Using publicity to inform. Unlike the book in Figure 12.3, the purpose here is not just to sell a product but to gain publicity for the winners of the Crayola-sponsored nationwide Kid's Visions of the Future art contest. Eight $4\frac{1}{2}'' \times 11''$ double-sided panels unfold to show dozens of the winners and their pictures, printed for easy reproduction in local and regional media to give publicity to the youngsters, the event, the sponsor, and news about next year's contest. (This DeChant media kit won that year's two top national PR awards.)

large hardly exists. Local firms and organizations get the attention that the *Chicago Tribune* neighbor lavishes on Toyota, IBM, and AT&T. Equally important, the local publishers, editors, and reporters live right next door. Because everyone who tells them anything has a "vested" interest in how it will be reported, local "real" news is not only needed but welcomed.

THREE WAYS TO GET NATIONAL COVERAGE

Essentially, there are three ways you may attain national coverage.

1. Have Fame Thrust On You

Practically every day, businesses, corporations, and organizations achieve instant (often unexpected) fame. *People* magazine lauds a product its producer thought would be limited to schools . . . and the phone rings off the hook. Cold fusion ignites a nationwide debate . . . and a university finds itself in the middle. An auto is downgraded by *Consumer Reports* . . . and a manufacturer's nightmare becomes reality.

The examples range from a small start-up business to a *Fortune* 500 corporation, from an enterprise that is not yet profitable to one that is nonprofit to one that is desperate for profit. But all have one thing in common: the need for expert response. In two of the three examples cited, that expertise was already on staff. In the third, the plug from *People* so totally overwhelmed its recipient's efforts to capitalize on it himself, that he forgot he had expert help on retainer for just such an emergency!

Fame does strike in most unexpected ways. Just don't panic. Do what *you* are good at. Treat a PR emergency—good or bad—exactly as you would a legal or medical crisis. Stay calm. Get help.

2. Find National Media That Want Your News

Trade media are magazines, journals, and newsletters devoted to a specific interest, trade, or profession. They are the most likely national publications to welcome your news, provided that it will appeal to their readers. So many of these publications exist, that even PR professionals need special directories to keep up to date on them. For instance, the SRDS directory *Business Publication Advertising Source* lists 58 magazines and trade papers devoted to metalworking, with cross-references to several hundred more in 17 related fields. Other topics in this directory have from 6 listings to 650—and that covers only the English-language periodicals from the United States plus selected magazines from Canada.

For PR purposes, the annual Bacon's media directories and *The Editor & Publisher International Year Book* are the most widely used references. Though somewhat overlapping, each has exclusive—and valuable—PR content, and most PR professionals get both. An industry bible, *Editor & Publisher* gives practically encyclopedic newspaper information worldwide, of which PR contacts are only one

Portland - Portland

822   Oregon - continued   Daily Newspapers

Portland - 437,319; County: Multnomah; DMA: Portland, OR; (23)

THE OREGONIAN (OR-D160)
1320 SW Broadway   **(503) 221-8100**
Portland, OR 97201-3499   Fax: (503) 227-5306

E-Mail: newsroom@news.oregonian.com
Home Page: www.oregonian.com
Circ: Morn: 355,980; Sat: 334,310; Sun: 431,137; **Audit:** ABC-Audit
Bureau of Circulations.

Coverage: Oregon & Southwestern Washington.
Owner: Newhouse Newspapers.
Wires: AP, NY Times, Knight-Ridder, Newhouse;   Publication
Available Online.
Ad Rate: $152.89; **Sub Rate:** $156.00.
Lead Times: Advertising - 1 week prior.
Publishes Special Sections Calendar.
Nationally Distributed Magazines: Parade.

Management/News Executives:
Publisher . . . . Fred A. Stickel (503) 221-8140
                                                    fredstickel@news.oregonian.com
Editor . . . . Sandra M. Rowe (503) 221-8400
                                                    srowe@news.oregonian.com
   Contact Notes: Mon-Fri, Between 10am and 4pm, *Preferred order:*U.S.
   Mail, Fax. She does not want to be contacted via e-mail.
Executive Editor . . . . Peter Bhatia (503) 221-8393
                                                    pbhatia@news.oregonian.com
Managing Editor . . . . Therese Bottomly (503) 221-8434
                                                    theresebottomly@news.oregonian.com
   Contact Notes: Oversees Daily News.
Managing Editor . . . . Jack Hart (503) 221-8229
                              Fax: (503) 294-5012
                                                    jackhart@news.oregonian.com
   Contact Notes: Oversees Weekend News.
Online Editor In Chief . . . . Kevin Cosgrove (503) 972-1014
                                                    kcosgrove@oregonlive.com
Special Projects Reporter . . . . Betsy Hammond (503) 294-7623
                                                    betsyhammond@news.oregonian.com

Columnist . . . . Bob Landauer (503) 221-8157
                                                    robertlandauer@news.oregonian.com
Opinion Page Editor . . . . . . Naomi Kaufman Price (503) 221-8433
                                                    oped@news.oregonian.com
   Contact Notes: Mon-Fri, *Preferred order:*U.S. Mail, Fax. No phone calls.
Commentary
   Editor . . . . Doug Bates (503) 221-8174
                                 Fax: (503) 294-4179
                                                    oped@news.oregonian.com
   Editor . . . . Pat Harrison (503) 294-4129
                                                    patharrison@news.oregonian.com
   Editor . . . . Giselle Price (503) 221-8150
                                                    letters@news.oregonian.com
National/International News:
News
   News Dept. Phone . . . . (503) 221-8100
   News Dept. Fax . . . . (503) 227-5306
   Assignment Editor . . . . Michael Arrieta-Walden (503) 221-8518
                                                    michaelwalden@news.oregonian.com
   Night Editor . . . . Randy Lemmerman (503) 412-7040
                                                    randylemmerman@news.oregonian.com
   Reporter . . . . Jim Long (503) 221-4351
                                                    jlong@news.oregonian.com
   Copy Chief . . . . Jerry Sass (503) 294-7602
                                                    jerrysass@news.oregonian.com
National News
   Senior Editor . . . . John Harvey (503) 221-8149
                                                    johnharvey@news.oregonian.com
   Weekend Editor . . . . Jim Camin (503) 294-5104
                                                    jimcamin@news.oregonian.com
   Section Editor . . . . Kathy Nokes (503) 294-5078
                                                    kathynokes@news.oregonian.com
   Wire Editor . . . . Howard Scott (503) 221-8192
                                                    howardscott@news.oregonian.com
International News
   Senior Editor . . . . John Harvey (503) 221-8149
                                                    johnharvey@news.oregonian.com
   Weekend Editor . . . . Jim Camin (503) 294-5104
                                                    jimcamin@news.oregonian.com
Investigative News
   Reporter . . . . Kim Christen (503) 221-5131
                                                    kchristen@news.oregonian.com
   Reporter . . . . Brent Walth (503) 294-5072
                                                    brentwalth@aol.com
   Wires Editor . . . . Howard Scott (503) 221-8192
                                                    howardscott@news.oregonian.com
Political Team Leader . . . . Bruce Hammond (503) 221-8525
                                                    brucehammond@news.oregonian.com
Political Assistant Team Leader . . . . . . Pete Lesage (503) 294-7609
                                                    petelesage@news.oregonian.com
Political Senior Reporter . . . . Jeff Mapes (503) 221-8209
                                                    jeffmapes@news.oregonian.com
Political Reporter . . . . Harry Esteve (503) 221-8226
                                                    harryesteve@news.oregonian.com

Bacon's Newspaper Directory - 2002

Figure 12.5 Typical (partial) listing, shown about 60 percent actual size, from *Bacon's Newspaper/Magazine Directory,* 2003 ed., covering virtually all North American and Caribbean daily newspapers and magazines. One of 13 directories listing more than 100,000 print and electronic media with nearly 350,000 media contacts throughout North America and Western Europe. Other Bacon's services include: MediaSource Internet, currently the most comprehensive media contact software and database in the industry; Media Monitoring, a broad-based monitoring service of print, broadcast, Internet, and analysis in one account; and Bacon's Distribution Service for multimedia custom list development and press. (Contact Bacon's Information, Inc., (800) 621-0561.)

part. There is also extensive information on newspaper suppliers, news services and syndicates, newspaper organizations, and schools of journalism. Bacon's print media directories (vol. I, *Magazines,* and vol. II, *Newspapers*) covers U.S. and Canadian print media and includes midyear updates. An example for the same newspaper from *Bacon's* and *Editor & Publisher* is shown in Figures 12.5 and 12.6.

Use Regional and Local References
As of September 2002, *local* references seem plentiful. Ask any local media representative whether one exists for your community.

The Oregonian
(all day-mon to fri; m-sat; S)
The Oregonian, 1320 S.W. Broadway, Portland, OR 97201; tel (503) 221-8327; fax (503) 227-5306; e-mail oreeditors@ aol.com. Advance Publications group.
Circulation: 333,654(a); 323,478(m-sat); 441,086(S); ABC Sept. 30, 1995.
Price: 35¢(d); 35¢(sat); $1.50(S); $12.00/4wk.
Advertising: Open inch rate $126.90(a); $126.90(m-sat); $131.69(S). **Representative:** Newhouse Newspapers/Metro Suburbia.
News Services: AP, LAT-WP, NYT, NNS, KRT.
Politics: Independent. **Established:** 1850.
Magazine: Parade (S).

CORPORATE OFFICERS

President	Fred A Stickel
Vice Pres	Theodore Newhouse
Treasurer	S I Newhouse III
Asst Treasurer	D W Palmer
Asst Treasurer	Richard E Diamond

GENERAL MANAGEMENT

Publisher	Fred A Stickel
President	Patrick F Stickel
Controller	D W Palmer
Manager-Credit	Betty Kirk
Manager-Human Resources	Tom Whitehouse
Director-Public Affairs	Stephanie Oliver
Purchasing Agent	James Brown

ADVERTISING

Director	Dennis Atkin
Manager-Retail	John Mannex
Manager-General	Debi Walery
Manager-Classified	Gayle Timmerman

MARKETING AND PROMOTION

Director-Marketing Service	Steve Hubbard

TELECOMMUNICATIONS

Audiotex Manager	Marsha Davis

CIRCULATION

Director	Patrick L Marlton

NEWS EXECUTIVES

Editor	Sandra Mims Rowe
Asst Editor	Richard C Johnston
Managing Editor	Peter Bhatia
Recruiting Director	George Rede

EDITORS AND MANAGERS

Audiotex Editor	Jeff Wohler
Books Editor	Ellen Heltzel
Business Editor	Patrick Chu
Columnist	Steve Duin
Columnist	Jonathan Nicholas
Columnist	Margie Boule
Copy Desk Chief	Jerry Sass
Editorial Cartoonist	Jack Ohman
Entertainment Editor	Karen Brooks
Editorial Writer	Nanine Alexander
Editorial Writer	Phil Cogswell
Editorial Writer	Larry Hilderbrand
Editorial Writer	David Reinhard
Editorial Writer	David Sarasohn
Editorial Writer	Wayne Thompson
Editorial Page Editor	Robert J Caldwell
Food Editor	Virginia Johnston
Graphics Editor	Michelle Wise
Librarian	Sandy Macomber
Photo Director	Serge McCabe
Public Editor	Bob Caldwell
Senior Editor-Enterprise	Jacqui Banaszynski
Senior Editor-Features	Mark Wigginton
Senior Editor-Production	John Harvey
Senior Editor-Spot News	Dennis Peck
Senior Editor-Training	Jack Hart
Suburban Editor	Quinton Smith
Sports Columnist	Dwight Jaynes
Sports Columnist	Julie Vader
Sports Editor	Dennis Peck
Systems Director	John Hamlin
Team Leader-City Life	John Killen
Team Leader-Crime	David Austin
Team Leader-East	Kathleen Glanville
Team Leader-Environment	Jacqui Banaszynski
Team Leader-Family/Education	Sally Cheriel
Team Leader-Government	Michele McLellan
Team Leader-Health	Therese Bottomly
Team Leader-Living	Michael Rollins
Team Leader-Nation/World	John Harvey
Team Leader-North	Beth Erickson
Team Leader-Presentation	Galen Barnett
Team Leader-South	Michael Arrieta-Walden
Team Leader-West	Wilda Wahpepah
Travel Editor	Sue Hobart
Television Editor	Stan Horton

MANAGEMENT INFORMATION SERVICES

Director-Computer Service	Carol Howard
Manager-Production Systems	Dick Rickman
Manager-Communications	Arthur Dummor

PRODUCTION

Manager	Ed Hagstrom
Manager-Ad Service	Larry Wilson
Asst Manager-Ad Service	John Bailey
Superintendent-Plant	Joe Crawford
Superintendent-Composing	Richard Dorr
Superintendent-Mailroom	James Holman
Superintendent-Platemaking	Dan Tucker
Superintendent-Pressroom	Dennis Russell
Asst Superintendent-Mailroom	Ed Spencer
Asst Superintendent-Mailroom	Will Sousley
Asst Superintendent-Pressroom	Herman Etzel
Coordinator-Quality	John McKinney

Market Information: Zoned editions; Split Run; TMC; Operate audiotex.
Mechanical available: Offset; Black and 3 ROP colors; insert accepted — preprinted; page cutoffs — 22¾".
Mechanical specifications: Type page 13" x 21½"; E - 6 cols, 2¹⁄₁₆", ⅛" between; A - 6 cols, 2¹⁄₁₆", ⅛" between; C - 10 cols, 1¼", .07" between.
Commodity consumption: Newsprint 90,470 short tons; widths 55", 41¼", 27½"; black ink 1,774,000 pounds; color ink 451,200 pounds; average pages per issue 84(a), 164(S); single plates used 470,000.
Equipment: EDITORIAL: Front-end hardware — 4-CCSI/CPU, DEC/PDP 11-70, 2-HI/Pagination; Other equipment — 213-CCSI/112 BS, 22-HI/2100. CLASSIFIED: Front-end hardware — 4-CCSI/CPU, 3-DEC/PDP 11-70, 1-DEC/PDP 11-84; Other equipment — 100-CCSI/CT97. AUDIOTEX: Hardware — Brite Voice Systems. DISPLAY: Adv layout systems — In-house; Front-end hardware — Cx; Other equipment — 14-Cx/Sun Breeze. PRODUCTION: Typesetters — 1-MON/MK IIi, 4-MON/Express, 4-III/3850; Plate exposures — 2-WL/III; Plate processors — 2-WL/38-D; Electronic picture desk — Lf/AP Leaf Picture Desk; Scanners — 2-ECR/Autokon; Production cameras — 1-C/Marathon; Film transporters — LE; Digital color separation equipment — CD/646, Lf/Leafscan 45, Nikon/3510.

Figure 12.6 Typical listing from *The Editor & Publisher International Year Book,* shown about 60 percent actual size. Some 20 percent of this listing, giving technical details on printing presses and other mechanical details, is not shown here. Contents cover U.S. and Canadian newspapers in detail, plus basic information about newspapers worldwide. The *Year Book* is also available on CD-ROM and with listing capabilities that let you create your own mailing lists based on multiple criteria. Contact Editor & Publisher International Year Book, 11 West 19th Street, New York, NY 10011–4234, (212) 675–4380.

Check 'em All

Only the larger PR departments are likely to need both *Bacon's* and *Editor & Publisher.* Their publishers offer excellent descriptive literature. Ask for it if you are unfamiliar with a guide. Be sure to request an *actual-size* sample page, too. This will make it much easier to compare styles and thoroughness of reference.

Local News Welcomed

With endless pages to fill, trade publication editors welcome your local news and features related to their special interest. To the specialist, "local" may have broader implications than even we, the senders of the news, realize—and which of us doesn't enjoy being in the know about *everything* in our field? After all, that's what makes us experts!

For stories that are more than routine, call the editor of the most important publication in your field (probably the one most widely read in your own organization), and offer an exclusive. Of course, you'll put a deadline on their acceptance, one that will permit you a wider distribution if the publication says no to your offer. Thank the editor for considering the offer. You want his or her goodwill for your nonexclusive releases, too.

INSIGHT 69

Publicists at companies and organizations should do telephone follow-ups with trade media. Get to *know* them. With this group, calling is more important than writing.

---

3. Use National Release Services

What National Release Services Do

Several services provide the nation's media with a constant stream of stories, articles, features, and cartoons of such broad interest that they can appear almost anywhere yet still be of local interest. Depending on the season, these items may include stories on gardening or snow blowers, June wedding dresses or Thanksgiving turkey stuffing, child safety seats in automobiles or new gears for seniors' bikes. The subject list is endless.

Unlike news services that employ reporters and charge media for the use of their stories and features, release services get their materials from public relations offices and get paid to distribute them for free use by the media. But don't be alarmed. The media hasn't sold out. Everyone involved knows the sources and the rules. Release services accept only materials that have wide appeal. Otherwise their primary audience, the editors looking for interesting "fillers," will stop considering what they submit. Release service customers, the companies paying to have their stories distributed, will remain customers only if the materials they distribute actually appear in print. What you, as a customer, are paying for is a combination of professional preparation, specified distribution, and a reasonably friendly reception in editorial offices. You eliminate the expense of an up-to-date mailing list and the duplication and distribution of your individual stories or features.

Where to Find a Release Service

Look in the Yellow Pages under "Publicity Services" for local and regional release services. They'll know that territory best. For national services, check the major city directories. Chicago's Associated Release Service ((312) 726−8693) is a well-established firm typical of the national group.

Who Uses Release Service Materials

Some release service materials find their way into electronic media and newspapers of major cities, especially in specific interest sections, such as gardening, home-making, automotive, and cooking. The most widespread use of these materials, however, is in smaller communities. There they are appreciated not only for their content but also because they can be used exactly as received, without new typesetting or editing—a considerable benefit in a budget-conscious office.

How to Learn Where Your Story Appears

Clipping services are in the business of reading practically every newspaper and magazine and, for specified fees, "clipping out" items that mention a specific subject. When you receive from them the stories you've ordered clipped (some 10 days to 3 weeks after they're first published), each has attached the name of the publication in which the story appeared, its circulation, and when the story ran. For organizations that wish to document the local, regional, or national success of their PR efforts, these services, listed under "Clipping Services" in major-city Yellow Pages, are about the only way of keeping track of those efforts. Analogous services also exist for radio and TV.

INSIGHT 70

Remember why you want national media PR:
1. To serve a specific purpose beneficial to your firm or association;
2. To have *national* material to duplicate and distribute to the audience you hope to influence;
3. To let the market for your product or service know it is there or is coming.

GETTING MORE PR FROM YOUR PUBLICITY

- Any mention about you in a national publication—even a trade journal—will get reported in your local press . . . provided that you make it known to them. Do it!
- Employees love to read about themselves and their successes. Post such stories prominently on special "Good News Bulletin Boards" . . . then invite everyone to post their personal good news there also—weddings, births, graduations, anniversaries, or whatever. Let them decide!
- Mail copies of your national coverage to persons important to you or your organization. Be sure to include local political leaders, the financial community, and your employee and union newsletter.

INSIGHT 71

Few publicity stories have truly national appeal. Don't sink your time and dollars into expectations that just won't be realized. Feeding an ego as big as the world is an appetite few of us can—or should—afford.

SUMMARY

- Local media want and need your news especially when you give it a local angle: Your audience is always interested first in themselves and second in everything that affects them.
- Think of your trade media as another local market, with the "locality" being its specialized interest. Then write accordingly.
- For national coverage, get to know specific media contacts, and then translate your news into a story or feature that meets *their* needs and preferences. Trust hard work and creativity rather than luck.

WHEN NOT TO DO IT YOURSELF

We began this chapter by defining the task of public relations as being "to limit harm and, where possible, to neutralize harm or turn it into good." That "harm" is the way we are viewed by a specific part of the public and the actions they might take because of that perception. Thus, PR has two tasks. One is to forewarn its own company or organization against (and possibly prevent) harmful PR consequences that can be foreseen. The second and more frequently called on task is to neutralize the public's perception of something—foreseeable or not—after it has occurred. Notice that the focus is on "something," rather than "us." An aircraft failure caused by a usually harmless lightning bolt may cause the same wreck as poor engine maintenance, but the public's perception of mechanics, the flight crew, and the airline affected will be markedly different in the two cases. If you think this is too radical an example to apply to *you,* consider the fact that it is the expected PR emergency for a specific industry. For an airline, PR surely should not be handled by amateurs—just as the PR critical to *you* demands equally expert attention. So when you are in need of PR:

- **Consider the stakes.** Are you trying to climb from a 60 percent to a 65 percent market share or halt a precipitous decline?
- **Consider the personalities.** Is the CEO more likely to accept PR guidance from an "objective" outside pro than from inside staff . . . especially when the results are painful as well as necessary?
- **Consider the location.** Will an outsider raise suspicions, whereas local expertise would gain a friendly welcome?
- **Consider your own abilities.** Balance what you can do, and do well, against what *only you* can do, and direct yourself accordingly.

But let's not be "firefighters," waiting to be summoned to PR disasters. PR and publicity can and should be used to create goodwill—among employees, customers, clients, and the community as a whole. This may mean sponsoring or helping publicize a golf tournament, a health fair, a scout outing, a contest for kids, and so on. It may also involve, depending on policy, making public your charitable contributions or involvement by management in public service. You probably do much more good than anyone suspects . . . so let the world know!

YES, YOU CAN DO YOUR OWN PR . . . SOMETIMES

Doing your own publicity can be both rewarding and a great deal of fun, and nothing said here should keep you from it. There are, however, times when your expertise should concentrate on finding PR professionals who can handle a project better than you can and then making sure that that's what they do.

The biggest mistake made by firms when hiring outside PR professionals is not to tell them the *whole* story. Usually, professionals are called in to help overcome a bad image, a falling market share, or unfavorable publicity. Many firms think that they won't get a good job out of the pros if they really tell them *all* the "bad news." So they send them into battle unaware. Of course they do learn—the hard way—from the media! They wind up looking foolish, and their employers look worse. Think of the pro as your good-guy hired gun. Don't arm him or her with blanks!

INSIGHT 72

When assigning any task, search for someone who's better at it than you. And don't worry about being shown up: Organizations are desperate for managers who recognize talent and tend to reward that more liberally than just doing a good job yourself. Good managers get promoted. Good workers get more work.

NOTES ON THE PUBLICITY/PUBLIC RELATIONS CHECKLIST

These notes are a supplement to the material presented in this chapter. They are not a substitute for that material. The checklist is presented in Figure 12.7.

1. **Audience.** The audience(s) you want to reach and which—if any—to address specifically, rather than as part of the whole. Differentiate between the same message keyed to different interests and different messages.
2. **Focus.** Decide both what the message is to say and what it is to accomplish. Set realistic PR goals, not those for advertising.

PUBLICITY/PUBLIC RELATIONS CHECKLIST

Project Title _____ **Date** _____

Project Description _____ **Project #** _____

_____ **Checklist #** _____

Overall Supervision By _____ **Deadline** _____

Budget _____ **Completion Date** _____ **Start Up Date** _____

Project Focus (Mark A–Z in order of importance): ☐ Managers ☐ Other Employees ☐ Immediate Community ☐ Broader Community ☐ Stockholders ☐ Other Financial ☐ Suppliers ☐ Customers ☐ Clients ☐ General Press ☐ Trade Press ☐ Financial Press ☐ _____ ☐ _____ ☐ _____

MANAGEMENT DECISIONS	ASSIGNED TO	DUE	IN	MUST APPROVE	BY DATE	IN	INFO COPY ONLY	SEE ATTACHED
1. Audience(s)	_____	___	☐	_____	___	☐	_____	☐
2. Focus	_____	___	☐	_____	___	☐	_____	☐
3. Project(s)	_____	___	☐	_____	___	☐	_____	☐
4. Time Line	_____	___	☐	_____	___	☐	_____	☐
5. Cost–Quotes/Actual	_____	___	☐	_____	___	☐	_____	☐
6. Project Supervision	_____	___	☐	_____	___	☐	_____	☐

PRODUCTION

	ASSIGNED TO	DUE	IN	MUST APPROVE	BY DATE	IN	INFO COPY ONLY	SEE ATTACHED
7. Components	_____	___	☐	_____	___	☐	_____	☐
8. Copy	_____	___	☐	_____	___	☐	_____	☐
9. Layout	_____	___	☐	_____	___	☐	_____	☐
10. Type	_____	___	☐	_____	___	☐	_____	☐
11. Duplication	_____	___	☐	_____	___	☐	_____	☐
12. Disk/New Art	_____	___	☐	_____	___	☐	_____	☐
13. Printing	_____	___	☐	_____	___	☐	_____	☐
14. Interview Practice	_____	___	☐	_____	___	☐	_____	☐
15. Audio Creative	_____	___	☐	_____	___	☐	_____	☐
16. Video Creative	_____	___	☐	_____	___	☐	_____	☐
17. AV Duplication	_____	___	☐	_____	___	☐	_____	☐

DISTRIBUTION

	ASSIGNED TO	DUE	IN	MUST APPROVE	BY DATE	IN	INFO COPY ONLY	SEE ATTACHED
18. Phone Contacts Assigned	_____	___	☐	_____	___	☐	_____	☐
19. Phone Contacts Made	_____	___	☐	_____	___	☐	_____	☐
20. Media Kit Packaging	_____	___	☐	_____	___	☐	_____	☐
21. Lists Ordered (mail/phone)	_____	___	☐	_____	___	☐	_____	☐
22. Shipping Assigned	_____	___	☐	_____	___	☐	_____	☐
23. Postage OK	_____	___	☐	_____	___	☐	_____	☐
24. Personal Contacts Assigned	_____	___	☐	_____	___	☐	_____	☐
25. Personal Contacts Made	_____	___	☐	_____	___	☐	_____	☐
26. Mailing Lists Checked	_____	___	☐	_____	___	☐	_____	☐
27. Phone Lists Checked	_____	___	☐	_____	___	☐	_____	☐
28. Legal Clearance	_____	___	☐	_____	___	☐	_____	☐

REPORTS

	ASSIGNED TO	DUE	IN	MUST APPROVE	BY DATE	IN	INFO COPY ONLY	SEE ATTACHED
29. Quotes/Estimates	_____	___	☐	_____	___	☐	_____	☐
30. Actual Costs	_____	___	☐	_____	___	☐	_____	☐
31. Checking Bureau Assigned	_____	___	☐	_____	___	☐	_____	☐
32. Results Received/Distributed	_____	___	☐	_____	___	☐	_____	☐

Figure 12.7 The publicity/public relations checklist.

3. **Projects.** Link the project(s) to #1 and #2. Define the media for each audience in relation to the "cash value" of achieving each goal. Not only dollars but staff and staff time are limited, too.

4. **Time line.** Almost anything can be done—given that nothing else is needed. If due dates demand an absolute concentration of effort on one particular project, make sure that management knows that no other project can receive attention.

5. **Cost control.** This is the centralized budgeting control, especially for multimedia projects such as items 12 through 18. This is not budget setting (that's supposed to be done), but deciding how expenditures are tracked and monitored. Don't do these projects without such a system!

6. **Supervision.** Note here if this is different from the overall supervision and how both work in developing items 1–5.

7. **Components.** Spell out each project's components. Not, for instance, just "media kit," but every detail. This includes the type of outer envelope along with its size and message; the color of the pocket folder and the number of pockets it has; any special design or standard format; and what each pocket contains and in what order. Mention also any additional enclosures—both new and existing—and the order in which they appear. Specify *everything.* Give every item an ID code and use it on that item.

8. **Copy.** Writing for PR is a specialized skill. Frequently, it can be found or developed in-house. Because its message is most often aimed at print and electronic media, experience even on high school or college newspapers, and/or radio, or TV, is invaluable.

9. **Layout.** When PR requires layout or type, treat them with the importance given to everything else that represents your organization. If it's not worth doing right . . . why do it at all?

10. **Type.** Most PR projects can be produced by desktop publishing.

11. **Duplication.** This is for the simpler quick-print projects and office duplication. For more ambitious outside printing, use #12 and #13.

12–13. **Disk/New art.** When PR requires the creation of major new printed pieces, use the separate checklists included for such projects in Chapter 5. For production and duplication, use the printing checklist in Chapter 16. The use is determined not by the quantity printed but by the complexity of the work.

14–17. **Radio, TV/cable.** Practice for likely contacts with electronic media with a *realistic simulation,* especially if you are new to radio and TV broadcasting. Unless you're a pro, do not do this cold! (For creating, producing, and/or duplicating your own taped materials, use the information and checklist from Chapter 13. Don't even think of doing it yourself without reading that chapter first.)

18–19. **Phone contact.** Most PR telemarketing involves in-house invitations or follow-up on news material. When the list or effort seem overwhelming, use the information and checklist in Chapter 9. That's why they're there.

20–27. **Must-do reminders.** These are a project reminder more than a personnel assignment in most instances. Save personal contact (#25) for something really worthwhile and for media who ignore everything else. If you're a beginner, ask colleagues who in the media that is. It's never a secret.

28. **Legal clearance.** Consider every claim and promise a legal commitment. If in doubt—and even when not—get legal clearance.

29–30. **Cost OK's.** Official report on estimates and decision on approvals. Due dates for this are established as part of #4.

31–32. **Results.** Consult with several checking bureaus regarding what it is possible to learn about results. They're most often the only way to check on PR *distribution* and its *use.* Gauging PR *effectiveness* is beyond the scope of this book.

13 | Media Creativity and Production
Video, CD, TV, Radio, and Web Site

> This chapter has been brought up to date with the help of **William Holtane**, founder and president of Sound/Video Impressions, Des Plaine, IL. Founded in 1976, the studio is expert in audio, video, and computer-based media production. It is a full-service facility, from concept to writing, shooting recording, editing, graphics, animation, and interactive programming, to final output in all formats for distribution and order fulfillment. www.soundvideoimpressions.com.

FINDING A MEDIA "PARTNER"

If, like most of us, you're a novice at purchasing audio and video services, you'll need someone at the creative and production end who will become your "partner"[1]—someone whom you can trust to give you your money's worth, especially when you have no way of knowing what that "money's worth" is. Selecting such a person has to be based on finding an organization that can demonstrate a consistent level of results over an extended period of time within an established price range. Shopping by cost is easy: You can always find someone who will do it for less. But not knowing whether you can *use* what you'll be buying is where disaster awaits. An advance deposit with progressive payments is standard practice. You seldom can allow time to do a project over. You have little recourse if you do not like what you get.

The Boutique Factor

Downsizing, especially in corporate media/audiovisual (AV) departments, has led to much "outsourcing," frequently to former employees at new one- or two-person media boutiques. Without in any way disparaging their creative abilities, their business know-how is frequently somewhat less. When working with such a boutique, make sure your working agreement states that you own all videotapes and audiotapes shot for your project, as well as everything converted to disks. After

---

[1]Holtane, president of Sound-Video Impressions in Des Plaines, II, (847) 297–4360, became, and contines as, my "partner." He not only helped guide me from ignorance to competence but is largely responsible for the wisdom in this chapter.

they have finished your job, take physical possession of disk and tapes. Store them in a cool, fire-resistant location, perhaps the same place you store your disks of backup computerized records.

The Longevity Factor

Don't hesitate to work with a start-up company that can demonstrate its ability at a lower than expected cost, if they have expertise in *all* that you'll need. The key words are *demonstrate* and *all*. The time and dollars spent in finding new help, then fixing or finishing, can be a budget buster. Many new audiovisual suppliers have undercharged themselves out of business before they learned the true cost of what they were doing! For long-term projects, work with suppliers who've shown their ability to survive the past five years.

The Basic Skills

Your media projects require four distinct skills. Each of them has both a *mechanical* and a *quality* factor: Synergy happens when you get a happy marriage of both.

1. **Preproduction.** The script with sound (such as a slamming door) indicated and a cartoon-style storyboard visual concept.
2. **Production.** Videotaping or recording the project—on location, in the studio, or both.
3. **Postproduction.** In-studio or do-it-yourself editing.
4. **Duplication.** As required.

Each of these four skills can be (and often is) provided by different organizations, especially when overall supervision of the project lies with an advertising agency experienced in media production as well as creativity. As an in-house supervisor, look for a "partner" company that can provide all three of the creative functions, from scripting through editing. Duplication is best given to experts in that field. Depending on what is being duplicated, media firms are often your best source, even for large quantities. In getting other quotes, be sure they speak with the media company about what will be needed. Get firm quotations—in writing—on time, quality, and costs. For minor cost differences, stick with the creating studio. It's their reputation (brand), too!

The Do-It-Yourself Quality Factor

Video editing requires computer equipment with a *huge* memory; that is, definitely *not* a typical home or office desktop computer. "Amateur" systems can be as low as $100 for an editing program you can install on your home computer, but it is *very* limited and without the ancillary items such as input, output modules, audio, and so on. Quality low-end systems begin at about $5,000 but are still quite limited at that level. In 2002, serious studios pay in excess of $60,000 for basic professional systems, $100,000 with ancillary gear. Excellent quality not only costs more, it demands the skills and experience to use it.

For clients with an in-house graphics department, today's media firms use more client-created material than in recent years, though usually not the video. Today there is much less of the "Let's write a script, let's do a video, let's put it on VHS," and so on. Now there is more working with in-house graphics staff, creating and using their materials. Rather than creative competition, there is much more of a partnership.

Why You (Probably) Need Outside Help

INSIGHT 73

Before you begin any media project, decide on the *results* as well as the *quality* of the message you wish to achieve. Discuss *both* with your media experts. *Listen* to their suggestions, too! Decide—then let them do their job.

Despite the advent of computer-based media systems that in-house personnel find easier to use, companies often learn—in mid-project—that they do not have the expertise to create and produce truly professional work. On anything complicated—and practically everything is becoming more complicated!—you may get a project started, then find you cannot finish the job. To mention just three common examples:

1. You try to synchronize video with audio, only to discover that unless you do it on a daily basis, it's not as simple as the manuals suggest.
2. In work with smaller digital cameras, often the picture quality is good, but just as often the shooting techniques are bad. Using a professional camera does not necessarily make us professional photographers.
3. To create a disks yourself and duplicate properly, you must learn *and follow* the industry standards for creating the original. Otherwise, you may have pieces that will not assemble and need a very expensive studio job of unscrambling and reassembling, then creating a new original. As a do-it-yourselfer, first go to an expert to learn. You'll probably get charged, but at least you'll get the parts right!

Finding Suppliers

In larger markets, if no other guidance seems available, begin with the business Yellow Pages under "Audio-Visual Production," "Recording Services," or "Video Production Services." In smaller communities, you're unlikely to find the same level of experience or sophisticated equipment, but you will be able to find *someone* who can help. Begin by deciding how "big city" you really have to be. Your commercials will actually be seen on television. Instructional and informational "infomercials" are shown on monitors using the same screen. Your audience, without consciously realizing it, expects the technical quality they get from that screen every day in regular programs, other commercials, and feature films. The ability to approach that quality within your budgetary and creative restrictions is what your initial search is all about.

A Wealth of Suppliers

Video and audio production facilities are practically everywhere. Community colleges, some high schools, many hospitals, local radio, TV, and cable companies, and, of course, local video and audio production companies all offer their services. Look for special promotions in which radio or TV stations—including some in the largest markets—offer to create and produce your commercial without additional charge, provided that you purchase a specified amount of broadcast time. You may even get to use their work on another station! In all probability, though, their end product, while competent, may be very packaged—one of a limited number of set solutions to any promotion problem. If what you want is some variation of "Good morning! We're so and so. Here's our address. Come in or give us a call," this may well be all you need. Much local automotive, home builder, and retail promotion is done exactly that way.

The use of on-air personalities in media projects requires quite different considerations. Broadcasting—especially local television—demands mechanical skills. Its expertise lies in sending a signal to listeners, subscribers, and viewers. With the exception of some news and sports, few television broadcasts originate locally. Local staff have neither the need nor the talent for much creativity. Radio's call-in and disk jockey personalities do tend to be excellent sales "voices," especially on their own programs. Elsewhere, however, use local talent with caution.

Skills for Multimedia Planning and Use

In-house or outsourced, you must have or find a studio or production company that has the ability to work with many different forms of media—from input to output. Today's planning often *begins* with producing for a single medium, but can and should look far beyond a single use for that material. If you do a spot commercial, consider its application on a Web site, a DVD, a CD-ROM, or other media. Thanks to digital technology, companies are multitasking all their media, and not just for advertising! Therefore, from the planning stage on, you need someone who can bring you to all those outlets. Just because it's digital doesn't make the usability automatic. Think of the variety of Web access speeds and the different computers on which someone will try to play your media and how to make it compatible for at least the vast majority. We are nowhere near the point where everything is as standard as the cassette player.

A CASE HISTORY

A client wanted a video on how to unpack and install a piece of their equipment. As diplomatically as possible, Sound/Video asked, "Shouldn't your marketing department be involved in this, too? Why don't you ask them and maybe they'll split the cost." It was the latter point that won the day. When marketing saw the project, they immediately recognized its value for showing the features, advantages, and benefits of the product to potential customers, as well as how the machinery was packed, delivered, and installed to those who'd already bought it. The finished video became a top sales tool and a crowd stopper when shown on a giant screen at their next trade convention. Being digital, unlike the older film process, individual frames also were perfectly clear pictures for print advertising, direct mail, and catalogs.

For Infomercials

For longer infomercials, that is, informational programs or commercials that delve deeper into your product or service, you must use people who are, first and foremost, creative. You need a true video or recording production company, preferably one that specializes in the infomercial field. Thousands of producers can hold an audience for 30 seconds. Thirty *minutes* is a quite different skill. For TV home-shopping-type selling, infomercial producers who specialize in this field almost always work on a percentage-of-profit basis. They can get as much as 50 to 60 percent of the sale—perhaps more! Have your attorney read the contract before you sign, and realize you will have to relinquish some creative control over both product and packaging.

Tape versus CD versus CD-ROM

Commercials and infomercials are produced according to set standards. They do not require *your* decision on tape versus CD. However, before deciding to produce your sales presentation, point-of-sale, or other media materials on CD or CD-ROM rather than standard tape, consider all of the following:

- You are not producing a music or movie disk. You are producing a commercial message for computer reproduction.
- Before creating and distributing a CD-ROM, survey the recipients' computer capabilities to make sure they can use it.
- Many older computers do not have CD capabilities.
- Even with newer equipment, CD does *not* have a uniform system for computer reproduction. Unless you have a one-to-one fit, your CD message may not work well, if it works at all.
- CD-ROM requires an immense amount of computer memory for end user access. The more enhanced your message with sight, sound, and motion, the longer it takes to appear. "Rendering" takes time! If you want to give your end users access to your information, how long do you expect them to wait?

SUMMARY

- Much media production works on the honor system. Find suppliers who will act as "partners," guarding your interests as well as their own.
- If you are unfamiliar with costs, preview work by suppliers in various price ranges. Establish your budget *after* you see what different dollars can buy.

THE CLIENT AND MEDIA CREATIVITY

Management Commitment

Production within a studio is comparatively easy. However, for on-location shooting, management must be absolutely committed to the project. Thanks to the new "chip cameras," true colors now can be shot without an immense amount of lighting specially placed for shooting. However, distracting extras, whether people or things, still must be removed from the picture. Work, traffic, and possibly sound must be stopped or redirected. Electrical cables must be permitted in strange places, and imperfect strangers must be allowed to give orders *to everyone,* whether they're in the video or not . . . and get their releases if they are.

INSIGHT 74

Consider asking employees for a written release at the time of employment, granting permission to picture that person in promotional materials. Many organizations do this. However, check with your attorney first.

Without on-the-scene cooperation, on-location shooting can become literally impossible. So be committed, and make that commitment known!

Begin with introspection: Let the producer or media company know how the clients see themselves, especially if the client is you. Are the clients so serious about what they do that the least touch of whimsy is out of character? Do they feel branded as stodgy and want a lighter image? Generally, senior managers don't review anything until it's completed. The last thing your media supplier wants to hear *from them* is "but that's not *us.*" There has to be a knowledgeable person from the client's side directly involved in *ongoing* creativity, not to tell the producer how to run the train, but to help redirect it when it's on an obviously wrong track.

What Media Creativity Is All About

In low- to medium-priced media organizations, the writer, director, and producer often are one and the same. But whether there is one, two, or a team, media creativity is the ability to *use* media to tell a story. It begins with the ability to create a script—to write the words that are spoken while sound effects, music, and visual images are received by the audience. It demands from the producer and director technical expertise in acting, filming, and editing. It requires visualizing what the entire project will achieve as individual segments are produced and then making it happen.

For on-location shooting, the writer and producer *must* visit the site not only before shooting but even before writing to learn whether filming there is practical, both for reasons of safety and to remain within the budget. Once reassured, they put their imagination to work. Immediately, they start seeing shots, hearing words, and visualizing action. Suggested scripts from the agency or the client are actually helpful at this stage. Far from hindering the writers, they tell them what the client wants and how they see themselves in relationship to that project. It focuses creativity within specified limitations, rather than letting it expend time, energy, and costs on efforts that are sure to be rejected.

The Critical Site and Sound Check

When shooting must be on location, it can be unavoidably disruptive to your workplace. So for anything more critical than a company picnic, work only with a producer/director who insist on a site and sound check before beginning your project. Both client and media crew require advanced planning so you don't have a *very* expensive film crew (as well as in-house employees) simply waiting while media rewrites the script to fit the location.

- **Lighting.** Outside lighting is unpredictable for interior filming, so windows must be covered and lighting created. New equipment requires less lighting and is less cumbersome, but this is not the case for the hand-held cameras used in many shots.
- **Sound.** Is there work and ventilating noise or outside traffic, especially in flight paths? If audio is recorded on site, all those noises you thought would not be a problem demand a solution.
- **Mechanical.** Often heavy cameras and lighting must be used and moved during filming, requiring room for portable tracks.

INSIGHT 75

Give your media producers suggestions, directions, and even scripts as a base on which to build. If *their* creative ability can't improve on *your* efforts, ask yourself whether you are really that good or whether someone else should decide between the two of you.

Openness to Criticism

No media professional expects a first script to be accepted without change or comment. It's for discussion. Both client and scriptwriter are like chefs given the same ingredients. One may not recognize the full possibilities, while the other may take them a bit too far. The key is to be open to each other's tastes. Argue, and even fight about the scripts, but just don't forget the audience for whom you are "cooking."

Amateur versus Professional Talent

How and where your media will be used may well determine whether amateur talents are an option. Not only do amateurs tend to get frustrated quickly, but contractual obligations for professional talent may be a factor. Your producer, charged with finding the talent, will be aware of these factors. When the option to use amateurs does exist, you can screen them from among actors, musicians, singers, and dancers in colleges, local drama and music groups, and fraternal organizations. Often, it's not a question of talent as much as it is of a client's wishes and priorities.[2] Keep in mind that what does make the professional different is the ability to follow directions: To a professional, doing or saying the same thing 10 or 20 times or more isn't deadly boring; it's part of the job. The result doesn't deteriorate with repetition; it gets better.

INSIGHT 76

Amateurs require inspiration. Professionals do it with a headache.

SUMMARY

- Differentiate between producing your idea and being open to alternatives. Be honest with yourself, and let the producer know *before* they begin.
- Be candid about how you see yourself. Be open to achieving your aims in unexpected ways.
- When either professional or amateur talent is an option, let the producer decide. "Talented" relatives tend to cost most of all.

ON-LOCATION SHOOTING

Endless Shooting

On-location shooting for the average piece, no matter what its length, will be from one to three days. Generally, there is a minimum crew of three: the producer/director, the camera operator, and an expert all-around assistant.[3] Their task is not only to shoot the project but to *overshoot* everything—the clock on the wall, the view from the window, the notices on the bulletin board, the receptionist's smile, the loading clerk's wave, the office, the hallway, the factory sweeper, and the jeweler's polishing—

---

[2]Try not to impose talented relatives on your producer. One of my more costly commercials needed a quartet (for which I had not budgeted) to outsing a client's daughter attempting to turn a simple radio spot into grand opera.

[3]If cost is no object, or the project demands it, a crew can expand to include makeup artists, hairstylists, carpenters, and electricians—indeed, almost any specialist you can name. The reason movies often list a hundred or more credits is that every single person named was *needed* to do *that* film. What "that" means for your project will determine *your* crew and *your* cost.

whether it seems to have a connection with the final piece or not. Though seemingly random, this shooting, known as "B-roll," is far from haphazard. It provides a wealth of raw, "cutaway" footage to be found and inserted wherever there is a need for a smooth transition between scenes. (Lack of such footage becomes obvious only when transition shots are missing or the same ones are endlessly repeated.) For the postproduction editor, there is never too much variety in *good* raw footage.

THE ART AND CRAFT OF EDITING FOR MEDIA

It is in postproduction editing that your project is actually created. The process involves a series of steps, some mechanical, some judgmental, and some both.

Time Code

Most often, video editing begins with the placing of a small time-code "window" onto each frame. The window shows the hour, minute, second, and frame for that video and looks like this: 03:16:32:05. Video is edited to 1/30 of a second. That is, there will be 30 frames *for each second.* But first comes the decision to edit for picture or sound. If the visual is the important thing, make the sound match it. If, on the other hand, you begin with a script that must be followed, tune the video to the sound track. Either is equally possible, provided that the postproduction editors know what is needed.

WARNING! FOR DO-IT-YOURSELFERS

Video editing requires the standard SMPTE frame-by-frame time code, produced automatically while shooting. Most consumer-grade cameras, however, do not have a time code that is readable for editing! When planning in-house shooting, check with your production company on the compatibility of their editing equipment with your camera. It's much cheaper to rent the right camera than to retime all your shooting!

- Use a tripod! Leave handheld video to the pros.
- Shoot three times as much as you think you'll need. You'll need it.

Voice and Teleprompters

The sound of your project—especially the spoken words—demands the same attention and skill as the picture. Decisions must be made on using the sound from the location or from studio recording. Anyone speaking directly to the audience should use a teleprompter located on the camera. They'll be much more comfortable and, even more important, will be forced to look directly through the lens and at their audience. Teleprompters and tiny lapel microphones that ensure good sound take a bit of practice but have made in-house stars out of many an unlikely candidate.

Sound Editing

Sound editing involves first finding the best available sound from on-location shooting and then knowing *and using* sound-quality techniques to improve, or "sweeten," what your location gave you. Incidental, ambient sounds, such as a door closing or footsteps approaching, almost always require "sweetening." Fortunately, they're also the easiest sounds to fix. Voices have fewer options. "Lip sync" recording is so difficult for amateurs, it should not be planned nor allowed for. Music, if any, can wait for the final combination of words and pictures.

Easier Visual Editing

Some new technology permits the director/producer to indicate the relative merits of the shots while shooting. Each is computer marked and rated, and the best two or three can later be assembled automatically. Rather than having to return to the studio and review everything, only the very best shots need be seen again, saving huge amounts of time and, of course, money!

As in sound editing, in visual editing all the steps are determined by the producer. Generally, it is the producer/director who views raw footage and determines which sections fit the script best, how to handle transitions, and when to add special effects or enhancements.

Final Editing

Final editing almost demands the presence of both the producer and the client. Audiotapes for radio commercials or information and training are easily edited and changed by simple cut-and-splice techniques. However once the sound and picture are brought together in final form, any change, no matter how seemingly trivial, may require starting from scratch. Audiovisual editing is not done on actual film; rather, it is done digitally, with electronic impulses, from which a final film is created. To make changes, sound and pictures must once again be synchronized from a dozen different sources. You must make synchronization decisions during editing, not afterward, or else not only will everything take longer than it takes but it will surely also cost more than it costs.

INSIGHT 77

About animation: Disney-type animation costs about $2,500 per *second* for the animation alone. That's $12 million for a one-hour feature film, a comfortably low cost by film standards. For a 30-second commercial, it's $75,000 and perhaps twice that by the time the project is done. Don't try and do it for less. If budget is the problem, stick with quality and do something else.

SUMMARY

- On-location shooting is invariable disruptive. Management must make its commitment known and enforced *before* the crew appears on the scene.
- Editing is often more costly than shooting. Keep it in control by being there when it happens, not correcting it after it's done!

THE ART AND CRAFT OF DUPLICATION

Many media production companies now have facilities and equipment for duplicating large quantities. In evaluating duplication companies, check all of the following costs before you decide:

- **Setting up.** Preparing tapes and equipment before duplication can begin.
- **Video and CD/CD-ROM duplication.** Make certain that your duplication company knows how the finished product will be used and can provide that service. Anyone can duplicate for a VCR. For anything else, from installing antipiracy protection to knowing TV requirements abroad, find and use specialists.
- **Audio duplication.** The duplication processes for audiocassettes and CDs (compact discs) are so different that each must be handled as a separate project. Because CD replication (copying) uses digital processes and cassettes use linear techniques, CDs require a somewhat costly master to reproduce from the same original master. Before you consider a CD because it's the contemporary thing to do, consult a CD replication service. Be sure you learn about the process before you begin.
- **Labeling.** Preparing camera-ready type and art, if any, plus duplicating labels both for the cassette itself and for individual audio- or videocassette containers.
- **Containers.** Boxes for audiocassettes. Use softer "albums" or more sturdy "library cases" for videocassettes.
- **Handling.** Putting everything together as a finished package.
- **Shipping.** Be sure to specify how the complete packages are to be shipped. Many duplication companies routinely ship air express, unless instructed *in writing* to use a less expensive method.
- **Scheduling.** Your responsibilities, as well as theirs, should be specified in writing. What happens if either one of you is late?
- **Savings.** The possible savings on a package cost for creative, production, and duplication.

Finding the Duplication Service You Need

Video/CD and audio duplication services are either small-or mass-quantity suppliers. Unlike printers, a middle size hardly exists. Because they may seem much alike to the uninitiated buyer, here are some guidelines:

1. Have your video or audio producer recommend a duplicating service (perhaps itself). Get a quote on the project *based on your producer's specifications* before production begins. If quantities and dollars are low, you can probably stop right there. For large quantities or large dollars, get additional quotations.

2. When evaluating new video or audio duplication companies, have them produce an approval copy (like a printing proof), from *your* original if time permits. Let them know that you will compare it with one or two other suppliers and that you will use it as you would a proof to check the complete run.

3. In my experience, videocassette/CD duplication services repay the evaluation effort. An obvious winner has always been easy to determine. When cost has been a factor, less expensive labels and containers have produced major savings. Consider purchasing them yourself only if your suppliers' sources fail to give them an obvious price advantage. (They're not purchasing just for you; they should get larger quantity discounts.).

4. In my experience, audiocassette services are fairly comparable to one another for *voice* duplication. If music is a critical part of the sound, however, get help in the evaluation. But keep a perspective on what it is that you are producing and the extraordinary cost of perfection when a good product will do.

5. For mass duplication—from thousands to millions of copies—go to a major national company. Before 1990, videocassettes had to be duplicated in real time; that is, a two-hour tape took two hours to copy. Larger producers had to have thousands of duplication machines to handle this. After 1990, high-speed duplication of videocassettes (as had been the case for audio and CD) was finally perfected, with quality every bit as good as the previous real-time system. If quantities warrant, ask your producer to recommend such sources, or check Allied Vaughn ((847) 595–2900). This firm has offices and facilities from Florida to California.

> ### SUMMARY
> - For small quantities, the cost of a new setup may be more than the cost of duplication. Check with your production service before you go elsewhere. Get *total* costs from both—for the finished package, not just the tape or CD.
> - To evaluate audio or audiovisual duplicating ability, comparison shop by having *your current project* copied. It's worth the extra cost and will give you a proof against which to check the production run.
> - Mass duplication needs a mass producer. Check several, not just the one closest to home.

NOTES ON THE MEDIA CREATIVE AND PRODUCTION CHECKLIST

These notes are a supplement to the material presented in this chapter. They are not a substitute for that material. The checklist is presented in Figure 13.1.

MEDIA CREATIVE AND PRODUCTION CHECKLIST

Project Title ______________________________ **Date** ______________
Project Description ______________________________ **Project #** ______________
______________________________ **Checklist #** ______________
Overall Supervision By ______________________________ **Deadline** ______________
Budget ______________ **Completion Date** ______________ **Start Up Date** ______________

MANAGEMENT DECISIONS	ASSIGNED TO	DUE	IN	MUST APPROVE	BY DATE	IN	INFO COPY ONLY	SEE ATTACHED
1. Purpose	________	___	☐	________	___	☐	________	☐
2. Client Self-Image	________	___	☐	________	___	☐	________	☐
3. Budget	________	___	☐	________	___	☐	________	☐
4. Project Supervision	________	___	☐	________	___	☐	________	☐
CREATIVE								
5. Focus	________	___	☐	________	___	☐	________	☐
6. Audience(s)	________	___	☐	________	___	☐	________	☐
7. Desired Response(s)	________	___	☐	________	___	☐	________	☐
8. Supplier Selection	________	___	☐	________	___	☐	________	☐
9. Client Script Ideas	________	___	☐	________	___	☐	________	☐
10. Client Contact/Supervision	________	___	☐	________	___	☐	________	☐
11. Script/Storyboard Approval	________	___	☐	________	___	☐	________	☐
12. Suggested Length	________	___	☐	________	___	☐	________	☐
13. Creative/Production Time Line	________	___	☐	________	___	☐	________	☐
PRODUCTION								
14. On-Site Contact	________	___	☐	________	___	☐	________	☐
15. Production Supervision	________	___	☐	________	___	☐	________	☐
16. Editing Supervision	________	___	☐	________	___	☐	________	☐
17. Actual Length	________	___	☐	________	___	☐	________	☐
DUPLICATION								
18. Supplier Selection	________	___	☐	________	___	☐	________	☐
19. Supplier Contact	________	___	☐	________	___	☐	________	☐
20. Label Copy with ID	________	___	☐	________	___	☐	________	☐
21. Label Design	________	___	☐	________	___	☐	________	☐
22. Distribution	________	___	☐	________	___	☐	________	☐
23. Duplication Time Line	________	___	☐	________	___	☐	________	☐
24. Report(s)	________	___	☐	________	___	☐	________	☐
______________	________	___	☐	________	___	☐	________	☐

Figure 13.1 The media creative and production checklist.

1. **Purpose.** The purpose of the project from management's point of view—especially *what* it is to achieve. *How* that is to be accomplished is best left by management to the pros.

2. **Client self-image.** Be open about the self-image you wish to project. If there are different suggestions within management, rank them. More than one may fit.

3. **Budget.** Be certain that management knows what its proposed budget can actually buy. If the budget is too limited for the quality desired, rethink your media needs.

4. **Project supervision.** The project supervisor is charged with managing everything from #5 on. Where supervision is delegated, the project supervisor makes the assignments.

5–7. **Basic approach.** How the purpose of #1 is to be addressed to a specified audience to achieve a specific response. Put #5 through #7 into writing before evaluating suppliers. If you are unsure about focus—soft sell or hard sell, for instance—leave it until after #8. Just be sure which options exist for you. Not everything will work.

8. **Suppliers.** It's not a question of which suppliers are best at what *they* do, it's who's best at what *you* need done. Evaluate your potential supplier from that perspective! (A teenager's rock group that's best for his friends may be a disaster as a dance band for parents.)

9. **Client's script.** Nothing presents the client's self-image more clearly than his or her ideas for scripts. The more detailed, the better they are. Urge management to participate, perhaps in a brainstorming session. Most of us know we're not scriptwriters. Keep it informal.

10. **Client's contact.** The client's one contact person—and keep it at one only!—with whom outside services may deal. Media production is just too difficult, time consuming, and costly to fix to permit uncoordinated instruction.

11. **Script approval.** Who *must* be involved? Who *may* be involved? Surely, not everyone who *wants* to be involved!

12. **Length.** This is primarily an "infomercial" decision that's often determined by the needs of the sales department. For on-air commercials, determine all the likely uses (say, 60-, 30-, or 15-second spots) before writing begins. It's much easier, and much less costly, to plan now, rather than as an afterthought during editing.

13. **Creative/production time line.** This time is determined by the client's needs, the supplier selected, and the variety of the end product. (A 30-second commercial may take as much time as a 30-minute infomercial.) To reserve duplication time, order duplicates to be made by #18 *now,* based on the #13 schedule, and notify everyone if there are delays. Everything in media generally takes longer than you expect.

14. **On-site contact.** Designate who is authorized to act for the client during on-site shooting, especially at the client's site. Also, appoint a backup. Film crews and recording producers get paid by the day . . . whether you make it possible for them to work or not.

15. **Production supervision.** Designate a project supervisor for management who can make on-the-spot filming and taping decisions. Others may have to be consulted, but the management's project supervisor *decides.*

16. **Editing supervision.** After filming and taping, editing achieves the final project. A number of product specialists may be present, but only the management's project supervisor speaks for the client.

17. **Length.** For "infomercials," the actual length is determined during editing. Do not, however, let this vary by more than 10 percent from the projected length in #12 without approval. Sales personnel, for instance, may not be able to use something twice as long, no matter how good it is. Even public service announcements often must fit set time slots. Don't just do. Check!

18–19. **Supplier/contacts.** If they are different, hold final approval of the production and duplication suppliers until you know that they are mechanically compatible with each other. Have them speak to one another. Make them explain what they decide.

20–21. **Labeling.** Duplication suppliers from #18 are generally the best source for labels and labeling. If special designs are wanted, let your duplicating service know. But find out the effect on production time. Consider routine but quick labeling for immediate needs, with customized labels thereafter.

22. **Distribution.** When the duplication supplier also ships the goods, find out the supplier's routine way to distribute them. Many send everything by air express, unless ordered to do otherwise in writing.

23. **Duplication time line.** Don't spare the details for larger projects or multiple shipments. Something will be forgotten, if it isn't specified here.

24. **Reports.** Note especially what has been learned that can be applied to future efforts. Put it in writing so that others may learn, too.

14 | Conventions, Trade Shows, Consumer Shows, and Meetings

> The photos of trade show exhibits featured in this chapter have been updated with the support of **Mike Thimmesch,** director of marketing for Skyline Displays (www.skyline-exhibits.com). Skyline is a major provider of exhibits, graphics, and services based in Eagan, MN, with offices in every major city in the United States and Canada—135 offices worldwide.

HOW THEY DIFFER AND WHY IT MATTERS

This chapter is about exhibiting at conventions, trade shows, and meetings.[1] In industry jargon, they're all called "shows," but they do have important distinctions.

Conventions

The main purpose of a convention is to advance skills, to increase knowledge, or to promote a cause, and sometimes all three. Heart surgeons, political parties, and associations tend to have "conventions."

Many conventions include exhibits. Your evaluation of such conventions will depend on the interest shown in the exhibits by those attending the convention.

Trade Shows

The main purpose of a trade show is business-to-business—that is, to bring together exhibitors with a preselected audience of customers and prospects. Manufacturers of office equipment and T-shirts, as well as breeders of horses and dogs, have trade shows.

Many trade shows also include convention-type activities, such as seminars, but the primary focus is still on the exhibits.

Consumer Shows (for the General Public)

Auto shows and the larger home and garden shows are examples of exhibits for the general public. They almost all charge admission, and many of them sell products

---

[1] The terms *exhibit* and *display* are used interchangeably by just about everyone concerned with either. The traditional distinction of *display* as a verb and *exhibit* as a noun (e.g., to display at an exhibit) is still found in some dictionaries as the primary definition but is ignored in current practice. Thus, a company in the field might be called General Exhibit and Display.

directly from their booths. The information in this chapter is applicable to consumer shows, but it does not deal with them directly. It concentrates on trade shows, conventions, and meetings.

Meetings

A meeting may be a convention, a show, or neither. Check the description in the meeting prospectus before you attend.

WHY YOU CARE

As a new exhibitor or one unfamiliar with a specific show, you don't care what it's called. You want to know what such shows do and how much importance is placed on the exhibits. (See Figures 14.1 and 14.4.) So check the descriptive literature, and then speak to the sponsoring organization—always remembering that they make money only if you decide to go. You'll want answers to at least two questions:

1. **Exhibits-only time.** What times are set aside exclusively for visiting exhibits? (Be aware that many shows that are successful for exhibitors have no such set-asides. Those attending make time. But it's one factor you'll want to consider.)
2. **Conflicts.** What special events by the sponsoring organization, other exhibitors, or anyone else are scheduled? If they do not know, ask for the

Figure 14.1   A large island exhibit created by Skyline Exhibits uses modular truss to carry colorful, lightweight fabric graphics. This creates a sense of mass and brings the company name into view from across the trade show floor.

previous year's final schedule. This type of activity tends to follow similar patterns each year. For instance, if noon to 2 P.M. is set aside to visit exhibits, is someone enticing away your prospects with a two-hour buffet, or will they gulp a cup of coffee and rush to the exhibits . . . and how can you know?

TRADE SHOW MARKETING

"Doing business" at trade shows is an increasingly important part of many integrated marketing programs. "Shows have emerged," according to David Kaminer, a widely published, nationally recognized expert in the field,[2] "as an increasingly significant component in companies' total marketing and selling strategies and budgets, as well as places where information is exchanged and major buying decisions are made within given industries. Trade shows today are a major way companies doing business in America—or wanting to do business in America—position themselves and seek to establish and increase their share of market."

Reasons for Increased Importance

"Cost efficiency," according to Kaminer, "is *the* major reason companies are participating in more trade shows, as well as stepping up their profiles at the events. Shows have proven to be three times more effective than a sales call—over 50 percent of trade show leads don't require a sales call to close. And well over 80 percent of the visitors now have buying influence for their companies or organizations."

Attendance

The days when low-level managers were sent to trade shows are gone . . . if they ever existed. Research in the 1990s by the Center for Exhibition Industry Research[3] (formerly the Trade Show Bureau) shows predominant attendance is by business leaders with buying power . . . who can and do buy at shows.

- 25 percent-plus of attendance is by top management—presidents, owners, partners, vice presidents, general managers.
- 50 percent-plus of attendance is by middle management.

Marketing Media

Trade shows ranked number 2 as the "most useful" marketing media according to American Business Press research.[4] The seven leaders, ranked in order, were:

---

[2]David A. Kaminer is president of The Kaminer Group, White Plains, New York, a PR and consulting firm specializing in trade shows ((914) 684-1934).

[3]Check them on the Web at www.ceir.org.

[4]Reported in *Business Marketing* magazine.

Percent

76.4 percent—Specialized business publications

67.6 percent—Trade shows

67.1 percent—Salespeople

61.4 percent—Conventions, seminars

56.4 percent—Direct mail

46.8 percent—Business directories

35.7 percent—General business publications

INSIGHT 78

When you exhibit, have your own key executives there to meet with comparable key customers and prospects one-on-one. Don't expect this to just happen! Schedule the meetings. Keep them brief. Have a top salesperson there to answer questions . . . and sell.

Information-Driven Growth

The demand by customers and prospects for instant, detailed information has brought about both an explosive growth in the number of trade shows and in the services they are expected to provide their audiences. Customers and prospects want the shows taken to them, rather than having to spend extra time and dollars traveling cross-country to attend. That's why the number of shows has more than doubled since 1980—from under 5,000 to more than 10,000, with the majority of the growth in a local or regional format. Equally important, computer access to their "at-home" databases by *both buyers and sellers* makes on-the-spot purchasing practical.

- Buyers can *immediately* match or modify exact needs to best offers without returning to check in-office files. Thanks to the laptop and increasingly the Internet, the "files" either travel with them or are only a modem away.
- Sellers can *immediately* match their capabilities against buyers' needs and, often within minutes or hours, propose solutions, including pricing and delivery time.

INSIGHT 79

The computer has led to demands that information requests be met with immediate answers. Staff your booth with salespeople totally at home with your on-computer files. At a successful show, "cold calls" are thrust at staff dozens of times each hour. Over 50 percent of these walk-in leads require no follow-up sales call to close[5] . . . providing you have the information and the staff to sell it!

---

[5]Center for Exhibit Industry Research.

IS IT WORTHWHILE ATTENDING?

Despite the explosive growth in trade show exhibiting, few exhibitors attend *every* convention or trade show in their field. Before exhibiting at a meeting of unknown value, ask the sponsoring organization to send you a copy of the previous year's program and, if separate, the list of that year's exhibitors. Call a few exhibitors with interests similar to yours and ask for their evaluation. Are they going back? If so, is it for business or "political" reasons? You'll know whether the same reasons apply to you.

When you've decided where to exhibit, you can start planning what will happen before and after you get there. Industry research shows that one-third of trade show leads can come from your own preshow promotion! One thing is absolutely certain: It won't happen if you don't plan.

SUMMARY

- Conventions focus on knowledge.
- Trade shows focus on product information and services.
- You care not about what it's called—only about what they do.
- Ask previous exhibitors for their evaluations. They paid the bill.

INSIGHT 80

The First "Secret" of Successful Exhibits: "Lack of resources" is an invitation to invent excuses. Forget resources and remember goals. In planning your exhibit, keep your focus on your goals and make the resources fit them.

WHY YOU AND THEY ARE THERE

The planning of your exhibit begins with a search for the answers to two questions:

1. Why are they—my clients and prospects—there?
2. What can I gain from being there with them, and how do I do it?

Figure 14.2 summarizes some appropriate answers to these questions.

In all probability, a trade show held in Las Vegas in mid-February will get less *display* attention than the same show held in Iowa City in August. But less is far different from none. Many of the most successful conventions and trade shows are very deliberately held in seemingly distracting locations. That's how they draw such huge attendance. Taking advantage of that attendance despite the attraction of outside interests requires detailed planning. Especially important is the setting of specific goals that will focus your efforts.

Why Clients and Prospects Attend	How to Turn It to Your Advantage
To make a careful evaluation of exhibitors' and competitors' products and services. Increasingly, to buy.	Your customers aren't the only ones who have competitors. Get out of your booth long enough to see what your competitors are doing. Take photographs of their displays and any others that seem especially interesting, to learn what they do right.
To learn.	Make your displays a learning opportunity by helping *your* customers look smarter to *their* colleagues, employers, and/or customers.
To meet with friends and colleagues.	Become a friend by being active in the organization sponsoring the meeting. The very fact of your being there makes you a colleague.
To get a tax-deductible vacation.	Don't wine and dine guests without a specific purpose in mind. Their goal may be a fancy, free meal; yours has to be totally business centered.

Figure 14.2   Why clients and exhibitors attend conferences.

HOW TO FOCUS YOUR EFFORTS AND THEIR ATTENTION

Success with trade shows and conventions is mostly about focusing attention—yours and that of the people you hope to attract and persuade. To demonstrate the problem, imagine yourself at the annual New York or Chicago Premium and Incentive Show. Of the more than 1,000 exhibitors, some 27 specialize in T-shirts and caps, 27 more in watches and clocks, 31 in pens and writing materials, and 19 in some kind of food. In addition, 60 exhibitors have a combination of one or more of those products. If you are a buyer deciding among T-shirts, pens, watches, and edibles as a premium, how do you decide with whom to spend your time? Conversely, if you are one of those exhibitors, how do you get that buyer to spend time with you when he or she can't possibly evaluate every single display? The answer lies in one word: *focus.*

Focus on Focus

The single most effective way to succeed as an exhibitor is to aim for a particular type of prospect and to give them an instantly recognizable reason for thinking that you can solve the problem that took that prospect to the show. If all you want is to draw a crowd, just give a crisp, cool, delicious apple to anyone who comes to your booth. You'll be inundated with visitors. That may be your goal if you are the leading supplier in your industry and are exhibiting to retain and build on goodwill. But if you are new or one of the lesser players, you don't want *visitors,* you want *prospects.* Make that your focus.

Focus on Prospects

It is, of course, possible that everyone attending a trade show or convention is a prospect for your product or service. Booksellers viewing exhibits from publishers or hardware retailers given their choice of different brands of nails seem likely examples. But no bookseller can stock every title, and few hardware stores have more than a few brands of nails. How you bring attention to *your* titles, *your* nails, *your* brand of ice cream, *your* microwaves, or *your* earthmoving equipment depends—often at first sight—on your prospects' view of you. Focusing that view so they see you as a solver of their problems is the key to your success.

Focus on Customers: They're "Prospects," Too!

Your existing customers are almost always easier to sell than the new prospect . . . if they give you the chance. Don't take them for granted. Treat them as your most important prospects that still have to be sold. Decide what is most helpful to your existing customers and how to attract them to your display when they think they already know all about you. Make this a key part of your planning. There's much help in the pages that follow.

Focus on Your Prospects' Problems . . . and Solve Them

Think of your prospects as buyers who, in turn, must please a specific kind of customer. This is true whether their "customer" is within their own organization (seeking new furniture for the offices or new locomotives for the trains) or outside (buying a new line of children's shoes or a new line of lawnmowers). Pleasing these ultimate customers should be the focus of everything your prospects do at a show. Your success lies not in appealing to them as a buyer but in assuring their success as a seller. Convince them that you can make them look good to their ultimate customers, and you'll turn prospects into customers, to your benefit . . . and theirs.

"Trade show selling is extremely fast-paced and highly competitive," reports trade show sales trainer Keith Resnick.[6] "The average sales opportunity lasts only three to five minutes. And the prospect often leaves your booth to visit with your biggest competitors."

To make those few minutes work to your best advantage, Resnick urges a consistent eight-step approach:

1. Immediate contact. Let your entire body language invite and welcome the visitor.
2. Open the sales call with a handshake, a smile, and an introduction.
3. Identify the prospect's company. Make sure you are spending your invaluable time with a prospect, not a competitor!
4. Qualify, as time permits.

---

[6]Keith Resnick, president of Creative Training Solutions, Gibbsboro, New Jersey (www.creative training.com), conducts workshops and seminars on trade show selling throughout the country.

5. Present just enough to arrange a follow-up call. If visitors want more, they'll ask.
6. Arrange the next step, from an appointment to a demonstration to buying right there . . . whatever the prospect wants.
7. Close the sales call with a pleasant thank-you and a smile.
8. Record results *immediately,* perhaps on a tape recorder, before spending time with anyone else.

Failure to Follow Up

Center for Exhibit Industry Research statistics indicate that 80 percent of trade show leads are not followed up, despite the fact that higher-level prospects are attending. The problem lies in a combination of poor lead-form design ("What do I do with this garbage?") and lack of a system to ensure lead follow-up ("I don't have time to make my regular calls now. Which ones do you want me to drop?"). The solution, suggests Resnick; lies in getting lead forms designed by the sales representatives who get them after the show, plus establishing a system that makes follow-up practical—and financially rewarding—for everyone involved.

INSIGHT 81

Decide who your real prospects are by focusing on what they want from the show and on whether you can provide it. Then look at your display through their eyes. If it doesn't trumpet you as the best answer to their needs, you're looking at either the wrong prospects or an ineffective display.

SUMMARY

*   Discover and fill your customers' and prospects' needs. It's the most likely way to fill your own.

THE BILLBOARD APPROACH TO SUCCESS AT EXHIBITING

No one has learned better than the producers of billboards how to focus fleeting attention. Just think of the problems of selling *in print* to drivers whose lives depend on keeping their eyes on the road! Here's how it's done:

1. **Use one simple message only** . . . the simpler the better. If ever there was a time for the KISS principle to (keep it simple, stupid) this is it.

2. **Keep it single.** Let everything reinforce the same message. Products, words, visuals, colors, and design all work together to achieve a single goal. Make *integrated* marketing communications work for you!

3. **Keep it short.** The fewer words and images you have, the better off you are. Keep it focused. If you can get along without it, do.

What This Book Can Do to Help

Neither this book nor any other guide can design, stock, or staff your exhibit. But it can give you a method for applying the billboard technique to your display from its original preshow concept, to every step along the way, and to your postshow evaluation. Here's how.

1. Assume that you will be placed in the middle of five exhibitors showing what appears to be a product or service identical to yours. To make things easier, assume that you all have the same amount of space.

2. Assume that a temporarily blinded prospect goes to each of you and asks that you tell her *just one thing,* on the basis of which she'll decide whether or not to return after her vision clears up later that day. That one thing is your "billboard"—the featured words that are part of your display and that tell your prospects that you know who they are and that you can solve their problems.

3. Now assume that a temporarily deaf prospect goes by each of your displays. He'll also return to one of you when his hearing clears up. He sees your signs, but he also sees your entire exhibit. Do they both send the same message? Do they reinforce each other? Or do they contradict or ignore each other, as if different persons with different goals had been in charge of preparing your display? You have a one-in-five chance of getting the prospect back if you leave it to luck and if your competitors do the same. Because they're unlikely to do that, however, you'd better not count on it either.

INSIGHT 82

Use the billboard technique. Don't be fuzzy, and hope for the best. Be focused and plan for the most.

SUMMARY

- Think of your display as a billboard with room for a single, simple message.
- Know what you want to say and to whom you want to say it. Then make everything send the same signal. "Your problem solved here!"

When You Are Limited to Saying Just One Thing, Make It a Benefit

Examples

- *You* develop a larger computer screen.
  Your prospects want greater productivity through less eye fatigue.
- *You* offer biodegradable paper.
  Your prospects want packaging materials they can brag about.
- *You* offer frozen gourmet dinners for restaurants.
  Your prospects want four-star meals with a nonstar chef.

INSIGHT 83

Features are what you put in. Benefits are what they get out. Features explain and instruct. Benefits attract and sell. Use benefits.

SUMMARY

- Concentrate on learning the real reasons your prospects are at a show, and focus your presentations on meeting that need (Yes, we said this before, but it's worth repeating.)
- Think of your exhibit as a billboard. It will focus everything you do.

TARGET YOUR PROSPECTS FOR PERSONAL ATTENTION

There's More to Exhibiting Than Exhibits

How much personal attention you give to specific customers and prospects will depend on five factors:

1. **Identify your targets.** Know the key customers and prospects who are likely to attend. The easiest way to find out is to ask them in advance.
2. **Make two lists.** List one has the clients and prospects you have targeted for special attention, with the reasons they should give it to you (what you have to offer) and what you hope to get out of it. List two has the persons from your company who will attend the show.
3. **Decide what "special attention" means for everyone on list one.**
4. **Focus.** Assign your staff, if any, to specific individuals on list one, with detailed instructions about focusing and goals. Give everyone, including yourself, *objectives you must document!*
5. **Invite the targeted men and women.** Invite them to your booth and to any "special attention" events. Call, then follow up in writing. Do it well in advance of the show, and then confirm their acceptance just before the date. (Don't say, "You can make it, can't you?" Say, "I'm really looking forward to our lunch.")

If You're Few and They're Many

If there are just too many customers and prospects to give all of them personal attention, invite them to a grand breakfast in the centrally located hotel. You'll want a private suite or dining room decorated with your products and literature. But don't give them a hard sell. It's breakfast time, and how would you like a sales talk with your cereal!

Since lunch and dinner invitations abound, your "Breakfast Club" is likely to be more appreciated—and remembered—than something fancier and more expensive later in the day.

Breakfast is also a great way to give a second invitation to anyone who can't join you at a different time. ("I'm really sorry you can't make it for dinner, but perhaps you can join us for an informal breakfast at the Savoy Drop-In Suite. Anytime between 7 and 9 A.M. on Monday and Tuesday. I'll send you a reminder before the show.")

INSIGHT 84

You and your staff are *not* there to have breakfast! You are there to meet specifically targeted individuals, introduce them to senior management (if that's other than you), generally make them comfortable . . . and set up a specific time to "do some business" later.

It Doesn't Have to Have Food

The wooing of customers and prospects doesn't *have* to be centered around a meal. Be inventive! Consider a sports event, a play, or a disco. They'll relax with colleagues and entertain each other. When they are back home, drop each one a note by mail or fax. Broadcast fax, described in Chapter 9, is perfect for this. Tell them how much you enjoyed their company and how *they* helped the group have a good time. That will remind them who was their host, something often forgotten in the rush of parties at many trade shows and conventions. Of course *you* use the event to focus on your business goals and obtain specific objectives you can document.

There's Always Lunch or Dinner

When the ultimate in individual attention is called for, that usually means lunch or dinner. Here are some suggestions to make those meals more effective as *business* events:

- **Make reservations in advance.** Check a standard guide of restaurant listings. Because the more desirable places fill up early, make your reservations two months in advance of the show dates. If you are unfamiliar with the location, ask for an approximate time and distance from your hotel. You'll want to remain fairly close for lunch.
- **Fewer is better.** Have a maximum of six persons per table. Invite fewer people, rather than use larger tables. When there are more than six per

table, comfortable conversation is limited to the persons seated next to you. As host, you lose control of the table as a whole.

*   **Be "guest wise."** Generally, a ratio of one host to two guests is preferable to the reverse. There are, of course, exceptions, and your own good sense will tell you when they apply. In assigning guests to hosts, weigh the difference between flattering your guests with attention and intimidating them by sheer weight of numbers.

It is a fact, overlooked at our peril, that much business is done over lunch and golf. That's not because customers or prospects are being "bought." Rather, other things being equal—as they often are—we'd rather do business with our friends, and few things seem to build business friendships faster than a shared activity or a relaxing meal.

INSIGHT 85

NEVER let staff socialize with each other at an event attended by customers and prospects. It is insulting to your guests to have "the help" find itself more interesting than the men and women they invited!

Focus for Individual Attention

Most of this chapter is concerned with your exhibit and you as an exhibitor. But some of your most valuable exhibiting contacts can be made through individual and small-group "business socializing." Like everything else about exhibiting, this requires careful advance planning. You pick the shows to attend because they bring your key customers and prospects to the same location. It's your chance to meet with them individually or collectively, formally or socially, briefly or extensively, as your schedule and theirs permit. Don't pass up the opportunity to cement a business relationship with some personal attention.

INSIGHT 86

Your best prospects and customers are your competitiors' most likely key targets. If you don't go courtin' . . . they will.

SUMMARY

*   Plan for personal contacts, and then follow them up to make them happen.
*   Hold staff—and yourself—responsible for specific targeted results from social events. *Your guests go* to parties, *you* produce business-based events.

YOUR EXHIBIT SPACE

As an exhibitor, you have quite a variety of options for developing your display, but no matter which one you choose, there are certain rules of thumb about the space, generally referred to as "floor space," your exhibit will actually occupy.

Booth Size

Exhibit space is made up of units called "booths," with one booth the minimum space available. At most shows, booths are 10 feet long by 10 feet deep, but always check for variations. If you're attending more than one show and will provide your own exhibit, plan it around the smallest space and build from there.

Booth Height

Almost all standard booths have a maximum height of 8 feet at the back of the booth and then drop rather quickly to a 30-inch table height, to permit visibility along an entire row of displays. The object is to keep exhibitors from blocking their views of each other by erecting "fences" between their booths. The height rule is often different for "peninsula" and "island" displays, as explained shortly.

Aisles and Visibility

The aisle between rows of booths is generally 8 to 10 feet wide. This width becomes an important factor in planning signs and determining what your audience can actually take in when they see your booth from the middle of an aisle. Work with your display company or other professionals to determine the best size and colors for the signs and their lettering as well as how high they should be placed. (As a general rule, make the top row of letters no more than six feet off the ground . . . but there are lots of exceptions.) If local sources for signs seem inadequate, check the nearest major city Yellow Pages.

Exhibit Space Configuration

Exhibit space is available in three configurations (see Figure 14.3):

1. **Back wall.** These in-line configurations are any number of booths lined up next to each other. The booths are usually 10 feet wide by 10 feet deep. Occasionally sizes differ, so be sure to check the show guide. The height of the booth is generally limited to 8 feet at the back and table height or 30 inches at the front.
2. **Peninsula.** Peninsula displays have aisles on three sides. Different rules and restrictions apply if they abut another peninsula, versus if they abut two rows of back wall booths. Check the show rules for what is permitted. The management will often create a larger peninsula space on request by borrowing from abutting back wall booths.

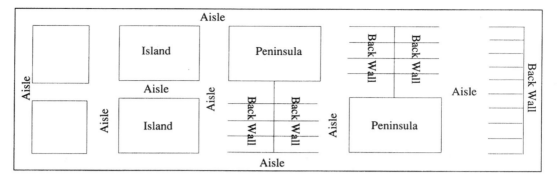

Figure 14.3 Sections of floor plan showing three types of booth configurations

3. **Island.** An island, as the name implies, is surrounded by aisles on all four sides. Special rules apply to islands, but they tend to be quite liberal, as islands are the most expensive spaces to rent and management wants to encourage their use. Height limitations are often highest for island displays, making them the space of choice for tall products or exhibits. Regardless of the height of the ceiling, there are always strict limitations on space you may use. Check before you plan and before you ship your booths.

Hanging Signs

Many shows permit signs that are elevated (see Figure 14.1) or that hang above a display. Exhibitors use them to call attention to themselves from locations where their display cannot otherwise be seen. Hanging signs are controlled by show rules and fire regulations but are very effective additional exposure.

Space for New Exhibitors

Unless you purchase a major island or peninsula area, prime space goes to regular exhibitors. Newer exhibitors, through repeat exhibiting, must earn their way to the more desirable locations. But don't get mad. Increase the number of visitors to your booth with better preshow promotion. Here are some suggestions:

- Over 25 percent of trade show visitors go to specific booths to which they have been invited.
- Write a month before the show and give your prospects *a reason* to visit you. Prizes, contests, a key to open "Treasure Island" all are proven winners.
- Write two weeks before the show, reemphasize the benefits a visit to your booth offers, and enclose a 3″ × 5″ map to your location.
- Fax a reminder three business days before the show. Use broadcast fax for a large list.
- Make sure your booth signage and display reemphasizes your promised benefits the instant they are seen. If ever there was a need to make the right first impression, this is it!

SUMMARY

• Check the show rules for any display you plan to use. Do not assume that last year's rules still apply. Try to limit surprises to pleasant ones.

YOUR DISPLAY

As an exhibitor, you have five options for developing your display. Which one you select—and many exhibitors use more than one kind—should depend on your goals, budget, and availability of staff, probably in that order.

Custom-Built Displays (Option 1)

Custom-built displays are generally designed, built, and maintained by companies specializing in that field. They (and their cousins, the rental display companies, described shortly) are almost always the most impressive exhibits at a show. The most successful displays are designed with a specific goal in mind, and that is their strength, as long as the exhibitor's focus remains constant. A new focus may require a new display. Generally, displays wear out physically in about five years, so the likelihood of their outliving their usefulness is slight.

Modular Design

For displays longer than 10 feet (a single booth), consider a modular design that is organized around 10-foot or 20-foot units. This gives you flexibility in case of budgetary contraction or expansion: You can subtract or add units without rebuilding an entire exhibit and use individual sections for smaller shows.

What Display Companies Do

Exhibit design.   Display companies can design your exhibit or consult with you in its design. They are architects, as well as builders, of exhibits. A display company should always be consulted before any design for an exhibit is approved, because of the company's knowledge of exhibit rules and pitfalls.

Exhibit construction.   Display companies construct exhibits and, equally important, the customized, padded containers for shipping your display with minimal damage. Anyone who has ever watched a display being delivered to an exhibit site knows that "no damage" is but a dream.

Show planning.   A display company will act as your agent in all contact with the exhibit site, *except for ordering the actual floor space.* This space is always paid for in advance and then assigned on a first-paid basis. Payment is the responsibility of the exhibitor. Any question as to the size or height of your display, electrical hookups, furniture or other rentals, shipping, setting up and tearing down (dismantling) the display, and shipping the display to the next show or returning it for storage can be handled by the display company as your single "turnkey" source of supply. You will want to know what the charges for these services are, and you might decide to do some of them yourself. However, ask yourself what *you* get paid for (even if it's by yourself), then use *them.*

On-site supervision.   The display company can send an in-house expert to supervise set-up—the on-site assembly of your display. You are charged for the supervisor's time, transportation, and living expenses while there, but the ability to expedite the assembly of the display and make on-the-spot modifications and repairs often actually saves the additional cost. The peace of mind of knowing that supervision is being done by the original construction company is priceless. This same degree of supervision may not be required for dismantling the display, depending on the complexity of its construction, on whether the same crew did the setting up, and on whether the crew was made aware of any repacking problems.

Provide storage.   A major function of display companies is to ship and store displays between shows. With so many parts and pieces to manage, good inventory control is critically important.

Repair.   Display companies refurbish, repair, or modify displays and shipping creates as required.

ABOUT SPECIAL EVENTS

In addition to working on displays, many display companies have become their clients resource of choice for handling special events. Rather than use their own time and staff, companies use their display company to arrange trade show and convention meetings, dinners, and festivities, and to set up sales meetings, board presentations, employee's picnics, and so on. What began by doing a client a favor has, in many display companies, become an additional successful business.

Costs Involved in Using a Custom-Built or Rental Display

For the purpose of establishing costs, a rental display will go through the same steps to get ready for a show as a custom-built unit. The costs involved in this process may actually be higher than the cost of the floor space the display will occupy. Savings are, of course, possible by using fewer booths. In fact, many displays are unitized—that is, made up of modules that can be assembled into various configurations and sizes, depending on the importance of a show. However, there are always some start-up costs, and the savings may not be proportional to the number of booths used. Your display company can give you accurate estimates to help you decide.

A Dozen Cost Factors

1. **Planning meetings.** Take advantage of your display company's expertise by getting it involved at the earliest stages of planning. Though it is

possible to produce almost anything by using the JTWGCHD system ("Just think what God could have done if He'd had our money"), a conscientious representative will forewarn you about costs, time requirements, and other constraints.

2. **Final agreement** on the display and on modifications, if any.

3. **Removing the display from storage,** unpacking it from its crate(s)—for their own protection, displays are stored in their padded shipping crates—and inspecting, repairing, and modifying the display. Because display graphics—the art and signs—are seldom used the same way twice, a detailed inspection is not done until all modifications and new graphics are agreed on.

4. **Assembly for inspection** of the complete display as repaired and modified. This is an optional, fairly expensive step. Usually, only the new graphics and major modifications need client approval.

5. **Repairing** the shipping crate and packing the display.

6. **Contacting the trucking firm** and reserving space for a guaranteed arrival time. Depending on the number of days and routes available, the display will be shipped one of two ways:

    *   **Direct van.** This refers not to the size of the truck but to the method of routing. Direct van shipments remain on the same truck from pickup to delivery, minimizing handling and the resulting damage. This is usually the fastest way to ship and, if required, the easiest to trace. It is more expensive, however, than common carrier, the next method to be discussed.

    *   **Common carrier.** The shipment may be transferred to a different truck to combine materials going to a common destination. Although this is the less expensive way to ship, it generally results in more handling, with possible costly damage.

7. **Shipping the display and unloading it at the destination.**

8. **Assembling the display.** At most shows, the exhibitor's own staff may *not* assemble major displays. This work may be supervised by the exhibitor, a display company representative, or an on-site supervisor. Work rules vary widely in right-to-work states. Check before you do anything yourself!

9. **Making on-the-spot repairs and adjustments.**

10. **Preparing for return shipment.** The bills of lading and labels for shipping the display to its next destination or its return to storage are prepared. This paperwork is usually completed in advance by the display company.

11. **Tearing down the display.** The display is disassembled and repacked into the original crates.

12. **Arranging for next use or return shipment.** The crates are checked against the number in the original shipment and, if there is no discrepancy, are sent to their next destination(s) or returned to storage. If returned to storage, repairs are not made at this time, but await possible modification with the next use of the display.

Rental Displays (Option 2)

Many display companies have displays that can be rented and customized to meet an exhibitor's needs. These displays range from impressive island exhibits to single-booth units. They can be very effective where you wish to make a one-shot impact without taking on the cost of designing, constructing, and storing your own display—especially one with limited use.

Off-the-Shelf Displays (Option 3)

Dozens of companies, including many exhibit builders, have standard off-the-shelf displays that can be personalized at little cost, usually by adding the exhibitor's name and some simple graphics. (See Figure 14.4). Many of these displays are truly portable in that they disassemble into suitcase-size units that fit into the trunk of most midsize or larger cars . . . but measure the trunk before you buy. You'll find the names of the manufacturers in any major city's Yellow Pages, under "Exhibits and Displays." Ask several to send you their catalogs.

Pipe and Drape Displays (Option 4)

A curtained backdrop draped from a pipe and holding a sign with the exhibitor's name is supplied by the show as part of your contract for exhibit space. There is no fancy backdrop. There is no special lighting and no unique graphics—just the exhibitor and the products or services. Sometimes a table and/or chairs is also part of the package. Some of today's major exhibitors started just this way.

Although pipe and drape is the least costly booth space, there is no limit, within show rules, to the enhancements that you may put into the area. Off-the-shelf and smaller-space customized displays, or one or more modular sections from large-space displays, are used in many pipe-and-drape booths. Your only limits are your imagination and your budget . . . and with the display suggested in Option 5, even budget should be no problem. Read on!

THE THROW-AWAY DISPLAY

> The newly popular one-show, throw-away display described here was developed in 1990 by **Jack Heimerdinger,** a gifted independent creative director, now living in Plainfield, Ill. (815) 436–5137, jheimerdinger@ameritech.net.

The One-Show, Leave-Behind Display: An Invitation to Adventure (Option 5)

With a custom-built or rental unit, much of the cost is made up of fees for storage, shipping, assembly, dismantling, reshipping, repair, and general maintenance. Constructing a leave-behind display that is of low weight and bulk, easy to assemble, and sturdy and attractive is not an impossible assignment for an imaginative designer. Since the display will always be brand new, you eliminate the cost of repair and maintenance. Because it's light and compact, you save a major portion—if not all—of the cost of storage, shipping, and handling. Because it's

Figure 14.4   Exhibits of all sizes—from portable tabletops and back walls to modular islands—are available for purchase or rent and can be customized with many kinds of graphics. Cases for Skyline's pop-up displays can even be turned into cost-efficient tables. Call Skyline to receive a free copy of their 86 page *Trade Show Marketing Idea Kit.* Skyline Exhibits: 1-800-328-2725

Figure 14.5   Example of a one-show, leave-behind display. Original concept and design by Jack Heimerdinger.

left behind, you save the total cost of return shipment and subsequent handling. You may, depending on exhibit rules, have to use show personnel for assembling the display, but that would also be true of a custom-built display. You will want to tear down or disassemble your display before you leave, or there's a very good chance that show personnel will repack it and ship it to you at your expense. Just tear it apart, and put a few signs reading "Throw Away! Do Not Ship!" where they can't be missed. See Figure 14.5 for an example of a throw-away display.

Constructing Your One-Show Display

Triangular Columns

The triangular column, shown in Figure 14.6, is made from a standard sheet of $\frac{3}{8}$-inch-thick, 4 × 8-foot Foamcord. This exceptionally strong yet light display material is stocked by many sign suppliers. Keep the wording on the columns and signs to an absolute minimum. The fewer words, the more likely it is that they will be read and noted.

The one-show, leave-behind display seen in Figure 14.5 cost less than 25 percent of just the shipping charges associated with using the company's custom-built display.[7] The entire leave-behind display was produced on site, where the show took place, eliminating storage and shipping costs. Only two suppliers were needed: one made the columns and signs and the other was a "home store" retail outlet. Both were found in the Yellow Pages.

To give the columns of the display stability, use the design shown in Figure 14.6. The original board is eight feet tall, but you need use only six feet for the column. That leaves 24 × 48 inches that you can use to make a sign.

---

[7]To be fair, lightweight construction materials used in newer displays have dramatically reduced the cost of shipping.

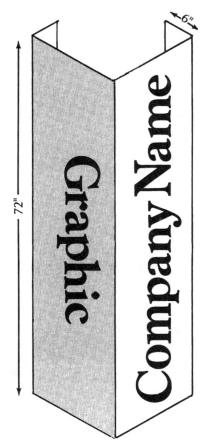

Figure 14.6 Triangular column design.

Shelved Cases

Not every exhibitor can make use of the easily assembled bookshelf-type cases pictured between the columns in Figure 14.5, but if you can, they are available at low-cost home furnishings stores for about $100 each. Check the Yellow Pages for a source. When ordering, specify cases with or without doors, and ask how much the cost will be to deliver the units assembled. The supplier can probably also provide inexpensive gooseneck lamps and extension cords for lighting. Use the same delivery instructions as for the columns. Everything is an off-the-shelf retail item.

Tables and Chairs

If tables or chairs are needed, rent them from the show. Chairs can also be purchased from the outlet that provides the cases. Purchasing is slightly more expensive but may have greater eye appeal.

A REMINDER: THROW IT AWAY!

Avoid the temptation to save the columns and signs. Unless you can use them again immediately, they will get damaged or frayed or simply be in the way. Throw them out, even though it hurts. The cases, lamps, and—if purchased—chairs are another matter. Before the show is over and you have to rush off, contact a local charity that can use these items and have them picked up. You'll get a tax write-off that will make you proud!

SUMMARY

- Explore all your options, from purchasing custom-built to rental to leave-behind displays, for the shows you attend. There may be a variety of "best" solutions to your display needs.
- Work with an exhibit company if your budget permits. It will let you concentrate on the selling for which your display is just the background.

ORDERING A NEW DISPLAY

The purchase or rental of displays is one of the most exciting projects for any promotion manager. Here, in outline form, is a basic schedule for this project. A special checklist is provided at the end of the chapter.

1. **Getting in-house agreement on the basics of the display.** Get agreement on the following items:

- Type of display: custom built, rental, tabletop, modular, leave-behind, and so on.
- Number of booths or running feet of display space.
- Budget. (Get advance cost and time estimates from several possible suppliers, and then add 10 percent.)
- Materials and services to be featured.
- Purpose of the display, beyond showing materials or services. For instance, will there be conference or sales areas and/or a safe storage section?
- Visual impact desired, such as high-tech or warm and friendly or both.
- Frequency of expected use of all or of portions of the display during a three-year period. Will smaller modular units be used more often than the whole? How many? How often?
- Expected life of the display.
- Approval procedure. Who must be consulted and who will give final budgetary and design approval? When will they be available? Who has approval authority in their absence? (There is little point in waiting until March 9 to approve an exhibit for a show that was over on March 8.)

2. **Putting it in writing.** Put the display basics in writing, and get approval of this description from all concerned. If there are disagreements about your description of what was decided on, resolve the difficulties before going any further.

3. **Finding an exhibit company for custom-built or rental.** If you have never before worked with an exhibit company or are unfamiliar with those in your area, ask for recommendations from your competitors (this is not a noncompetitive industry), your colleagues, trade associations, or media representatives (they know a surprising amount). Or simply check the Yellow Pages.

Send each candidate a copy of your display basics from No. 1 and your New Display Construction checklist from page 288. Ask for a *written* response, by a specified date, including the following information:

- The candidate's experience with the type of display you have outlined. Have them include pictures you'll return, costs of displays shown, dates of construction, and persons to contact for recommendations.
- Design and construction personnel. Are they employees or outside contractors and designers? The latter is not necessarily negative, but you will want to take it into consideration.
- Where and by whom the display will be stored.
- Basic storage charges, with costs for removing the display from storage or returning it after a show.
- Estimated maintenance charges.
- Who the candidate's account executive will be and that person's experience in the exhibit field.

Make absolutely clear that you will not accept a personal presentation in place of the information you have requested, but that you are prepared to answer by phone any further questions the candidate may have.

4. **If you have an existing display.** For most companies, purchasing a new display is such a large expenditure that multiple bids are mandated, even when they

have an excellent relationship with a particular display house. If your company is in such a position, have lunch with your account representative and break the news as gently as possible. No one lives a business life of more threatened security than an account executive, so assure the AE that his or her firm will get "most favored nation" consideration. But ask for exactly the same information you're requesting from everyone else. Few decisions that are at least partly aesthetic can be totally objective, so it is best to begin with a level playing field.

INSIGHT 87

If you are dissatisfied with your current display house or its account executive, try to resolve the problem by going to the senior management of that display house, rather than leaving them out of the picture. Account executives for any kind of supplier sometimes become apologists for their employers, rather than expediters and problem solvers for their clients. That is an excess of loyalty only employers can solve—as they will, but only if you let them know a problem exists. You don't want your account executives fired. You do want them working for *your* best interest.

---

5. **Narrowing the field and final inspections.** Narrow the number of candidates to a reasonable number, and then arrange for a personal visit to each. Take along the New Display Construction checklist from this chapter with the candidates' mail, fax, or phone responses already filled in. You won't mind their having put their best foot forward, but reality mustn't be too far from what you've already been told.

Satisfy yourself about the ability of the firm you ultimately choose to work together with you. Be prepared to answer some questions about your firm, your credit rating, and your promptness in paying bills. Designing and constructing displays involves such a preponderance of up-front, out-of-pocket costs for the exhibit company that it customarily gets a one-third down payment before beginning a job, a second third at a specified time during construction, and the final third on completion.

Select the finalists—probably three, usually no more than four—and invite them, individually, to visit you for a turnaround inspection in which they will get answers to any questions they may have about you and your project, plus a final project specification form that includes the following:

- General directions, with any modifications from the original version already seen by them.
- The schedule for presentation of their design concept, plus time for at least one revision before a final rendering. Do not discuss the competing presentations with the competitors. *Exhibit design is the intellectual property of the exhibit company until you buy it!* It is unethical to show a design or even discuss its approach with a competing exhibit company.
- The date for the presentation of the final rendering and a scale model. The production of a model is customary and, like the customized ship-

ping containers, is included in the overall cost. The model becomes invaluable in visualizing different configurations and the relationships of various elements to each other. Have each presenter specify the following:

- The date when all copy and graphics to be used in the actual display must be given to the exhibits house.

- The date when the display will be ready for a first inspection, with adequate time for modifications before shipment.

- The presentation date for all concerned—the final show and tell.

- The date of shipment of the display to the first show. Certain suppliers may wish to trade a shorter production schedule for more time to prepare a presentation. Don't do this. It's unfair to you, as it forces a faster decision-making process, and it's equally unfair to other candidates who prefer a normal work schedule. Extraordinarily fast production is an invitation to shortcuts and shoddy workmanship. Avoid it wherever possible.

INSIGHT 88

Get at least three bids for creating your display, and pay each company an agreed-on amount for its presentation. Few of us do our very best work on speculation.

In 1992, I supervised the competition that produced a major new display. The display companies were authorized to charge up to $5,000 each for their presentation designs. Each was given a maximum budget of $200,000 for a completed 100-foot display. Actual cost estimates from each supplier were not a part of management's decision. To management's surprise and delight, the winning display, unanimously agreed on, proved to be $50,000 less than they had budgeted. (I had told the competitors that within budget, price would not be a factor.)[8]

SUMMARY

- Put everything in writing.
- Get in-house agreement on basics of the display and the assignment of responsibilities—and don't go further until you do.
- Personally visit likely candidates to inspect all aspects of their operations. Insist on the "show" part of the show and tell.
- Prepare a workable schedule for all concerned, and monitor it continually. When all has finally gone well and your new display is a success, put your thanks to all concerned in writing, too.

---

[8]Despite my warnings when I saw preliminary concept drawings, the winning display was the only one that actually followed the outlined specifications. Two out of three were so creative that they were useless.

NOTES ON THE NEW DISPLAY CONSTRUCTION CHECKLIST

Unlike the other checklists in this book, this one (Figure 14.7) needs no annotation. The following notes may, however, be helpful:

- Use a separate copy of this checklist for each potential supplier. Fill in #2–14 for each kind of project. Duplicate as needed.
- The type of display (#1) can be determined in advance or by the information provided in #2–14. Be prepared to make some modification from what you want to what is more practical and less costly, even when the display is custom built or left behind and thrown away.
- You'll need #16–31 primarily for custom-built and major rental displays. That's where you require the most detailed knowledge about your supplier. You ask #17 because you do want that company there a month or a year from now, when it's time to use the display again!
- Modify #15 in accordance with the type of display you order. You certainly won't need it for the pipe and drape display, which comes with the show.

NOTES ON THE CONVENTIONS/TRADE SHOWS/ MEETINGS CHECKLIST

These notes are a supplement to the material presented in this chapter. They are not a substitute for that material. The checklist is presented in Figure 14.8.

1. **Exhibit focus.** Determine why you are at *that* show at *that* time. The answer must determine everything else you do . . . every other point on this checklist. It therefore comes first.

2. **Total budget.** The complete-for-everything show budget. If the cost of a new display, whether rented, purchased, or custom built, is included, use the checklist on page 289 for that amount. (See point #10. Custom-built construction is generally a *capital,* rather than a one-show cost. Determine which before including it here.) *Do not let final budget approval delay action on #3 and #4!*

3–4. **Booth space/location.** Unlike real estate, location may not be the most important factor for display booths, but it certainly helps. Find out the why's of space assignments. Just ask! Then be the first to follow the rules and meet the deadlines.

5. **Space reserved/confirmed.** This refers to official notification from a show that specific space has been assigned to you. If you plan something unusual in size, shape, traffic flow, or electrical or other service requirements, don't wait for that "official" notification. Make sure to get approval far enough in advance to change if the answer is "no." The show organizers want you to attend and will try to help. Give them the chance!

6. **Display company order.** One person at your end deals with one person at the display company's end. Put everything in writing. Get it con-

NEW DISPLAY CONSTRUCTION CHECKLIST

Project Title _____   Date _____
Project Description _____   Project # _____
_____   Checklist # _____
Overall Supervision By _____   Deadline _____
Budget _____ Completion Date _____   Start Up Date _____

1. **STYLE:** ☐ Custom Built ☐ Rental ☐ Portable ☐ Pipe & Drape ☐ Throw-away
2. **DATE NEEDED:** _____ 3. **QUANTITY NEEDED:** _____ 4. **BUDGET:** $_____
5. **SIZE:** _____ Booths/ ____ Running feet 6. **MODULAR:** ☐ Yes ☐ No
7. **BASIC CONFIGURATION:** ☐ Back Wall ☐ Island ☐ Peninsula
8. **MATERIALS TO BE SHOWN—RUNNING FEET OR DIMENSIONS:** _____
_____
_____
_____

9. **STORAGE SPACE NEEDED:** _____
_____

10. **LITERATURE BINS & OTHER GIVE-AWAYS:** _____
_____

11. **EXPECTED FREQUENCY OF USE:**
   (Indicate all or part of display. Be specific.) 1-year _____
   3-years _____
12. **SEATING/HOW MANY & WHERE:** _____
_____

13. **OTHER REQUIREMENTS:** _____
_____

14. **OVERALL "FEEL":** ☐ Contemporary ☐ Traditional ☐ VERY High Tech ☐ User Friendly
   (Check all that apply) ☐ Male ☐ Female ☐ Other

---

15. **APPROVAL PROCESS: DESIGN AND BUDGET**
   First Presentation _____
   Second Presentation _____

   Signatures   FINAL DESIGN OK _____ Date _____
                  FINAL BUDGET OK _____ Date _____
                  CONSTRUCTION OK _____ Date _____

---

16. Exhibits Co. Candidate _____ Contact _____
    Address _____ Phone _____
17. Years in business _____ 18. ☐ Own Designers 19. ☐ Outside Design 20. ☐ Own Construction
21. ☐ Outside Construction 22. ☐ Own Storage 23. ☐ Outside Storage
24. ☐ Photos Received 25. ☐ Cost Information Received 26. ☐ Recommendations Checked
27. AE & Experience _____
28. Other _____
29. Date Visited _____ 30. By: _____ 31. Recommendation (+5/–5) _____

See Attached Concerning Nos. ___ ___ ___ ___ ___ ___ ___ ___ ___ ___ ___ ___ ___ ___

Figure 14.7 New display construction checklist.

CONVENTIONS/TRADE SHOWS/MEETINGS CHECKLIST

Project Title _____ **Date** _____

Project Description _____ **Project #** _____

_____ **Checklist #** _____

Overall Supervision By _____ **Deadline** _____

Budget _____ **Completion Date** _____ **Start Up Date** _____

	ASSIGNED TO	DUE	IN	MUST APPROVE	BY DATE	IN	INFO COPY ONLY	SEE ATTACHED
EARLIEST DECISIONS								
1. Exhibit focus	_____	___	☐	_____	___	☐	_____	☐
2. Budget approved	_____	___	☐	_____	___	☐	_____	☐
3. Booth space/configuration	_____	___	☐	_____	___	☐	_____	☐
4. Booth location	_____	___	☐	_____	___	☐	_____	☐
5. Space reserved/confirmed	_____	___	☐	_____	___	☐	_____	☐
6. Display company notified	_____	___	☐	_____	___	☐	_____	☐
7. Hotel reservation requested	_____	___	☐	_____	___	☐	_____	☐
8. Direct billing requested	_____	___	☐	_____	___	☐	_____	☐
BUDGET DETAIL OK								
9. Booth $	_____	___	☐	_____	___	☐	_____	☐
10. Display $	_____	___	☐	_____	___	☐	_____	☐
11. Travel $	_____	___	☐	_____	___	☐	_____	☐
12. Product $	_____	___	☐	_____	___	☐	_____	☐
13. Collateral $	_____	___	☐	_____	___	☐	_____	☐
14. Lodging/Food $	_____	___	☐	_____	___	☐	_____	☐
15. Hospitality $	_____	___	☐	_____	___	☐	_____	☐
PERSONNEL/HOSPITALITY								
16. VIP list	_____	___	☐	_____	___	☐	_____	☐
17. VIP responsibilities assigned	_____	___	☐	_____	___	☐	_____	☐
18. Hospitality plan OK	_____	___	☐	_____	___	☐	_____	☐
19. Hospitality ordered/reserved	_____	___	☐	_____	___	☐	_____	☐
20. Hospitality invitations creative	_____	___	☐	_____	___	☐	_____	☐
21. Invitation printing	_____	___	☐	_____	___	☐	_____	☐
22. Invitation mailing/distribution	_____	___	☐	_____	___	☐	_____	☐
23. Hospitality confirmed/cancelled	_____	___	☐	_____	___	☐	_____	☐
24. Personnel attenting OK'd	_____	___	☐	_____	___	☐	_____	☐
25. Personnel notified of plan and assignments	_____	___	☐	_____	___	☐	_____	☐
26. Hotel confirmed/cancelled	_____	___	☐	_____	___	☐	_____	☐
EXHIBITING DETAIL								
27. Display design for setup	_____	___	☐	_____	___	☐	_____	☐
28. Signage ordered	_____	___	☐	_____	___	☐	_____	☐
29. Product ordered	_____	___	☐	_____	___	☐	_____	☐
30. Product shipped	_____	___	☐	_____	___	☐	_____	☐
31. Collateral ordered	_____	___	☐	_____	___	☐	_____	☐
32. Collateral shipped	_____	___	☐	_____	___	☐	_____	☐
33. Physical display ordered	_____	___	☐	_____	___	☐	_____	☐
34. Physical display shipped	_____	___	☐	_____	___	☐	_____	☐
35. Show services & rentals	_____	___	☐	_____	___	☐	_____	☐
36. Service & rentals ordered	_____	___	☐	_____	___	☐	_____	
37. Set up/Tear down	_____	___	☐	_____	___	☐	_____	

© 2003, Fred Hahn

Figure 14.8 The conventions/trade shows/meetings checklist.

firmed. Get the work schedule. Check to make sure that it's being followed.

7.   **Hotel space/tentative.** Request reservations *the day they may be ordered.* Find out when is the last moment they may be canceled. *One* person deals with both of these points.

8.   **Direct billing OK.** Who is authorized to charge what to your company? What control is there, if any, on those authorized to charge?

9.   **Space $ OK.** Display *space* tends to be the least costly of items 9–15. Add more space and place your display within it, perhaps in an island configuration, for extra impact. Even a single extra booth can work for smaller budgets.

10.   **New display $.** See the separate new display checklist for ordering or building a new display. Treat the costs involved as a capital expense, or add them under the total budget in #2. Use #10 for costs associated with maintenance, modification, shipping, setup and dismantling, and reshipping of the display, as well as returning it to storage. For record keeping, separate routine items and one-time costs to make future planning easier.

11.   **Attendance/tentative.** Who goes? Who gets them there? How is it paid for?

12–13.   **Product/collateral.** If at all possible, send product samples and promotional materials with the display. For both control and huge savings, a single shipment is by far the best thing.

14.   **Lodging/food $.** Limitations or rules regarding the cost of daily meals. Lodging is handled under #7, but must be recorded here for purposes of budgeting.

15.   **Hospitality $.** Estimated or quoted costs for items 16–23. Have a single person *in charge* of hospitality though any number of individuals may have specific responsibilities.

INSIGHT 89

16–23.   **Hospitality details.** Have a reason for hospitality. If you can't justify entertaining the persons in #16 . . . *Stop!* Don't give a party. Go to theirs.

INSIGHT 90

Schedule rehearsal time for *everyone* attending to ensure familiarity with their responsibility, the display itself, the sales message(s), and the location of products and collateral materials. Do role playing, including actual filling out of follow-up reports.

24–25.   **Attendance assignments.** Are your personnel attending the show determined by hospitality or other needs? Have a reason for everyone's being there—a cash-effective reason!

26.   **Hotel confirmed.** The decision in #24 may be someone else's. The confirmation or cancellation is done by the same person as in #7. Make sure that everything is in writing and everything is confirmed.

27.   **Space design.** Exactly how will the display look, and where will the products and collateral materials go? If possible, code every carton or item by number, keyed to a specific location.

28.   **Signage.** What do the signs say and where do they go? Ship them with the display.

29–32.   **Products/collateral ordered and shipped.** Who is responsible? If this person is different from the one responsible for #27, let #27 know if anything is not available. Don't make a half-empty display your convention surprise!

33–36.   **Display shipping/handling.** Generally the responsibility of a single person. When using a display company, let it handle #28, #30, #32, and #34–36. They do it every day, know exactly how, and will save you *lots* of money.

37.   **Setup/tear down.** Let your display company supervise, if practical. Keep house kibitzers away. Show personnel are *very* expensive and get paid by the hour.

FOLLOW-UP

Eighty percent of leads found at trade shows are never followed up! Put in place a system to make sure yours are. If yours are not because of lack of personnel, see the chapters on telemarketing, direct mail, and broadcast fax.

15 | Moving Your Project from Disk or Art through Film and Printing

The prepress and printing section of this chapter has been brought up to date with the help of **Joe Erl,** vice president of ColorImetry, a full-service prepress and printing company in Chicago, IL (www.colorimetry.com, Joeerl@colorimetry.com).

FILM SEPARATION AND PROOFING

Modern printing begins with a "prepress" prepublishing process that changes type and pictures into a computer digital format that lets you see them on a computer monitor. Rather than moving type and illustrations the old-fashioned way, by "cutting and pasting," your designer and film house do it with the click of a mouse.

Film preparation begins with one or more of three kinds of materials:

1. *Final art.* All the type and illustrations with instructions on how they are to be combined to create an ad, catalog page, brochure, and so on. Color art and transparencies are scanned and put into two digital formats. First, for ease of handling and saving in computer server capacity, a low-resolution file often is prepared in-house. Then, when all corrections and positioning are done and using the low-res as place holders, a full-resolution, full-size file is created by a prepress service for color proofing and printing.
2. *Electronic file.* Some or all of the materials to be printed that are prepared on a computer. Type is practically all set this way. Adding illustrations requires specific kinds of equipment and skills.
3. *Digital photography.* Studio-quality photography using special new cameras that produce computer-compatible images rather than film.

Whichever process or combination is used, the final image is transferred either onto a film and from there to a printing plate or, increasingly, directly onto the plate by the computer-to plate (CTP) process from which the actual printing is done. If colors are to be used in printing, there are two options:

1. *Specific colors:* Select from or have the printer create a special color. Thousands of such colors exist.

2. *Process colors:* Print by one of several color systems in which all printed colors are a combination of just four inks. "Process printing," which uses the four "process" colors, is the best known such system.

It is the job of the prepress filmmaker to create the films or digital file from which the printing plates are prepared. Use specialists for anything in full color or an otherwise complicated workflow. With widely available and inexpensive systems you can do routine one- or two-color projects, but let the prepress service quote on that too. What follows tells how this is done.

INSIGHT 91

Discuss the capabilities and limitations of their separation system with your pre-press supplier *before art or photography is assigned.* It's a lot easier and cheaper than attempting to fix the product after it is delivered.

From New Art to Film or File

- *Paste up,* the twentieth-century method of preparing work for printing, has been replaced by the computer-generated *electronic file.*
- *New art* is the term for anything supplied as original art for reproduction, anything that has not yet been scanned and digitized.
- The transfer of film to plates is rapidly becoming obsolete. It is being replaced by digital page proofs or one of a variety of digital files that skip film and go directly to plates through *computer-to-plate* (CTP) systems.
- These systems, on disk or hard drive, often are supplied by the printers and preset for their needs. Using CTP, printers can skip much of the expensive, time-consuming "make ready," go directly to print, and save their clients time and money.
- Electronic files can be supplied to prepress or printers in a variety of formats, but not all can handle every variety. As always, check for compatibility *before* you begin!

Reproducing something in color for film or file begins by separating the original image into its four process colors. For instance, an ad or catalog page that is reproduced from a combination of type, drawings, photographs, and slides is quite typical. Each of these preliminary scannings must be correctly sized, then positioned for printing. There are two ways of doing this:

1. *Laser scanners.* This more sophisticated method of seeing and separating the original art for printing became widespread in the 1970s. This quickly became the primary way of preparing film for printing.
2. *Digital photography.* In the 1990s, computerized film preparation revolutionized the prepress (preprinting) process. Computer-prepared type and art, plus digital photography elements, are combined onto a single com-

puter image. The images are brought onto an oversized high-resolution viewing screen and positioned as called for on the original design. Here, clients, artists, designers, and others can see the page(s) before the film or file is made.

At this stage, *anything* can be changed at the click of a mouse . . . copy, position, color, size—anything! This latest process has huge advantages over previous systems:

- Work done by the digitized system can be seen as "work-in-progress" on a high-quality computer screen for on-the-spot major and minor retouching. There is no need to wait for final film and its proofing before errors are corrected.
- Film created from a digitized format can always be "re-created" (duplicated) or modified to its original fidelity. There is no "second-generation" copying loss, whereas previous film duplication lost some of the fidelity of the original. Now every regenerated "copy" is, in fact, another original.
- The computer-stored images can be repurposed (used) or modified for any promotional activity: Web sites, brochures, ads, slides, transparencies, and billboards and other out-of-home promotions.

Many design studios also produce computerized final art and film. Although not quite as technically advanced as a color separator, they are excellent for many individual ads, flyers, and brochures. For major projects such as catalogs or sophisticated art, the color separator is the answer.

INSIGHT 92

For clarity and legibility, *always* mark your original art "SHOOT ALL TYPE AS LINE." Without this instruction, type may be screened routinely, giving it the appearance of a series of fuzzy dots rather than continuous lines. Your color separator knows this but is not permitted to avoid it without your instructions!

Ownership

Specify on your purchase order *your* ownership of the digitized file or film on payment. This does not require you to take physical possession of the film unless you want to do so. It does, however, give you complete freedom to use and move your file or film as you wish.

Proofing before Printing

Once the film or file is ready for printing, it is used to make one or more prints for a final check. The sample that is checked is called a *proof.* For CTP, you get an electronic proof. For film to plate, your proof is printed as in the past. For catalogs and other material that will be folded, at least two kinds of proofs are made for the same project.

Color Proof

When two or more colors are to be printed, a color proof shows how the printed piece will look and how it compares with any original art or photographs. This comparison is not checked on the computer screen. To show what the finished piece will look like, this proofing is done on standard proofing paper or, through "waterproofing," on the same paper on which the project will be printed. The comparison to the original art and design should be made under industry-specified controlled lighting to give specified, uniform conditions for comparisons, rather than the random light sources that are available wherever you happen to be. Your prepress firm will have such a light source.

For multicolor projects, it is quite common to begin with a *random proof.* This shows, to size, the illustrations and photographs only, before they are placed into position. These are viewed and corrected for color density and detail. Any substitution or other change at this point is less costly than after everything is in place. After corrections are made, a second random proof is done only if the changes are major. More often, the second proof shows everything in position, that is, as it will appear in print. This proof is checked again, both for the specified corrections and for any other changes and corrections that may still be needed. Most often, none of the latter are needed, and this is the proof that goes to the printer.

INSIGHT 93

Accidents can happen any time anyone works with film or file. Don't just check for your corrections—check *everything.* But don't change anything unless *absolutely* necessary. The process is costly and requires equally careful checking every time.

The proof is accepted, dated, initialed, and marked "OK for printing" or "OK as corrected." (*Note the difference!*)[1] It becomes the guide against which the project is checked while it is actually being printed. In reviewing proofs, be mindful that "what you see is what you get." Do not give your approval until you are satisfied with what you see!

Of course you will let your print production and art departments take the lead in proof checking and approvals. If such departments are not available, use your design source. It is *their* area of *expertise.* It is *your* area of *responsibility.*

---

[1] Typical "as corrected" notations will indicate that a color is to be slightly darker or lighter, that something has been removed, that a number or letter has been changed, and so forth.

Single-Color Proofs and Folding Dummies

Where only one color will be used in printing, the color chosen and the sophistication of design will determine how closely the proofing must match the printed piece. An exact proofing match of a specific color (or something as close as the prepress service can provide) is more costly than a routine monotone, but like multicolor proofing, it is the only way to *know* what you will see when you print.

The folding proof is produced in one color on the actual stock or on paper that is thin enough to fold easily. The proof is folded or formed into the exact shape and format of the final printed product. It is this folded proof that lets you see how facing pages actually look when all the elements are present and that lets you check whether all those elements are the way they were specified.

Always check the following elements on folding proofs:

- ☐ Are all pages present and in consecutive order?
- ☐ Do elements that run across the center of facing pages (across the gutter) line up?
- ☐ Does the index or table of contents reflect where the elements are? If not, which one is wrong?
- ☐ Do all the elements work together? (Do the materials fit into envelopes? Are items that bind together the proper size and shape? Etc.)
- ☐ Are comparable elements positioned properly?
- ☐ Are all page numbers (called "folios") in the same spot?
- ☐ Is the use of page or section headings consistent? If not, was this deliberate?
- ☐ Do all cross-references check out?
- ☐ Do the captions match the pictures? Are both in the right place?
- ☐ Is all mailing information present and accurate?
- ☐ Is all ordering information present and accurate? Phone, fax, E-mail, Internet? Addresses? Legal and self-protection requirements (e.g., "Printed in USA," "Prices subject to change," etc.)?

This is your final chance to see the job as a whole before printing. Take the opportunity to *check everything.*

A Continuous Process

The preparation of film or file for use in advertising or printing and the printing itself are so interrelated that we shall treat them as continuous, with the previous list and the notes that follow a part of the basic information. Whereas in other chapters checklist notes are supplemental, here they are a significant part of the text.

The proof delivered by the prepress firm and accepted by the printer carries an implied guarantee that the film or file will produce what the proof shows. Many printers inspect the film or file and proofs carefully before agreeing to accept them. Once accepted by printers, any problem in producing what the proof shows is to be solved by them and the prepress firm, not by the client. Be mindful, however, that the printer is matching a proof, not original art! The time to settle questions concerning the artwork is when it is first seen by whoever makes the film or

PREPRESS FILE/FILM PREPARATION CHECKLIST

Project Title _____ Date _____

Project Description _____ Project # _____

_____ Checklist # _____

Overall Supervision By _____ Deadline _____

Budget _____ Completion Date _____ Start Up Date _____

	ASSIGNED TO	DUE	IN	MUST APPROVE	BY DATE	IN	INFO COPY ONLY	SEE ATTACHED
1. Project Manager	_____	___	☐	_____	___	☐	_____	☐
2. Tentative Schedule	_____	___	☐	_____	___	☐	_____	☐
3. Start-up	_____	___	☐	_____	___	☐	_____	☐
4. Supplier Selection	_____	___	☐	_____	___	☐	_____	☐
5. Final Schedule	_____	___	☐	_____	___	☐	_____	☐
6. Completion	_____	___	☐	_____	___	☐	_____	☐
7. File/Film/Printer Contact	_____	___	☐	_____	___	☐	_____	☐
8. Prepress Art Check	_____	___	☐	_____	___	☐	_____	☐
9. Final Prefilm/ Pre CTP Check	_____	___	☐	_____	___	☐	_____	☐
10. Random Proofs	_____	___	☐	_____	___	☐	_____	☐
11. Final Proofs	_____	___	☐	_____	___	☐	_____	☐
12. Dylux Sample	_____	___	☐	_____	___	☐	_____	☐
13. Delivery	_____	___	☐	_____	___	☐	_____	☐

© 2003, Fred Hahn

Figure 15.1   The prepress file/film preparation checklist.

file. A professional prepress firm forewarns you about how art will actually reproduce and suggest ways of doing it better. If not, they may be wrong for the job. Note that certain colors or inks probably cannot be matched in standard process printing. They simply will not reproduce as seen. So warn your colleagues. For the sake of your printer's sanity and yours, do not try to "fix" it on press!

> Newer, increasingly popular systems eliminate both film and printing plates through digital printing technology. This generally allows personalization and variable data wherever and whenever wanted. However, as this is written, there are limitations as to paper size and some personalization placement. Check with both prepress/printing and direct mail production specialists about this constantly improving field.

NOTES ON THE FILE/FILM PREPARATION CHECKLIST

Unlike notes on most other checklists, these notes are not a supplement to the material presented in the chapter. Rather, they are an integral part of the chapter. The checklist is presented in Figure 15.1.

1. **Project manager.** The direct technical supervisor. If the client has no one in this capacity on staff, use the person or studio that prepared the final art.

2. **Tentative schedule.** The schedule prepared before the prepress firm is selected. This is generally done at the very beginning of the project, during its planning stages. For anything complicated or more than a few pages, have a prepress firm give a ballpark *time* estimate to help your planning. The prepress vendor probably can't estimate costs without more facts.

3. **Start-up.** The date the prepress firm can begin processing materials and, if different, when all the final piece will be delivered.

4. **Supplier selection.** If you are new to the field or to the geographic location, here are workable suggestions for selecting a prepress supplier.
   - Find out whom your company or organization has used in the past. Don't change without a reason.
   - Call several printers in the area and ask for their recommendations.
   - Ask the nearest local direct marketing association. To find it, call the Direct Marketing Association in New York at (212) 768-7277. Ask for the "DM Clubs and Association Network."
   - Ask the promotional director of some local businesses.
   - Check the Yellow Pages under "Printing—Color Separator" or "Prepress."

   For simple one- or two-color projects, almost anyone recommended should do. So shop for price and schedule. For full-color or complicated projects, call first to learn the kind of work the various suppliers do. (Think twice before having a podiatrist do brain surgery or a brain surgeon look at your feet.) Get references. Check! Get samples. Give your final candidates written specifications, including deadlines.

5. **Final schedule.** Prepare a schedule that you, your prepress firm, and your printer can meet to get the project done on time. If all else fails, negotiate.

6. **Completion.** The date the client is responsible for approving the final proofing. Be sure to allow for at least two proofings on *everything*.

7. **File/Film printer contact.** File/film must be prepared to match the printer's need. Choose your printer as early as you do the prepress firm, and have both agree on how material is to be delivered (for instance, as 4-, 8-, or 12-page units).

8. **Prepress art check.** The prepress vendor should check the drawings, paintings, and other original art so as to foresee problems in duplication and to discuss their solutions. (It is sometimes better to begin with a color photograph, rather than with the original.) Also, the prepress vendor should select the most reproducible photograph or transparencies when several are available. Often, the choice is between contrast and detail. In printing, the printed photographs and drawings are called halftones because they are made up of dots of various sizes lined up in rows, with from 65 to 400 dots per inch. The fewer the dots, referred to as line,

screen, halftone, or any combination of the three ("65-line screen," "200-line halftone" etc.), the less detail can be shown. But specific lighting and camera settings also control results. Without instructions, prepress color separators tend to work for a middle ground. For advertising and promotional purposes, we almost always prefer high contrast. When numerous illustrations will be used, have the firm shoot and proof samples in a range of modes before you make a decision on which to use.

For rougher stock newspapers, 65- to 85-line halftones are standard. In general commercial offset work, 133 to 200 dots are typically used. Two hundred- to 400-line reproduction is used only in the highest quality printing, almost always to show detailed illustrations to exceptional advantage. For any advertisement or for your own commercial work, check on the maximum number of lines *the printer can use.* Each printing press works best at a specific line value. Know what that is, and make certain that no finer screening is ordered from the prepress firm. Fewer lines may give you less of an impact, but it is never a *printing* problem. On the other hand, more than the maximum number of lines for a particular press tends to produce random ink blots that reduce rather than enhance detail.

9. **Prefilm file/new art check.** Except on the simplest of projects, do not just ship final materials to the prepress firm. Rather, take your artist or art director with you to meet with them and go over *each* instruction. Ask the film/file maker to point out potential difficulties *in printing,* including the printing of multicolor type as well as costs not covered by the estimated total. Using some color combinations within type can be a register problem for the printer.

10. **Random proofs.** When transparencies are the art against which proofs are compared, they are generally placed on a "light box," which illuminates them as if they were projected onto a screen. *No printed proof can possibly match the intensity of the colors this produces!* Visualize the originals that the transparencies show, and make *that* the basis for judging.

INSIGHT 94

Prepress firms expect to do two random proofings for advertising agencies, but only one for most other clients, and quote accordingly. Specify your likely needs when you describe the project, and have those needs reflected in writing in the quotations.

---

11. **Final proofs.** Final proofs show the project as it is to be printed. The corrected illustrations are in position, and everything should match what was asked for on the material checked in #9. Make sure to:

   • Compare the corrected illustrations against the previous version, using the uniform lighting source.

- Check the proof against every instruction given on the material. Literally check them off to make certain that none are missed.

- Make a final inspection of every color, to be certain that no obvious errors were made. (For instance, green will turn into blue if yellow has been erroneously located on the film.) If the color of the products is important, have someone who knows about colors check with you. We often see what we expect to see—especially the tenth time we look at it!

Full-Color Proofing

Seven types of proofs are possible for most full-color projects. If you are unfamiliar with any of them, ask to see a sample of all seven ways, with the cost difference for each. The types of proofs are:

1. *Digital on-screen proofing.* The only proofing system that permits as-you-watch retouching, changes, and corrections. It is followed by ink on paper "hard copy" for on-press checking.
2. *Waterproofing.* A new process that proofs regular process colors on the stock on which the project will be printed, no matter how thick or thin, dull or shiny; even on plastics and cloth. The first proofing process other than actual printing that can show a project on two or more different stocks before stock is ordered.
3. *Match print.* This closely matches what will be printed. It is not as popular as it should be, probably because many clients prefer the flashier Cromalin.
4. *Cromalin.* This is the most accurate proofing for non–"process color" printing. It produces a very high-gloss surface that can be somewhat deceptive in its feel as a printed piece.
5. *Color key.* This technique results in layers of film, one showing each printing color, positioned on top of each other to reflect what happens in the actual printing process. The colors are slightly muted through effects of the film itself. This was the original color proofing process and is the least expensive of the film color systems available.
6. *Reading or Dylux proof.* In this technique, proofs are used to make the samples described in #12 for a final check of all copy, and for the positioning of all illustrations. Depending on the colors used, this proof can be made from just one or two of the four colors used in printing.
7. *Kodak approval.* A digital system only, unlike the others, which can work with film also. The preferred system for CTP printing.

Two-Color Projects

In many two-color projects, single-color "reading proofs" are adequate. Where only the color of the type is affected—for instance, red headlines or blue handwriting—color is often indicated as a gray, less dense image that is still easy to read.

Illustrations

Where illustrations are to be shown as duotones, that is, in two colors, one of which most often is black, at least a color key should be used for proofing. The two ways of achieving the final color have quite different effects:

- **Fake duotone.** The illustration is printed in the darker of the two colors and then covered with a light layer, or screen, of the second color. This is the easier way to print and is less expensive for film.
- **True duotone.** A halftone image is made on film for both colors and is then printed with all the care used in full-color projects. True duotones require specialized knowledge and skills by the prepress firm. The technique does not simply use the same film for each color. To give prepress instructions and to help check results, you need an art director who is familiar with the process.

12. **Dylux sample.** This is the *only* preview of how the final project will look in its actual size and with all pages or elements in proper order. All other proofs are presented with wide margins for notations and can be very deceptive. (Dylux is a trade name, and your printer may use a different process. Check for nomenclature.)

    Everyone with whom you work will have a near heart attack when you dare to fold or cut a Cromalin to see what a page actually looked like, although it was never what they thought they had seen in the untrimmed version. (Cut very carefully with a sharp razor, and you can tape it back together almost like new. Remember, we give you absolution: "Hey! It's not a sacred relic! It's just a proof!").

13. **Delivery.** You are responsible for providing the address of the destination. Let the prepress service be responsible for shipment or delivery to media and printers. The last thing you want to hear is, "It was perfectly fine when you picked it up." So don't!

NOTES ON THE PRINTING/BINDERY CHECKLIST

Unlike notes on most other checklists, these notes are not *a supplement to the material presented in the chapter. Rather, they are an integral part of the chapter.* The checklist is presented in Figure 15.2.

1. **Printing budget.** The portion of quoted or estimated costs allocated to printing, even if printing and binding are given to a single supplier. You will want this figure for future comparison shopping. Be mindful of probable savings in getting a printing-binding package price.
2. **Start-up date.** When the project will actually go to press. Dates materials must be received by the printer are covered in #7.
3. **Completion date.** When the *printing* portion of the project is to be done. Any bindery work that is to follow is checked off in #12 on.

PRINTING/BINDERY CHECKLIST

Project Title _____ Date _____
Project Description _____ Project # _____
_____ Checklist # _____
Overall Supervision By _____ Deadline _____
Budget _____ Completion Date _____ Start Up Date _____

PRINTING	ASSIGNED TO	DUE	IN	MUST APPROVE	BY DATE	IN	INFO COPY ONLY	SEE ATTACHED
1. Printing Budget	_____	___	☐	_____	___	☐	_____	☐
2. Start-up Date	_____	___	☐	_____	___	☐	_____	☐
3. Completion Date	_____	___	☐	_____	___	☐	_____	☐
4. Project Manager	_____	___	☐	_____	___	☐	_____	☐
5. Tentative Schedule	_____	___	☐	_____	___	☐	_____	☐
6. Supplier Selection	_____	___	☐	_____	___	☐	_____	☐
7. Final Schedule	_____	___	☐	_____	___	☐	_____	☐
8. Paper	_____	___	☐	_____	___	☐	_____	☐
9. Inks/Colors	_____	___	☐	_____	___	☐	_____	☐
10. Coating	_____	___	☐	_____	___	☐	_____	☐
11. Shipping	_____	___	☐	_____	___	☐	_____	☐
BINDING								
12. Bindery Budget	_____	___	☐	_____	___	☐	_____	☐
13. Bindery Start-up	_____	___	☐	_____	___	☐	_____	☐
14. Completion Date	_____	___	☐	_____	___	☐	_____	☐
15. Project Manager	_____	___	☐	_____	___	☐	_____	☐
16. Schedule	_____	___	☐	_____	___	☐	_____	☐
17. Folding	_____	___	☐	_____	___	☐	_____	☐
18. Binding	_____	___	☐	_____	___	☐	_____	☐
19. Shipping Dates & Methods (skids, cartons, etc.)	_____	___	☐	_____	___	☐	_____	☐
20. Postage	_____	___	☐	_____	___	☐	_____	☐
21. Reports	_____	___	☐	_____	___	☐	_____	☐

Figure 15.2   The printing/bindery checklist.

4. **Project manager.** When in-house technical expertise is available, use it, always asking to be a spectator *permitted to learn.* When printing decisions are thrust on you before you feel quite ready for them, ask the printer to be your guide. Never involve yourself in how-to questions! Remember the client's magic words: "I know what we have to achieve. I couldn't begin to tell you how to get there."

5. **Tentative schedule.** This schedule is generally prepared at the beginning of the project, before suppliers are chosen, and helps guide in their selection. Some flexibility must be built in, depending on the complexity of the project.

6. **Supplier selection.** Follow the same procedure as that suggested for selecting a prepress supplier on page 298 and then add the following considerations:

   - **Sheet or web printing.** Sheet-fed printing uses precut individual sheets. Web printing uses paper taken from huge rolls. Web printing almost always prints on both sides of the paper at the same time, with folding continued as part of the same printing process. Commercially, web printing is used for larger quantities—generally, no less than 25,000 for printing one or two colors and 50,000 for full color.

     Sheet-fed printing has many advantages of its own. It tends to be much more flexible in quantity, number of pages to be printed, size of the pages or printed sheet, stock to be used, and number of suppliers than does web printing. The "quick print" shops found almost everywhere are sheet-fed printers, as are commercial printers in smaller communities.

   - **Check for the right printer for each job.** No single printer can do everything! Visit the plants you asked for quotations. If you are unfamiliar with anything you see, ask. If the plant is not spotless, leave.

7. **Final schedule.** Prepare a schedule that you and your prepress supplier, printer, bindery, and distribution source can achieve to get the project done on time. If all else fails, negotiate. Remember to differentiate between how and when!

8. **Paper.** Selecting paper, or stock, is one of the most critical aspects of any printing project. There are literally thousands of different stocks, many available in a variety of thicknesses or weights. The lower the weight, in units of pounds, the thinner the stock. Thus, paper used in most office copy machines is 50-pound offset, or 50# stock, which means that 1,000 25″ × 38″ sheets weigh exactly 50 pounds. To keep life from being too simple, different kinds of stock use different weight criteria, but each is consistent within itself and shows thinner to thicker (light to heavy weights) as smaller to larger numbers.

INSIGHT 95

Before making a final decision on paper, get stock samples and dummies—that is, actual-size samples—from the paper merchant or printer. Have *them* label each paper type and weight. Include that sample stock when you order. Let your order read: "80# cover and 70# body *as per samples herewith*" if you don't want 70# cover and 80# body and want no excuses for getting them confused.

Buying Paper Yourself

Paper and other stocks can be purchased through the printer or, for large jobs, directly by the client from wholesalers or paper mills. If you are inexperienced in purchasing paper or judging among suppliers, get expert help. Merchants are listed in major cities' Yellow Pages. Information is available from your advertising or direct marketing organization or trade publications in the graphic arts.

Here is a short checklist for purchasing paper:

Paper Supplied by Printer
- ☐ Availability
- ☐ Cost
- ☐ Alternative comparable stocks, including their availability and cost

Paper Supplied by Client
- ☐ Minimum order required
- ☐ Cost of specified paper and comparable stock
- ☐ Delivery schedule and guarantees
- ☐ Storage and handling
- ☐ Responsibility for quality
- ☐ Insurance
- ☐ Alternatives if delivery or quality fails

Many organizations and companies purchase their own paper. Others take advantage of their printers' house stocks, purchased in huge quantities at equally huge discounts. But *when only one stock will do, allow enough time for its acquisition.* Paper can seldom be manufactured overnight, no matter who orders it. If it's not on hand, it must wait until the manufacturer's production schedule says it's ready to be produced.

There are many types of paper, including the following:

- **Cover stocks.** These are heavier papers used for catalog covers and similar projects.
- **Offset or matte papers.** These have a duller finish, though not necessarily less white, than that of the glossy alternatives. Most books and newspapers are printed on offset stock.
- **Enamel papers.** These are glossy papers used in many magazines and promotional mailings and on book jackets and other retail packaging. Printed on enamel, color illustrations achieve more sparkle, and even black-and-white illustrations seem to have more life. Enamel papers range from having a lesser gloss, used where materials have to be read as well as seen, to having practically mirrorlike finishes, called chrome coats, where attention-getting ability is the major criterion.
- **Textured stock.** Few things are as underused as textured papers to give an immediate impression of elegance and good taste. Their very touch conveys prestige. Perhaps a fear that textures will cause difficulties in reproduction is why they are not more used. However, this fear is most often groundless, whether reproducing type or illustrations. Ask to see printed samples, then be pleasantly surprised at how little more it costs for this added impact.

- **Colored stock.** The more popular offset stocks tend to be available in dozens of colors, at a somewhat higher cost than white. Most enamel stock, unless specially prepared by the paper mills, is white only.

Advantages and Disadvantages of Color

The major advantage of colored over white stock lies in its being different—in its standing out from the majority of paper people look at. The disadvantage lies in the way printing on color mutes type and illustrations, especially photographs. (Because many art directors are interested in how something looks, rather than how easily it can be read, be especially mindful of this problem.)

Fortunately, there is a solution that produces both unmuted illustrations and color stock: printing the color and leaving the areas to be illustrated white. To do this, you need merely instruct the prepress facility to match a particular light color or use a "screened," light tone of one or more inks that are already part of the job. The process is quite simple and adds little, if anything, to the overall cost of printing. For example, you can mark the final art, "Screen entire background 20 percent blue, but drop (remove) color behind all illustrations." This not only gives your illustrations their maximum visibility but also frames them in color for even more impact.

9. **Inks/Colors.** In addition to the five-color presses discussed in #10, many new presses can print even more colors in a single press run. This permits combining four-color process with metallic and other colors for special effects and at comparatively low costs. If unfamiliar with everything new in the field work with a printer's representative who will keep you up to date.

10. **Coating**[2] Coating on paper has the same results as varnish on wood: protection, durability, and special visual effects.

    - **Protection.** Touching uncoated printing, especially on enameled glossy stock, tends to leave fingerprints on the paper. The darker the ink, the more obvious the fingerprints will be. Catalog covers are the most common example. Adding an inexpensive, easily applied coating totally eliminates this problem. Many four-color (full-color) printing presses have a fifth-color unit that can be used for this purpose. More often, the coating is applied on a single-color press after the ink has dried. Both methods are effective. Using the latter, however, permits an actual fifth color in the printing. Few of us are able to resist that temptation.

    - **Durability.** Fingerprints are far from being the only danger to uncoated printing. Scuff marks, caused by pieces rubbing against each other during shipping, can make anything appear used or damaged, much as if you were asked to accept a new car with a blotched paint surface. I have seen thousands of presentation folders thrown out because their printing buyers had not known about press coating. You do. Use it!

---

[2]Much more expensive plastic coatings are possible but almost always unnecessary.

- **Special effects.** Coatings can be glossy or matte. No explanation will be as effective as seeing the difference, so ask your printer for samples. Either will give protection. More important is the use of "spot coating," which adds a striking gloss to a portion of the page, usually its illustrations. In trade terms, "spot" can be any size and any quantity, as long as it does not cover the whole page. Here, too, seeing is much better than describing, so ask several printers for examples and costs. Comparatively few of them have a wide range of samples.

11. **Shipping.** Many printers have their own bindery departments. Those with major direct marketing clients may also have an in-house mailing departing. This can eliminate the time and cost of one or two shipping and handling moves: from the printer to the bindery and from the bindery to a mailing service. In getting quotations, factor in all these variables. I have always urged clients to pay slightly more to keep everything under one roof—with one supplier held responsible.

12. **Bindery budget.** Find out the bindery portion of the estimated or quoted costs, even if printing and binding are given to a single supplier. You will want this figure for future comparison shopping. Be mindful of possible savings through a printing and binding package price.

13. **Bindery start-up.** Start-up does not necessarily, nor often, occur the moment printing is done. Be there, or ask[3] to see the first completed pieces. Show them to the mailing service or department as a final safety check.

14. **Completion date.** Specify what "completion" means: the day a job is finished at the bindery or the day it is received at the next destination, usually the mailing service. Go for the latter.

15. **Project manager.** Costly outside creative direction should not be needed here. Do-it-yourself management again comes into its own.

16. **Schedule.** Whether work is done by the printer or contracted with a separate bindery, get a schedule that shows the following:
    - The time and cost (if any) for shipment from the printer to the bindery.
    - The time and cost of specialized outside services, such as die-cutting or embossing, before bindery work can begin. If practical, have the printer run those portions first. They can be finished outside while the rest of the printing is being completed.
    - The time and cost of all standard bindery work.
    - The time and cost (if any) from the bindery to the finishing house (mailing service) and all other destinations.

17. **Folding.**[4] Before ordering folds on pieces that are to be mailed, especially if they will be placed in an envelope, show them to the bindery

---

[3]As in all outside work, if samples must be delivered to you for approval, you pay for the "holding" (waiting) time until work can continue. Be there!

[4]A variety of folds available through most printers and binderies is shown on page 56.

and to the finishing house. Almost any fold is possible; some, however, may be very expensive because they cannot be made by a single run through the folding machines. Your finishing house will tell you if a folded piece can be handled by their automated addressing and envelope stuffing equipment. Some folds can't! Don't insist on using your paper-folding ingenuity without assurance from both the bindery and the finishing house.

18. **Binding.** For multipage promotional pieces, such as catalogs and brochures, there are three binding or fastening options.[5]

- **Saddle stitch.** Pages are folded and stapled together with a metal fastener through the spine.
- **Perfect binding.** This is the system used on most paperbound books. Where thickness permits (different binderies have their own minimums), perfect binding is the method of choice for appearance and ease of printing. Where it is used, it produces a flat spine that should be imprinted as if it were a book, for instance, a highlights index on the spine. Many perfect bound catalogs are filed vertically, on bookshelves, rather than in filing cabinets.
- **Press glue.** On some web presses, pages can be glued together at the spine as they are folded. When printers have this equipment, and unfortunately few do, it is an excellent—and inexpensive—way of binding 24 or fewer pages.

19. **Shipping dates and methods.** Discuss with your warehouse and other bulk destinations how they want their shipments sent to them—in cartons, on skids, and so on—and how each unit is to be marked. Get their instructions in writing. Discuss this with the bindery before you approve. If the bindery suggests a better way, let the bindery people discuss it with the people at the destination. As always, don't pretend to an expertise you do not have. But learn and get it!

20. **Postage.** How much postage and other shipping costs must be paid in advance? Where? When? How is the proof of mailing or shipping documented and recorded?

21. **Reports.** In a brief form, reports are for management. A more detailed version is for do-it-yourselfers. Give yourself time to review such reports at a later date. All too often, they are done, filed, and forgotten. Remember a critical difference between a professional and an amateur: Where a professional has, say, 10 years' experience, an amateur has 1 year's experience 10 times.

---

[5]A variety of binding options is shown on page 132.

16 | Distribution
On Working with Your DMPC
(Direct Mail Production Company)

> The direct mail production section of this chapter has been brought up to date with the help of **Bill Krafcheck,** vice president, Service Graphics, a full-service, nationwide direct mail production company, headquartered in Oakbrook Terrace, Ill. (www.servicegraphics.com, sgibill@servicegraphics.com).

Lettershops began as mail-handling services that could print your letter and reply card or order form, address the letter on the bulky and noisy mechanical systems then in use, insert the pieces into envelopes (often by hand), seal the envelopes, and deliver them to the post office. Today's lettershop still does much of that work. But what a difference the computer age has brought to you and with it, the DMPC (Direct Mail Production Company). The DMPC/lettershop Checklist that follows will help you both in evaluating potential suppliers and in scheduling their responsibilities—and yours—once they are selected.

Three-Column Checklist Format

The DMPC/lettershop/distribution checklist is not complete in itself, except for the simplest of mailings. Its purpose is to guide you through at least one preliminary and final planning meeting with your DMPC. Additional checklists and schedules will be needed for creative design, printing, acquisition of mailing lists, and your in-house handling of responses and their evaluation. Make liberal use of the third column, "See Attached." Where possible, use the other checklists in this book. Where none exists, use them as models and make your own.

Evaluating the DMPC

The type of work DMPCs do has remained fairly consistent since our first edition. *How* they do it has changed dramatically for the better. Before planning your promotion, arrange a visit to several DMPCs that handle your quantity mailing, plus a multimillion unit mailer, if yours is much smaller. Ask for a guided tour to learn what is now possible and practical.

On Postage Savings

The chart in Figure 16.1 is based on the rates of July 1, 2002 and is scheduled to be in effect for three years. Though rates may change and should be checked with

Compliments of your friends at

SERVICE GRAPHICS, INC.

17W045 Hodges Road, Oakbrook Terrace, IL 60181

630/941-2899 • 630/941-1634 Fax

Postage Rate Chart *(in effect June 30, 2002)*

FIRST-CLASS MAIL (Not over 1 oz)

		AUTOMATION		NONAUTOMATION	
		Letters	Postcards	Letters	Postcards
Letters	Carrier Route	27.5	17.0	–	–
	5-Digit	27.8	17.6	35.2	21.2
	3-Digit	29.2	18.3	35.2	21.2
	AADC	30.1	18.7	–	–
	Mixed AADC	30.9	19.4	–	–
	Single Piece	37.0	23.0	37.0	23.0
Flats	5-Digit	30.2	–	35.2	–
	3-Digit	32.2	–	35.2	–
	Basic	33.3	–	35.2	–

STANDARD MAIL (A)

		AUTOMATION			NONAUTOMATION		
	Sort Level		Entry			Entry	
		None	DBMC	DSCF	None	DBMC	DSCF
Letters	5-Digit	19.0	16.9	16.4	24.8	22.7	22.2
3.3 oz or less	3-Digit	20.3	18.2	17.7	24.8	22.7	22.2
	AADC	21.2	19.1	18.6	–	–	–
	Mixed AADC	21.9	19.8	–	26.8	24.7	24.2
Flats	3/5-Digit	26.1	24.0	23.5	28.8	26.7	26.2
	Basic	30.0	27.9	27.4	34.4	32.3	31.8

Flats/Irregular Parcels

Pieces more than 3.3 oz, per lb.		70.8	60.8	58.3	70.8	60.8	58.3
	3/5-Digit	11.5 additional per piece			14.2 additional per piece		
	Basic	15.4 additional per piece			19.8 additional per piece		

ENHANCED CARRIER ROUTE

		None	DBMC	DSCF	DDU
Letters	Auto Basic	17.1	15.0	14.5	13.9
3.3 oz or less	Basic	19.4	17.3	16.8	16.2
	High Density	16.4	14.3	13.8	13.2
	Saturation	15.2	13.1	12.6	12.0
Nonletters					
3.3 oz or less	Basic	19.4	17.3	16.8	16.2
	High Density	16.9	14.8	14.3	13.7
	Saturation	16.0	13.9	13.4	12.8
Nonletters					
Pieces more than 3.3 oz, per lb.		61.0	51.0	48.5	45.3
	Basic	6.8 additional per piece			
	High Density	4.3 additional per piece			
	Saturation	3.4 additional per piece			

Postal Reference

Postcards
- Minimum postcard size is 3-1/2 x 5
- Maximum postcard size is 4-1/4 x 6
- Minimum thickness is 0.007
- Minimum thickness over 4-1/4 x 6 is 0.009
- Maximum thickness is 0.016

Letters
- Minimum letter size is 3-1/2 x 5
- Maximum letter size is 6-1/8 x 11-1/2
- Maximum thickness is 0.25
- Minimum thickness is 0.007 up to 4-1/4 x 6, and 0.009 if more than 4-1/4 inches high or 6 inches long, or both

Flats
- For height, no more than 12 or less than 6 inches long
- For length, no more than 15 or less than 5 inches long if from 6 to 7-1/2 inches high
- Minimum thickness is 0.009
- Maximum thickness is 0.75

5/02

Figure 16.1 In addition to merge/purge, note the huge savings available through a variety of mail handling options. Discuss this with your in-house or mail handling services! This superb postage chart, based on June 2002 rates, was prepared by Service Graphics ([630] 941-2899). Nonprofit mailing costs are approximately 50 percent of those shown. Check your lettershop, DMPC, or post office for the exact rates and detailed rules. (Reprinted with permission from Bill Krafcheck, Service Graphics, Inc.)

your post office, one thing is certain to remain the same. The more of the preliminary sorting and handling work you do, the less your mailing will cost. Keeping your mailing list up to date and in nine-digit ZIP code order is the easiest way to get these savings. Postal regulations state that presorted first class mailing lists *must* be corrected for address changes and full ZIP coding every six months. As you'll see in checklist point #6, this has great advantages for standard bulk-rate mailings, too! If you are not familiar with this process, contact a mailing list company (from your Yellow Pages), and ask for directions.

For your evaluation, visit prospective suppliers while they are working. Note especially their degree of supervision, the relationship of supervisors to line workers, and the esprit de corps in the shops. Mailing service work demands unflagging attention to detail by *everyone* involved. Look for that first. Where it exists, the rest is likely to follow.

NOTES ON THE DMPC/LETTERSHOP CHECKLIST

Unlike notes on most other checklists, these notes are not *a supplement to the material presented in the chapter. Rather, they are an integral part of the chapter.* The checklist is presented in Figure 16.2.

1. **Discussion of project specifications.** Your DMPC can be an unexcelled source of *free consultation* on the mechanical aspects of direct mail. Involve it in your preliminary planning. If you are not a direct mail pro, tell the DMPC people! Ask for guidance in mechanical and postal specifications that will help your more detailed planning as you proceed. For lowest mail-handling costs and postage, envelopes must be of a certain size, with flaps in a certain position, larger materials must be folded in certain ways, and addressing cannot be affixed to specific areas of the envelope. Your DMPC can be invaluable in helping you plan. See Figure 16.3 for standard envelope sizes, but do not plan to use *any* envelope before discussion with your DMPC! Even if you are a pro, the one way to keep up in this volatile industry is to ask.

2. **Dummy copy for estimate/quotation.** Show your dummies—samples of the exact size and stock you plan to use—to the bindery and DMPC. Discuss with them possible cost-saving changes and get estimates or quotations. Often a small change in size or stock can mean huge savings. Estimates are just that—an *approximation* of what the project will cost. *Quotations* demand *exact specification* of every item on this checklist.

3. **Date mailing is to get to recipients.** The date mail *must* be received by the recipients controls all your decisions. Tie-ins with scheduled events or traditional promotion times are obvious examples. Fourth of July sales are announced in June. Seed catalogs arrive in January. Every business product has its own season, and some bloom all year long. Do not, without careful testing, mail anything out of season. The reason everyone in your industry mails at the same time is . . . because that's when everyone decides what to buy.

DMPC/LETTERSHOP CHECKLIST

Project Title _____   Date _____

Project Description _____   Project # _____

_____   Checklist # _____

Overall Supervision By _____   Deadline _____

Budget _____ Completion Date _____   Start Up Date _____

SUBJECT	PLANNING	FINAL	SEE ATTACHED
1. Discussion of project specifications	_____	_____	_____
2. Dummy copy for estimate/quotation	_____	_____	_____
3. Date mailing is to get to recipients	_____	_____	_____
4. Scheduling	_____	_____	_____
5. Quantity to be mailed	_____	_____	_____
6. Source and type of lists	_____	_____	_____
7. Merge/purge and other list control	_____	_____	_____
8. Type(s) of addressing	_____	_____	_____
9. Personalization–wanted/required	_____	_____	_____
10. Class of mail (First/Standard/Non-profit)	_____	_____	_____
11. Date(s) printed materials must be at lettershop and how delivered (skids/cartons/etc.)	_____	_____	_____
12. Printing and bindery work to be provided by DMPC/lettershop	_____	_____	_____
13. Date mailing list(s) required by DMPC/lettershop	_____	_____	_____
14. Outgoing mail permit(s)	_____	_____	_____
15. Incoming mail permit(s)	_____	_____	_____
16. Postage amount(s)	_____	_____	_____
17. Date(s) postage is required	_____	_____	_____
18. DMPC/Lettershop charge(s)	_____	_____	_____
_____	_____	_____	_____

ELEMENTS OF MAILING	QUANTITY	SUPPLIER	ID#
Self-Mailer			
Outgoing Envelope			
Reply Envelope			
Reply Card/Order Form			
Letter			
Flyer/Brochure			

Figure 16.2   The DMPC/lettershop checklist.

STANDARD ENVELOPE SIZE REFERENCE CHART

Please use this chart to see if your envelope is a standard size.

Commercial & Officials	
No.	Size
5	3-1/16 x 5-1/2
6-1/4	3-1/2 x 6
6-3/4	3-5/8 x 6-1/2
7	3-3/4 x 6-3/4
7-3/4	3-7/8 x 7-1/2
Monarch	3-7/8 x 7-1/2
8 Check	3-5/8 x 8-5/8
9	3-7/8 x 8-7/8
10	4-1/8 x 9-1/2
11	4-1/2 x 10-3/8
12	4-3/4 x 11
14	5 x 11-1/2

Booklet Envelopes	
No.	Size
2-1/2	4-1/2 x 5-7/8
3	4-3/4 x 6-1/2
5	5-1/2 x 8-1/8
6	5-3/4 x 8-7/8
6-1/2	6 x 9
7	6-1/4 x 9-5/8
7-1/4	6-1/2 x 9-1/2
7-3/8	7 x 10
7-1/2	7-1/2 x 10-1/2
8	8 x 11-1/8
9	8-3/4 x 11-1/2
9-1/2	9 x 12
10	9-1/2 x 12-5/8

Catalog Envelopes	
No.	Size
3 Catalog	7 x 10
6 Catalog	7-1/2 x 10-1/2
8 Catalog	8-1/4 x 11-1/4
9-3/4 Catalog	8-3/4 x 11-1/4
10-1/2 Catalog	9 x 12
12-1/2 Catalog	9-1/2 x 12-1/2
13-1/2 Catalog	10 x 13
14-1/2 Catalog	11-1/2 x 14-1/2
15-1/2 Catalog	12 x 15-1/2

Baronial	
No.	Size
4	3-5/8 x 5-1/8
5	4-1/8 x 5-1/2
5-1/2	4-3/8 x 5-3/4
5-3/4	4-5/8 x 5-15/16
6	4-3/4 x 6-1/2
6-3/4	4-3/4 x 6-3/4
7-1/2	5-1/2 x 7-1/2

Announcement Envelopes	
No.	Size
A-2	4-3/8 x 5-3/4
A-6	4-3/4 x 6-1/2
A-7	5-1/4 x 7-1/4
A-8	5-1/2 x 8-1/8
A-10	6 x 9-1/2

Remittance or Collection Envelopes		
No.	Size	
6-1/4	3-1/2 x 6	[3-3/16" Flap]
6-3/4	3-5/8 x 6-1/2	[3-1/4" Flap]
9	3-7/8 x 8-7/8	[3-5/8" Flap]

Figure 16.3 Standard envelope size chart by Service Graphics. Because of the desire to stand out by being different, many mailers depart from these standards in size, window placement, etc. Before *you* do, check with your DMPC to find out both what is possible and what is practical. Even when money is no object, some things won't work.

4. **Scheduling.** Based on your "must be received" dates, work through this checklist with the DMPC. Most suppliers will have standard cost, expedited, and *emergency* schedules and rates. Note that your DMPC has no control over your outside suppliers. Item #11 especially will demand its own schedule. Try for the DMPC's standard time line. Not only does it have the lowest costs, but if anything does arrive late, it has built-in time for expedited or emergency action. If you begin on the fastest track and something goes wrong, how can anyone make up the time?

5. **Quantity to be mailed.** The total quantity of your mailing is not the only question to be decided here. Will you test? If so, what quantities and what potential rollout? Different equipment and planning may be needed for different-sized lists. Can your DMPC do both economically? If not, should you try to find a different shop that can or use two suppliers? If two shops are used, who will supervise the second—your primary DMPC or you? There are lots of questions. *Now,* in the planning stage, is the time to get answers. The major advantage of using a full-service supplier (such as a direct marketing agency or production company) is limiting work to a single source. It is *their* expertise. Make them use it. Hold them responsible.

6. **Source and type of lists.** If anything more than simple addressing in is required, discuss with your DMPC what it can do, how much it costs, how long it takes, and how the list must be supplied to make it all possible. Before agreeing, contact your list sources to see whether they can meet those needs and at what cost. Do not pretend to expertise you do not have. Let your DMPC speak with sources of lists and translate for you.

"MOVE UPDATE" YOUR LISTS!

About 1997, the post office was handling so much presorted but misaddressed first class mail, that the forwarding cost was more than the presorting saved. The result was a new ruling. Now, any list used in such a mailing must be "move updated" within the past six months by an organization such as the National Change of Address service (NCOA). Because bulk mailings are not forwarded without *you* paying the cost, they are not bound by this ruling.

But how much money are you willing to throw away on *any* mailing for unneeded printing, mail handling, and postage? In late 2002, such list updating cost about $5 per thousand, with a minimum charge of $200. At 50¢ each, you have to correct just 400 pieces on a 40,000-piece mailing to break even. Depending on the list, consider this updating insurance for smaller mailings, too.

Before using any list, make sure you check on NCOA or a similar update. Some lists, such as current—*not* lapsed—magazine subscribers, update automatically. Most lists of prospective or past buyers, rather than *current* customer, don't. There is a standard update guarantee form that must be used to mail presorted first class. Get the same form for every list you use . . . including your own!

UPDATE TO "UPDATE"

In early 2004, the U.S. Postal Service is scheduled to make Move Update savings possible for standard (bulk) and periodical mailings. The savings are so large that they are subject to audit, and you will need compliance records to make your discount audit-safe! Check this with your post office's direct marketing expert and keep up-to-date in periodicals such as *DM News*. Large-volume mailers can contact Bob Swick at rbsemperfi@aol.com, for a no-cost Power Point presentation on the Move Update and Compliance issue. It's the closest thing to free money you're likely to find.

---

7. **Merge/purge and other list control.** A way of eliminating duplicate addressing when using more than one list, merge/purge is a computerized system that can save you money on postage and on mountains of printed material. They cannot be provided economically—if at all—from nondigital sources. Before any of these operations are specified, give your DMPC a contact at the location of each list source and let them determine what is *possible.* You must decide what is *practical.*

HOW TO USE MERGE/PURGE FOR MAXIMUM SAVINGS

Any merge/purge (M/P) system will give you a single list that eliminates duplicates, insofar as a computer can detect them. However, without explicit—and easy—instructions to the computer, this will not give you the most *economical* results! Here are the things you want to take into account

A. When purchasing lists for a M/P mailing, you pay only for the names you actually use. But there will be a minimum charge, usually for 5,000 to 10,000 names. It is the cost of that minimum and then everything above that number that tells you how much you pay.

B. Rank your lists from lowest to highest charges. Lists are purged one at a time. Instruct your mailing service or department to use the lowest-cost list as the control, then purge the other lists in their lowest to highest cost order. In other words, because you pay only for what you actually use, you want to add the names from the most expensive list last.

C. If you are purging against a list of your own, or another one that costs you nothing, make that your control. (We apologize for stating the obvious, but we've seen this ignored because no one pointed it out.)

- **Merge only.** It is often less costly to create a single large list (without purging duplicate names), than it is to handle several lists individually. Although this list will include all the duplicate names, it may qualify more of your list for postal presort discounts. Merge only definitely is less expensive *as a system* than merge/purge for lists of 100,000 or less. Check with your DMPC about this.

- **Test selected items.** The *nth* name, ZIP code, or other test selection from larger lists may be less costly when done by a DMPC rather than the list source. Let both quote, but get *all* costs involved.

- **Coding of source list.** If the lists are delivered uncoded, it still may be possible to code them. Check. It is impossible to check on the results of individual uncoded list, if more than a single such list is included.

- **Presort and ZIP code qualifications.** Sorting from alphabetical order into ZIP code, combining for individual mail carrier delivery, and refining into ZIP code plus four, or plus six bar code, generate substantial savings. The bar code on mail permits automatic sorting by the post office. It is refined to individual mail carrier routes in block-by-block (or floors of larger buildings) street number order. Not every mailing needs this much sophistication, but find out what your DMPC can do, the costs, and savings in postage.

8. **Types of addressing.** You can address on peel and return labels, simulate typewriter or handwriting, and address onto envelopes, reply forms, or

letters that show through windows. There are lots of options, different requirements, and costs. Know *why* as well as *how* if you decide to test.

9. **Personalization.** Practically everyone loves to see their name in print, no matter how obviously it is mass produced. New computer technology is making personalization increasingly more versatile and less costly. Learn what your printer, bindery, and DMPC can do and what they will need—and charge—to do it. Test.

10. **Class of mail.** Check with your post office, as well as your DMPC, on the requirements and costs for different classes of mail. You may need postal permits to show mailing from a specific location, or you may be able to use the DMPC's. Most *business* mailings will produce essentially the same results whether mailed first class or not. But don't take it for granted. For *your* mailing . . . test. Believe the numbers.

11–13. **Deliveries to the DMPC lettershop.** Determine the specific dates by which outside materials must be received by the DMPC to maintain the dates and costs that were quoted. On-time delivery is *your* responsibility for printing, bindery work, and mailing lists. Some DMPCs can provide printing or binding in addition to mailing services. Consider outside shipping and handling in your costs. Find out the DMPC's capabilities, especially in regard to personalizing materials you might not otherwise give that special touch.

14–15. **Mail permits.** New mail permits may be required, depending on where and how you mail your material. Check with both the post office and the DMPC at the beginning of your planning, and then incorporate the permit numbers into your printing. Certain preprinted permits may simulate an *undated* first class meter. Let your DMPC be your guide.

16. **Postage amounts.** Should you overpay postage, making out your check to the postmaster rather than to your DMPC will cause long delays in getting a postage refund. A refund of any overpayment requires a written request, whereas under-payment *by any amount* may cause refusal of the entire mailing. If you mail regularly from the same post office, establish an account there, and always deposit a bit more than you think you'll need. For a one-time mailing only, ask your mailing service how best to handle the postage, whether to deposit postage with your DMPC or at the post office before it receives the mailing. If a check accompanies the mailing and there is any question raised about it, the mailing may be refused.

17. **Dates postage is required.** Deposit checks at the post office several days in advance of the mailing, to give them time to clear. (A cash payment may require references!)

18. **DMPC charges.** *Any* change between what your DMPC saw for estimating and what it actually receives may change costs. Get samples to the DMPC so it can confirm or requote prices in advance of the actual mailing.

INSIGHT 96

Code *every piece of every mailing,* whether that piece changes within the mailing or not. Place the code where it can be seen (on the outside, not the inside of the brochure). Ask the DMPC's mailing service where the code must be placed. It's the best—and often the only—way of getting the right pieces into the right envelope addressed with the right list. Code reply cards and order forms *on the ordering side.* For test mailings, copy each reply (that's why you put it on the ordering side) before it goes to the order fulfillment department. Use those copies to check any computer analysis reports. This time, don't believe the numbers. Check!

Index